THE ARCHAEOLOGY OF NATIVE NORTH AMERICA

The Archaeology of Native North America presents the ideas, evidence, and debates regarding the initial peopling of the continent by mobile bands of hunters and gatherers and the cultural evolution of their many lines of descent over the ensuing millennia. The emergence of farming, urban centers, and complex political organization paralleled similar developments in other world areas. With the arrival of Europeans to North America and the inevitable clashes of culture, colonizers and colonists were forever changed, which is also represented in the archaeological heritage of the continent. Unlike others, this book includes Mesoamerica and the Caribbean, thus addressing broad regional interactions and the circulation of people, things, and ideas.

This edition incorporates results of new archaeological research since the publication of the first edition a decade earlier. Fifty-four new box features highlight selected archaeological sites, which are publicly accessible gateways to the study of North American archaeology. These features were authored by specialists with direct knowledge of the sites and their broad importance. Glossaries are provided at the end of every chapter to clarify specialized terminology.

The book is directed at upper-level undergraduate and graduate students taking survey courses in American archaeology, as well as other advanced readers. It is extensively illustrated and includes citations to sources with their own robust bibliographies, leading diligent readers deeper into the professional literature. *The Archaeology of Native North America* is the ideal text for courses in North American archaeology.

Dean R. Snow is Professor Emeritus and former Head of the Department of Anthropology at The Pennsylvania State University, USA. His archaeological research interests are in Iroquoian and Algonquian ethnohistory, American historical archaeology, paleodemography, and rock art. He has conducted research projects in Mexico, northeastern North America, and Europe.

Nancy Gonlin is a Mesoamerican archaeologist who specializes in household archaeology, ritual and ideology, and archaeology of the night. She is a Professor of Anthropology at Bellevue College, Washington, USA. Her research and publications have centered on commoners in complex societies, whether working in Mexico, El Salvador, or Honduras.

Peter E. Siegel is Professor and Chair of Anthropology at Montclair State University, USA. He is a New World archaeologist with research interests in historical ecology, ethnoarchaeology, spatial analysis, and cosmological and political organization. He has conducted projects throughout eastern North America, much of the West Indies, lowland South America, and eastern Bolivia.

THE ARCHAEOLOGY OF NATIVE NORTH AMERICA

Second edition

Dean R. Snow, Nancy Gonlin, and Peter E. Siegel

NEW YORK AND LONDON

Second edition published 2020
by Routledge
52 Vanderbilt Avenue, New York, NY 10017

and by Routledge
2 Park Square, Milton Park, Abingdon, Oxon, OX14 4RN

Routledge is an imprint of the Taylor & Francis Group, an informa business

First edition published by Pearson Education, Inc. 2010 and Routledge 2016

Library of Congress Cataloging-in-Publication Data
Names: Snow, Dean R., 1940– author. | Gonlin, Nancy, author. | Siegel, Peter E., author.
Title: The archaeology of Native North America/Dean R. Snow, Nancy Gonlin, Peter E. Siegel.
Description: Second edition. | Milton Park, Abingdon, Oxon; New York, NY: Routledge, 2019. | Includes bibliographical references and index.
Identifiers: LCCN 2018056350 (print) | LCCN 2018059724 (ebook) | ISBN 9781315101156 (ebook) | ISBN 9781351588256 (web pdf) | ISBN 9781351588232 (mobi/kindle) | ISBN 9781351588249 (epub) | ISBN 9781138118850 (hardback : alk. paper) | ISBN 9780367175979 (pbk.: alk. paper)
Subjects: LCSH: Indians of North America–Antiquities. | North America–Antiquities. | United States–Antiquities.
Classification: LCC E77.9 (ebook) | LCC E77.9 .S565 2019 (print) | DDC 970.01–dc23
LC record available at https://lccn.loc.gov/2018056350

ISBN: 978-1-138-11885-0 (hbk)
ISBN: 978-0-367-17597-9 (pbk)
ISBN: 978-1-315-10115-6 (ebk)

Typeset in Bembo
by Newgen Publishing UK

Visit the eResources: www.routledge.com/9780367175979

To the first Americans and their descendants
D.R.S.: to Jan, Kate, Barb, and Josh;
P.E.S.: to Rosa, Diana, and David;
N.G.: to the next generation of students – Penelope, Jack, Gloria, Andrew, Allison, Elizabeth, Mahin, Bryce, Marlon, Walter Yuki, Jasmine, Vanessa, Michael, Melissa, Holly, Amy, and David.

CONTENTS

FIGURES

TABLES

PREFACE

We, the coauthors of this book, have spent our adult lives studying what Columbus called the "other world," what we now call North America. Between us we have had hundreds of undergraduate and graduate students and are familiar with the texts available to support the courses we have taught. There are some very good books in print on this subject. The current book was written in its first edition by Dean Snow during a 2005–2006 sabbatical leave. The original publisher, Prentice-Hall, passed the rights to Pearson, which subsequently passed them along to Routledge, our current publisher. By then, a decade of new archaeology had accumulated, and our editor, Matthew Gibbon, asked for an updated edition. Dean Snow persuaded Peter Siegel and Nancy Gonlin to come aboard as coauthors of the new volume.

Two things are different about this book and its predecessor. First, it covers all of North America, including Mesoamerica, the islands of the Caribbean, and Greenland, not just the United States and Canada. Second, it is organized around the themes of evolution and ecology. It is important to explain the past in terms of scientifically valid conclusions. To that end we have done our best to avoid merely repeating the obvious or limiting ourselves to pretty pictures and basic descriptions. American archaeology features many perspectives and research agendas, but there is general consensus regarding research challenges for the next decade or two, articulated in a seminal article in volume 79, number 1 (2014) of our flagship journal, *American Antiquity*, "Grand Challenges for Archaeology."

This book is largely about the continent before it was dominated by descendants of the Europeans who established modern nation states, before epidemics devastated its native inhabitants and many of the landscapes lapsed into wilderness, before it was the America familiar to us from history books. This book is also about the archaeology and heritage of a continent, not a book about how to do archaeology. Many readers will want to know more about how we have reached a particular conclusion or, more importantly, how to solve specific problems themselves. The numerous chapter references provide such details. Readers can also refer to the many good books on archaeology as a discipline to learn more about how we apply both archaeological science and the several related sciences upon which archaeologists depend. There is no substitute for the scientific method in archaeology, even though there are many worthy supplements to it provided by literature and the arts. Numerous such contributions enhance the central themes of this book.

There are many ways to organize a book like this. While its organization allows for most chapters to be read out of order, it is nonetheless constrained by our decisions about how best to tell the story of Native America. We could start with the most recent and most securely known part of that story and work backwards in time, but the trajectory of Western linear time flows in the opposite direction and pushing upstream against it would hinder efforts to address evolutionary processes.

We could also have presented a data-intense text with minimal discussion regarding underlying social and ecological processes. We chose to avoid that option, thus excluding turgid descriptions of pottery and projectile point types and local cultural sequences that fill site reports, technical articles, and regional syntheses. Readers wishing for these details may find them in articles, chapters, or books listed in the bibliography; in the companion website to the book with links to supplementary materials; or visit key archaeological sites discussed in the box features.

Generally trustworthy articles worth pursuing are published in peer-reviewed journals. Books are another matter because quality depends upon the nature of the press. University press publications are peer reviewed and usually high quality and reliable. Some commercial presses are no more trustworthy than tabloid newspapers with goals of securing high-sensation markets and great profits and not for achieving interpretations based on sound evidence. Reviews in professional journals usually help one to evaluate books. If the reader does not find evidence of Viking runestones, African megaliths, Irish monasteries, or ancient astronauts in the current book, be assured they have been left out for good reason. The study of archaeology is, as it should be, about using evidence to confirm or disconfirm hypotheses and not twisting evidence to fit fantasies. One is about doing good science; the other is at best about writing science fiction and at worst about presenting to the unsuspecting public junk science.

We have dedicated this book to the American Indians, who left all Americans of today such a rich archaeological legacy, and to people that have supported us in our work. They have tolerated archaeological vacations, countless museum visits, sunburns, tortured humor, Spartan accommodations, blood-sucking insects, and life-threatening illnesses far from home, often for our sakes.

ACKNOWLEDGMENTS

So many people have helped each of us in our archaeological careers that it is not possible to list them all here. Those closest to us know who they are, as do those who have helped us along the way. We do wish to acknowledge more specifically the people who took the time and effort necessary to produce the 54 box features that highlight key North American sites. The sites included are not just essential to the story of American archaeology but are protected and open to the public, such that everyone can learn more by visiting them. The contributors are: James Adovasio, Kenneth M. Ames, Anthony F. Aveni, Jack W. Brink, Ian W. Brown, Christopher Carr, Rafael Cobos, Michael B. Collins, L. Antonio Curet, Ann Cyphers, Kathleen Deagan, William H. Doelle, Glen H. Doran, Don E. Dumond, David H. Dye, Brian Fagan, Michael Galban, Patricia A. Gilman, Diana M. Greenlee, Scott W. Hammerstedt, Lisa M. Hodgetts, Lara Homsey-Messer, Dennis L. Jenkins, John R. Johnson, Adam King, Timothy A. Kohler, Brad Lepper, Roberto López Bravo, Linda R. Manzanilla, William H. Marquardt, George R. Milner, Paul E. Minnis, Jeffrey M. Mitchem, Paul R. Picha, Nelly M. Robles García, Amy L. Rosebrough, Bret J. Ruby, Sissel Schroeder, Lynne Sebastian, Andrew M. Stewart, David Hurst Thomas, Roberto Valcárcel Rojas, Michael R. Waters, Michael E. Whalen, and Nancy Marie White. Finally, we thank the individuals and organizations that provided us with images and their permissions to reproduce them. Each of them is specifically recognized in the list of figures and credits.

Dean R. Snow
Nan Gonlin
Peter E. Siegel

1

INTRODUCTION

It was bitterly cold on the continent, snow fell heavily, and wooly mammoths roamed the landscape. Yet, a trickle of humans was able to successfully navigate this dangerous terrain over 14,500 years ago to reach what we now call the North American continent (Figure 1.1). They pushed southward from Beringia, the land bridge that connected Siberia on the Asian continent and Alaska. Biologically modern humans have roamed the earth for tens of thousands of years. Small groups expanded, slowly multiplied, and eventually spread to all corners of the American continents. Like people everywhere at the time, these earliest Americans were hunter-gatherers, but from that time forward their histories developed separately from the rest of humanity. Their descendants lived in almost complete isolation from the rest of the world until a mere five centuries ago, yet the trajectory of their independent cultural evolution in the Americas paralleled those of other peoples on other continents. This similarity should be reassuring to all of us, for it means that human potential is universally shared on this planet.

This book is about the archaeological past of the native peoples of North America (Figure 1.2). **Archaeology** is the scientific study of historic or prehistoric peoples by analysis of their material remains. Our goal is to provide a concise introduction to the generally accepted framework of the archaeology of native America. It has thus been important to restrict discussion to topics in which certainty is most strongly established and professional agreement is most abundant. This approach consequently emphasizes the findings of archaeological **science** as the foundation for further discussion. Partly because of advances in the natural and physical sciences, we are able to address with some certainty topics related to chronology, architecture, **artifact**s, human evolution, and human **ecology**. Advances and insights from cultural anthropology and other social sciences allow for observations approaching the same level of certainty, although frequently accompanied by rational alternatives. When they encounter multiple possibilities, archaeologists seek data and new methods to test alternative explanations for patterns identified in the archaeological record.

Books on North American archaeology have traditionally covered the United States and Canada, extending southward into Mexico to roughly the Tropic of Cancer. Here, coverage also includes Greenland in the Far North and Mesoamerica and the Caribbean Islands to the south. The archaeology of North America cannot be fully understood in truncated form. Mesoamerica

FIGURE 1.1 A full-scale diorama at the New York State Museum depicts a band of hunter-gatherers as they might have looked 14,500 years ago. Courtesy of the New York State Museum

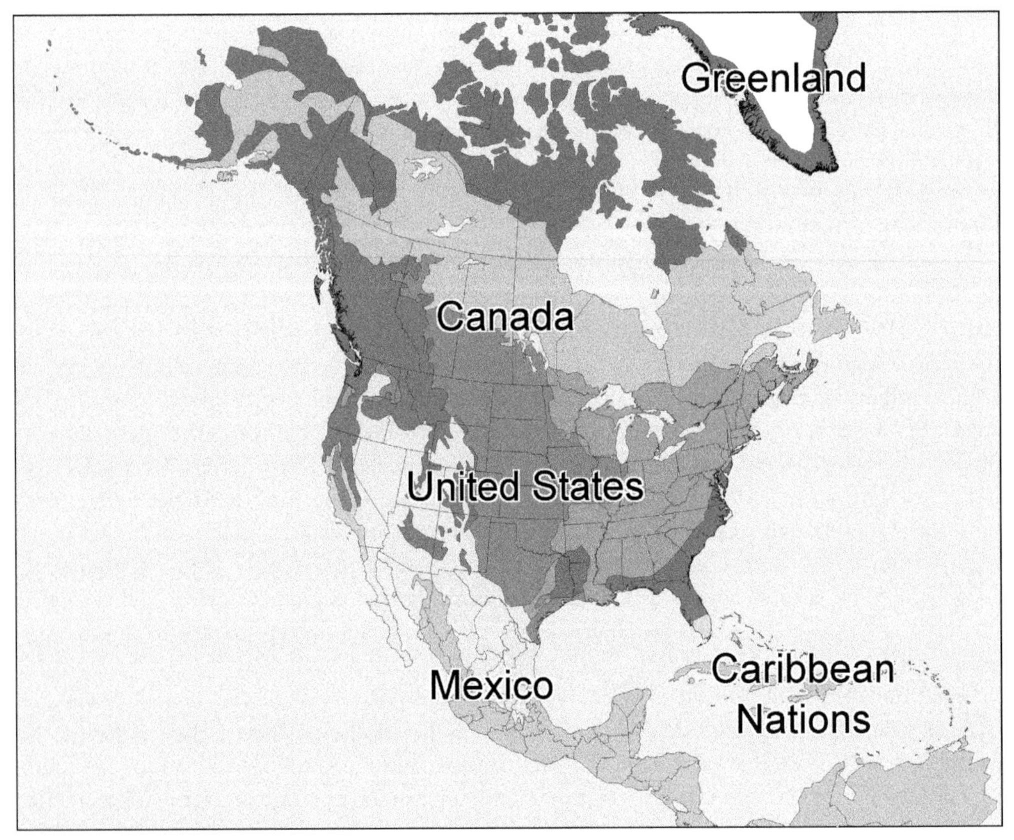

FIGURE 1.2 The major modern nations of North America

especially was a cornucopia, the fruits of which nourished the majority of people living in all of North America in 1492 and earlier. Including Mexico and the Caribbean allows coverage of regions that were origins of crops and other influences that profoundly affected the peoples of more northern regions of the continent. Their inclusion too allows examination of influential nation states and **empire**s that would otherwise be excluded from consideration in the historical trajectory of most native North Americans.

The long preliterate history of the American Indians and its remarkable parallels with developments elsewhere in the world have seized the imaginations of many people over the years. But it takes more than imagination and anecdotes to explore this saga. It takes careful application of archaeological science and related natural and social sciences. In the following pages, we introduce the ways in which native North American cultures evolved and adapted to environmental changes and to shifting opportunities afforded by their own technological and social innovations. Further, we explore the ways in which archaeology reveals those ancient developments. Other topics build upon this foundation and serve as major subheadings in the chapters that follow:

- Environment and Adaptation
- Demography and Conflict
- Subsistence and Economy
- Architecture and Technology
- Culture, Language, and Identity
- Art and Symbolism
- Resilience and Collapse

This textbook offers a scientific perspective on the archaeology of North America by exploring the environment of this vast continent and how ancient peoples adapted to the wide variety of ecosystems. The changes in their populations (**demography**) left their mark on the landscape. The opportunities and challenges of exploiting the environment manifested themselves in the diversity of how people made a living and fed themselves and how they conducted economic transactions with others. There were numerous technological inventions, including innovative architecture, some of which has survived until today. Aspects of social organization and other cultural characteristics can be envisioned through material remains. For some peoples, language and identity persist into the modern world. The rich record of art and symbolism permeates the artifacts produced by ancient peoples. Like groups the world over, games were part of one's culture and tied in with symbolism, politics, and society. While some ancient cultures disappeared entirely, others persisted, and modern descendants attest to their resiliency.

The archaeology of North America matters to those who live on the continent today because it is embedded in the landscape we all share. It is part of our common heritage simply because we are all residents on the land. Like the forests, grasslands, birds, mountains, and streams all around us, the evidence of the past gives context to our lives. The growing popularity of public archaeological **site**s as tourist destinations is clear evidence of public appreciation for the past. Over 500 Native American archaeological sites are open to the public. A companion website for this book includes an electronic map and detailed directions.

The material remains of the human past have special importance in North America to people of Native American descent because such remains tie in more directly with their past and heritage. The resurgence of American Indian cultures during the twentieth century revived broader appreciation for their role in the history of the continent and underscored the connection between the distant past and living cultures.

In addition to the significance of the North American past for all of us, it is important because it provides an independent perspective on the study of the evolution of human societies from simple **band**s of hunter-gatherers to large urbanized **state** societies with all the trappings we have come to think of as defining **civilization**. Without the evidence from the Americas, we might never have been sure that the explosive growth in the size and complexity of human society was not a single unique phenomenon, a combination of singular lucky happenstance followed by wholesale imitation. But the appearance of cities, literacy, technological traditions, organized religion, and state polities in North America occurred with little if any influence from South America and virtually none from the rest of the world. American archaeology reveals that all of these traits were latent in the biologically modern but thinly scattered hunter-gatherers that made up the world's entire human population 15 millennia ago. An American Indian gift to the world is the assurance that complex human societies arose independently in the past in all populated areas of the world and that even after some future global catastrophe they would do so again so long as modern humans survived as a species.

Archaeological Science

While acknowledging multiple different meanings that American archaeology may have for us as individuals, this book is grounded on archaeological science. At the foundation of scientific thought lies the certainty that there is a correct answer to any question, even though the available evidence might allow for only the uncertainty of multiple possibilities. This approach requires a researcher to be comfortable with uncertainty and revision and also driven to find ways to exclude possibilities, thus increasing the probabilities for the alternative explanations that remain. Opinion tends to converge over time as the collective effort disposes of alternatives.

Archaeological science involves the development of principles and procedures for the systematic development of **theory**, which involves the recognition and formulation of problems, the systematic collection of data through observation and experience, and the formulation and testing of **hypotheses**. Theory is indispensable, and we all use it all the time. If a person points to something and says that it is a "bus," they are not making a factual statement so much as using their perceptions along with a theoretical model of what a bus is in order to make sense of those perceptions. Humans do this easily all the time, and we have generally agreed that we will treat such observations as factual, at least until we disagree. If someone else says that it is not a bus but rather a truck and they both have time on their hands, they might argue about it. Fortunately, we generally take each other's word for such things. Likewise, in archaeology we use our experience to say that something is a **projectile point**, a hearth, a burial mound, or a ball court that we are comfortable will be taken at face value. But it is in the nature of science to provide a means to argue about both this and propositions that are more complicated than bus identification and to provide a means to force choices between alternative propositions that are mutually exclusive.

Perhaps the most important scientific rule is that a theory, if it is to be worth spending time on, must be able to generate testable hypotheses. If the theory is not testable because it does not fulfill that criterion, it will not interest a scientist. What may be unsettling about this situation is that no matter how many times a theory is scrutinized and relevant hypotheses are tested, it can never be proven. It remains only the best currently known explanation for some particular set of phenomena, always subject to disproof and revision in light of new data.

Coping with Incomplete Information

A big problem for archaeologists is that they must often make do with very spotty and incomplete data and connect the dots to produce a recognizable picture. If all that is known about an object is when and where it was made, and when and where it was deposited in the ground, the archaeologist has no choice but to use broader theoretical understandings about how things move through space and time to describe the object's most probable history. Much of what we do is connecting the dots in this way, and that explains why theory is so important to archaeological science. The elements of human culture are mutually contingent, and theory specifies those contingencies. For the archaeologist, the task is often to acquire more data through excavation or to reduce the scope of the problem so that it becomes solvable. The alternative is to be content with the uncertainty of two or more alternative hypotheses, to accept that for the time being there may be two or more mutually exclusive explanations and no way to force a choice between them.

The Use and Misuse of Evidence

Empirical archaeological science requires evidence, and negative evidence simply will not do. Perhaps in religion and politics one can get away with the view that an absence of proof is not proof of absence, but one cannot get away with such a statement in science or, for that matter, in a court of law. This constraint is a serious and seemingly unreasonable one in some instances. When rising sea levels are likely to have destroyed or made inaccessible all evidence of early coastal sites it is logical to argue that while there is nothing there now, there probably was once much evidence of human settlement along the coast. That might be true, but one cannot build a convincing argument based on an untestable **hypothesis**. Skepticism about negative evidence prevents science from being overtaken by fantasy, just as in law, it forestalls convictions in the absence of evidence.

Mistakes and Fakes

It is also the case that an open mind allows for ideas to be tested and rejected, whereas dogged advocacy of a particular wrong idea too often leads others to reject not just the idea but its advocate. By taking the approach of seizing upon a single hypothesis and promoting it as a thesis, researchers in effect make themselves rather than their hypotheses the things that must be tested and discarded by others if found wanting. The advocate strategy of research has littered the history of some disciplines with many failed advocates. The casualty rate is high, and this kind of approach to research is thus at best very inefficient because single-minded advocates disappear as a result of their errors rather than learning from them.

Unfortunately, many popular books and articles on North American archaeology have resulted from the advocate approach, a frequent source of **pseudoarchaeology**. This is defined as description of the past that claims to be based on fact but is actually fictional or a deliberate distortion of observations for some nonscientific purpose. Some colossal stone heads along the Gulf Coast of Mexico do indeed look superficially African, but there is no archaeological, linguistic, or genetic evidence to support the proposition that they portray African immigrants who arrived there three millennia ago. A Norse rune stone turned up a century ago in Minnesota, but there is no archaeological, linguistic, or genetic evidence to support the proposition that a crew of Norse adventurers presaged the settlement of the region by later Norwegians. In the latter case, people later admitted to faking it.

Roman coins, fake inscriptions, superficial resemblances, religious innovations, and endless wishful thinking have all contributed to the pseudoarchaeology that is mixed in with reputable

North American archaeology on the shelves of libraries and bookstores (Mainfort and Kwas, 2004). Disappointed advocates will continue to complain that professional archaeologists are narrow-minded, hidebound, and unwilling to consider alternative viewpoints. And they will continue to publish the occasional new imaginary revelation. It is up to each of us to sort through the contradictory literature and to apply the scientific method that separates sense from nonsense (Feder, 2013).

Biological and Cultural Evolution

The theory of **evolution** is the single most important established scientific theory needed to understand what follows in this book. Other perspectives are included as appropriate, and in this sense, the book takes a broad view of the past. An ecological perspective underlies other topics in the book because it is a useful way to describe the basic story of North American prehistory while at the same time explaining why and how it all unfolded as it did.

To understand the long pageant of humanity over time and space, we must distinguish between the different processes of biological and cultural evolution. The two often work together, cultural forces stimulating biological changes and vice versa, to coalesce in biocultural evolution (Ames, 1996; Durham, 1991; Shennan, 2000). Biological and cultural evolution are conceptually different in detail, and to truly understand how they interact, one has to understand how each operates independently. In both, the unit of selection is the individual human being (Snow, 2002). But beyond that, the basic principles differ because individuals can change culturally. Instead of being well-bounded breeding populations, the social groups in which cultural evolution works are numerous, often not well bounded, overlapping, and highly variable. Individual humans form cultural groups of many sizes, of highly variable permanence, and for many purposes. For cultural groups, which vary greatly in size, membership can be quite fluid. Individuals can often join or leave a hunting band almost at will as they seek marriage or other partnerships. Sibling bonds are strong, but bands often contain many unrelated individuals (Hill et al., 2011).

Individuals can transform themselves culturally, through religious or cultural conversion and the like. People can also belong to many groups simultaneously, some of which are subsets of others, and they will assert membership in any or all of them situationally. Unlike biological evolution, cultural evolution is clearly marked by a trend toward increasing complexity. That said, it must be admitted that measurement and assessment of human complexity at any scale has proven to be difficult (Premo, 2016). There is a very strong correlation between growth in human populations and growth in complexity as measured by the number of their constituent social groups and the elaboration of social networks. A hunter-gatherer from 20,000 years ago plunked down in one of the world's modern megacities would be no less intelligent or less capable than the average modern person, and they would have no trouble recognizing that modern society is more complex than that of 20 millennia ago.

It is also the case that the products of cultural evolution cannot be classified hierarchically in the same way that the products of biological evolution can. A.L. Kroeber long ago depicted the difference in terms of the trees in Figure 1.3 (Kroeber, 1948:260). The origins of new species through biological evolution produce hierarchical branches in the tree that remain separate forever, gradually growing and splitting further into new branches. No such branching model can be used to illustrate cultural evolution because the endpoints can be the result of many recombinations of elements. Cultural evolution allows for both reconvergence and swapping, so a branching model is often inapplicable. Another difference is that while biological evolution is a mindless process, cultural evolution is the result of the usually rational choices made by intelligent human beings.

FIGURE 1.3 A.L. Kroeber's models for biological evolution (left) and cultural evolution (right)

Basic Concepts for the Study of Cultural Evolution

Basic anthropological terms for sociocultural changes that embrace the simplest form of organized society to the most complex include the concepts of "band," "**tribe**," "**chiefdom**," "state," and "empire." Such terms have been used to classify polities that evolved in North America over the last 14 millennia (Service, 1962). This theoretical construct is a progression of forms from small to large, simple to complex. Each of these types conveys aspects of organization and is meant as a heuristic device (Table 1.1). In this continuum, overall polity size matters, but there is significant overlap among these categories due to demographic events. For example, a larger and more complex form such as a chiefdom can suffer misfortune and shrink in population, but still retain the organizational complexity of a chiefdom, or a boatload of castaways familiar with the formal characteristics of state organization may well retain them on an island refuge rather than revert to simpler band organization. However, it is difficult to retain a tribal form of sociopolitical organization if the population rises into the thousands. One solution is for a supersized tribe to split into two or more new manageable tribes. But if competition for space from other surrounding societies makes this plan impossible, then innovations leading to chiefdom organization may resolve the situation. **Circumscription** can constrain physical expansion and force growing populations to increased density, which in turn encourages the organizational innovations of tribes, chiefdoms, and states (Carneiro, 1970).

Economics might also drive the evolution to more complex organization, even in the absence of rising population density. Examples are societies that enjoy abundant seasonal foods that must be stored and redistributed or that develop large irrigation systems that must be maintained, either of which in turn may require centralized authority and management that they can acquire only by moving to more complex organization.

Table 1.1 lists many of the characteristics of each societal type in very simplified form. It is necessary to remember that the individuals involved and their everyday lives are equally complex

TABLE 1.1 A simplified chart of characteristics of five levels of sociopolitical complexity

	Band	*Tribe*	*Chiefdom*	*State*	*Empire*
Settlement Type	Mobile	Mobile/Fixed	Fixed	Fixed	Fixed
Settlement Size	Camp	Village	Town	City	City
Social Organization	Kin	Kin	Kin/Rank	Rank	Rank
Social Stratification	No	No	Usually	Yes	Yes
Leadership	Informal	Big Man/Woman	Formal	Formal	Formal
Bureaucracy	No	No	Simple	Complex	Complex
Standing Army	No	No	Yes	Yes	Yes
Languages	1	1	1	1+	2+
Formal Religion	No	No	Yes	Yes	Yes
Food Production	No	Sometimes	Usually	Yes	Yes
Trade & Exchange	Reciprocal	Reciprocal	Redistributive	Redistributive	Redistributive
Public Architecture	No	No	Yes	Yes	Yes
Writing	No	No	No	Yes	Yes

regardless of the complexity of the society in which they happen to live. One can choose to live a simple life in a complex state or, alternatively, a complex life as a member of a small band.

Specialists quibble about the specifics in Table 1.1, but most agree with the basic outline. It allows the use of standard terms without having to repeatedly define or characterize them. The most useful feature of this chart is that the implied sociocultural evolution occurred independently many times around the world. Figure 1.4 shows the rough distribution of these sociopolitical forms in North America around 1500 CE, the time of first contact with Europeans.

Figure 1.5 depicts forms of sociopolitical integration in a very simplified shade-coded hierarchy. Once societies are classified according to the traits shown in Table 1.1, the resulting five categories can be scaled according to population levels, shown on the vertical axis. These are not precise, and authoritative opinion about specifics will vary. One should note that the population scale is logarithmic such that values increase by powers of ten (orders of magnitude). There is not much doubt that a band can shrink to no fewer than a single person before it ceases to exist. Small bands are at great risk of extinction simply because they are so vulnerable to random events (Wobst, 1974). The weakest bands, those having populations of ten or fewer, are represented as a lighter shade, whereas strong bands have 10–100 members. There are cases of bands that exceed 100 people, but these are rare and unstable.

Five hundred is both the approximate minimum number of people needed to maintain a viable social system and the maximum number of personal contacts maintained by the average human being (Hunn, 1994). Bands typically must maintain close interactions with other bands. Overlapping networks called "connubia" meet this need (Williams, 1974). A **connubium** is thus an abstract concept, a unit made up of a band and its neighboring bands, each of which is also the center of its own connubium.

Above 100 members there is a strong tendency for a population to acquire the organizational characteristics of a tribe. A group smaller than that might adopt tribal characteristics even in the absence of population pressure if its members are familiar with other tribes and they perceive benefits to doing so. An unlucky tribe might lose population yet cling to tribal characteristics, such as food production and village life. There are remnant tribes known to have populations as low as 25. In both cases these are weak tribes, shaded lighter than strong tribes in Figure 1.5. Tribal societies start to show signs of instability when populations exceed 1,000, and few remain above 2,000. There are only rare cases in a worldwide sample of tribes that reach 3,000 (Hays, 1998).

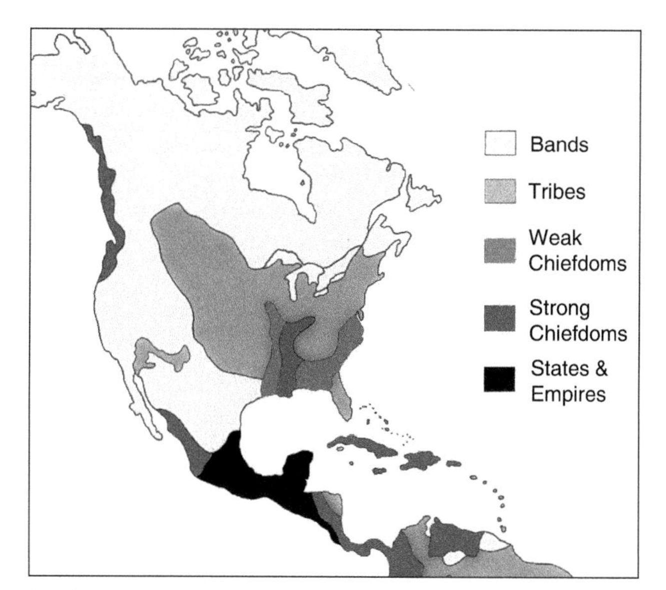

FIGURE 1.4 The distribution of bands, tribes, chiefdoms, states, and empires around 1500 CE

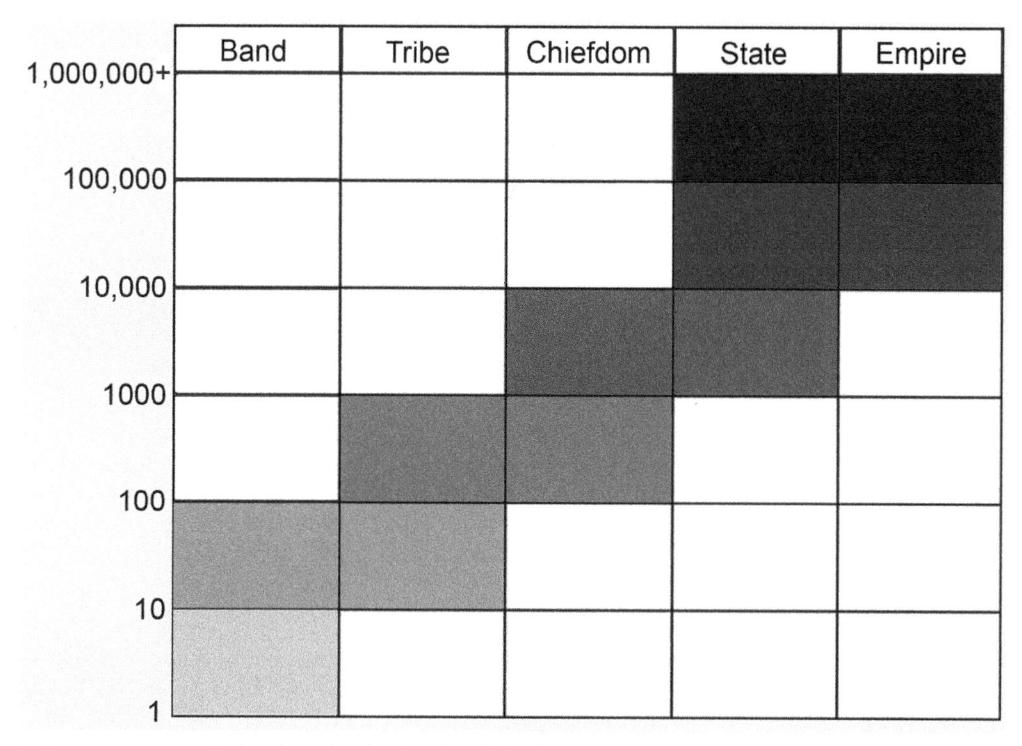

FIGURE 1.5 Simplified scale of levels of sociopolitical integration

There is a strong tendency for large tribes to adopt the characteristics of chiefdoms, including social ranking and the storage and redistribution of food. As in the case of tribes, copycat chiefdoms can form when tribes are in contact with chiefdoms and competition or perceived benefits prompt them to adopt chiefdom characteristics even in the absence of other pressures. As in the case of tribes, chiefdoms in reduced circumstances may cling to ranking and other customs rather than reverting to tribal modes of operation. There are known cases of chiefdoms having maximum community sizes as low as 200. Most are much larger, ranging up to a maximum of 10,000. Weak chiefdoms are represented by the lighter cell in that column of Figure 1.5 (Earle, 1991).

Populations above 10,000 tend to acquire complex bureaucracies, standing armies, and other characteristics of states. The upper size limit for states has not yet been reached. Modern China is a thousand times bigger than a million, and it is still increasing in numbers. States can also arise spontaneously through imitation or be spun off by colonial empires (Smith, 2004). Large states can be diminished through misfortune. Smaller, weaker states are shown as lighter shades in Figure 1.5.

Empires are typically multiethnic superstates that grow by conquest. They can fragment easily into independent states, as the British Empire and later the Soviet Union did so spectacularly in the second half of the twentieth century. Alternatively, they can sometimes evolve into large, well-integrated state organizations.

Implicit in Figure 1.5 is the observation that each of the five societal types is subordinate to those (if any) that are to its right and dominant over those (if any) to its left. Occasionally a strong chiefdom can dominate a weak state, at least temporarily. The same exception is true in the other three cases of adjacent columns. The pastoral nomads of Eurasia used military and technological advantage to intimidate the more complex societies of Europe and China several times. The absence of large domesticated animals in North America prevented the development of this dramatic exception to the general rule until the colonial period. Ultimately, there was too little time and too many epidemics to allow pastoralists to develop and become a significant threat to states in North America.

The theory represented in Figure 1.5 is simple and imperfect but serviceable and testable. Hypotheses derived from it can be tested against ethnographic data (Ember, 1963; Hays, 1998; Murdock, 1962; Murdock and Provost, 1973; Naroll, 1956). In practice, it is necessary to define types of societies according to the criteria summarized in Table 1.1, and only then scale them by population size. This process avoids the circularity inherent in simply naming societies according to their sizes. North American archaeology affords many examples of each of the five sociopolitical types.

Theoretical Approaches

Ecology is the study of the interrelationship of organisms and their environments. It helps explain and place into context the past for archaeologists. This approach is also relevant to the future, particularly now that there is concern over how we are going to adapt to a changing world, especially as human activities increasingly drive that change (Kintigh et al., 2014). Problems of a historical nature also drive much archaeological research, such as the Norse exploration of North America or battlefield archaeology (Cobb, 2014; Snow, 2016). However, historical approaches also frequently entail the forcing of choices between incompatible competing hypotheses. Scientific logic works in these cases too, but owing to the complexity of problems and the difficulty in controlling variables, choices between reasonable alternative explanations are not always possible given available evidence.

Generally, climate change has driven environmental change in North America, and this in turn has been the context for evolving human adaptation. Several lines of evidence have allowed

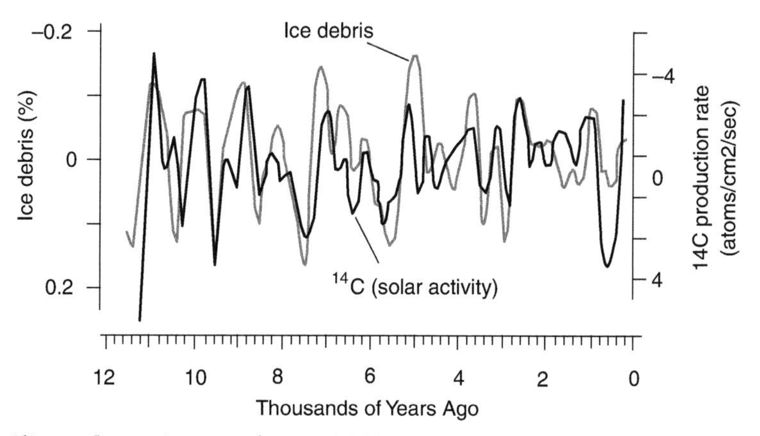

FIGURE 1.6 Climate fluctuation over the past 12,000 years

researchers to reconstruct the timing and extent of past climatic changes with increasing accuracy. The last 11,700 years following the Ice Age, or **Pleistocene** epoch, are particularly well understood. We now have a climate curve for the past 12,000 years linked to human populations that are always slightly off balance in their evolving efforts to settle on an optimal adaptation. The conditions to which they were adapting were always a moving target, sometimes moving more quickly than other times. Unlike some organisms that may have strictly bounded environmental parameters within which they can survive, humans are inherently flexible in their behavioral strategies, thereby allowing them to adapt to a broad range of shifting climatic conditions.

The curve in Figure 1.6 begins on the left with the end of the **Younger Dryas** episode (Bond et al., 2001). The Pleistocene had come to a false finale 12 centuries earlier, 12,900 years ago when disruption of ocean currents caused average temperatures to plunge to Ice Age levels once again during the Younger Dryas. The cold episode switched off again over the course of just a few years around 11,700 years ago, marking the beginning of the **Holocene**. The Holocene has been punctuated by cool episodes at a frequency of about 1,500 years, give or take a few centuries. Figure 1.6 shows that there have been nine such cooling spells over the last 12 millennia.

Warm episodes between the cold cycles have sometimes been very hot and dry. A series of three peaks between 7000 and 3500 BCE have been referred to as the **Altithermal** period within the Holocene. The three peaks were separated by relatively mild cool cycles, so the entire 3,500-year period was a time of unusually hot and dry conditions that turned parts of North America into uninhabitable deserts and put severe stresses on human adaptations in other parts of the continent. In some regions, the Altithermal period produced conditions that actually made life a bit easier for bands of hunter-gatherers.

Around a thousand years ago, Europe and North America were in the midst of the **Medieval Maximum**, an extended spell (950–1250 CE) of warm conditions that made life harder for some people but opened up possibilities for farmers in regions where previously conditions had been too marginal for farming. This was followed by the **Maunder Minimum**, popularly known as the "Little Ice Age," a cool period that lasted roughly from 1430 to 1850 CE. We are now in the **Anthropocene** epoch, a new episode of rapidly increasing warmth, this one caused by humans, mainly through our burning of fossil hydrocarbons.

These long-term climatic cycles have consequences for human populations, albeit consequences that are not often perceived as they are happening. Individual human memory is simply too short to take account of changes that occur on a scale of centuries. Shorter cycles, such as the El Niño phenomenon, are scaled much more noticeably to human lifetimes. El Niños occur every two to eight years, and cores from lakes in Peru indicate that this cycle has been going on for the last five millennia. These events were weaker and much rarer before that (Rodbell et al., 1999).

Humans adjust to changes with varying degrees of success, often depending on the speed of change and how stubbornly they cling to responses that have worked in the past. If 5% of a population perceives a new opportunity and acts on it, the other 95% may die off, leaving the prescient small group as the founder population for a new adaptation. This is something that might not happen often but produces a change in the archaeological record when it does. In this example we can see the potential for more nuanced studies of such processes played out at a human scale.

There is no shortage of interest in societal collapse and other forms of catastrophic change. Such episodes produce discontinuities in the archaeological record that are hard to miss even with our impaired hindsight. These are the tipping points between boom periods of well-being and bust periods of misery that produce a ratchet effect in human adaptation over the long term. They inform researchers interested in general processes as well as those interested in historical specifics. Whether general or specific, there are two sides to human adaptation, one conditioned by environmental forces and the other driven by potential for innovation and organization that resides in human culture. Each of the two sides of human adaptation is necessary, but by itself, each is insufficient to allow a clear understanding of the whole. Both culturally endogenous (internal) and exogenous (external) factors have to be considered in any complete explanation. Human behavior is much more than just adaptation to changing environments, for innovation often combines with individual or collective ambition to produce cultures that go beyond what is necessary for simple survival. Culture is **emergent** in the sense that it generates large patterns from the interactions of simple basic principles. Environment constrains and conditions that process, but it does not determine it in any strict sense. Environments set limits, but human innovations can and often do overcome those constraints.

Because of the complexity of past climate change, the unexpected ways in which that change can affect environment, and the unpredictable cleverness of people, the comprehension of adaptations of humans to their environments is a complex undertaking. The chapters that follow will sometimes distinguish between **focal adaptation**s, such as the brief single-minded dependence of mounted nomadic Plains Indians on bison herds, and **diffuse** (broad or generalized) **adaptation**s, like those of Great Basin hunter-gatherers. Similarly, settlements can range from highly nucleated to highly dispersed. Because density varies, the physical size of the community can vary independently of the number of inhabitants, although density does tend to remain fairly constant within a given culture (Figure 1.7).

Intensive adaptations, which are usually focal, tend to remain that way as long as they can. But focal adaptations are subject to catastrophic collapse because they lack diversification. Extensive (diffuse) adaptations can either remain so or shift toward intensive over time. Generally, societies tend to opt for intensification when the opportunity arises. The problem with increased complexity and/or increased intensity is that both tend to involve (focal) specialization. This change may result in fatally maladaptive solutions in the long run. For example, if the bison herds disappear, or extended drought wipes out the maize crop year after year, or a landslide ends salmon runs, focal adaptations that depend on these resources will collapse as well. When conditions change, more extensive (diffuse) adaptations are favored, and cultures facing them sometimes have to scramble to readapt. It is not always possible for them to do so, particularly if important technology needed for a more generalized adaptation had long since been abandoned, forgotten, or never developed in the first place. Stable environments are necessary for intensive, focal, and specialized adaptive systems to emerge and persist, and the long histories of all the regions of North America document

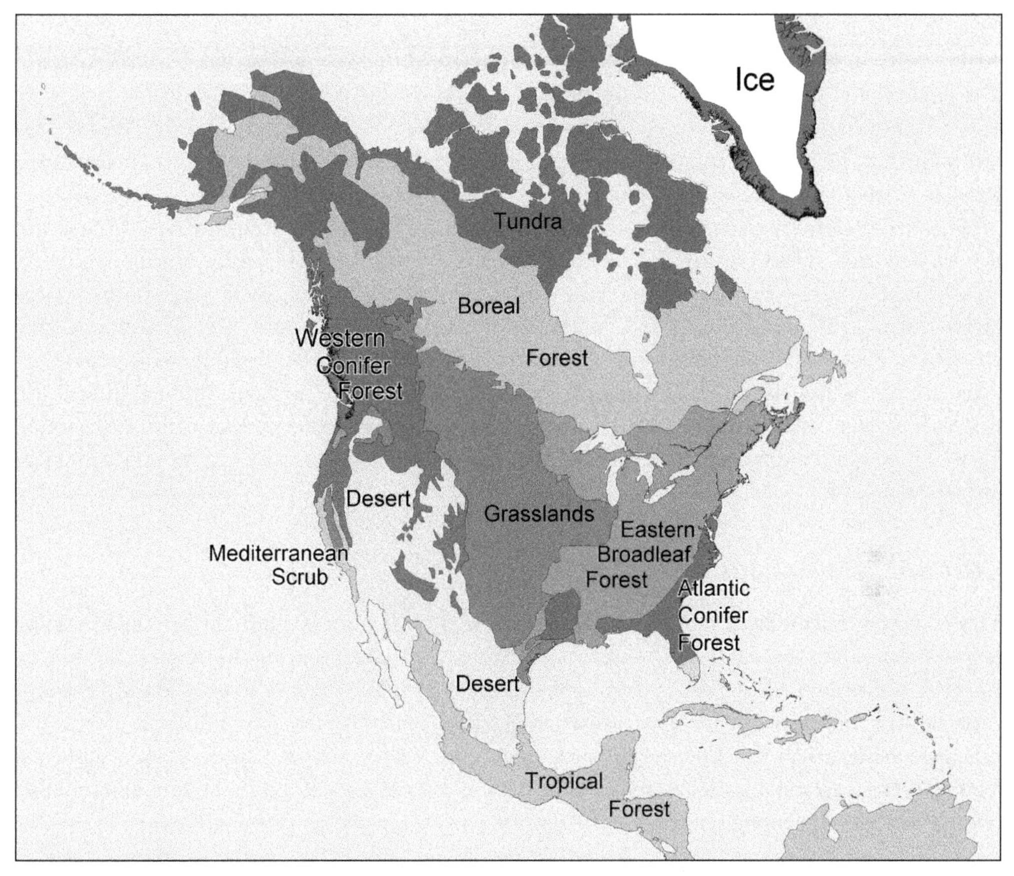

FIGURE 1.7 Modern ecozones of North America between the Arctic and Mesoamerica

the usually cautious evolution of conservative societies in that direction as their environments stabilized over the long term. The potential for catastrophe also explains why generalist hunter-gatherers persisted for so long, particularly in regions where resources have never been abundant or sufficiently predictable (Whitlam, 1983).

Generally, the larger the scale the less risky the long-term prospects. A band of two dozen people is at high risk of extinction simply because it is so small and subject to random events. A state organization of millions has much better odds for long-term survival simply because of its size and internal adaptability. At the same time, the extinction of a small band is not likely to leave a major discontinuity in the archaeological record, but the collapse of a state society is a large-scale event that is likely to be archaeologically visible. Examples of both types of cultural change appear in this book.

North America and Human Potential

That brings us back to the prior question: How and why did human cultural evolution develop as it did in North America, independent from, but along tracks that paralleled those of Eurasia and Africa? The answer probably lies not in finding what triggered the intensity of food gathering that eventually led to agriculture in so many places but rather in finding what prevented it from happening earlier. Biologically modern humans evolved in Africa perhaps 200,000 years ago, left

Africa by around 60,000 years ago, and spread across much of Eurasia and as far as Australia by 40,000 years ago (Nielsen et al., 2017). By as early as 30,000 years ago, they had reached Beringia. The capacity for all the human achievements that followed must have been latent in all of these early *Homo sapiens sapiens*, so what took them so long? What held them back until the last several millennia? The answer appears in the conditions of the planet: the hostile and unpredictable climates of the Pleistocene.

The glacial climates of the Pleistocene epoch were dry and low in atmospheric CO_2, even in regions well away from the vast ice sheets. Further, they were unpredictably variable over short time spans. Under these conditions, humans could not respond to their own population pressures by intensifying the production of food plants, a first step toward domestication. Conditions were not conducive to such intensification in many parts of the world. This constraint disappeared in many regions at the end of the Pleistocene, and the intensification of food production took off wherever suitable plants existed (Richerson et al., 2001). We might recoil from this observation for its apparent environmental determinism, but a convincing alternative explanation has yet to surface.

Calendric Conventions and Basic Terms

This book generally follows the convention of referring to past time by BCE (before the Common Era) and CE (Common Era), which are equivalent to the older, more culture-bound BC and AD usages. Radiocarbon dating is part of modern archaeology, but there is an important difference between raw radiocarbon age determinations, which often deviate from calendar years, and calibrated radiocarbon dates that have been made consistent with calendar years. Archaeologists tend to prefer calibrated radiocarbon dates because calendars and other dating techniques keyed to them become increasingly important as one approaches the present in North American archaeology. Some of the sources cited, particularly geological and climatological ones, may refer to calendar years **BP** (before present), which is set by convention to 1950 CE, as it is for radiocarbon age determinations. Thus, 10,000 BP (years before present) converts to 8050 BCE. "Before present" has the same meaning as "**YA**" (years ago).

Calendar dates are preferred in this book, which means that all radiocarbon dates have been calibrated, preferably by the investigators who paid for them, published the results, and best understand their associations with archaeological remains. Calibration should make understanding easier for most readers.

Special terms are identified in bold face as they are introduced in this book, and a glossary list at the end of each chapter provides definitions. Some terms are used rather loosely in order to facilitate communication. Archaeologists often use the word **complex** when naming a specific tool industry. The term **culture** can imply that we know more about our subject than we actually do, but it remains handy and widely understood.

The names we use to label things matter at a particular time, but often turn out later to be inappropriate. In time these names take on their own new meanings such that their origins become mere curiosities. Names are also sometimes charged with unintended meanings, banished from the generally accepted vocabulary, insisted upon for political reasons, and so forth. A brief discussion of the name game is important because archaeologists habitually name things and because names have consequences in broader contexts.

In the case of North American Indians, only "North" has some chance of not being controversial. The term "America" did not exist until 1507, when Waldseemüller used it to honor Amerigo Vespucci on his *Universalis Cosmographia* map (Waldseemüller, 1507). Columbus reached the islands of the Caribbean in 1492, but he thought that he had landed in the East Indies. The mistake led him and later writers to refer to the people of the Americas as "Indios," in English "Indians." Thus, the human subjects of this book are usually known as American Indians because of some combination of deceit and error committed over five centuries ago.

Many American Indian cultures acquired names that resulted from mistranslations, mistakes in pronunciation, or deliberate insults. Names in unfamiliar languages ensured that even honest attempts by Europeans to call groups by the names they used for themselves often failed. One result is that in several cases modern American Indian nations are asking that the rest of us call them by more appropriate names. It is a small and reasonable request, but it can confuse readers trying to use both recent and older sources when the sources use different names for the same people (see the companion website).

Archaeologists often name sites after landowners, but not always. Recent sites sometimes have the names they had when people were still living on them, but naming a site according to one found in a historical document carries with it the assumption that one has correctly identified the site. There is risk in that assumption, and there are many cases of sites that have been inappropriately named. This problem is an especially significant one for many sites that were named in the nineteenth century, when enthusiasm raced far ahead of caution in the name game. Sites still known as Aztalan, Montezuma's Castle, and Toltec in the United States are a few of the more egregious examples. All three were named according to mistaken identifications with Mexican cultures.

Whole archaeological cultures are often named for their type sites, which are considered to be exemplars. Archaeological cultures are often equivalent to or subdivided into developmental **phase**s. A temporal series of related phases can be strung together as a named **tradition.** The older archaeological literature sometimes contains terms such as "branch," "focus," or "aspect" that once had narrow definitions but are no longer used.

Projectile point types and pottery types are often named after locally significant place-names or geographic features, supplemented by some descriptive term. Often their names are the same as the sites on which they were initially defined. Examples of the results are names like "Steubenville Stemmed" points and "Red Mesa Black-on-White" pottery. They were important a few decades ago when key types were necessary for **cross dating.** Today radiocarbon and other independent techniques for dating have largely replaced cross dating. There has never been a central authority for the approval and registration of type names. That means that a single projectile point type might have two names, one in each of the two adjacent states in which it is found. Or a single type might have different names, depending on which archaeologist is authoring a publication in which the type is mentioned.

Oral Tradition

The history of American Indian cultures is largely undocumented except by archaeology, but the **oral tradition**s of their living descendants can sometimes supplement and enrich the story. The problem with archaeology, of course, is that its evidence is extremely fragmentary and indirect at best or completely silent about some topics we might wish to understand. Oral tradition can sometimes flesh out details and meanings that would otherwise remain unknown, but there is risk in this undertaking. Oral traditions, unlike traditions frozen in ancient documents, are subject to change over time. Despite the hazards, oral traditions can be helpful if used carefully. For example, the interpretation of **petroglyph**s can sometimes be illuminated by oral tradition. However, the rock art of the Great Basin was probably not left by the immediate ancestors of the region's historic inhabitants, so in this case oral tradition is either nonexistent or not applicable. While oral tradition is generally irrelevant to remains that are millennia old, it has proven to be invaluable at more recent sites. At the very least, oral tradition regularly presents archaeology with an additional source for testable hypotheses.

Art and Symbolism: Rock Art

Rock art comes in two basic forms, which are only rarely combined. Petroglyphs are pecked or engraved on rock faces. **Pictograph**s are painted on rock surfaces. Both forms occur by the thousands across the North American landscape, common in some regions but rare in others. Recording and preserving rock art has become a part- or full-time activity for many researchers.

Many North American archaeologists have traditionally avoided the study of rock art, yet it is often the most visible evidence of religion, cosmology, and symbolism in the American Indian past. Many rock art sites are open to the public, and people unfamiliar with anything else relating to the archaeology of the continent more often than not find rock art to be fascinating. Interest in it appears to be high, at least in part because, while it is physically accessible, the intellectual accessibility of rock art often seems to lie tantalizingly just beyond our reach.

This simultaneously explains why rock art is popular and why many professional archaeologists tended to avoid it until recently. Rock art is often separate and disconnected from the deposits archaeologists excavate and unassociated with the specimens and samples archaeologists use to date and understand their finds. But careful contextual analysis can sometimes overcome those constraints (Toner, 2016). As examples mentioned above and others in the chapters that follow will show, rock art sometimes cannot be related to the historic cultures of the same region. In cases where a link can be demonstrated, interpretation of rock art can be unconvincing.

However, some sites have begun to yield more reliable evidence that can be used to tie rock art more securely to the broader domain of archaeology. Careful excavation can sometimes relate rock art to datable deposits containing other kinds of archaeological evidence. Paint from rock art can sometimes be dated directly. The symbols in rock art can sometimes be directly related to ones in the ethnographic or ethnohistoric records or oral tradition (Boyd, 2016). This is good news because although most archaeological deposits are the unintentional or inadvertent results of past human activity, rock art like monumental architecture was certainly intentional. The maker of any example of rock art surely intended to communicate something meaningful, however poorly we might be able to perceive it today (Keyser and Whitley, 2006).

Many impressive rock art sites are now protected in public parks. Nearby American Indian tribes often take an active role in preservation, even when those sites lie outside reservation lands. Unfortunately, many rock art sites are at remote locations, particularly in the West, where they are vulnerable to vandalism. However, volunteer organizations are doing much to preserve and protect even sites that are remote and difficult to access. Rock art is increasingly an important public face for North American archaeology (Stewart, 2015, Loendorf et al., 2005).

Glossary

Altithermal A long series of high-temperature climatic episodes, 7000–3500 BCE.

Anthropocene The current epoch, which followed the Holocene with the onset of climatic changes caused by human activity, especially the generation of greenhouse gasses.

archaeology The scientific study of historic or prehistoric peoples by analysis of their material remains.

artifact A portable object that has been used or intentionally modified by a human being.

band The smallest human society, characterized by egalitarian relationships and typically composed of fewer than 100 people.

BCE A date before the Common Era, equivalent to BC.

BP Before present, which is set by convention to 1950 CE.

CE A date in the Common Era, equivalent to AD.

chiefdom A society of 1,000–10,000 people, characterized by social ranking and ascribed or inherited leadership.

circumscription Constraints on population expansion imposed by surrounding features of geography or other human groups.

civilization A social and political entity with a large population, institutionalized social inequality, formal legal apparatus, autocratic powers of repression, high degree of occupational specialization, permanent standing military or police force, and highly developed artistic and architectural styles or traditions.

complex A distinctive set of cultural materials that typically occur together in excavated assemblages.

connubium (pl. connubia) An abstract social unit consisting of a band and related surrounding bands.

cross dating The inferential dating of a deposit at one site to the age of a similar deposit at another site by means of shared artifact types.

culture A coherent way of life shared by members of a population that often speak the same or related languages.

demography The study of the characteristics of a human population in terms of growth, decline, and structure.

diffuse adaptation A human adaptation that is focused on a broad array of resources.

ecology The study of the interrelationship of organisms and their environments.

emergent Produced by the bottom-up formation of large, complex patterns from simple, fundamental rules.

empire A multiethnic superstate, typically created by the conquest of one or more subordinate states by a dominant state.

empirical Based on evidence and observation.

evolution Change in a reproducing population resulting from differential reproductive success.

focal adaptation A human adaptation that is focused on a narrow range of resources.

Holocene The geological epoch following the Pleistocene, which began 11,700 years ago and continued until the onset of the Anthropocene.

hypothesis (pl. hypotheses) A proposition inspired by some combination of evidence and theory that is potentially disprovable.

Maunder Minimum A cool period that lasted approximately 1430–1850 CE.

Medieval Maximum An episode of climatic warming that lasted approximately 950–1250 CE.

oral tradition Cultural traditions that are passed along from generation to generation in spoken form rather than recorded in writing.

petroglyph Rock art made by pecking or engraving.

phase An archaeological culture, limited in space and time, and often one of a developmental series.

pictograph Rock art made by painting.

Pleistocene The geological epoch lasting from 1.8 million to 11,600 years ago, popularly known as the Ice Age.

projectile point A sharp point, often made of stone, attached (hafted) to a projectile, such as a spear or arrow.

pseudoarchaeology The selective use of archaeological evidence to promote nonscientific accounts of the past.

science A set of principles and procedures for the systematic development of theory, which involves the recognition and formulation of problems, the systematic collection of data through observation and experience, and the formulation and testing of hypotheses.

site An archaeological location containing a concentration of remains.

state A society numbering over 10,000 people, having social ranking, permanent leadership, bureaucracy, and a standing army.

theory An internally consistent and well-substantiated explanation of some aspect of the world that is capable of producing testable hypotheses.

tradition A series of two or more phases representing a developmental continuum over time.

tribe A society of two or more bands, having impermanent leadership and a population typically between 100 and 1,000.

YA Years ago, equivalent to before present (BP), which is set by convention to 1950 CE.

Younger Dryas A return to Ice Age conditions that occurred 12,900–11,700 BP.

References

Ames, K.M. (1996). Archaeology, Style, and the Theory of Coevolution. In: H.D.G. Maschner, ed. *Darwinian Archaeologies*. New York: Springer.

Bond, G., Kromer, B., Beer, J., Muscheler, R., Evans, M.N., Showers, W., Hoffmann, S., Lotti-Bond, R., Hajdas, I., and Bonani, G. (2001). Persistent Solar Influence on North Atlantic Climate During the Holocene. *Science*, 294, pp. 2130–2136.

Boyd, C.E. (2016). *The White Shaman Mural: An Enduring Creation Narrative in the Rock Art of the Lower Pecos*. Austin: University of Texas Press.

Carneiro, R.L. (1970). A Theory of the Origin of the State. *Science*, 169, pp. 733–738.

Cobb, C.R. (2014). The Once and Future Archaeology. *American Antiquity*, 79, pp. 589–595.

Durham, W.H. (1991). *Coevolution: Genes, Culture, and Human Diversity*. Stanford, CA: Stanford University Press.

Earle, T. (1991). The Evolution of Chiefdoms. In: T. Earle, ed. *Chiefdoms: Power, Economy, and Ideology*. New York: Cambridge University Press.

Ember, M. (1963). The Relationship between Economic and Political Development in Nonindustrialized Societies. *Ethnology*, 2, pp. 228–248.

Feder, K. (2013). *Frauds, Myths, and Mysteries: Science and Pseudoscience in Archaeology*. Boston, MA: McGraw-Hill Mayfield.

Hays, D.G. (1998). *The Measurement of Cultural Evolution in the Non-literate World*. New York: Metagram Press.

Hill, K.R., Walker, R.S., Božičević, M., Eder, J., Headland, T., Hewlett, B., Hurtado, M., Marlowe, F., Wiessner, P., and Wood, B. (2011). Co-Residence Patterns in Hunter-Gatherer Societies Show Unique Human Social Structure. *Science*, 331, pp. 1286–1289.

Hunn, E. (1994). Place Names, Population Density and the Magic Number 500. *Current Anthropology*, 35, pp. 81–85.

Keyser, J.D., and Whitley, D.S. (2006). Sympathetic Magic in Western North American Rock Art. *American Antiquity*, 71, pp. 3–26.

Kintigh, K.W. et al. (2014). Grand Challenges for Archaeology. *American Antiquity*, 79, pp. 5–24.

Kroeber, A.L. (1948). *Anthropology*. New York: Harcourt, Brace and Company.

Loendorf, L.L., Chippindale, C., and Whitley, D.S. (eds.) (2005). *Discovering North American Rock Art*. Tucson: University of Arizona Press.

Mainfort, R.C., and Kwas, M.L. (2004). The Bat Creek Stone Revisited: A Fraud Exposed. *American Antiquity*, 69, pp. 761–769.

Murdock, G.P. (1962). Ethnographic Atlas. *Ethnology*, 1 ff.

Murdock, G.P., and Provost, C. (1973). Measurement of Cultural Complexity. *Ethnology*, 12, pp. 379–392.

Naroll, R. (1956). A Preliminary Index of Social Development. *American Anthropologist*, 58, pp. 687–715.

Nielsen, R., Akey, J.M., Jakobsson, M., Pritchard, J.K., Tishkoff, S., and Willerslev, E. (2017). Tracing the Peopling of the World through Genomics. *Nature*, 541, pp. 302–310.

Premo, L.S. (2016). Effective Population Size and the Effects of Demography on Cultural Diversity and Technological Complexity. *American Antiquity*, 81, pp. 605–622.

Richerson, P.J., Boyd, R., and Bettinger, R.L. (2001). Was Agriculture Impossible During the Pleistocene but Mandatory During the Holocene? A Climate Change Hypothesis. *American Antiquity*, 66, pp. 387–411.

Rodbell, D.T., Seltzer, G.O., Anderson, D.M., Abbott, M.B., Enfield, D.B., and Newman, J.H. (1999). An ~15,000-Year Record of El Niño-Driven Alluviation in Southwestern Ecuador. *Science*, 283, pp. 516–520.

Service, E. (1962). *Primitive Social Organization*. New York: Random House.

Shennan, S. (2000). Population, Culture History, and the Dynamics of Culture Change. *Current Anthropology*, 41, pp. 811–835.

Smith, M.E. (2004). The Archaeology of Ancient State Economies. *Annual Review of Anthropology*, 33, pp. 73–102.

Snow, D.R. (2002). Individuals. In: J.P. Hart and J.E. Terrell, eds. *Darwin and Archaeology: A Handbook of Key Concepts*. Westport, CT: Bergin and Garvey.

Snow, D.R. (2016). The British Fortifications. In: W. Griswold and D.W. Linebaugh, eds. *The Saratoga Campaign: Uncovering an Embattled Landscape*. Lebanon, NH: University Press of New England.

Stewart, T. (2015). Putting the Petroglyphs in Context. *American Archaeology*, 19, pp. 39–45.

Toner, M. (2016). A Sense of Place. *American Archaeology*, 20, pp. 13–19.

Waldseemüller, M. (1507). *Universalis Cosmographia*. France: Saint-Dié-des-Vosges.

Whitlam, R. (1983). Models of Coastal Adaptation: The Northwest Coast and Maritimes. In: R.J. Nash, ed. *The Evolution of Maritime Cultures on the Northeast and Northwest Coasts of America*. Vancouver: Department of Archaeology, Simon Fraser University.

Williams, B.J. (1974). *A Model of Band Society*. Washington: Society for American Archaeology.

Wobst, H.M. (1974). Boundary Conditions for Paleolithic Social Systems: A Simulation. *American Antiquity*, 39, pp. 147–178.

2

EURASIAN ORIGINS

This chapter traces the movements of early human beings from their origins in Africa to the threshold of America in the far-off reaches of northeastern Siberia. Humans evolved in Africa, expanding multiple times from that continent to Europe and Asia. Modern *Homo sapiens* expanded farther than earlier forms could, adapting to cold conditions and reaching northeastern Siberia by around 30,000 BCE (Pitulko et al., 2014). Genetic, dental, and linguistic evidence is all consistent with the archaeological evidence that humans entered western **Beringia** by 21,000 BCE. There was a broad Ice Age isthmus joining Alaska and Siberia, which is today largely under water.

Over the course of the next 5,000 years, the population of Beringia expanded to 8–10,000 people (Mulligan and Kitchen, 2014). By at least 14,500 BCE, the ancestors of the American Indians were living in eastern Beringia, now Alaska, and were unknowingly poised to expand southward across two continents on which humans had never before walked (Graf et al., 2015). Domesticated dogs joined these human bands by at least 10,500 BCE, possibly earlier (Frantz et al., 2016).

Geological Background

It took a long time for us to get our turn at life on this earth. The earth is about 4.6 billion years old, and for all but the last sliver of that time, around 100,000 years, it got along just fine without modern humans. But the human past is what archaeologists study, so it is that last sliver that is our focus here. The human past in North America is an even smaller sliver of the longer saga of humanity.

Geologists have long since blocked out the major eras, periods, epochs, and stages of geological time. By the nineteenth century, the geological sequence had been divided into four great eras: the Primary, Secondary, Tertiary, and **Quaternary**. It was later discovered that the first two covered immense periods of time that were much longer and more complicated than was generally appreciated at first, so they were replaced by other terms. The Tertiary and Quaternary were recast as shorter "periods" and made parts of the more inclusive Cenozoic Era. Everything earlier was assigned to one or another of two very long eras that were named for their dominant forms of life, as shown in Table 2.1. The Cambrian period became the earliest period of the Paleozoic (Ancient Life) era. Later generations would put everything in Table 2.1 into the even more inclusive Phanerozoic eon and add earlier eons not shown here. For the time being, the absolute ages

TABLE 2.1 Recent periods of geological history. Everything here makes up the Phanerozoic eon. The Anthropocene epoch is not shown because the dating of its onset is unsettled

Eras	*Periods*	*Epochs*	*Stages*	*Began*		*Ended*	
Cenozoic	Quaternary	Holocene	Recent	11.6	tya[1]	0	tya
		Pleistocene	Late	128	tya	11.5	tya
			Middle	750	tya	128	tya
			Early	1.8	mya[2]	750	tya
	Tertiary			65	mya	1.8	mya
Mesozoic				250	mya	65	mya
Paleozoic				543	mya	250	mya

1 Thousand years ago.
2 Million years ago.

of these great building blocks of geological time were unknown. The geologists of the nineteenth century had to be content with a relative chronology, one that had all the pieces in the right order from oldest to youngest, but that lacked absolute dates.

The discovery of radioactive elements around the beginning of the twentieth century made it possible to date the components of Table 2.1 and create an absolute chronology for the geological sequence. The results astounded some physicists and delighted most biologists. Darwin had said that immense time was needed for biological evolution to work, but many nineteenth-century physicists had argued that the earth was too young to accommodate it. The new dating techniques showed that there was more than enough time for life to have evolved as Darwin had said. They also revealed that in geology, as in written history, those events closest to us in time are known in greatest detail. Mammals did not dominate until the onset of the Tertiary, which began a mere 65 million years ago, but we now know that period well enough to divide it into five epochs. The Quaternary period began only 1.8 million years ago, divided into the Pleistocene and Holocene epochs, as mentioned in Chapter 1.

The Expansion of Early Humans

Humans originated in Africa during the Pleistocene, later spreading out from there, first along the tropical fringe of southern Asia and into Europe. *Homo erectus*, the direct ancestors of *Homo sapiens*, evolved in Africa around 1.7 million years ago. These people looked like us in most respects, but their skulls were more robust and their brain cases were smaller. It is likely that they did not have language as we know it, for their tools were simple, crude enough to have been made by people who learned by simply mimicking one another. But they probably cooperated with each other, driven to it for mutual support in the millennia before they evolved from a prey species to a predator species (Brooks et al., 2005). They might have been able to control fire, and they were adaptable enough to spread out of Africa to other warm parts of the Eastern Hemisphere. This expansion of the *Homo erectus* population was an adaptive radiation that carried them into southern Europe and across southern Asia to the Indonesian archipelago. The first *Homo erectus* skull found was the famous Java man, but others have since been found elsewhere across southern Europe and Asia (Figure 2.1).

The zones of climate and vegetation of Asia tend to be east–west bands that facilitate movement in those directions by animals adapted to them. Even today moving north or south in Asia more often requires greater adaptation than moving east or west. For humans these may be largely cultural

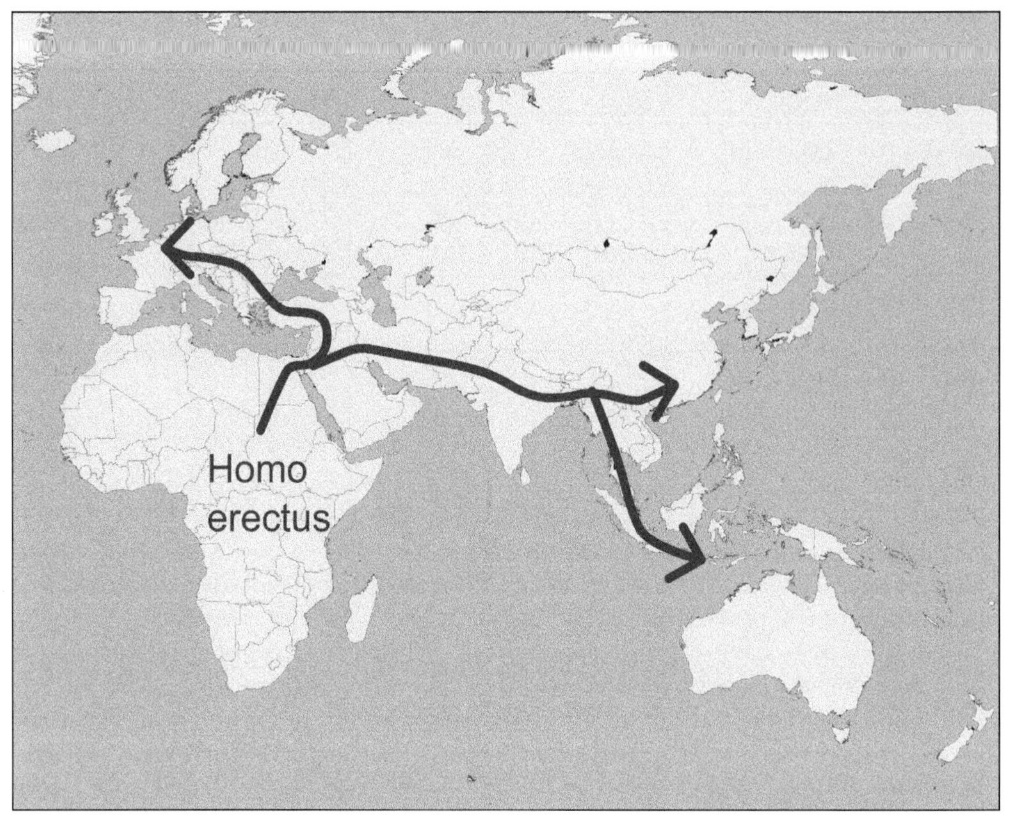

FIGURE 2.1 *Homo erectus* expanded out of Africa to Europe and southern Asia after evolving in Africa

adaptations, but some biological adaptations were also entailed in the distant past. Moreover, adaptation to new environments by early human populations was harder the farther they penetrated into the higher latitudes. Because virtually all of Asia lies north of the equator, the higher latitudes were mostly northward.

Early branches of *Homo sapiens*, people popularly called Neanderthals and Denisovans, moved northward into Eurasia beginning around 180,000 years ago (Figure 2.2). The Neanderthals were equipped with at least stone tools and minimally adequate clothing for colder regions. Recent evidence has shown that these and perhaps other populations of early *Homo sapiens* later dwindled to extinction (Stringer and Galway-Witham, 2018).

Based on current evidence, it is most likely that our branch, *Homo sapiens sapiens*, evolved in Africa prior to 100,000 years ago. Our ancestors could communicate easily with each other, empathize, and even anticipate each other's actions, probably more effectively than the Neanderthals and other earlier branches of *Homo sapiens*. They collaborated, created friendships with nonrelatives, shared food, and in short did all those things that today set humans apart from all other living species.

The earliest art is associated with *Homo sapiens sapiens*, and our capacity for modern language might have emerged then as well. The adaptive advantage of a gene or small set of genes that produce these and other capabilities was so extraordinary that it must have spread rapidly, both as people having them bred with those lacking them and as populations having them expanded and displaced the earlier human populations. No new feature arises *for* anything, so like birds, which

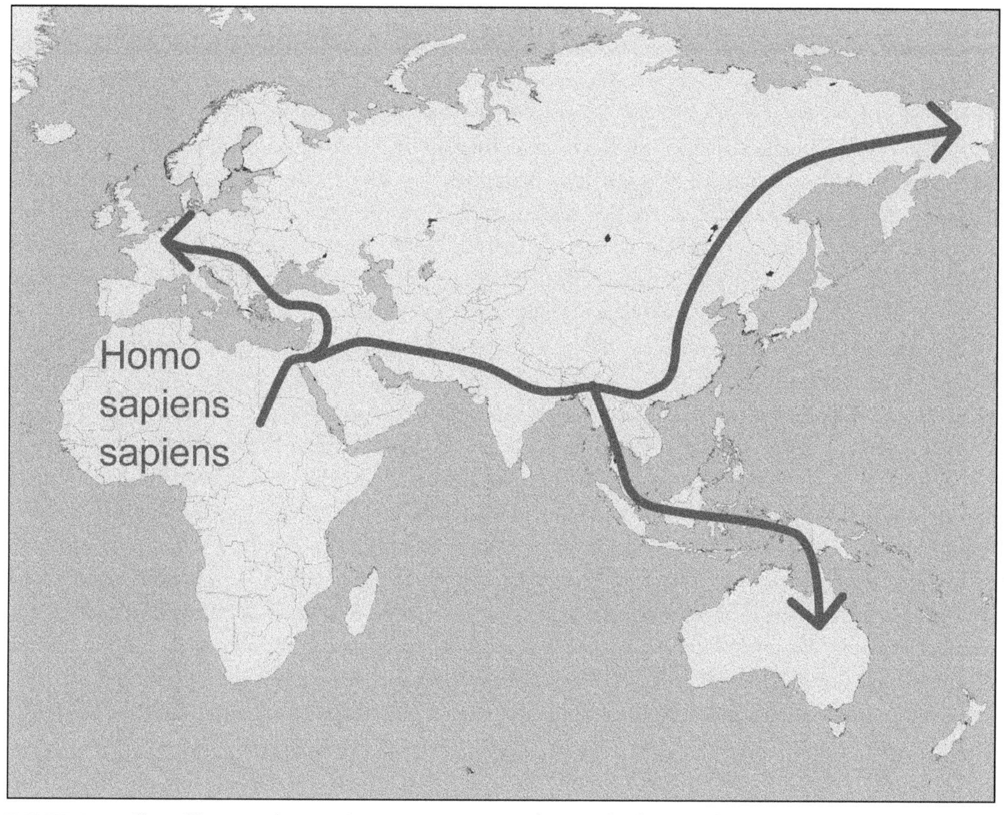

FIGURE 2.2 Our *Homo sapiens sapiens* ancestors spread out of Africa and across the tropical and temperate parts of Eurasia, reaching northeastern Siberia by 30,000 years ago

evolved flight based on feathers that evolved for other reasons, we got lucky when random mutation made tiny but key changes in some remote ancestor's brain (Bae et al., 2017).

Environment and Adaptation

Most of what this book covers is relegated to the Holocene, but the roots of the human presence in the Americas go back to the late Pleistocene, sometime prior to 14,500 BCE. The climate history of North America has always set the moving parameters of environmental conditions to which people have had to adapt. The environments that result from the interactions of climate, physiography, vegetation, animal species, and latitude do not determine human adaptation, but they do set limits to it.

The single most dominant feature of the North American landscape prior to 11,600 years ago (9650 BCE) was glacial ice. Vast dynamic Pleistocene ice sheets spread out of northern Canada and down from the Rocky Mountains, carrying along pulverized earth and rock like a slow-motion conveyor belt, spewing torrents of meltwater from their leading edges, depressing the landscape hundreds of meters under their enormous weight, forming vast glacial lakes, and casting a chill upon the continent. The depression of the landscape, and the rebound that occurs after glacial ice disappears, is called **isostatic** change.

The coastlines of North America and other continents moved seaward with falling sea level during the Pleistocene, as more and more of the earth's water was locked up on land as glacial ice.

The balance of snowfall and melting was shifted by cooling climate so that year after year snow accumulated and compacted into glacial ice in the Far North and in the higher mountains, in some places to thicknesses measurable in kilometers rather than meters. Sea levels lowered to 100–150 meters (m) below their current levels. Glaciers spread because the weight of accumulation in the ice caps forced ice to flow slowly out from the centers of accumulation, creating dynamic moving lobes of ice, some of which moved southward until they reached warmer regions where melting balanced the rate of advance. There the debris carried by the moving ice accumulated in large **moraine** deposits that can still be recognized today. New York's Long Island is one such end moraine deposit. Others stretch westward from there to the Midwest, marking the lines where the dynamic margins of the great moving ice sheets stood for long periods.

The largest North American ice sheet was the Laurentide sheet, which formed over what is now north-central Canada (Figure 2.3). Another, the Cordilleran ice sheet, formed over the Rockies and the other major mountain ranges of western North America. This sheet expanded out of the mountains until its eastern margin collided with the Canadian Laurentide sheet advancing westward. On its western side, tongues of the Cordilleran sheet advanced down mountain valleys to the Pacific, often pushing out across a continental shelf laid bare by lowered sea levels. The last major advance along the Northwest Coast peaked 14–16,000 BCE. Melting rates overtook rates of ice advance by 12,000 BCE, and by 10,000 BCE, most of the coastline of the Northwest Coast was no longer under glacial ice. By 7500 BCE, Cordilleran ice was almost entirely confined to the mountains. Similar dates mark the peak size and later retreat of the Laurentide sheet. The shrinkage of the massive ice sheets at last permitted humans to expand southward easily. However, just when and how the first Americans arrived remains the topic of continuing archaeological research and debate.

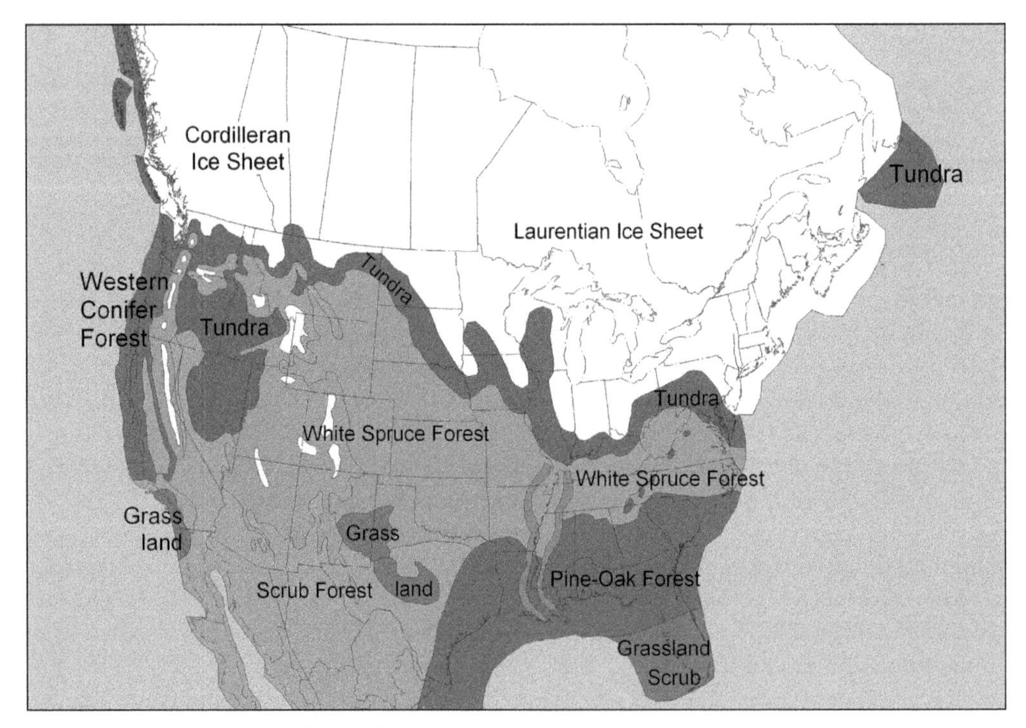

FIGURE 2.3 Pleistocene ice sheets of North America at their maximum extent

The archaeological record of the first arrivals was complicated by a temporary setback in environmental conditions. Pleistocene climate did not come to a graceful end. Its last gasp, the Younger Dryas climatic reversal, lasted fourteen centuries. This episode of colder conditions lasted from around 12,900 to 11,700 YA (10,950 to 9250 BCE), a span that turns out to have been contemporary with the first widespread archaeological culture of North America, the Paleoindians. That culture is reasonably well known today, but what preceded it prior to 12,900 years ago is still much less well understood.

The human expansion northward and eastward toward America depended upon cultural adaptation to colder regions, new technology, and clever use of it. Just when and how this happened continues to be the focus of current archaeological research. No convincing evidence exists for any premodern humans in the Western Hemisphere despite some recent claims (Holen et al., 2017). Most archaeologists agree that people did not reach Beringia until after 25,000 years ago and thus well after modern *Homo sapiens* had emerged and earlier humans forms had all but disappeared. Only modern humans had the cultural capacity to expand into and live in the cold reaches of northeastern Eurasia, the only route to the Americas at a time when humans still lacked advanced seagoing boats. The Americas had lain well over the horizon and far beyond the theater of human evolution until near the end of the last Ice Age.

Genetic Evidence

The evidence of DNA, particularly evidence from **mitochondrial DNA** and **Y-chromosome** DNA, has helped clarify the origins of modern American Indians. We all carry loops of mitochondrial DNA (mtDNA) in our cells in addition to the nuclear DNA that encodes our physical makeup. We inherit the mtDNA strands from our mothers. The strands are more abundant than nuclear DNA and thus easier to extract and study. Rare mutations over the long term have created different lineages of mtDNA, which can be used to trace descendant populations back to their geographic origins. The genetic variants, or **haplotype**s, that define the lineages are relatively few and very useful for this purpose.

Haplotypes in mtDNA cluster into a handful of diagnostic **haplogroup**s (A, B, C, D, and X) that are found in varying proportions in sample populations drawn from the Americas and Asia. The proportions found in American Indian populations are most similar to those of central Asia. Another form of haplogroup X is present in certain European populations, and it appears to be 35–14,600 years old. The haplogroup X variant is diverse, though, and the American variant is distinct from the European one. There are also two useful haplogroups (C and Q) on the Y-chromosome, a nuclear chromosome carried only by men and inherited through the male line. These too point to American Indian origins in northeast Asia. However the details are eventually resolved, it is clear that the genetic evidence confirms the Siberian origins of American Indians.

Geneticists are able to date the ages of haplogroups because they can estimate the rate of mutations that produced them. That is how they estimate that haplogroup X is at least 14,600 years old. Thus, the genes of American Indians tell us that they have been a distinctive population for at least that many years. Even the ancestors of the Nadene and Inuit populations, long considered to be more recent arrivals, were part of the founding population of ancient Beringia. The genetic evidence generally agrees with the archaeological evidence, indicating that Beringia was occupied no more than 23,000 years ago and that the ancestors of American Indians were isolated there for no more than 8,000 years. Thus both the upper and lower limits on the peopling of the Americas are understood (Raghavan and Al, 2015).

The Evidence of Languages

Languages also inform us about the human past because historical linguists are able to not only show how they split and multiplied over time but to even reconstruct parts of extinct ancestral languages. There were probably about a thousand distinct languages being spoken in the Americas in 1492. Of these, perhaps 400 were being spoken in North America (Figure 2.4). These seem like very large numbers until it is remembered that about 800 languages are being spoken today just on the island of New Guinea. The propagation of new languages is something that occurs naturally as populations expand and fragment. Related speech communities become isolated from one another over time, and when this happens, the languages drift apart due to their own internal evolutionary dynamics.

The rate at which languages drift apart can be measured in terms of the half-lives of words. This is the amount of time required for there to be a 50% chance that a word will be replaced by a new

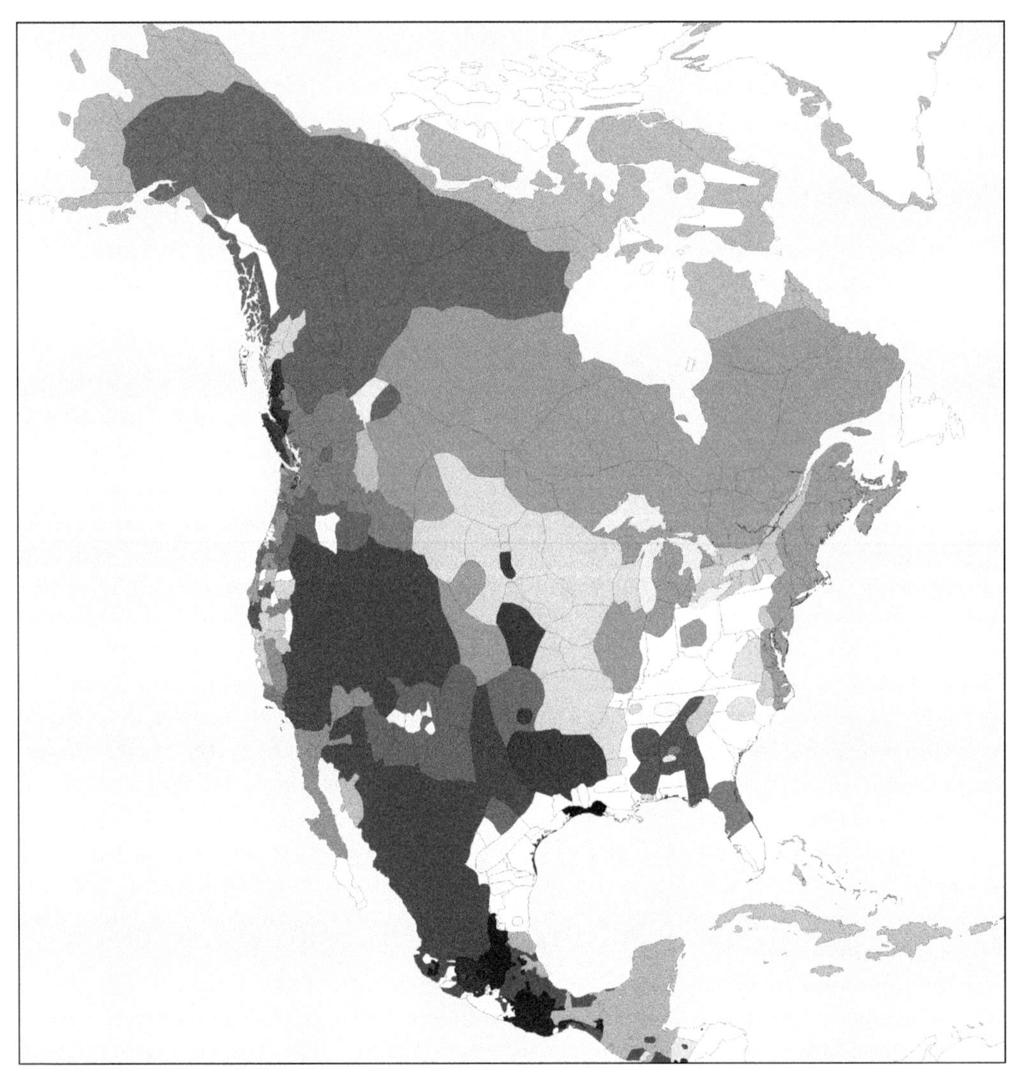

FIGURE 2.4 Language families of North America at the time of European contact. See the Companion Website for a color version

word. For most words, the half-life is about 2,000 years, but for a few very conservative words, it might be greater than 10,000 years (Gray, 2005). A problem is that even though a word might survive for thousands of years it will change as sound systems evolve, making them recognizable only to experienced linguists. Thus, the linkages between related languages are often very difficult to trace after a few thousand years. This severely limits the usefulness of languages in tracing more ancient origins, but their discussion is included here because of well-known attempts to use them in that way (Cavalli-Sforza and Cavalli-Sforza, 1995; Greenberg, 1996).

Linguists have more recently debated the time necessary for the known diversity of American languages to have evolved. While some estimates put the required time at 50,000 years, others set it at only half that, and the debate is not yet resolved. Even 25,000 years would require some of that diversification to have played out in Siberia or Beringia to make it fit the archaeological evidence.

The process of language diversification is amplified by increasing population density, decreased mobility, the rise of political barriers, and geographic isolation. All of these apply to the agricultural groups of New Guinea, where there are many languages. The reverse is found in eastern subarctic Canada, where thin, mobile populations have existed for many centuries. In this case, a single language, Cree-Montagnais-Naskapi, has persisted for a very long time over a large region because tiny widespread mobile bands have stayed linked to one another. Easy communication persisted over the long run between adjacent bands, but a Naskapi person from the east and a Cree person from the west would have some difficulty communicating if they were suddenly thrown together. In this case, the language is so variable over space that some linguists refer to it as a language complex, and it is clear that if something caused the complex to split into two or more isolated populations, separate and mutually unintelligible languages would form. But because population density is low, mobility is high, distances are great, and isolation is low, the Cree-Montagnais-Naskapi language complex persists.

By studying language structures and vocabularies, linguists have been able to group most American Indian languages into families. Related languages can be shown to descend from common ancestors called **protolanguages.** Linguists can even reconstruct parts of the vocabularies of protolanguages from the vocabularies of the daughter languages, based on known rules of sound change over time. This kind of analysis has been verified many times by reference to language families that have long histories of writing. Thus, for example, the English word "hound" is **cognate** with the German word "hund," and the sound changes that occurred in both after the breakup of their common protolanguage can be traced with considerable accuracy. Many such cognates exist between related languages, but occasionally they are replaced over time by completely different words, sometimes words borrowed from other languages, sometimes internally generated neologisms. Thus "hound" has taken on a narrower usage in English, and the **semantic** equivalent of the German "hund" is now "dog" in English. "Dog" originally referred to just a particularly powerful breed in Old English. If for some reason our descendants all come to prefer the Spanish word "perro," future linguists will have to dig even deeper to understand what happened.

It is not just word replacements and sound changes that interest linguists; semantic shifts (changes in meaning) can push a word to a corner of the vocabulary where it might not be noticed. For example, one might conclude that the Spanish word for horse (*caballo*) did not derive from earlier Latin roots until one realizes that it derives from a Latin word for "nag" that replaced the Latin term for horse (*equus*) over time.

The Northern Iroquoian language family is an informative case. There are over a dozen Northern Iroquoian languages known; some of them are still spoken. The differences between them are about as pronounced as the differences between the closely related Romance languages of Europe, which include Spanish, Portuguese, French, Italian, and some others. Thus the time depth since the breakup of the Northern Iroquoian protolanguage is probably about equivalent to the time it has taken the Romance languages to emerge from various colonial forms of Latin, more than one but less than two millennia. Some other American Indian language families have constituent languages that are as closely related as the Northern Iroquoian languages are, but others do not hold together nearly as well, usually because they broke up longer ago. Linguists still debate whether the Penutian language family of the Far West really holds together, and those that think it does argue that the common protolanguage was probably spoken more than 6,000 years ago (Nichols, 2002). In addition, there are isolates, some of which cannot be easily classified with any other languages. Cherokee is the only surviving example of Southern Iroquoian, related to Northern Iroquoian to be sure, but without close sister languages. Tsimshianic and Zuni are both small isolates that might or might not be distantly related to the Penutian family, depending upon which linguist one consults. Similarly, Beothuk, the extinct native language of Newfoundland, might or might not have been related to the Algonquian language family, but too few words of it are known for anyone to be sure. Some such isolates that are now extinct will probably never be linked to other languages because we lack and cannot acquire the necessary information. Others will be linked by way of ancient connections only after much more research.

We know that people have been in the Americas for several millennia, so it is no surprise that we have many language isolates and little consensus among linguists about how language families were connected in deep time. A few have been willing to assume that most American Indian languages descend from the same very ancient protolanguage. But this solution leaps over problems of classification rather than specifying solutions for them. Most linguists take a bottom-up empirical approach, preferring to establish language families as sets of demonstrably related languages before moving on to link families into larger units. There are no fewer than 21 families and many unclassified isolates that they could have listed as the sole survivors of still more families (Campbell and Mithun, 1979). Volume 17 of the authoritative *Handbook of North American Indians* inventories no fewer than 62 language families and isolates (Goddard, 1996:4–8).

If a protolanguage can break up into, say, ten daughter languages over the course of a millennium, then it would be easy for many more than the 400 or so known languages to have resulted in the time available since the first peopling of North America. In fact, such a rapid rate of new language formation would predict that there were many now unknowable languages, and even some language families, that must have appeared and then gone extinct over that much time. If the rate of language splitting can be measured, we have another dating technique, but attempts to gauge rates of linguistic change are notoriously inaccurate. **Glottochronology**, which uses standard rates of word replacement in vocabularies as a means to estimate the age of the split between any two related languages, works convincingly only some of the time and only for closely related languages.

It is clear that comparative linguistics has difficulty finding connections between languages that have been separate for more than a few thousand years. Even the most optimistic linguists set the limit at 8,000±2,000 years (Dunn et al., 2005). The good news is that using language structure, sound systems, and grammar, rather than vocabularies, might allow historical linguists to extend the time depths at which languages can be linked. At least for now, archaeology provides the best reliable means for dating the peopling of the Americas.

Languages also define speech communities, the networks of individuals that normally interact with one another and think of themselves as both related to one another and different from the foreign others that reside beyond the barrier of easy communication. The speech community is a handy concept because it typically approximates the concept of archaeological culture that is used in this book. The concept also accommodates the phenomenon of language switching, when a community shifts from speaking one language to speaking another, sometimes in a matter of only three generations.

The Evidence of Bones and Teeth

There are several sets of human remains known for the earliest American Indian inhabitants of North America. Generally speaking these remains reflect the same Siberian origins as modern DNA and native language analyses. As the celebrated case of Kennewick Man demonstrates, research on ancient skeletal remains has been fraught with controversy in recent decades (Meltzer, 2015). Some of the reasons for this are discussed further in the last chapter of this book.

When reconstructed by a forensic specialist, the face of Kennewick Man did not look particularly American Indian to many of the people who saw it. But DNA analysis showed that the remains were consistent with Native American and Siberian heritage. Ancient bones can also reveal much about individual diets, geographic origins, and other details of individual life histories and the histories of the populations to which the individuals belonged. But as Kennewick Man has shown, expected physical features can change over the course of a few thousand years.

Curiously, teeth are perhaps more reliable than other skeletal features. Human teeth are much more variable than most of us think, and distinctive dental characteristics also point to Siberian origins for the American Indians. We are all aware that many people lack some or all of their third molars, or wisdom teeth. But molars also can vary in the number of cusps or roots they have. A supernumerary root on lower first molars (3RM1) is common in northeast Asia, present in 6% of Native Americans, but very rare or absent in modern and prehistoric Europeans. Incisors can vary by the degree to which their back (lingual) sides have shovel-shaped ridges, also common in northeast Asia and the Americas but absent elsewhere (Powell, 1993; Turner II, 1989; Turner II, 2002).

Demography and Conflict

People first expanded into Siberia from the south, lured by the game that roamed there but constrained by environment and the limitations of their technology. Siberia is a bleak place today, but it was an even more challenging environment 30,000 years ago. Vast continental ice sheets in western Eurasia and North America locked up much of the world's water, exposing continental shelf and land bridges that today lie covered by shallow seas. The Bering Strait did not exist then, but the term "land bridge" misrepresents Beringia. The isthmus connecting Siberia and Alaska was actually 1,600 km (1,000 mi) across, not at all a narrow bridge. Small ice caps existed here and there, but for the most part the regions of northeastern Siberia and western Alaska that made up much of Beringia were parts of a single, largely unglaciated, landmass the size of Australia. Figure 2.5 shows the approximate location of the Pleistocene shoreline of Beringia and the locations of sites mentioned in this chapter.

Researchers have made a strong case for boat travel in the Late Pleistocene. After all, by 65,000 years ago, people had made it to New Guinea, Australia, and nearby islands, something that they could not have done without at least crude boats, even though they could have seen their destinations on the horizon. But open ocean crossings were another matter. The Pacific Ocean was a forbidding obstacle, and even hardy boaters would have stayed near the fringe of land. The more distant islands of Oceania, or for that matter Madagascar, would not be found and settled for thousands of years. For the human populations of eastern Asia 30 millennia ago, the Pacific was a vast obstacle that could be overcome only by expansion northeastward through the interior of Beringia or along its Pacific coast. Of course, nobody knew yet that Beringia was there, or that two unoccupied American continents laid beyond it.

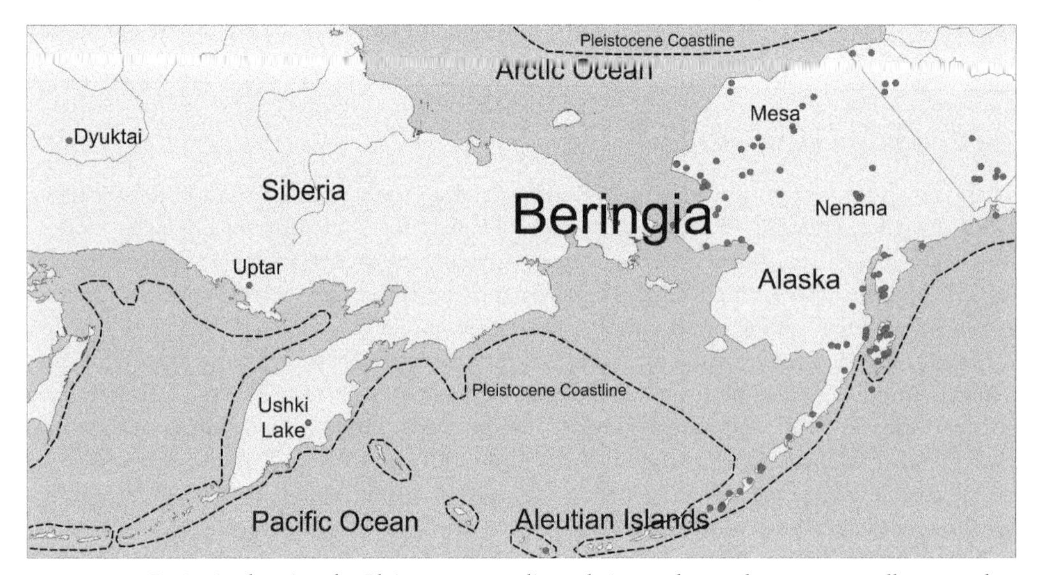

FIGURE 2.5 Beringia, showing the Pleistocene coastline relative to the modern one, as well as some key archaeological sites

Just as important, the slow expansion toward America was not intentional in the sense that they anticipated expansion into the Americas. The horizons of the hunter-gatherers of Siberia were limited to the scope of their personal experience and the information they could pick up from their relatives in other bands. Their decisions were short-range ones, conditioned by the opportunities and capabilities that they had at hand, but collectively those short-range decisions drew them farther and farther afield as their capabilities improved. Competition for game and a natural preference for relocation over conflict added to the attraction of game animals just over the horizon to drive the expansion of these bands of humans. The nature of band organization is discussed in greater depth in Chapter 3.

The rising human tide in eastern Asia carried the earliest American populations eastward out of Siberia. But the process was slow because the skills required to survive in northeastern Siberia were not easy to come by. Thin human populations expanded northward on to the northern steppe of Siberia, then fell back again more than once before reaching a latitude that would allow them to gradually expand eastward into America. Evidence from Bluefish Caves in Canada's Yukon Territory indicates that people were living there in small numbers by 24,000 years ago (Bourgeon et al., 2017). This is good news for geneticists and linguists whose research suggests that much time is needed to explain later observed diversity. Perhaps human bands were resident in Beringia from then on; perhaps humans expanded into the hostile Beringian environment more than once, falling back to Siberia when conditions required. Whichever possible scenario of Beringian occupation turns out to be more likely, archaeological evidence indicates that the way southward was blocked by massive ice sheets until after around 14,500 years ago (12,500 BCE).

Subsistence and Economy

The ecological zones of Eurasia were displaced by climate much farther southward in the Late Pleistocene than they are today. The ecozones of the north lie approximately in bands across the

TABLE 2.2 Ecozone bands of northeastern Siberia arranged north to south

Ecozone name	*Type*
Tundra (Arctic)	Tundra
Taiga	Boreal Forest
Forest-Steppe	Park Grassland
Steppe	Grassland

region, with the tundra band farthest north and the steppe farthest south (Table 2.2). During the Late Pleistocene, southern Siberia was a patchwork of these zones, with tundra on elevations and treeless steppe in the valleys. Northward was mostly an Ice Age environment often referred to as "mammoth steppe," a biome that supported mammoths and other large herd animals but was very cold, lacked edible plants for humans, and was short on wood for fuel and shelter. The people were generalized hunter-gatherers, taking Mongolian gazelles, argali sheep, horses, woolly rhinoceros, reindeer, steppe bison, and Siberian mountain goats as opportunities arose, but they undoubtedly gathered a few plants as well (Goebel, 1999: 215–216).

Traveling Companions

Dogs are the oldest domestic species, unless we count ourselves. Genetic evidence is still being evaluated to determine whether domesticated dogs arose from wolf ancestors only once or on two or more occasions (Frantz et al., 2016). However that eventually sorts out, larger genetic variation among dogs in eastern Asia suggests that this was a region in which an early population of dogs evolved, possibly as early 13,000 BCE. Several maternal DNA lineages were present in the population of domesticated dogs that diverged from wolves, and they persisted in the population that expanded with humans into the Americas.

One DNA lineage is unique to American dogs, indicating that it arose through mutation after dogs arrived in North America. This serves as further evidence that dogs came with the first humans, already hunting companions, camp cleaners, and sentinels. The unique American **clade** of domesticated dogs never spread back into Eurasia. It is also the case that it is largely absent from modern dog breeds in America, indicating that colonists from Europe discouraged breeding between their imported breeds and native American dogs (Leonard et al., 2002).

Dogs and humans communicate very well, better in fact than great apes, our closest living relatives, and humans do (MacLean and Hare, 2015). Puppies whine like human babies and have other behaviors that ingratiate them to humans. They are also very good at making eye contact and reading human cues, signals that help them find food in test situations or carry out commands that lead to food rewards. These abilities, which are present even in puppies who have had little prior human contact, are absent in wolves, even those that have been raised by humans. That means that there was strong selection for social and cognitive abilities during the course of dog domestication (Hare et al., 2002). But it does not necessarily mean that dog domestication was an intentional process on the part of ancient Asian hunters. It might have been fortuitous, emerging from chance associations between humans and a few unusual mutant wolves that happened to have the mental skills that preadapted them to cooperate with people. So far, the oldest archaeological evidence for domesticated dogs in eastern Siberia appears to be the 10,650-year-old dog burial at Ushki-1 (Dikov, 1996; Morey, 2006).

Architecture and Technology

Another byproduct of our ancestors' new capacity for language was technological. By around 50,000 years ago, hunters were making small projectile points that could be used to tip spears that could be launched at game or human enemies, a terrific advance over heavier thrusting spears (Brooks et al., 2005). Spear throwers were still being used in some places in the Americas when Europeans arrived. Aztec soldiers used them to launch torrents of spears against the Spanish invaders. It was a formidable weapon, and it eventually gave our ancestors as much advantage over *Homo erectus* people and the Neanderthals of Europe as guns would later give the Spanish over the Aztecs. Even better, our early ancestors had an improved intuitive grasp of the geometry of landscape and their three-dimensional world, a legacy shared today by all of us (Dehaene et al., 2006).

The spear thrower (called "atlatl" by the Aztecs) is typically a wooden shaft about as long as a forearm. At one end there is a handle or perhaps a couple of finger loops. At the other end is a hook designed to fit loosely into a socket at the end of a spear. The hunter (or warrior) holds the spear loosely in the same hand that holds the spear thrower, with the butt of the spear set against the hook (Figure 2.6). The spear is thrown with the same motion that one swings a tennis racket, except that as the spear thrower whips through the air, the spear is released so that it is propelled by just the far end of the spear thrower, which (like the head of a tennis racket) is moving at a much greater speed than the hunter's hand. Once launched, the spear is flying faster than the fastest javelin because of the boost provided by the spear thrower.

Spear throwers were made of perishable materials, so they are rarely found by archaeologists. The oldest one known probably dates to no more than 18,000 years ago (16,050 BCE), so the arguments in favor of its invention thousands of years earlier is inferential and based on the sizes of the stone projectile points that have survived. Small points would make no sense on heavy thrusting spears. However, there is a weight limit for those used on the lighter spears, sometimes called **dart**s, that were launched with spear throwers. The impact of a thrown spear was a product of its weight and velocity, so clever people could increase impact by significantly increasing velocity, even if weight was reduced somewhat.

Such were the weapons and the skills of early modern humans, some of whom expanded to the extreme northeast of Siberia. The bow and arrow would come later. Like every human alive today, they descended from common ancestors that lived not very long ago in the grand scheme of things. Thus the first Americans for the most part necessarily looked like us, talked like us, and thought like us. Sorting out the details of what happened next requires the use of several lines of evidence (Snow, 2009).

Not surprisingly, the earliest Siberian sites left by modern humans are south of 55° north latitude. The sites that interest American archaeologists most are the few later ones found to the north of that line (Figure 2.7). They are, for the most part, open sites on bluffs or terraces, looking out over broad floodplains. Hearths at the centers of larger rings of stone indicate that these people were living in skin tents. Their stone tools included **biface**s and long, slender blades struck from cores of fine-grained **chert**, a family of hard glassy stones that includes flint. The chert bifaces were

FIGURE 2.6 A time-lapse series showing how a spear thrower is used to launch a small spear or dart

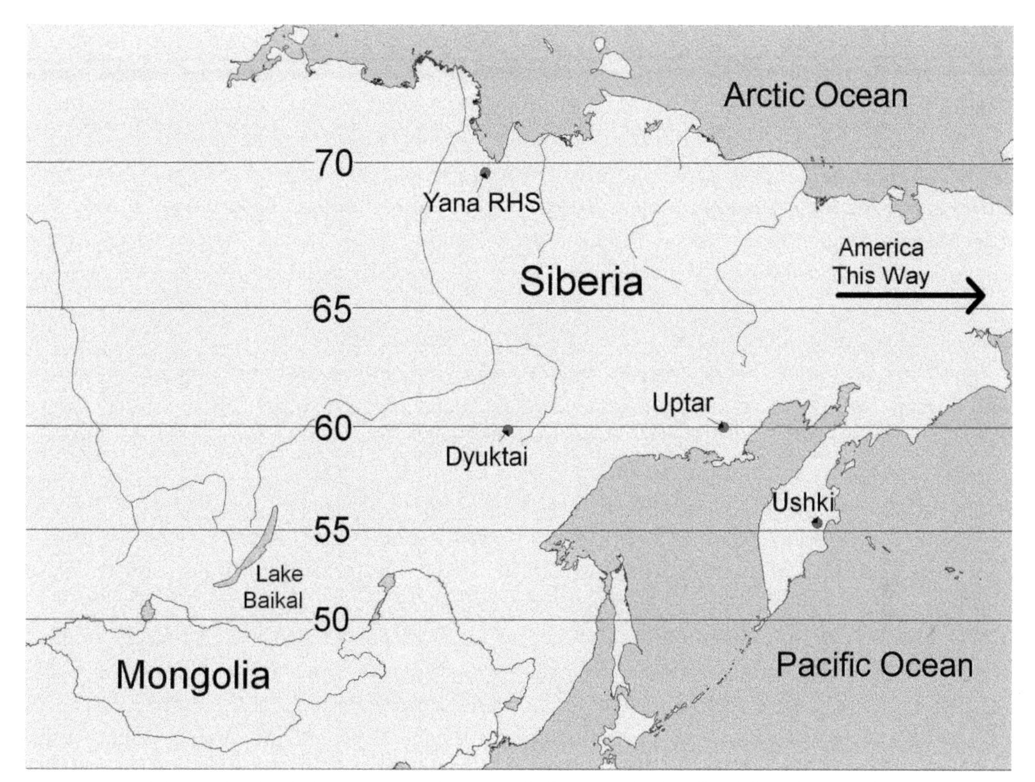

FIGURE 2.7 Lines of latitude in eastern Siberia. Early hunters had to be able to live as far north as 62° before they could expand across Beringia and into North America

probably used as knives, with ivory, bone, and antler points used to tip spears launched by spear throwers.

Chert blades were often worked further into end scrapers, side scrapers, **burins**, and points. Other tools were made from bone, antler, and ivory. These must have included needles, for the cold climate of even southern Siberia would have required tailored clothing (Goebel, 1999; Madsen, 2004).

The adaptive northern expansion of human bands might have been driven by nothing more than better clothing, better shelters, and improved knowledge of the environment and its resources. By this time they were clearly harvesting the full range of available fur-bearing animals, downy birds, and even killing the occasional mammoth (or at least dining on one found already dead).

Penetrating the Arctic was a task taken up unknowingly by hunters just trying to make a living, attracted by the possibility of game or food plants just over the next hill. On a conventional map, with north at the top, the rim of the Pacific looks like a hill to be climbed, but it is no more so than a high pressure "ridge" on a weather map. Yet the analogy is apt, for the barriers of ocean and glacial ice held back a rising tide of humanity for millennia, and even then allowed only a relative few to pass.

It is important to remember that in addition to climate and topography, there were also technological and social constraints on the expansion. No band could afford to move too far from related bands, on which they depended for information, assistance, marriage partners, and trade (Moore and Moseley, 2001). Sources of fine chert were left far behind in some cases, and trade in high-grade materials was necessary to keep hunters supplied. If recent hunter-gatherers are good analogies, then trade was probably couched as gift giving, an activity that reinforced the other linkages between related bands.

The Pleistocene waned, and the climate of Siberia slowly warmed in late glacial times, but it did so in long fits and starts separated by short reversals. People recolonized the areas that had been previously abandoned, but each time with more advanced technology. Wedge-shaped cores and **microblade**s of chert were new additions to the technology, which archaeologists see appearing first in the Lake Baikal region. Microblade technology is sophisticated and difficult to master, but mastery of the new skills was worth the effort given the effectiveness of composite tools and the difficulty of acquiring high-quality cherts (Yesner and Pearson, 2002).

The Yana RHS site holds evidence that people were in northeastern Siberia by around 30,000 years ago. The Dyuktai Cave complex is later and probably more relevant to the peopling of America. Unlike earlier people living in the Siberian Subarctic, the makers of the Dyuktai complex did not use a combination of larger base camps and smaller short-term camps. Instead archaeologists see evidence of a different strategy, one that emphasized small, temporary camps and highly mobile bands (Goebel, 1999: 223). This was a strategy that, with a modest population growth rate, would have allowed rapid expansion of a hunter-gatherer population without risk of it becoming too thin for interband connections to be maintained.

The people responsible for sites along the shoreline of Ushki Lake on the Kamchatka Peninsula might have expanded into the area from farther south along the eastern side of Asia. The Ushki complex is comprised of small, stemmed bifacial points, bifacial knives, and stone and ivory beads, all found on the floors of substantial houses (Goebel et al., 2003). Unlike the Dyuktai complex, this one lacked microblades and burins. The people who lived at Ushki Lake subsisted by exploiting both salmon runs and large terrestrial mammals. The Ushki Lake complex resembles the earliest Northern Paleoindian assemblages in central Alaska more than the Dyuktai complex does, in the view of some archaeologists.

Apart from timing, the issue is whether such an important technological advance as microblade manufacture would have been dropped by the Beringian descendants of the earlier Siberians that had it. Another possibility is that Northern Paleoindian complexes derived from some remnant of the people who lived in Siberia prior to 16,000 BCE and whose technology did not yet include microblades. That possibility even suggests a third hypothesis that some people made it into Beringia before the general Siberian retreat southward around 16,000 BCE, a possibility supported by the finds in Bluefish Caves.

Resilience and Collapse

Looked at from Siberia, although they could not have been aware of it, Asiatic people were finally poised to expand eastward into America. These mobile hunter-gatherers might have been already accompanied by dogs whose curved tails and tractable dispositions set them apart from wolves and advantaged their human partners. If not, dogs soon would join them, moving quickly through the networks that connected bands across the huge expanse of northeastern Siberia and Beringia.

In their hands the humans carried spears and spear throwers that made them lethal at a distance, particularly to game that had never before experienced being hunted by such a skilled predator. They wore cleverly tailored clothing and carried complex tools made of multiple materials and designed for mobility. And in their minds were stored the strategies, traditional knowledge, and skills necessary to survive, even thrive, on the great mammoth steppe of Beringia. Like any other well-adapted species, these early people were not necessarily on their way to being something else or somewhere else. They could have had no idea that they were on the threshold of a continent, that great things awaited their descendants, or that they had within them the capacity to demonstrate the potential of humans to thrive on their own in a new world. Over the succeeding millennia, the children of these few founders would demonstrate as no other branch of humanity could that the potential for the development of complex societies was inherent in all biologically modern people.

Glossary

Beringia The broad Pleistocene isthmus joining Alaska and Siberia, today largely under water.
biface A flat chipped-stone tool having two faces.
burin A chipped-stone tool made from a blade and used to chisel bone, antler, and ivory.
chert A glassy cryptocrystaline stone material that is well suited for making chipped-stone tools.
clade A taxonomic group of organisms consisting of an ancestor and all the descendants of that ancestor.
cognate A word in one language that is related to a word in another language by virtue of the two words having derived from a single ancestral word in their common protolanguage.
dart A small spear, larger than an arrow, used with an atlatl.
glottochronology The estimation of the timing of the breakup of related languages by measurement of changes in core vocabulary.
haplogroup A group of similar haplotypes that share a common ancestor with a single nucleotide polymorphism (SNP) mutation.
haplotype A set of single nucleotide polymorphisms (SNPs) that are statistically associated; in effect, a set of genes that occur together.
isostatic Having to do with the rise and fall of the landscape due to the presence or absence of heavy sheets of glacial ice.
microblade A small sliver with parallel sides, struck from a prepared core.
mitochondrial DNA Genetic material inherited by all animals from their mothers.
moraine Deposits of ground-up rock laid down along the sides and especially at the leading edges of glaciers.
protolanguage An extinct language reconstructed on the basis of evidence found in living descendant languages.
Quaternary The geological period containing the Pleistocene, Holocene, and Anthropocene epochs.
semantic Pertaining to meaning in language.
Y-chromosome A chromosome that determines male characteristics and is inherited by males from their fathers.

References

Bae, C.J., Douka, K., and Petroglia, M.D. (2017). On the Origin of Modern Humans: Asian Perspectives. *Science*, 358, pp. 1269.

Bourgeon, L., Burke, A., and Higham, T. (2017). Earliest Human Presence in North America Dated to the Last Glacial Maximum: New Radiocarbon Dates from Bluefish Caves, Canada. *PLoS One*, 12, pp. 1–15.

Brooks, A.S., Yellen, J.E., Nevell, L., and Hartman, G. (2005). Projectile Technologies of the African MSA: Implications for Modern Human Origins. In: E. Hovers and S. Kuhn, eds. *Transitions Before the Transition: Evolution and Stability in the Middle Paleolithic and Middle Stone Age*. New York: Kluwer Press.

Campbell, L., and Mithun, M., eds. (1979). *The Languages of Native America: Historical and Comparative Assessment*. Austin: University of Texas Press.

Cavalli-Sforza, L.L., and Cavalli-Sforza, F. (1995). *The Great Human Diasporas*. New York: Addison-Wesley.

Dehaene, S., Izard, V., Pica, P., and Spelke, E. (2006). Core Knowledge of Geometry in an Amazonian Indigene Group. *Science*, 311, pp. 381–384.

Dikov, N. (1996). The Ushki Site, Kamchatka Peninsula. In: F.H. West, ed. *American Beginnings: The Prehistory and Paleoecology of Beringia*. Chicago: University of Chicago Press.

Dunn, M., Terrill, A., Reesink, G., Foley, R.A., and Levinson, S.C. (2005). Structural Phylogenetics and the Reconstruction of Ancient Language History. *Science*, 309, pp. 2072–2075.

Frantz, L.A.F. et al. (2016). Genomic and Archaeological Evidence Suggest a Dual Origin of Domestic Dogs. *Science*, 352, pp. 1228–1231.

Goddard, I., ed. (1996). *Languages*. Washington, D.C.: Smithsonian Institution.

Goebel, T. (1999). Pleistocene Human Colonization of Siberia and Peopling of the Americas: An Ecological Approach. *Evolutionary Anthropology*, 8, pp. 208–227.

Goebel, T., Waters, M.R., and Dikova, M. (2003). The Archaeology of Ushki Lake, Kamchatka, and the Pleistocene Peopling of the Americas. *Science*, 301, pp. 501–505.

Graf, K.E., Dipietro, L.M., Krasinski, K.E., Gore, A.K., Smith, H.L., Culleton, B.J., Kennett, D.J., and Rhode, D. (2015). Dry Creek Revisited: New Excavations, Radiocarbon Dates, and Site Formation Inform on the Peopling of Eastern Beringia. *American Antiquity*, 80, pp. 671–694.

Gray, R. (2005). Pushing the Time Barrier in the Quest for Language Roots. *Science*, 309, pp. 2007–2008.

Greenberg, J.H. (1996). Beringia and New World Origins: I. The Linguistic Evidence. In: F.H. West, ed. *American Beginnings: The Prehistory and Palaeoecology of Beringia*. Chicago: University of Chicago Press.

Hare, B., Brown, M., Williamson, C., and Tomasello, M. (2002). The Domestication of Social Cognition in Dogs. *Science*, 298, pp. 1634–1636.

Holen, S.R., Deméré, T.A., Fisher, D.C., Fullagar, R., Paces, J.B., Jefferson, G.T., Beeton, J.M., Cerutti, R.A., Rountrey, A.N., Vescera, L., and Holen, K.A. (2017). A 130,000-Year-Old Archaeological Site in Southern California, USA. *Nature*, 544, pp. 479–483.

Leonard, J.A., Wayne, R.K., Wheeler, J., Valadez, R., Guillén, S., and Vilá, C. (2002). Ancient DNA Evidence for Old World Origin of New World Dogs. *Science*, 298, pp. 1613–1616.

Maclean, E.L., and Hare, B. (2015). Dogs Hijack the Human Bonding Pathway. *Science*, 348, pp. 280–281.

Madsen, D.B., ed. (2004). *Entering America: Northeast Asia and Beringia Before the Last Glacial Maximum*. Salt Lake City: University of Utah Press.

Meltzer, D.J. (2015). Kennewick Man: Coming to Closure. *Antiquity*, 89, pp. 1485–1493.

Moore, J.H., and Moseley, M.E. (2001). How Many Frogs Does It Take to Leap Around the Americas? Comments on Anderson and Gillam. *American Antiquity*, 66, pp. 526–529.

Morey, D.F. (2006). Burying Key Evidence: The Social Bond Between Dogs and People. *Journal of Archaeological Science*, 33, pp. 158–175.

Mulligan, C.J., and Kitchen, A. (2014). Three-Stage Colonization Model for the Peopling of the Americas. In: K.E. Graf, C.V. Ketron, and M.R. Waters, eds. *Paleoamerican Odyssey*. College Station: Texas A&M University Press.

Nichols, J. (2002). The First American Languages. In: N.G. Jablonski, ed. *The First Americans: The Pleistocene Colonization of the New World*. San Francisco: California Academy of Sciences.

Pitulko, V., Nikolskiy, P., Basilyan, A., and Pavlova, E. (2014). Human Habitation in Arctic Western Beringia Prior to the LGM. In: K.E. Graf, C.V. Ketron, and M.R. Waters, eds. *Paleoamerican Odyssey*. College Station: Texas A&M University Press.

Powell, J.F. (1993). Dental Evidence for the Peopling of the New World: Some Methodological Considerations. *Human Biology*, 65, pp. 799–819.

Raghavan, M., and Al, E. (2015). Genomic Evidence for the Pleistocene and Recent Population History of Native Americans. *Science*, 349, p. 841.

Snow, D.R. (2009). The Multidisciplinary Study of Human Migration: Problems and Principles. In: P.N. Peregrine, I. Peiros, and M. Feldman, eds. *Ancient Human Migrations: A Multidisciplinary Approach*. Salt Lake City: University of Utah Press.

Stringer, C., and Galway-Witham, J. (2018). When did Modern Humans leave Africa? *Science*, 359, pp. 389–390.

Turner II, C.G. (1989). Teeth and Prehistory in Asia. *Scientific American*, pp. 88–96.
Turner II, C.G. (2002). Teeth, Needles, Dogs, and Siberia: Bioarchaeological Evidence for the Colonization of the New World. In: N.G. Jablonski, ed. *The First Americans: The Pleistocene Colonization of the New World*. San Francisco: California Academy of Sciences.
Yesner, D.R., and Pearson, G. (2002). Microblades and Migrations: Ethnic and Economic Models in the Peopling of the Americas. In: R.G. Elston and S.L. Kuhn, eds. *Thinking Small: Global Perspectives on Microlithization*. Washington, DC: American Anthropological Association.

3

THE PEOPLING OF AMERICA

This chapter summarizes what is known about the earliest inhabitants of North America and the principal controversies surrounding their archaeological interpretation. There are, and probably always will be, an assortment of sites for which very early dates are claimed, but few of them stand up under close examination. The Paleoindian period spanned at least the centuries from 11,050 to 9750 BCE, and the Paleoindian foundation of North American archaeology is generally accepted. Clovis was the first widespread Paleoindian culture, and **fluted points** were its hallmark. A major archaeological problem today is the discovery of the origins of Paleoindians and assessing sites that appear to predate Clovis (Figure 3.1).

Clovis culture appears to have derived from Northern Paleoindian complexes in Beringia (Smith et al., 2014). Clovis tools resemble some European artifacts, but there is little or no support for the alternative hypothesis that its distinctive technology came from Europe (Straus et al., 2005). Claims for a few scattered sites elsewhere in both North and South America that are possibly older than Clovis are subjects of continuing debate. A recent claim for a human presence in North America 130,000 BP has not received general acceptance (Holen et al., 2017).

Empirical science by definition demands evidence, yet the special circumstances of the peopling of the Americas have made evidence especially hard to produce. The evidence we need was meager to begin with, subject to destructive forces, possibly under water today, and in any case scattered thinly on the landscape of a huge continent.

Environment and Adaptation

The biggest environmental obstacle to the expansion of people from eastern Beringia southward was glacial ice. The Cordilleran ice sheet of the mountain west and the Laurentian ice sheet of eastern Canada merged at glacial maximum sealing off an ice-free corridor between them. Tongues of ice pushed down to the sea along the West Coast, making travel by that route difficult or impossible as well (Figure 3.1).

Eastern Beringia, modern Alaska, was largely unglaciated, even when mile-high sheets of ice covered most of modern Canada (Table 3.1). As noted in Chapter 1, this part of Beringia was home to human bands prior to 14,500 BCE. Because of their importance for everything that came later, the sites left by these earliest Americans have been subject to intense archaeological research in recent years (Smith et al., 2014; Potter et al., 2014; Moreno-Mayar et al.; 2018). Bluefish Caves contain

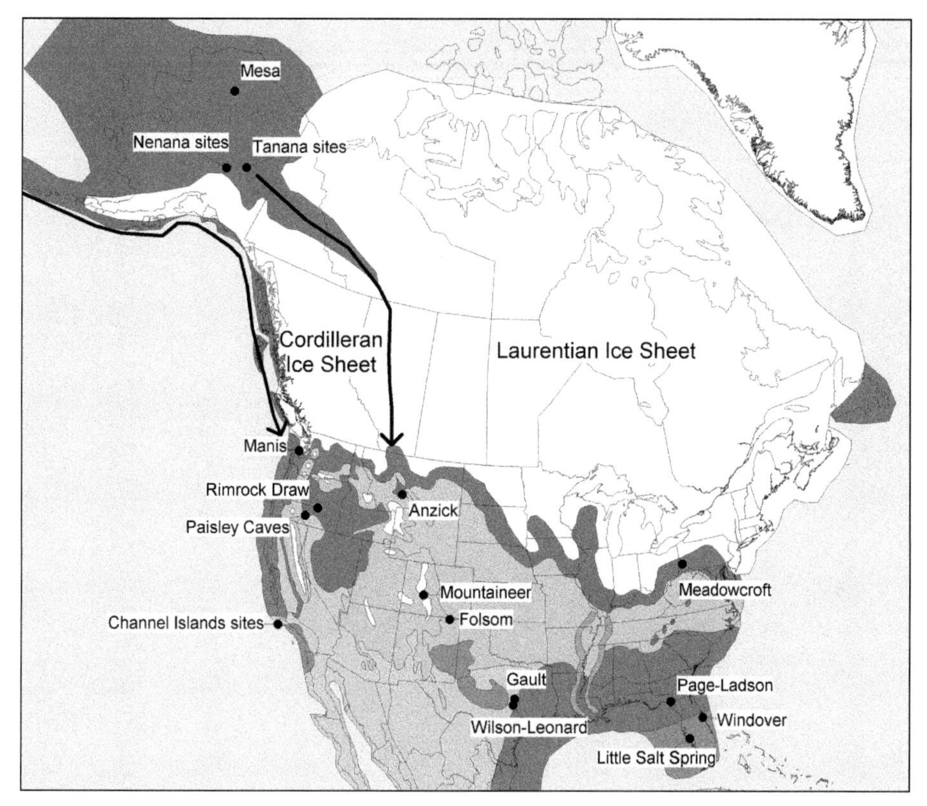

FIGURE 3.1 Ice Age North America, with sites mentioned in the text. Arrows show possible migration routes

bones bearing the marks of manmade tools (Bourgeon et al., 2017). A cluster of sites in the Tanana River valley, Mead, Swan Point, and Broken Mammoth, contain tools that are among the earliest known. Their derivation from the Siberian complexes mentioned in Chapter 2 are generally clear but complicated and the subject of much current debate. Swan Point appears derived from Dyuktai culture and dates to around 12,000 BCE (Lanoë and Holmes, 2016). The later relationships between evidence from Beringia and from the interior of North America lying to the south remain tenuous.

By about 13,000 years ago (11,000 BCE), there were complexes in Alaska that look enough like what we have long referred to as Paleoindian in the lower 48 states to call them "Northern Paleoindian" (Graf et al., 2015). The earliest of these, including Dry Creek, predate the appearance of Clovis Paleoindians south of the continental glaciers by a few centuries. Sites such as the Mesa sites and a cluster of sites in the Nenana Valley represent this development. To put it in context, the climate was warming as the Pleistocene waned, an episode known as the Late Allerød. But there was a sudden return to colder conditions around 10,950 BCE, the onset of the Younger Dryas climatic episode. Somehow some of the Beringian people had spread southward well before the beginning of the Younger Dryas. Later, others that we recognize as Northern Paleoindians also spread southward, but probably by a different route. How these expansions occurred is the focus of current archaeological investigation of environment and adaptation in these early years of the peopling of North America. Key to the resolution of the resulting debates are the acceptance or rejection of specific claims for supposed early sites.

Based on the evidence presented in Chapter 2, there can be little doubt that the roots of modern American Indian populations can be traced back to eastern Asia. The list of pre-Clovis

TABLE 3.1 A very simplified comparative chronology for understanding the relationships between the [illegible] of Beringia and interior North America. Some pre-Clovis sites might date to as early as 15,000 YA

Years Ago (YA)			*Years BCE*			*Climate*	*Beringia*	*Interior North America*
11,000	to	11,100	9050	to	9150	Holocene	Northern	Early
11,100	to	11,200	9150	to	9250		Paleoindian	Archaic
11,200	to	11,300	9250	to	9350			Cultures
11,300	to	11,400	9350	to	9450			
11,400	to	11,500	9450	to	9550			
11,500	to	11,600	9550	to	9650			
11,600	to	11,700	9650	to	9750			
11,700	to	11,800	9750	to	9850	Younger		Folsom and other
11,800	to	11,900	9850	to	9950	Dryas		Late Paleoindian
11,900	to	12,000	9950	to	10,050			Cultures
12,000	to	12,100	10,050	to	10,150			
12,100	to	12,200	10,150	to	10,250			
12,200	to	12,300	10,250	to	10,350			
12,300	to	12,400	10,350	to	10,450			
12,400	to	12,500	10,450	to	10,550			
12,500	to	12,600	10,550	to	10,650			
12,600	to	12,700	10,650	to	10,750			Clovis
12,700	to	12,800	10,750	to	10,850			(Early
12,800	to	12,900	10,850	to	10,950			Paleoindian)
12,900	to	13,000	10,950	to	11,050	Late Allerød		
13,000	to	13,100	11,050	to	11,150			Various Possible
13,100	to	13,200	11,150	to	11,250			Pre-Clovis Sites
13,200	to	13,300	11,250	to	11,350			
13,300	to	13,400	11,350	to	11,450		Various	
13,400	to	13,500	11,450	to	11,550		Beringian	
13,500	to	13,400	11,550	to	11,650		Sites	

candidates that were taken seriously for a while but then failed one test or another is a long one. The jury is still out about other pre-Clovis candidates, and they are the subjects of considerable debate (Bradley and Collins, 2014). Only a few of the more likely ones can be mentioned here. The Gault site complex in Texas clearly contains extensive Clovis strata with older human-made tools below them (Jennings and Waters, 2014).

GAULT SITE

Gault is a multicomponent site superficially typical of the common burned rock midden sites of central Texas (Figure 3.2). It is in Buttermilk Creek valley, southwestern Bell County, 40 miles north of Austin, Texas, near the eastern edge of the Edwards Plateau. Buttermilk is a perennial, spring-fed creek incised into the plateau limestone where abundant, high-quality Edwards chert crops out. Land clearing exposed the site ca. 1906. Looting began soon afterward, persisted until 1998, and virtually destroyed the large burned rock Archaic midden (ca. 10,000–500 BCE). J.E. Pearce excavated there in 1929 without penetrating beneath the midden.

Unknown until 1991, when a collector dug deeper, was up to 2 m of stratified premidden cultural strata in valley alluvium dating from ca. 15,000 BCE. Collins and colleagues

FIGURE 3.2 Gault cultural strata and tentative ages as exposed in excavation area 15. 1. Gault Assemblage 15,000–14,000 BCE; 2. sterile zone; 3. Clovis 13,500–12,900 BCE; 4. Late Paleoindian 12,900–10,000 BCE; 5–6. Archaic and Late Prehistoric. Photo courtesy of Michael B. Collins

(1991–present) have intensely studied these strata and their contents, under the auspices of the University of Texas at Austin and Texas State University (collections and records housed at both). Since 2007, the Archaeological Conservancy has owned a large portion of the site. Gault is also widely known for its incised stone and bone artifacts from Clovis and later Paleoindian contexts (Lemke et al., 2015).

Premidden strata are, from earliest to youngest, Gault Assemblage (GA), Clovis, Folsom, and multiple Late Paleoindian components. GA consists of ~150,000 lithic specimens (mostly debitage) but also 32 bifaces, 12 projectile points, 47 blades and blade segments, 5 blade cores, 4 burins, 12 burin spalls, 13 unifaces, and 12 gravers. This assemblage, like Clovis, centers on flake, blade, and core tools, but distinct technological differences suggest no direct historical connections with Clovis. An artificial stone pavement, 2 m x 2 m, with blade tools and associated toss zones of lithic and faunal refuse dated to ca. 14,000 BCE is considered to be of GA affiliation (Collins et al., 2014).

Michael B. Collins

The Manis site in Washington, the Paisley Caves in Oregon, and the Meadowcroft site in Pennsylvania, surely some of the most carefully excavated of sites, are three that have produced pre-Clovis evidence that is generally accepted (Waters and Stafford, 2014). So too are Florida's Page-Ladson and Little Salt Spring sites (Anderson and Sassaman, 1996). There is a curious pattern to many of these sites; convincing Paleoindian strata often overlie undated strata containing a few blades. In the absence of independent dates for these mysterious earlier strata, the best course is to conclude for now that they represent what some researchers refer to as the "pioneer" phase of colonization, which one should expect to have low visibility as compared to the later "residential" phase represented by Clovis culture (Adovasio and Pedler, 2016; Housley et al., 1997).

MANIS MASTODON SITE

At the end of the last Ice Age, the ice sheet that once covered the northern portion of Washington retreated as the earth warmed. Many ponds were created on the gravelly plains left by the glacial ice. In 1971, Emanuel Manis was excavating around one of these ponds on his ranch near Sequim and discovered the bones of a mastodon. Excavation of the site by Carl Gustafson in the 1970s revealed the remains of a nearly complete, male, adult mastodon.

The bones of the left side of the mastodon were still largely articulated, but the bones of the right side of the animal had been dismembered and moved upslope to the edge of the pond. These bones had been broken and stacked, and some bear cut marks. Gustafson concluded that this arrangement of bones was the result of prehistoric humans butchering or scavenging the right half of the mastodon.

The most important artifact from the site was a fragment of a rib with an embedded bone projectile point. High-resolution CT scanning technology showed that the bone point intruded 2.5 cm into the rib. Ancient DNA extracted from the point showed that it was made of mastodon bone which indicated that prehistoric hunters had fashioned hunting weapons from an earlier mastodon kill. Radiocarbon dating showed the Manis mastodon to be 13,800 years old.

The Manis Mastodon site is a rare and important site that is part of the story of the journey of the first people to enter and explore the Americas. Additional archaeological and ancient human genetic evidence shows that these first immigrants originated in Asia, crossed a land connection between Asia and the Americas, and then using boats traveled along the Pacific Coast south of the thick continental ice sheets that covered most of Canada.

Michael R. Waters

Research in the Paisley Caves in south-central Oregon has been especially productive. The nearby Rimrock Draw Rock Shelter has produced artifacts found stratigraphically under a volcanic ash layer dating to 15,400 BP, but work is still proceeding (Neely, 2015). Coastal sites in British Columbia and Baja California are also adding to the rapidly accumulating evidence for an early spread of people southward along the West Coast (Koppel, 2016).

PAISLEY CAVES, OREGON

The Paisley Five Mile Point Caves ("Paisley Caves") are located on Lakeview District, Bureau of Land Management administered properties in the Summer Lake basin of south-central Oregon. The site is best known as the location where ancient human DNA (aDNA) was extracted from 14,300 year old **coprolites**. The site was first investigated by University of Oregon (UO) professor Luther Cressman between 1938 and 1940. Finding camel, horse, bison, fish, and waterfowl bones around a small house floor containing **obsidian** artifacts, Cressman believed he had proven his case for Pleistocene occupation of the Northern Great Basin. However, his lack of adequate documentation and dating left his claims generally unaccepted. Renewed UO investigations under the direction of Dennis Jenkins began in 2002 and continue at present (Figure 3.3). While findings from Paisley Caves are generally accepted by professional archaeologists, the aDNA evidence has been questioned by a few. Consequently, research into the formation of site deposits and the potential for downward movement of aDNA from younger deposits into older nonhuman coprolites continues. Human aDNA has been extracted from 12 coprolites of Clovis age and older. Five of these are pre-Clovis, dating to before 11,050 BCE. The ice-free corridor through Canada was not open or viable for human occupation this early, suggesting that humans were either south of the continental ice sheet before it coalesced or they colonized the continent by following a coastal route around the glaciers. Regardless of how and when they arrived, recovery of Western Stemmed Tradition projectile points firmly dated to the Clovis era at the Paisley Caves demonstrates that by that early time there were at least two technologically, and possibly genetically, divergent cultural traditions in North America (Gilbert et al., 2008; Jenkins et al., 2012; Jenkins et al., 2013).

Dennis L. Jenkins

FIGURE 3.3 Paisley Caves during excavation. Courtesy of Dennis L. Jenkins, Museum of Natural & Cultural History, University of Oregon

Demography and Conflict

An exception to the largely dismissed claims for early South American sites is the remarkable case of Monte Verde, an early site in far-off Chile. It is one of those sites that has required a major rethinking of the archaeology of the entire hemisphere (Dillehay, 2014).

Alternative hypotheses to explain how Monte Verde might have derived from the early cultures of Beringia have been subject to contentious debate for several years. It was long thought most likely that population expansion southward from Beringia occurred after the Laurentian and Cordilleran ice sheets had melted back far enough to open a corridor through western Canada. But the corridor might not have been open and able to sustain bands of hunters until 12,600 years ago (10,650 BCE) by which time Clovis culture had already run its brief course farther south (Pedersen et al., 2016). The corridor might have been available from that time on, but some researchers argue that it could not have accommodated the origins of Clovis or other early Paleoindians, let alone earlier pre-Clovis evidence. This makes the relationship between the Northern Paleoindians of Alaska and the Paleoindians of the continental interior an important focus of future research and debate.

Expansion Along the Pacific Coast

We can be reasonably certain that complexes were present in central Alaska 4,000 years earlier than the occupation of Monte Verde. This site is over 15,000 km (9,300 mi) south, which seems like a daunting distance even today. But that amounts to only 150 km (93 mi) per century. Put that way, distance too seems to be within range of the possible, particularly if the earliest American Indians had a coastal adaptation that led them to expand along the coast as their population grew. Archaeologists who accept Monte Verde's 10,500 BCE date thus find themselves drawn to the Pacific Coast alternative when the subject of routes comes up. Paleoindians could have reached southern South America even before they expanded into the interior of North America (Scheib et al., 2018).

Evidence from Daisy Cave, California, suggests that early Paleoindians had seaworthy boats that were sufficient to allow them to get around barriers (Rick et al., 2001). Daisy Cave is on San Miguel Island, one of the Channel Islands off the coast of southern California. San Miguel was an island even during the Late Pleistocene, when sea levels were lower, but not low enough to provide a bridge to the mainland (Figure 3.4). To reach the closest of the Channel Islands, one must cross at least 19 km of open ocean, and San Miguel lies even farther out. Daisy Cave was occupied by people exploiting the rich maritime environment 9550–6550 BCE, so the site tells us that boats and fishing were in use at least that long ago (Rick et al., 2001: 609). Fishhooks from Baja California dating earlier than 10,000 BCE provide additional evidence for early coastal migration (Des Lauriers et al., 2017).

Fortunately for early migrants, there were pockets of unglaciated landscape along the Northwest Coast even at the height of Cordilleran glaciation. These were biological refugia, where plants and animals were isolated for centuries or even millennia. The northern Queen Charlotte Islands and Prince of Wales Island of British Columbia were one such **refugium** (Warner et al., 1982). In addition, portions of the coastline along the Gulf of Alaska were deglaciated and probably supplied with driftwood by 12,000 BCE (Mann and Peteet, 1994; Menounos et al., 2017). Yet a coastal route would not have been without its hazards. Malaspina glacier is an immense mountain glacier that still extends all the way to the ocean, where it stands as a 70-km-wide icy barrier to anyone trying

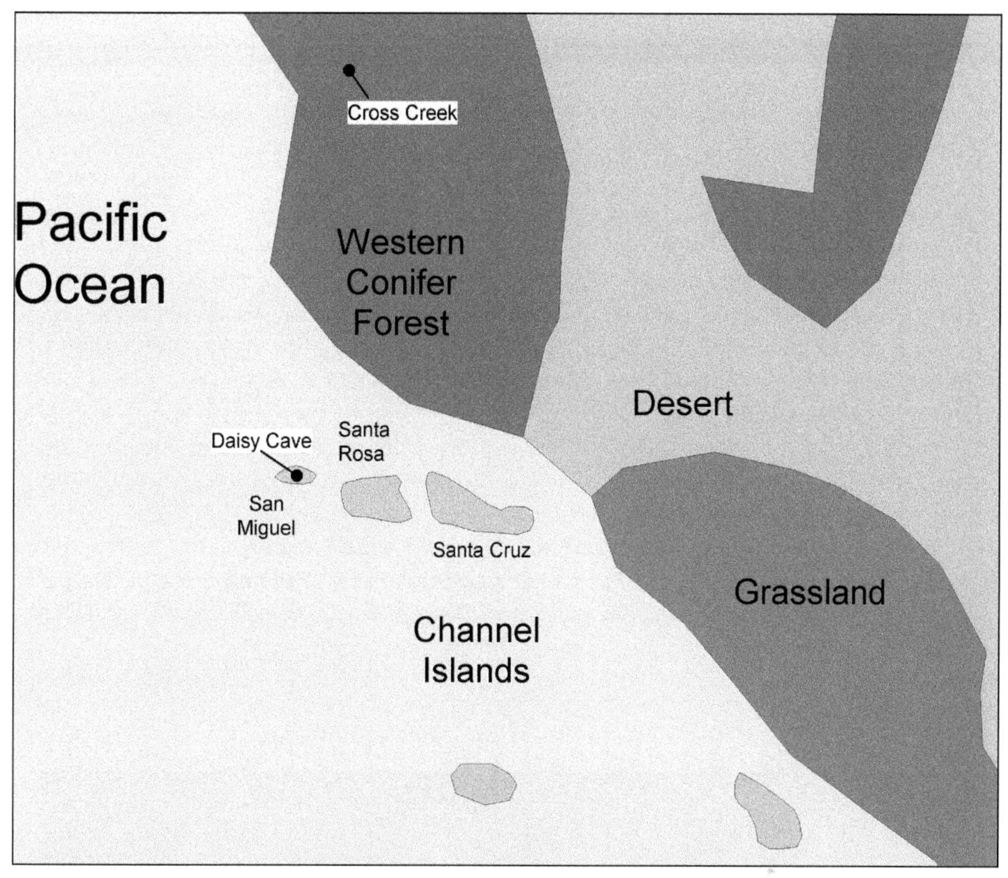

FIGURE 3.4 Channel Island sites on the southern California coast with evidence of early archaeology

to move south along the coast. Nevertheless, with sea levels substantially lower than today, boats presumably available, and stretches of unglaciated landscape for camps scattered along the coast, expansion along that route would have been possible.

Expansion into the Interior

Meadowcroft and a few other eastern sites show that people were in eastern North America before Clovis times. However, Clovis was the first widespread culture of the Paleoindian period, and it is well established that it was widespread across much of North America approximately 11,050–10,650 BCE (Waters and Stafford, 2014: 544). Clovis points occur all across the lower 48 United States, northern Mexico, and parts of Canada that had become free of glacial ice near the end of the Pleistocene. There is no evidence that Clovis culture spread to Central or South America. David Anderson and Michael Faught's inventory of 11,257 Paleoindian projectile points found up through 1997 shows that a preponderance of them were found east of the Mississippi River, confirming a pattern already suspected over four decades ago (Anderson and Faught, 1998). The total is now over 13,000 and still growing, but the West is where they were first found and where the best dated finds are located.

MEADOWCROFT ROCKSHELTER

Meadowcroft Rockshelter is a deeply stratified, multi-component site located about 30 miles southwest of Pittsburgh, Pennsylvania. The site is situated on the north bank of Cross Creek, a small tributary of the Ohio River, which lies 7.6 miles to the west. Field work began in 1973 and continued thereafter every year until 1978. Additional excavations were conducted in 1983, 1985, 1987, 1993–1994, 2003, and, most recently, in 2007 (Figure 3.5).

The 11 natural strata at Meadowcroft currently represent the longest occupational sequence in the New World. The site yielded a remarkable corpus of artifactual, floral, and faunal data firmly anchored by some 52 stratigraphically consistent radiocarbon dates spanning more than 15 millennia of autumn-focused, short-term visits. The site's earliest occupants are ascribable to the Miller complex.

The dating of the Miller complex is problematic. If the six deepest dates unequivocally associated with cultural materials are averaged, then the Miller complex is present at this site and in the contiguous Cross Creek drainage between ca. 12,605 BCE and 12,005 BCE.

The inventory of flaked-stone artifacts from lower and middle Stratum IIa at Meadowcroft contains small prismatic blades that were detached from small prepared cores. In 1976, a small, lanceolate biface, subsequently called the Miller Lanceolate projectile point, was found in situ on the uppermost living floor of lower Stratum IIa at Meadowcroft.

James Adovasio

FIGURE 3.5 Meadowcroft site after excavation. Photo courtesy of James M. Adovasio

Despite the thousands of fluted points known for the rest of the continent, Western Stemmed projectile points predominate along the West Coast, where Clovis points are very rare (Jones et al., 2002: 227). This makes sense if the West Coast was initially populated by early migrants moving southward along it. If the vast interior of the continent was settled by people expanding southeastward through the more recently deglaciated Canadian interior from Northern Paleoindian origins in Beringia, the cultural contrast between the coast and interior is explained.

The accurate dating of Clovis sites has been important but difficult. Only a few sites meet the most stringent requirements. It is generally accepted that Clovis components most likely date 11,050–10,650 BCE after **calibration** (Prasciunas and Surovell, 2014; Waters and Stafford, 2014). Fiedel (2014) argues for a somewhat narrower range. Resolution of the dating of Paleoindian sites containing Clovis points is important because our desire to know how this adaptation fits with the last gasp of the Pleistocene, the Younger Dryas cold spell. This episode of colder conditions lasted for about 13 centuries, 10,950–9750 BCE. The spell began and ended abruptly, each time perhaps over the course of just a handful of years. But while it lasted, it was an episode that conditioned human adaptation in ways that we do not yet fully understand (Alley et al., 2003; Taylor, 1999). Clovis culture appears to have flourished during the warm episode just before the Younger Dryas, apparently lasting into the early years of the cold spell. If current dating is correct then the rapid spread of Clovis culture across North America was something that occurred just before Younger Dryas began. This makes sense ecologically, for one should expect Clovis to have flourished when the climate was warming, not during a presumably more difficult episode of returning cold conditions. But we do not yet understand either the Younger Dryas or Paleoindian adaptation well enough to be sure (Meltzer and Holliday, 2010).

Architecture and Technology

The hallmark of Clovis culture, the fluted point, was an innovation that made artists of Clovis **knapper**s (Figure 3.6). The sudden appearance of Clovis culture around 11,050 BCE, and its rapid adaptive radiation across much of interior North America might need no more complex explanation than that, except that a secondary question remains. What was the specific mechanism of its

FIGURE 3.6 Clovis fluted points

spread? Did fluted points spread as the population of people making them grew and expanded across the continent, or did the technique spread independent of population spread, as knappers trained each other in the technique? Most archaeologists appear to assume that the Clovis points spread as the population carrying them fanned out across the continent. This hypothesis is at least consistent with the sudden appearance of Clovis points. But the widespread distribution of Clovis points and the brief four-century period in which they were made seems more consistent with the second hypothesis (Bradley and Collins, 2014).

Northern Paleoindian technology differed from Clovis technology only in the innovation of the fluting of Clovis points (Goebel et al., 1991; Hoffecker et al., 1993; Waters and Stafford, 2014). This might have occurred as an adaptation to big game hunting, but archaeologists are hard put to demonstrate that fluting was a technologically significant innovation. Experiments have revealed that it confers no particular advantage in either hafting or killing power (Adovasio and Pedler, 2005). However, recent experimental research does indicate that fluting makes hafted points more robust (Adovasio and Pedler, 2016; Thomas et al., 2017). Thus fluting probably had a technological function, evidence of more than human love of the beautifully impractical.

Heat treatment is another advance that enhanced both the workability of the cherts and other materials used in chipped-stone technology and often the appearance of the finished product. Heating cryptocrystalline raw material to make it easier to work has been known to human knappers for at least 72,000 years, and the first Americans must have brought that knowledge with them. But in addition to workability, heat treatment often also improves luster and color (Webb and Domanski, 2009). For example, the already pretty yellow ocher color of Pennsylvania jasper, a form of chert, changes to bright red with heat treatment.

Labor was probably divided much as it typically has been among more modern hunter-gatherers, largely along lines of sex and age. Everyone had a range of skills and tasks, and the band's survival depended upon a complementary mix of individuals. Tailored skins, without which no one could survive even the milder winters, required slender needles and clever tanning techniques (Erlandson et al., 2014; Lyman, 2015; Osborn, 2014). Needles were made from bone or antler, which in turn had to be worked using specialized **pièces esquillées**, gravers, burins, and scrapers to split, wedge, and carve the tough materials. These in turn required deft knapping techniques and sources of good-quality cherts.

Bands of highly mobile Paleoindians cannot be expected to have left behind much in the way of architecture. Rings of stone that held down the bottoms of hide tents can survive. Post molds and hearths turn up in both open contexts and in rock shelters. Most of the time bands probably sheltered in small structures intended for nuclear families or small extended families. A rare foundation ring, 5 m (16 ft) in diameter, at the Mountaineer site in Colorado, shows that later Paleoindians sheltered in temporary structures capable of holding more than just single families (Stiger, 2006). For further information we must await the discovery and evaluation of new evidence.

Subsistence and Economy

Their subsistence included hunting, but they were not exclusively big game hunters. Everything about them suggests that these were people who were doing their best to stay as flexible as they were mobile in a period of rapid and dramatic environmental change (Figure 3.7). Horse remains were found in close association with a human coprolite dated to 14,525 BP in Paisley Caves (Stewart, 2016). Clovis people in the Northeast were probably intercepting herds of caribou. But these were only their most obvious subsistence activities. They also must have hunted many smaller animal species, such as rabbits and hares, and harvested a limited range of plants they were familiar with (Cannon and Meltzer, 2004). The Gault site has revealed that they were using birds, turtles, frogs, and antelopes as well as large game.

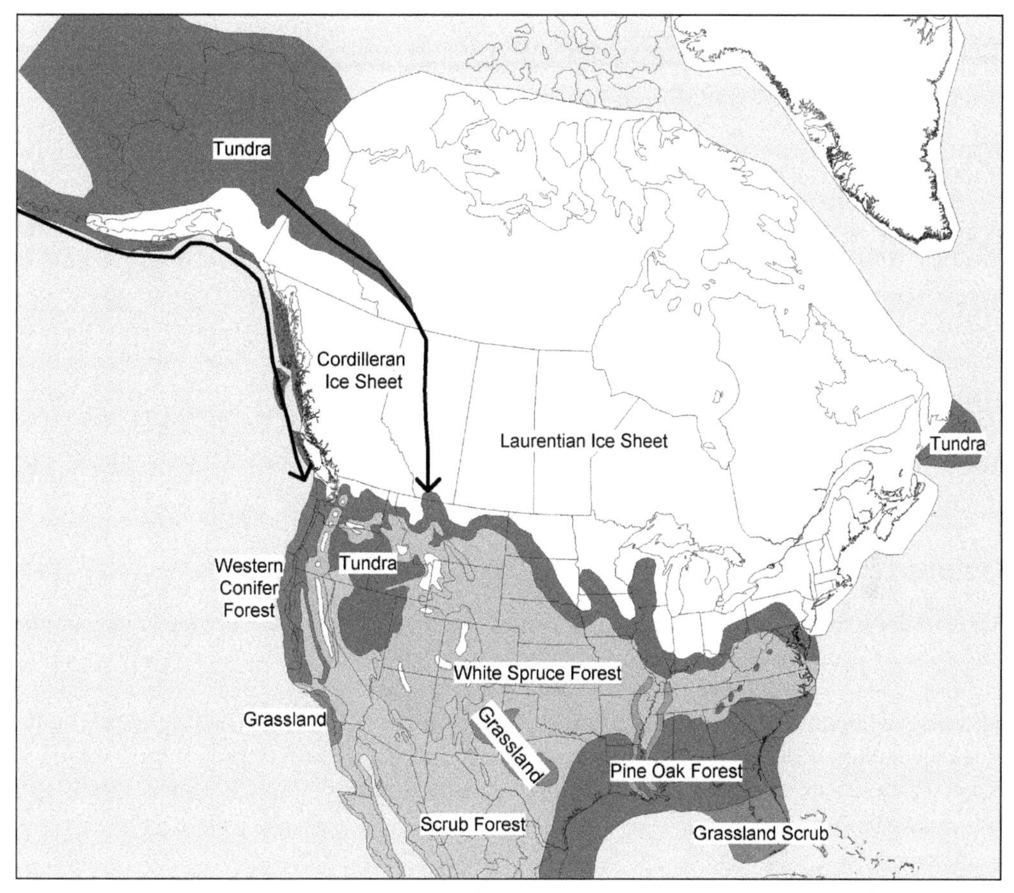

FIGURE 3.7 Late Pleistocene ecozones in North America

Despite the diversity of their animal and plant diet, what is missing in Paleoindian subsistence is any substantial dependence upon high-cost, high-return resources. Tough seeds that required laborious milling or the removal of toxins to be made edible were not yet exploited. Environments would have to stabilize and bands would have to settle in long enough for them to learn how to harvest and prepare such resources. Human adaptation was still young in North America, and more mature adaptations would take centuries to develop (Erlandson et al., 2014). Meanwhile, things were about to change dramatically.

The Great Extinction

Several dozen genera of **megafauna** went extinct at the end of the Pleistocene, some around the time that human hunters added themselves to the ecological equation, and researchers have debated the likely role of human hunters for several decades. The archaeological evidence is scanty; only a few sites show conclusively that humans were hunting species that subsequently dwindled to extinction (Grayson and Meltzer, 2015). However, computer simulations and the evidence of historic cases of megafaunal extinctions following human colonization suggest that hunting probably played an important role. An empirical approach to the problem, coupled with standard scientific skepticism, has led some archaeologists to doubt that Paleoindians could have been the major factor in Late Pleistocene extinctions. However, new evidence, the advent of DNA research, and advanced computer simulations have fueled new debate and have increased the likelihood of resolution of the question (Meltzer, 2015b; Surovell and Brund, 2012).

Paleoindian Skeletal Evidence

A 2014 inventory lists skeletal remains of 324 individuals dating to 8,000 radiocarbon years BP or greater (Lepper, 2014). These include the remains of 159 adults and 85 subadults, the others being uncertain. Sex can be determined for 72 males and 80 females, but the rest are also uncertain. The most famous is Kennewick Man, found in the state of Washington, which was the focus of litigation (Meltzer, 2015a; Owsley and Jantz, 2014). However, others such as Arlington Springs are older, securely dated, and likely to provide new knowledge about North America's earliest inhabitants. The post-discovery histories of these finds have varied considerably (Toner, 2017). The most important general observation from all of these is that their skeletal features and their DNA assays are consistent with Siberian origins.

Culture, Language, and Identity

The North Americans of 12 millennia ago are too far removed from the present to allow specific discussion of language and culture beyond the observation that they must have had both. The inclusion of funerary offerings with some subadult burials, such as Anzick and Windover Burial 90, are a clear measure of the grief experienced by people losing children (Lepper, 2014: 21). Their technology reveals skill in their material culture. Other remains in the meagre archaeological record of this distant time might reveal more about cultural identity through future archaeology.

Art and Symbolism

Like people everywhere, Paleoindians had artistic impulses, but their mobile lifeway limited their ability to express them. Incised stone, bone, and ivory artifacts found at the Gault site and several other Paleoindian sites show that design and decoration were part of their culture. They occasionally used **red ochre**, and there are a few cases of western petroglyph sites that probably date to Paleoindian times (Frison et al., 2018; Lemke et al., 2015).

It is revealing that modern knappers that have rediscovered and mastered the difficult technique of fluting are very proud of their work and that their points sell for high prices. In fact it is likely that a fairly large percentage of the fluted points in the antiquities market are modern fakes. Thus ancient Clovis points have all the attributes of a fad, probably America's first really big one. What we are seeing in this case is evidence of the human pursuit of excellence, the production of highly valued objects, and their use as both tools and gifts. Hunter-gatherers living in mobile bands typically couch exchange as gift giving rather than trade. People living in small-scale societies often share food and other resources freely, for in the long run there is much greater advantage in sharing than in hoarding, although the specific mechanisms are more complex than that statement might imply (Hawkes, 1993). Moreover, gifts constantly renew social bonds, as anyone ever invited to a wedding knows. A gift given or a favor done today might not be reciprocated for years, but it creates the kinds of obligations that hold societies together.

The dry caves of the Great Basin preserve scraps and sometimes whole specimens of cordage, basketry, and textiles. Woven bags show designs resulting from the selection of raw materials having different colors and textures, and their further modification through the use of natural dyes. Even sandals made of heavy cordage were made with more skill and design than necessary from a purely functional point of view (Connolly et al., 2016).

There are many rock art sites scattered across North America, but they are difficult to date and interpret. There are petroglyphs that clearly depict mastodons and camelids on the Colorado Plateau and in California. These are hunted species that have been extinct for 12,000 years. Patinas of natural desert varnish cover some of them to a thickness that makes recent carving, and thus modern forgery, unlikely. It is probable that at least some of North America's rock art dates to the Paleoindian period (Agenbroad and Hesse, 2004; Kooyman et al., 2012; Whitley, 2009).

Resilience and Collapse

Clovis fluted points probably came and went in less than four centuries. The ecological **niche** that was occupied by Clovis culture was broadly defined. Their adaptation was a general one compared to what came later, exactly what we should expect for a human culture adapting to an environment that was at once unfamiliar and still changing. As Clovis bands became more familiar with their local environments, they began to differentiate from one another. This must have pervaded all parts of their culture, from language to technology. Where we can observe it, of course, is mainly in the durable parts of their technology that have survived in the ground. Fluted points diversified from standard Clovis forms to a variety of regional types, which archaeologists have given names like Cumberland, Neponset, Nicholas, and Folsom.

Like earlier Clovis points, later Paleoindian Folsom points found in the western United States are bifacial and **lanceolate** in shape, fluted, and lacking either barbs or a stem (Figure 3.8). They too tend to be finely made from high-grade material, carefully chipped and ground along their

FIGURE 3.8 Folsom projectile points

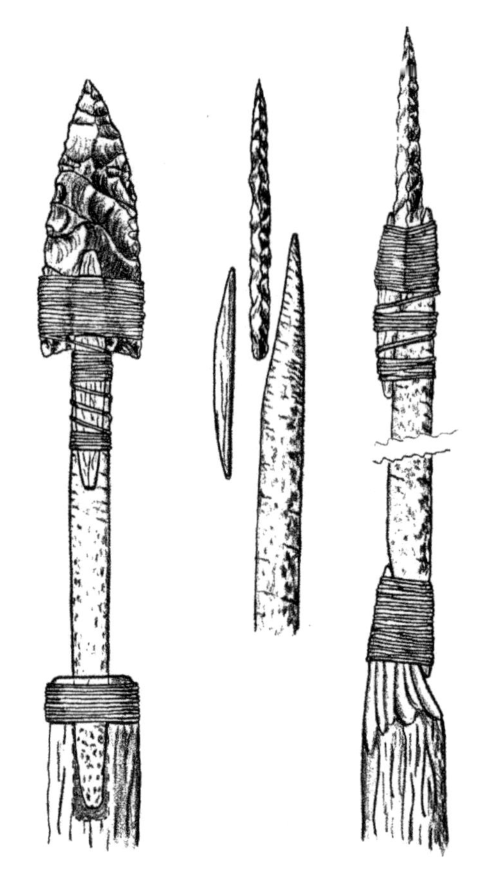

FIGURE 3.9 Reconstructed foreshaft and projectile point composites from the Anzick site, Montana.
Source: From Lahren and Bonnichsen, 1974: 149, Fig. 3. Reprinted with permission from the American Association for the Advancement of Science

lower edges to keep them from cutting through the lashing that would have been used to haft them to handles, spear shafts, or foreshafts (Figure 3.9).

Folsom culture persisted until around 9900 BCE, a few centuries before the Younger Dryas cold spell ended and the Holocene began. The pattern of monsoonal rains that had watered the Plains changed with the onset of the Holocene, disrupting established human adaptations (Lovvorn et al., 2001; Mann and Meltzer, 2007). Complex patterns of air circulation and precipitation produced other results in other areas, but on the High Plains generally warmer conditions caused Paleoindians to split into two adaptive modes. Those living in the foothills of the Rocky Mountains soldiered on, surviving over the long term by diversifying their subsistence to exploit plants and what animals remained after the largest of them became extinct. Those living on the open plains were dependent upon bison herds after the extinction of other large mammals. Bison kills declined after 6000 BCE, and human habitation of the High Plains nearly ended between then and 3000 BCE except for summer forays from the margins of this forsaken landscape (Lovvorn et al., 2001; Meltzer, 1999).

Elsewhere across North America other Late Paleoindian cultures that were derivative from Clovis also appeared as Holocene climate became established. Fluting was dropped as a knapping technique in most areas, although the production of finely made lanceolate points continued (Figure 3.10). Several unfluted lanceolate point types, such as Plainview and Agate Basin, are

FIGURE 3.10 Unfluted points of the Plano tradition

often lumped together by researchers and called "Plano points." In other areas knappers shifted to stemmed forms.

The Laurentian ice sheet retreated to a point at which the Laurentian lakes piled up along its southern margin drained catastrophically through the Hudson Strait into the North Atlantic around 6250 BCE. The event triggered cold, dry, and windy conditions on the Great Plains. The cooler conditions did not last, but the dryness did. Monsoonal rains returned after around 5850 BCE, breaking the long drought. The intense dryness of this episode altered plant communities, the animal populations that depended upon them, and the humans who depended upon both. Little wonder that the High Plains were virtually abandoned in favor of safer adaptations to the foothills to the west and the milder prairies closer to the Mississippi to the east of them during the long, dry period. Both the bison herds and their human hunters avoided the harsh High Plains for a long time (Lovvorn et al., 2001).

None of these changes were either simultaneous or universal across the continent. At the Wilson-Leonard site in Texas, a **stratum** containing stemmed Wilson points, nominally Archaic in character, is overlain by a later one containing Plano points, which is in turn overlain by other Archaic and still later strata. The best explanation is that there was a variety of cultures that shifted back and forth across the southern Plains around 8000 BCE, leaving behind a more complex record than we might have hoped for (Bousman et al., 2002).

The best way to end this chapter and move on to the next is to set its close at the onset of the Holocene 11,700 years ago (9750 BCE). Archaeologists agree that American Indians were certainly present across the continent in substantial numbers by that date, and the foundation of their long and complicated evolution into an array of hundreds of later cultures was set.

Glossary

calibration Specifically radiocarbon date calibration. The use of tree rings and other materials of precisely known age to calibrate radiocarbon age determinations to the modern calendar.

coprolites Dried fossil feces.

fluted points Projectile points bearing long, concave scars left by one or more flakes detached from the side.

knapper A person who manufactures stone tools by means of flaking and chipping using percussion and pressure techniques (knapping).

lanceolate Lance shaped. Usually applied to projectile points lacking notches or stems.

megafauna Very large animal species.

niche As used in ecology, the specific part of an environment to which an organism is adapted.

obsidian Volcanic glass.

pièces esquillées Flaked stone artifacts manufactured by the bipolar percussion technique, usually characterized by lenticular or wedge-shaped cross-sections.

red ochre A red pigment typically derived from hematite.

refugium (pl. **refugia**) A region where plants and animals survived during periods when conditions elsewhere were too hostile for them.

stratum (pl. **strata**) A depositional layer in an archaeological site, often one of several strata, the oldest at the bottom and the youngest at the top.

References

Adovasio, J.M., and Pedler, J. (2005). The Peopling of North America. In: T.R. Pauketat and D.D. Loren, eds. *North American Archaeology*. Malden, MA: Blackwell.

Adovasio, J.M., and Pedler, J. (2016). *Strangers in a New Land*. Richmond Hill, Ontario: Firefly Books.

Agenbroad, L.D., and Hesse, I.S. (2004). Megafauna, Paleoindians, Petroglyphs, and Pictographs of the Colorado Plateau. In: C.M. Barton, G.A. Clark, D.R. Yesner, and G.A. Pearson, eds. *The Settlement of the American Continents: A Multidisciplinary Approach to Human Biogeography*. Tucson: University of Arizona Press.

Alley, R.B., Marotzke, J., Nordhaus, W.D., Overpeck, J.T., Peteet, D.M., Pielke Jr., R.A., Pierrehumbert, R.T., Rhines, P.B., Stocker, T.F., Talley, L.D., and Wallace, J.M. (2003). Abrupt Climate Change. *Science*, 299, pp. 2005–2010.

Anderson, D.G., and Faught, M.K. (1998). The Distribution of Fluted Paleoindian Projectile Points: Update 1998. *Archaeology of Eastern North America*, 26, pp. 163–187.

Anderson, D.G., and Sassaman, K.E., eds. (1996). *The Paleoindian and Early Archaic Southeast*. Tuscaloosa: University of Alabama Press.

Bourgeon, L., Burke, A., and Higham, T. (2017). Earliest Human Presence in North America Dated to the Last Glacial Maximum: New Radiocarbon Dates from Bluefish Caves, Canada. *PLoS One*, 12, pp. 1–15.

Bousman, C.B., Collins, M.B., Goldberg, P., Stafford, T., Guy, J., Baker, B.W., Steele, D.G., Kay, M., Kerr, A., Fredlund, G., Dering, P., Holliday, V., Wilson, D., Gose, W., Dial, S., Takac, P., Balinsky, R., Masson, M., and Powell, J.F. (2002). The Palaeoindian–Archaic Transition in North America: New Evidence from Texas. *Antiquity*, 76, pp. 980–990.

Bradley, B.A., and Collins, M.B. (2014). Imagining Clovis as a Cultural Revitalization Movement. In: K.E. Graf, C.V. Ketron, and M.R. Waters, eds. *Paleoamerican Odyssey*. College Station: Texas A&M University Press.

Cannon, M.D., and Meltzer, D.J. (2004). Early Paleoindian Foraging: Examining the Faunal Evidence for Large Mammal Specialization and Regional Variability in Prey Choice. *Quaternary Science Reviews*, 23, pp. 1955–1987.

Collins, M.B., Stanford, D.J., Lowery, D.L., and Bradley, B.A. (2014). North America before Clovis: Variance in Temporal/Spatial Cultural Patterns, 27,000–13,000 cal yr BP. In: K.E. Graf, C.V. Ketron, and M.R. Waters, eds. *Paleoamerican Odyssey*. College Station: Texas A&M University Press.

Connolly, T.J., Barker, P., Fowler, C.S., Hattori, E.M., Jenkins, D.L., and Cannon, W.J. (2016). Getting Beyond the Point: Textiles of the Terminal Pleistocene/Early Holocene in the Northwestern Great Basin. *American Antiquity*, 81, pp. 490–514.

Des Lauriers, M.R., Davis, L.G., Turnbull III, J., Southon, J.R., and Taylor, R.E. (2017). The Earliest Shell Fishhooks from the Americas Reveal Fishing Technology of Pleistocene Maritime Foragers. *American Antiquity*, 82, pp. 498–516.

Dillehay, T.D. (2014). Entangled Knowledge: Old Trends and New Thoughts in First South American Studies. In: K.E. Graf, C.V. Ketron, and M.R. Waters, eds. *Paleoamerican Odyssey*. College Station: Texas A&M University Press.

Erlandson, J.M., Kennett, D.J., Culleton, B.J., Goebel, T., Nelson, G.C., and Skinner, C. (2014). Eyed Bone Needles from a Younger Dryas Paleoindian Component at Tule Lake Rock Shelter, Northern California. *American Antiquity*, 79, pp. 776–781.

Fiedel, S. (2014). The Clovis-Era Radiocarbon Plateau. In: A.M. Smallwood and T.A. Jennings, eds. *Clovis: On the Edge of a New Understanding*. College Station: Texas A&M University Press.

Frison, G.C., Zeimens, G.M., Pelton, S.R., and Walker, D.N. (2018). Further Insights into Paleoindian Use of the Powars II Red Ocher Quarry (48PL330), Wyoming. *American Antiquity*, 83, pp. 485–504.

Gilbert, M.T.P., Jenkins, D.L., Götherström, A., Naveran, N., Sanchez, J.J., Hofreiter, M., Thomsen, P.F., Binladen, J., Higham, T.F.G., Yohe II, R.M., Parr, R., Cummings, L.S., and Willerslev, E. (2008). DNA from Pre-Clovis Human Coprolites in Oregon, North America. *Science*, 320, pp. 786–789.

Goebel, T., Powers, W.R., and Bigelow, N. (1991). The Nenana Complex of Alaska and Clovis Origins. In: R. Bonnichsen and K.L. Turnmire, eds. *Clovis: Origins and Adaptations*. Corvallis: Center for the Study of the First Americans.

Graf, K.E., Dipietro, L.M., Krasinski, K.E., Gore, A.K., Smith, H.L., Culleton, B.J., Kennett, D.J., and Rhode, D. (2015). Dry Creek Revisited: New Excavations, Radiocarbon Dates, and Site Formation Inform on the Peopling of Eastern Beringia. *American Antiquity*, 80, pp. 671–694.

Grayson, D.K., and Meltzer, D.J. (2015). Revisiting Paleoindian Exploitation of Extinct North American Mammals. *Journal of Archaeological Science*, 56, pp. 177–193.

Hawkes, K. (1993). Why Hunter-Gatherers Work: An Ancient Version of the Problem of Public Goods. *Current Anthropology*, 34, pp. 341–361.

Hoffecker, J.F., Powers, W.R., and Goebel, T. (1993). Colonization of Beringia and the Peopling of the New World. *Science*, 259, pp. 46–53.

Holen, S.R., Deméré, T.A., Fisher, D.C., Fullagar, R., Paces, J.B., Jefferson, G.T., Beeton, J.M., Cerutti, R.A., Rountrey, A.N., Vescera, L., and Holen, K.A. (2017). A 130,000-Year-Old Archaeological Site in Southern California, USA. *Nature*, 544, pp. 479–483.

Housley, R.A., Gamble, C.S., Street, M., and Pettitt, P. (1997). Radiocarbon Evidence for the Late Glacial Human Recolonisation of Northern Europe. *Proceedings of the Prehistoric Society*, 63, pp. 25–54.

Jenkins, D.L., Davis, L.G., Jr., Stafford, T.W., Campos, P.F., Hockett, B., Jones, G.T., Cummings, L.S., Yost, C., Connolly, T.J., II, Yohe, R.M., Gibbons, S.C., Raghavan, M., Rasmussen, M., Paijmans, J.L.A., Hofreiter, M., Kemp, B.M., Barta, J.L., Monroe, C., Gilbert, M.T.P., and Willerslev, E. (2012). Clovis Age Western Stemmed Projectile Points and Human Coprolites at the Paisley Caves. Science, 337, pp. 223–228.

Jenkins, D.L., Davis, L.G., Thomas, W., Stafford, J., Campos, P.F., Connolly, T.J., Cummings, L.S., Hofreiter, M., Hockett, B., Mcdonough, K., Luthe, I., O'grady, P.W., Reinhard, K.J., Swisher, M.E., White, F., Yates, B., II, Yohi, .I M.B., Yost, C., and Willerslev, E. (2013). Geochronology, Archaeological Context, and DNA at the Paisley Caves. In: K.E. Graf, C.V. Ketron, and M.R. Waters, eds. *Paleoamerican Odyssey*. College Station: Texas A&M University Center for the Study of the First Americans.

Jennings, T.A., and Waters, M.R. (2014). Pre-Clovis Lithic Technology at the Debra L. Friedkin Site, Texas: Comparisons to Clovis Through Site-Level Behavior, Technological Trait-List, and Cladistic Analysis. *American Antiquity*, 79, pp. 25–44.

Jones, T.L., Fitzgerald, R.T., Kennett, D.J., Miksicek, C.H., Fagan, J.L., Sharp, J., and Erlandson, J.M. (2002). The Cross Creek Site (CA-SLO-1797) and Its Implications for New World Colonization. *American Antiquity*, 67, pp. 213–230.

Kooyman, B., Hills, L.V., Tolman, S., and McNeil, P. (2012). Late Pleistocene Western Camel (*Camelops Hesternus*) Hunting in Southwestern Canada. *American Antiquity*, 77, pp. 115–124.

Koppel, T. (2016). Stepping Into the Past. *American Archaeology*, 20, pp. 22–29.

Lahren, L., and Bonnichsen, R. 1974. Bone Foreshafts from a Clovis Burial in Southwestern Montana. *Science*, 186, 147–149.

Lanoë, F.B., and Holmes, C.E. (2016). Animals as Raw Material in Beringia: Insights from the Site of Swan Point CZ4B, Alaska. *American Antiquity*, 81, pp. 682–696.

Lemke, A.K., Wernecke, D.C., and Collins, M.B. (2015). Early Art in North America: Clovis and Later Paleoindian Incised Artifacts from the Gault Site, Texas (41BL323). *American Antiquity*, 80, pp. 113–133.

Lepper, B.T. (2014). The People Who Peopled America. In: D.W. Owsley and R.L. Jantz, eds. *Kennewick Man: The Scientific Investigation of an Ancient American Skeleton*. College Station: Texas A&M University Press.

Lovvorn, M.B., Frison, G.C., and Tieszen, L.L. (2001). Paleoclimate and Amerindians: Evidence from Stable Isotopes and Atmospheric Circulation. *Proceedings of the National Academy of Sciences*, 98, pp. 2485–2490.

Lyman, R.L. (2015). North American Paleoindian Eyed Bone Needles: Morphometrics, Sewing, and Site Structure. *American Antiquity*, 80, pp. 146–160.

Mann, D.H., and Meltzer, D.J. (2007). Millennial-Scale Dynamics of Valley Fills over the past 12,000 14C yr. in Northeastern New Mexico, USA. *Geological Society of America Bulletin*, 119, pp. 1433–1448.

Mann, D.H., and Peteet, D.M. (1994). Extent and Timing of the Last Glacial Maximum in Southwestern Alaska. *Quaternary Research*, 42, pp. 136–148.

Meltzer, D.J. (1999). Human Responses to Middle Holocene (Altithermal) Climates on the North American Great Plains. *Quaternary Research*, 52, pp. 404–416.

Meltzer, D.J. (2015a). Kennewick Man: Coming to Closure. *Antiquity*, 89, pp. 1485–1493.

Meltzer, D.J. (2015b). Pleistocene Overkill and North American Mammalian Extinctions. *Annual Review of Anthropology*, 44, pp. 33–53.

Meltzer, D.J., and Holliday, V.T. (2010). Would North American Paleoindians Have Noticed Younger Dryas Age Climate Changes? *Journal of World Prehistory*, 23, pp. 1–41.

Menounos, B., Goehring, B.M., Osborn, G., Margold, M., Ward, B., Bond, J., Clarke, G.K.C., Clague, J.J., Lakeman, T., Koch, J., Caffee, M.W., Gosse, J., Stroeven, A.P., Seguinot, J., and Heyman, J. (2017). Cordilleran Ice Sheet Mass Loss Preceded Climate Reversals Near the Pleistocene Termination. *Science*, 358, pp. 781–784.

Moreno-Mayar, J.V., Potter, B.A., Vinner, L., Steinrücken, M., Rasmussen, S., Terhorst, J., Kamm, J.A., Albrechtsen, A., Malaspinas, A.-S., Sikora, M., Reuther, J.D., Irish, J.D., Malhi, R.S., Orlando, L., Song, Y.S., Nielsen, R., Meltzer, D.J., and Willerslev, E. (2018). Terminal Pleistocene Alaskan Genome Reveals First Founding Population of Native Americans. *Nature*, 553, pp. 203–207.

Neely, P. (2015). Pre-Clovis Artifact Found in Oregon. *American Archaeology*, 19, p. 7.

Osborn, A.J. (2014). Eye of the Needle: Cold Stress, Clothing, and Sewing Technology During the Younger Dryas Cold Event in North America. *American Antiquity*, 79, pp. 45–68.

Owsley, D.W., and Jantz, R.L., eds. (2014). *Kennewick Man: The Scientific Investigation of an Ancient American Skeleton*. College Station: Texas A&M University Press.

Pedersen, M.W., Ruter, A., Schweger, C., Friebe, H., Staff, R.A., Kjeldsen, K.K., Mendoza, M.L.Z., Beaudoin, A.B., Zutter, C., Larsen, N.K., Potter, B.A., Nielsen, R., Rainville, R.A., Orlando, L., Meltzer, D.J., Kjær, K.H., and Willerslev, E. (2016). Postglacial Viability and Colonization in North America's Ice-Free Corridor. *Nature* 537, pp. 45–49.

Potter, B.A., Holmes, C.E., and Yesner, D.R. (2014). Technology and Economy among the Earliest Prehistoric Foragers in Interior Eastern Beringia. In: K.E. Graf, C.V. Ketron, and M.R. Waters, eds. *Paleoamerican Odyssey*. College Station: Texas A&M University Press.

Prasciunas, M.M., and Surovell, T.A. (2014). Reevaluating the Duration of Clovis: The Problem of Non-Representative Radiocarbon. In: A.M. Smallwood and T.A. Jennings, eds. *Clovis: On the Edge of a New Understanding*. College Station: Texas A&M University Press.

Rick, T.C., Erlandson, J.M., and Vellanoweth, R.L. (2001). Paleocoastal Marine Fishing on the Pacific Coast of the Americas: Perspectives from Daisy Cave, California. *American Antiquity*, 66, pp. 595–613.

Scheib, C.L., Li, H., Desai, T., Link, V., Kendall, C., Dewar, G., Griffith, P.W., Mörseburg, A., Johnson, J.R., Potter, A., Kerr, S.L., Endicott, P., Lindo, J., Haber, M., Xue, Y., Tyler-Smith, C., Sandhu, M.S., Lorenz, J.G., Randall, T.D., Faltyskova, Z., Pagani, L., Danecek, P., O'connell, T.C., Martz, P., Boraas, A.S., Byrd, B.F., Leventhal, A., Cambra, R., Williamson, R., Lesage, L., Holguin, B., Soto, E.Y.-D., Rosas, J., Metspalu, M., Stock, J.T., Manica, A., Scally, A., Wegmann, D., Malhi, R.S., and Kivisild, T. (2018). Ancient Human Parallel Lineages within North America Contributed to a Coastal Expansion. *Science*, 360, pp. 1024–1032.

Smith, H.L., Rasic, J.T., and Goebel, T. (2014). Biface Traditions of Northern Alaska and Their Role in the Peopling of the Americas. In: K.E. Graf, C.V. Ketron, and M.R. Waters, eds. *Paleoamerican Odyssey*. College Station: Texas A&M University Press.

Stewart, T.J. (2016). Extinct Horse Coexisted with Humans at Paisley Caves. *American Archaeology*, 20, p. 8.
Stiger, M. (2006). A Folsom Structure in the Colorado Mountains. *American Antiquity*, 71, pp. 321–351.
Straus, L.G., Meltzer, D.J., and Goebel, T. (2005). Ice Age Atlantis? Exploring the Solutrean-Clovis "connection". *World Archaeology*, 37, pp. 507–532.
Surovell, T.A., and Brund, B.S. (2012). The Associational Critique of Quaternary Overkill and Why It Is Largely Irrelevant to the Extinction Debate. *American Antiquity*, 77, pp. 672–688.
Taylor, K. (1999). Rapid Climate Change. *American Scientist*, 87, pp. 320–327.
Thomas, K.A., Story, B.A., Eren, M.I., Buchanan, B., Andrews, B.N., O'Brien, M.J., and Meltzer, D.J. (2017). Explaining the Origin of Fluting in North American Pleistocene Weaponry. *Journal of Archaeological Science*, 81, pp. 23–30.
Toner, M. (2017). The Fates of Very Ancient Remains. *American Archaeology*, 21, pp. 41–46.
Warner, B.G., Clague, J.J., and Mathewes, R.W. (1982). Conditions on the Queen Charlotte Islands, British Columbia, at the Height of the Late Wisconsin Glaciation. *Science*, 218, pp. 675–677.
Waters, M.R., and Stafford, T.W., Jr. (2014). The First Americans: A Review of the Evidence for the Late-Pleistocene Peopling of the Americas. In: K.E. Graf, C.V. Ketron, and M.R. Waters, eds. *Paleoamerican Odyssey*. College Station: Texas A&M University Press.
Webb, J.W., and Domanski, M. (2009). Fire and Stone. *Science*, 325, pp. 820–821.
Whitley, D.S. (2009). *Cave Paintings and the Human Spirit: The Origin of Creativity and Belief*. Amherst, NY: Prometheus Books.

4
ARCHAIC CULTURES

As a term defining early hunting-gathering-collecting-foraging-fishing cultures without pottery and **horticulture**, the "Archaic" was first applied by William A. Ritchie in northeastern North American archaeology (Ritchie 1932; Willey and Phillips 1958: 104–111). With ongoing research, Ritchie (1965: 31) found that pottery was in fact included in the repertoire of some Archaic assemblages, and he observed that

> Far from uniform ... the Archaic ... displays a surprising variety in the details of its content, reflecting in part local ecological adaptations, and probably also the inherent dissimilarities of the several historically diverse traditions involved in its composition, as well as the varying interactions which took place between cultures within, and ... outside, the area.
>
> *Ritchie 1965: 32*

In their review, Willey and Phillips (1958: 107) added that specialized collecting and processing of wild foods were often associated with "early experimentation in plant domestication" and in some early Archaic cultures are found "the first evidences of New World horticulture."

The Native Americans who lived during the Archaic period of North America were originally perceived by archaeologists to fill a niche between the long period of hunting and gathering adaptations that followed the Paleoindian period and preceded the time when they adopted horticulture and produced pottery. This perception was reasonable in a time when evidence was scant and researchers lacked radiocarbon and other independent dating techniques. The transition to the Archaic coincided with the onset of the Holocene at 11,700 years ago (9750 BCE). Thousands of new sites and radiocarbon dates show that horticulture and ceramics appeared at different times in different places. To accommodate this variability and its implications, this chapter is followed by regional ones whereby trajectories of cultural change derived from Archaic antecedents are discussed without expectations of continent-wide simultaneity. This chapter will carry us forward to around 3500 BCE, with the understanding that this date is only a general approximation for the onset of later developments discussed in the regional chapters (Bousman et al., 2002; Janetski et al., 2012).

Although many archaeologists have long used "Archaic" to indicate an entire period in North American archaeology, and frequently split into shorter Early, Middle, Late, and Terminal Archaic subdivisions, these names are unsatisfactory today because major evolutionary changes occurred in different regions at different times. Consequently, continued use of these subdivisions impedes our ability to make broad comparisons at large regional scales. The term "Archaic" is used here to reference Holocene hunter-gatherers as a broad culture type. Instead of using Archaic subdivisions, this chapter refers to the calendrical time scale as much as possible (Anderson and Sassaman, 2004).

Environment and Adaptation

During the six millennia from the beginning of the Holocene to 3500 BCE, Archaic peoples adapted to a wide variety of evolving environments. While the chronological framework differs from area to area, several general trends characterized this vast array of adaptations. Populations were affected by the many contingencies that influenced specific lines of cultural evolution. While the larger trends were generally predictable, the effects of random chance or locally contingent influences led to unpredictable specific outcomes.

Human-environmental relations were an important feature of Holocene reforestation. The Archaic peoples of North America adapted to and in many cases modified a diverse and environmentally dynamic landscape. The great ice sheets of the Pleistocene had compressed the ecozones arrayed south of them in what are now the 48 lower United States. Figure 3.7 shows a simplified version of forests and limited grasslands at the height of the Pleistocene. But every forest and grassland of that epoch was different from anything familiar to us today (Figure 4.1) in constituent species and their relative frequencies. For example, forests lumped here as "western conifer forest"

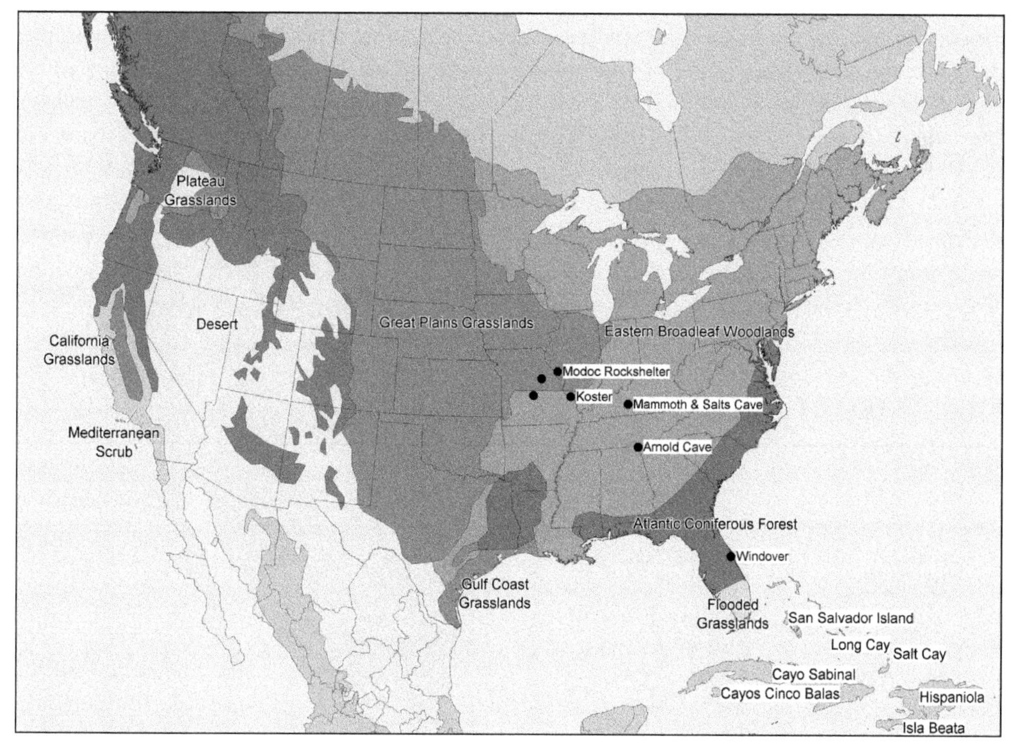

FIGURE 4.1 Contemporary ecozones of North America that emerged after the Pleistocene epoch and sites mentioned in Chapter 4. Mexican sites are shown in Figure 4.7. See the Companion Website for a color version

were unlike any variant of today's western conifer forest, just as the white spruce forests that spread across much of what are now the central and eastern United States were similar to but not nearly identical with, the modern boreal forests of Canada. The evolutionary history of the North American forests from the Pleistocene to today is a long tale with many strands (Bonnicksen, 2000).

The Holocene Release at the end of the Pleistocene enabled human societies everywhere to effectively exploit these new environments. In North America, Archaic adaptations were increasingly specialized on the sometimes-unique resources of regional environments, but they generally remained reliant on hunting and gathering. Advanced food processing technologies were developing during this time period. Later adaptations unfolded according to the special circumstances of each of the continent's many local and regional environments, which were still in flux because of changing climatic conditions. In some areas, Archaic adaptations continued until the arrival of European colonists.

In a few parts of the continent, Archaic peoples exploited plants that had potential for domestication. This development was broadly similar to other contemporaneous cases of early farming elsewhere in the world. Two major centers of crop domestication emerged in North America where people sought out and recognized appropriate plants: the Eastern Woodlands and Mesoamerica. Once domesticated, some of these plants were carried to regions beyond their geographical origins where they thrived in farming communities.

Periodic climatic stress, the constant pressure of population growth, and human ingenuity were there all along, but with the Holocene, environmental conditions favored or promoted the adoption of cultivation in some areas. With warming conditions approximately 11,570 years ago, humans adopted horticulture in some places, delayed its adoption in other areas, and in some places, groups did not adopt horticulture at all. If the sequence of tending, cultivating, domesticating, and intensifying production were all part of the process, why did the sequence unfold at different times at different rates in different regions? It turns out that **cultivation** arose first where conditions were demonstrably most favorable, later where conditions were more difficult, and still later where people were most challenged by the environment. There are many parts of the world where horticulture did not arise at all because of local conditions (Richerson et al., 2001).

Table 4.1 provides a list of regions where horticulture likely developed independently. Native Americans were completely isolated from Eurasian and African peoples while they were adopting horticulture, but there is growing evidence for stimulating influences of people and ideas within and between regions in each of these hemispherical domains (Duarte et al., 2007; Highsmith, 1997; Richerson et al., 2001; Smith, 2001; Smith, 2007b; Zeder et al, 2006).

TABLE 4.1 Selected regional centers of horticulture with approximate dates BCE

Hemisphere	*Region*	*Intensive Foraging*	*Initial Plant Domestication*
The Americas (New World)	Central Mexico	10,000	8000
	Eastern North America	6000	3000
	South Central Andes	5000	5000
	Amazonia	9000	8000
Eurasia and Africa (Old World)	Southwest Asia	12,000	7500
	North China	9600	5800
	South China	10,000	6500
	New Guinea	10,000	10,000
	Sub-Saharan Africa	7000	2000

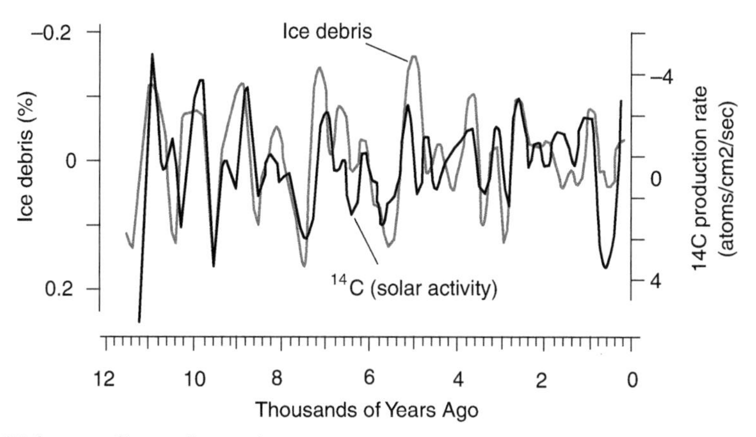

FIGURE 4.2 Holocene climate fluctuations

To better understand the reasons why food production was selected at different times and at different rates, we must examine details of the climatological record and variations in opportunity. The Younger Dryas ended abruptly about 9550 BCE, perhaps over only a few years and certainly within the lifetimes of many perplexed hunter-gatherers (Alley et al., 2003). The following Holocene epoch was less variable than previous interglacial periods. Devastating droughts, cold episodes, long-term variations in precipitation, and other environmental events were not as drastic compared to the Pleistocene. During the brief time of transition humans might even have noted that the emerging climate was relatively stable. Relative climatic stability and human ingenuity made dependence upon horticulture possible, if still sometimes episodic and precarious, and a viable solution to population growth.

Paleoclimatologists have been able to track the rise and fall of average annual temperatures using two independent lines of evidence: ice debris production of sediments on the ocean bottom and solar 14C production in the upper atmosphere. The two generally confirm each other (Figure 4.2). They both show that Holocene climate history was not a long relatively smooth trend toward modern environmental conditions. The 3,500-year period from 7000 to 3500 BCE saw three very high peaks in average temperatures, separated by mild cooler cycles. This period was called the "Altithermal" period in older archaeological literature but that has been shown to be too simplistic. The 35-century period of extreme climate swings heated and dried parts of North America severely, resulting in areas of uninhabitable deserts. Human survival strategies in other areas were difficult in centuries that were particularly hot or dry. While some western interior regions were too dry to be habitable, portions of the southeastern coastal plain were apparently depopulated for other reasons (Anderson, 2001). In contrast, there were parts of the continent where warmer and drier conditions were more advantageous for hunter-gatherers. The archaeological record reflects the vast array of adaptations of Native Americans. Consequently, there are many named Archaic cultures scattered across the continent, each of them an example of a specific adaptive trend.

Demography and Conflict

During the Holocene the composition and locations of North American forests shifted in response to a combination of human and natural forces. Human populations became generally denser, less mobile, and more diverse over time. Archaeologically these changes were expressed by a multiplicity of diverse projectile point types. Social and political boundaries appeared where they had not existed previously and specialized local adaptations emerged. Despite demographic increases and diverse adaptive strategies, there is little evidence that conflict was increasing significantly. There is no archaeological evidence for competition over critical resources during the Archaic period.

Managing Mobility

Human groups maximized the chances of encountering food resources and contacts with other bands by maintaining mobility. Under conditions where food resources were scarce, the overall population was broadly distributed over a large territory. Lacking easy ways to transport food, Archaic bands remained highly mobile. Band members had to weigh the expense of a move against its perceived benefits. Risk minimization was the driver behind mobility decisions. As resource-extractive strategies improved during the Archaic populations began increasing. It was no longer necessary for people to keep moving in order to stay in contact with related distant bands. Archaeologists see evidence of these decisions in the archaeological record as a long-term trend away from high mobility and very temporary habitations toward seasonal scheduling of moves and longer-term occupations of camps and villages.

Early on, hunter-gatherer groups would have buffered food shortfalls by moving frequently and sharing with other members of their connubia. The lack of clear linguistic or social boundaries would have precluded the exclusion of "others" from the group within which people were willing to share. People most likely first supported family members by sharing with consanguineal (blood) relatives, but any individual was unlikely to refuse any other person a helping hand because of long-term reciprocal obligations. Excessive food storage would have been regarded in this context as antisocial hoarding. But evolving Archaic adaptations gradually changed these earlier practices.

The practice of storing food meant that groups could displace consumption, either spatially or seasonally, by shifting it to another place or time. But the storage of surplus food was possible only when a group was able to (or forced to) abandon much of its mobility and to exclude hungry neighbors. Food storage was thus correlated with increased population size, more permanent camps, the establishment of social boundaries, and internal social innovations for maintenance and redistribution of stored food. Archaeologists see evidence for such changes during the long course of Archaic adaptation. At the same time, Archaic hunter-gatherers were shifting from economies that focused on a small numbers of obvious food resources like big game to broader arrays of less obvious ones, such as small seeds.

In ethnographically known cultures, degree of mobility and population distribution are known to affect social patterns, such as marriage. Generally, low-density, low-intensity foragers chose to marry partners who came from a distance, while high-density, highly invested cultivators tended to marry partners of local origin (Fix, 1999). These types of marriage patterns relate to specific kinds of mobility. Permanent **migration**, where an individual or group relocates to another area and does not return to the place of origin, is not cyclical and by definition it is not reversible. In contrast to migration, the concept of mobility connotes repetitiveness. There are different types of mobility applicable to the hunter-gatherer lifestyle. **Territorial mobility** refers to when the group shifts its range. This movement (which is not equated with migration) can occur over a period of years as groups take advantage of those areas with the most abundant resources and may return to the original territory. **Residential mobility** refers to the type of movement that occurs when the local band relocates within a known territory. **Logistical mobility** refers to the temporary dispatch of task groups to specific locations, usually for purposes of specialized hunting, fishing, or gathering activities. All of these types of mobility may vary in terms of frequency, duration, and, in the case of logistical moves, the composition of the task group. One can distinguish between **foraging** behavior, which involves moving residential or logistical camps to food resource areas, and **collecting** behavior, which involves bringing food resources back to the base camp (Binford, 1978). In short, during the Archaic period, people were overall less mobile than previously and employed strategies of various types of mobility to optimize resource extraction or social ties.

Evidence of central bases occurs in situations where humans exploited abundant food resources. Humans were also able to construct central bases where transportation innovations such as canoes allowed relatively rapid long-distance deployment of logistical task groups. Base camps usually contained the full range of chipped-stone tools and **debitage** (waste flakes) produced by knappers, whereas logistical camps typically contained only part of the full range of tools and debitage. The tools present in a logistical camp indicate the special activities carried out there and/or the nature of the task group. Two ethnographic examples include a hunting camp used mainly by adult men and a mast (acorn, hickory, and other nuts) processing camp used mainly by women.

Women processed tree nuts into several different types of highly nutritious food products that sustained the band. For example, acorns were processed into flour and hickory nuts into "hickory cream," a nutritious oil that was obtained by boiling crushed nuts in water. The dried hickory mash could also be used as flour and, like acorn shells, the hickory shells were a good source of fuel. Mammoth Cave, Russell Cave, Modoc Rockshelter, and other such sites in the central Eastern Woodlands show evidence of use that shifted from their use as occasional hunting camps to more intensely used mast processing camps during the course of Holocene warming prior to 3600 BCE (Homsey-Messer, 2015). Logistical use by largely or entirely female teams is suggested by both the inferred role of women in this kind of activity and the narrow seasonality of the mast resources. While mast was made into storable products at these processing sites, storage pits served to sequester processing equipment for future use. The food products were transported to residential sites (Wheeler et al., 2003).

MAMMOTH CAVE NATIONAL PARK

For over a hundred years, archaeologists have been fascinated by the intrepid Native Americans cavers who explored the dark reaches of Mammoth Cave, carrying only simple torches, a set of sophisticated caving skills, and an amazing level of courage. Some 405 miles (652 km) of Mammoth Cave have been surveyed, making it the world's longest-known cave system, much of which was traversed by Native American cavers (Figure 4.3). Scientific investigations of the dry cave passageways reveal preserved artifacts unheard of from earthen sites and shell middens along the nearby Green River (Watson, 1997).

Mammoth Cave's use was mostly restricted to the Archaic period, a time when hunter-gatherers who lived in the vicinity began venturing into the cave's remote recesses. Some 4500 to 5000 years ago, indigenous cavers began to explore fields of breakdown, massive rooms, and tight crawlways, aided only by simple cane and twig torches. Archaeologists find abundant evidence of exploration, often extending some 6–8 km (4.7–5.0 mi) underground, along the dry cave passageways. No other known caves show such an extent of underground trekking as the Mammoth Cave system. Patty Jo Watson, who has spent a lifetime studying the archaeology of the Mammoth Cave area, refers to the local Archaic people as "the world's greatest cave explorers" (Dye, 2008; Waston 1969).

Around 3,000 years ago, these hunter-gatherers began mining exotic minerals that had formed on the dry passageway walls. Extensive mining continued for over a thousand years as witnessed by chisel marks and stone and wooden tools left along the cave floor. For reasons currently unknown, exploration and mineral extraction ended around 2,000 years ago. Mammoth Cave, as an interconnected system of underground passages, continues to reveal important information about the indigenous cavers who scrambled over massive limestone breakdown and squeezed through tight, labyrinthine passageways to satisfy their curiosity and to mine valuable minerals.

David H. Dye

FIGURE 4.3 Salts Cave vestibule excavations in progress. Cave Research Foundation archaeological project. Digital image courtesy of the William S. Webb Museum of Anthropology, University of Kentucky. Original photograph by the Cave Research Foundation, c. 1969

Theoretically, the size of a local population is determined by the carrying capacity of the environment, technological adaptations, and social organization of that population. However, carrying capacity is not a concept that is easy to apply in real world situations (Bayliss-Smith, 1978) because all primates, humans included, for the most part live far below the objective carrying capacities of their environments.

We can better understand the vulnerability of small bands by modeling the processes in a general way. Small bands clearly face risk of extinction in the long run, and larger ones have better chances to survive and grow, but the demands of subsistence and mobility influence how large bands can grow. There are also what statisticians call **stochastic** variables, the random lucky or unlucky breaks that affect smaller populations more than bigger ones. For example, a band that has been doing well for generations might experience a high birth rate of baby boys that, 20 years later, leaves it short of women. Another example is a band that has for centuries been able to fall back on rabbits when other game is scarce, only to find out the hard way that the cycle of rabbit populations ranges from low levels to highs that are 25 times higher than the lows. If a low point in the rabbit population happens to coincide with the kind of killer winter that comes along every few decades, the results could be fatal for such a band.

Because of these factors, averages are misleading in the world of hunter-gatherers. It is the extremes that are lethal, and death is a one-way door. Thus, of all the bands that were alive and well around 8000 BCE, it is likely that many shrank and had to join with others. Many others must have simply dwindled to extinction, while a few lucky ones thrived and left living descendants. The cycles of boom and bust explain why there is so much variability in the projectile point styles they left behind, and why there is so often evidence of change over time in the archaeological record for which we are unable to specify the reasons.

Subsistence and Economy

Environments changed considerably during the Holocene. The very existence of horticulture in pre-Columbian America means that, given the Holocene Release of people everywhere from the adaptive constraints of the Pleistocene, they were able to refine their techniques for acquiring more and better food. Large low-hanging fruits and large sluggish animals are easy to take, but rarely encountered. More food was available from less accessible sources, but such sources were also less easily obtained, even when close at hand. For example, there was more meat per **hectare** running around the Eastern Woodlands in the form of mice and other small rodents than in the form of white-tailed deer; the problem is figuring out how to hunt and consume such an alternative resource (Kennett and Winterhalder, 2006).

Most plant foods are like mice, in that they are seemingly difficult to harvest in quantity and once harvested, are often difficult to convert into palatable food or to store for future consumption. But humans are not merely good at exploring environmental details, they are also inclined to tinker with them. The result was that hunter-gatherers constructed their own ecological niches as they learned more about their environments (Smith, 2007a). Over time people of the Eastern Woodlands learned how to make good use of nuts and acorns (mast) from at least 30 tree species, and the fleshy fruits and berries of at least another 20 species (Abrams and Nowacki, 2008).

The forests and grasslands of eastern North America are full of potentially nutritious plants, but they are also full of dangerous ones. A popular field guide to edible wild plants in North America warns of about nine species that can cause severe dermatitis, of which poison ivy is the best known (Peterson, 1978). No fewer than 90 species are poisonous to humans, and 24 of them are known to have caused fatalities. Some plants, like acorns, are not listed as poisonous because humans

FIGURE 4.4 Edible and poisonous plants that resemble each other. Caraway and wild carrot (top) are nutritious, while fool's-parsley and poison hemlock (bottom) are poisonous. Adapted from Britton and Brown (1923: 625–659)

have learned to leach the tannins from them to make them edible. The wild ancestors of modern watermelons and potatoes were unpalatable too, and it must have taken both time and luck for their food potentials to be realized.

Caraway and wild carrot are nutritious species that resemble each other, but they also look very much like the poisonous species of fool's-parsley and poison hemlock, which are lethal (Figure 4.4). Many mushrooms are tasty, but some are deadly, and it takes an expert to tell the difference. Examples like these are numerous. The point is that hunter-gatherers could not simply settle into a region and exploit the available animal and plant resources without going through a long and complicated learning process. There is a tendency to underestimate the time required for this process, given the many plants available and the natural caution of any pioneer gatherer. One can imagine that some of the consequences must have been tragic, but the people of North America like people everywhere else slowly became more adept at using the plant and animal resources they found around them. Given the natural variation in those resources from one region to another, it is no surprise that groups became regional specialists. Cultures and languages began to specialize and diverge from one another as a result, and in a few cases, people took the first steps toward domestication.

The emergence of domesticates may not have been a conscious process for gatherers, at least not in the beginning. The process led to interactions between plants and gatherers that would have led in turn to unconscious artificial selection. Gatherers tend to harvest the plumper juicier berries or the larger tastier tubers. Discarded seeds might grow into unusually healthy plants in the garbage deposits surrounding campsites, leading to still more careful selection by gatherers. Fruits that are bigger, less bitter, or sweeter will be favored over time. Gatherers might have even discouraged competing plants. Over the long term, they favored plants that grew quickly and were easy to harvest, store, and convert into food. The selective process also favored self-pollinating plants, as opposed to those that depended upon cross-pollination, because self-pollinators pass on their own desirable genes unchanged and respond more quickly to selection.

An important question is how the process led to better food plants if the best were constantly selected out for consumption rather than being allowed to reproduce. The answer is that the people doing the harvesting inadvertently propagated desirable plants in patches where the plants would not have otherwise reproduced naturally, like garbage middens. People eventually knew enough to encourage the strains with heightened food value. It did not have to be a conscious process. For example, plants that disperse their seeds easily when they mature will tend to be seedless by the time a human gatherer comes around, so those that hold their seeds longer and more tightly stand a better chance of being gathered. Over time the human gatherers will inadvertently select for plants that produce bigger more tightly bound seeds, plants that are less efficient at reproducing in the wild but more desirable to gatherers. Thus, over time humans and their domesticated plants have developed a strong mutual dependence.

Russell Cave, in northeastern Alabama, yielded an 8,000-year-long sequence that illuminates the Eastern Woodland variation on the Archaic theme. Acorns were processed for food and fuel. Elsewhere in the Eastern Woodlands, Archaic peoples focused on other food resources to maximize their production. In Kentucky they scoured rivers for freshwater mollusks and left behind extensive middens of discarded shells. These sites are typically located in places where local resources were particularly rich. People were eating not only mussels but also birds, fish, deer, and a range of domesticates and near domesticates.

RUSSELL CAVE

Russell Cave is located in northeastern Alabama, approximately 7 miles from the Tennessee River (Figure 4.5). The site is notable in part due to an extensive and well-preserved record of human occupation. Excavations by the Smithsonian Institution and National Geographic Society in 1953, followed by the National Park Service in 1962, revealed 3 m of cultural deposits, dating from approximately 6700 BCE to 1050 CE, and spanning the Early Archaic through Middle Woodland Periods. Like many limestone cave sites in the American Midsouth, the nonacidic environment of Russell Cave has preserved delicate faunal and botanical remains, numerous feature types, and bone tools such as needles and fishhooks. Although miles of back passageways exist, occupants throughout time restricted their activities primarily to the spacious shelter entrance. The earliest occupations likely functioned as ephemeral hunting camps for mobile bands of hunter-gatherers during the fall and early winter (Griffin, 1974: 4878). Over time, site use intensified and archaeologists see evidence for many cultural changes characterizing caves and rockshelters during the Archaic period, including a decrease in hunting paraphernalia, intensive exploitation of nut resources (e.g., walnut, acorn), the appearance of storage pits, and an increasingly logistical mobility strategy in which caves and rockshelters such as Russell Cave served as processing locales. Work parties likely lived at these sites for a few weeks each fall, processing plants and nuts into storable forms to provision base camps located elsewhere. These activities left behind a characteristic "fingerprint" of plant processing features, nutting stones, and storage pits. So pervasive was nut exploitation in the American Midsouth that Walthall (Walthall, 1998: 225) writes that "the interior

FIGURE 4.5 Russell Cave (left) and the human-occupied Russell Cave Shelter (right). Courtesy of Steve Marcos

floors of rockshelters … are literally riddled with Middle Archaic storage and processing pits." Today, Russell Cave is administered and protected by the National Park Service as a national monument. Visitors can take a guided tour, view museum exhibits and films at the visitor's center, and hike surrounding interpretive trails to identify plants used prehistorically for food, basketry, and other daily activities (Anonymous, 2018).

Lara Homsey-Messer

Where Boston, Massachusetts, now stands, Archaic people built **weir**s of closely set stakes to impound fish when the tide went out. Other seafoods were available here too, but most of the wild plants that had potential as domesticates were not. This northeastern variation on the more general Archaic theme of intensification and specialization in subsistence activities was productive, but it would not lead directly to farming.

WINDOVER SITE

Eight thousand years ago some people in central and south Florida were interring their dead in shallow ponds. There are only a few known **wet site**s like Windover (Figure 4.6). So far, all such sites date to the Early Archaic or early part of the Middle Archaic and are restricted to central and south Florida. The bodies were accompanied by bone, antler, wood, lithic, dentary artifacts, and an array of hand woven fabrics. Bodies were placed in scooped out depressions in peat deposits and pinned in place with modified pine stakes. Continuous peat deposition

FIGURE 4.6 The Windover wet site during excavation. Courtesy of Glen Doran

further entombed them in an anaerobic continuously saturated nearly neutral medium providing near optimum preservation. The organic inventory of bags, matts, and other items, including an oak mortar and pestle, document a sophisticated technology. The five stone tools (four bifaces and a biface tip) are overshadowed by a robust perishable technology seldom glimpsed in terrestrial sites. Wet sites provide a sobering illustration of what perishes in all but the most extreme environments – wet, dry, or cold.

Diet reconstruction and the artifact inventory reveal a terrestrial and freshwater pond and riverine orientation with a minimal use of marine resources. The climate was drier and a bit more temperate than today. Florida's modern fire prone climate appeared about 6,000 years ago, and this is clearly recorded in the pollen and peat petrographic record.

Windover's 168 individuals, with about 50% subadults and a nearly 50/50 adult sex ratio, provide an unparalleled opportunity to understand human health and disease. Multidisciplinary investigations with a heavy emphasis on biocultural and health reconstructions were possible because of the interest of the EKS, Inc. development firm, which helped with logistical support and funding from 1984–1987, as well as support of the Florida legislature. The site is a National Historic Landmark (Doran, 2002; Doran et al., 1990; Tomczak and Powell, 2003).

Glen H. Doran

Of 148 mammalian candidates for domestication worldwide, 72 occurred in Eurasia and only 24 in the Americas. Apart from the turkey, there were no naturally occurring animals suitable for domestication in North America. In addition to this constraint, Archaic people adapting to post-Pleistocene environments here necessarily had fewer large species to hunt than did their Paleoindian ancestors. This was because animal populations thinned as they shifted northward with the retreating tundra.

Centers of Plant Domestication

Archaic adaptations persisted for millennia in some parts of North America, in a few cases until the early twentieth century. However, in the Eastern Woodlands and in Mesoamerica, the Archaic adaptations laid the groundwork for a transition from hunting and gathering to food production. As elsewhere, the Archaic peoples in these two regions of North America shifted to more diversified diets, using increasingly complex technology to exploit resources that were productive but tricky to harvest. They modified their environments, especially through the use of fire to renew plant succession, they increased food storage, and buffer zones developed as ranges shrank, local populations increased, and supportive connections with neighboring groups became less vital to long-term survival.

Wild teosinte evolved into maize through artificial selection. Some domesticates remained viable only south of the deserts of Northern Mexico, but maize, beans, and squash eventually were carried north and became staples in diets as far north as the Great Lakes.

Although the archaeological evidence for early domestication comes primarily from the Mexican highlands, the earliest complex societies developed in the hot, wet coastal lowlands (Figure 4.7). There domesticates brought down from the highlands flourished in the rich humid soils of cleared tropical forest, yielding two crops a year.

In the Eastern Woodlands and Mesoamerica, some of the plants people had close to hand were species that had potential for domestication, but gatherers during the early part of the Archaic may not have known that. They were just trying to make a living, unaware that in the process their interactions with certain plants would yield quite unexpected results over the

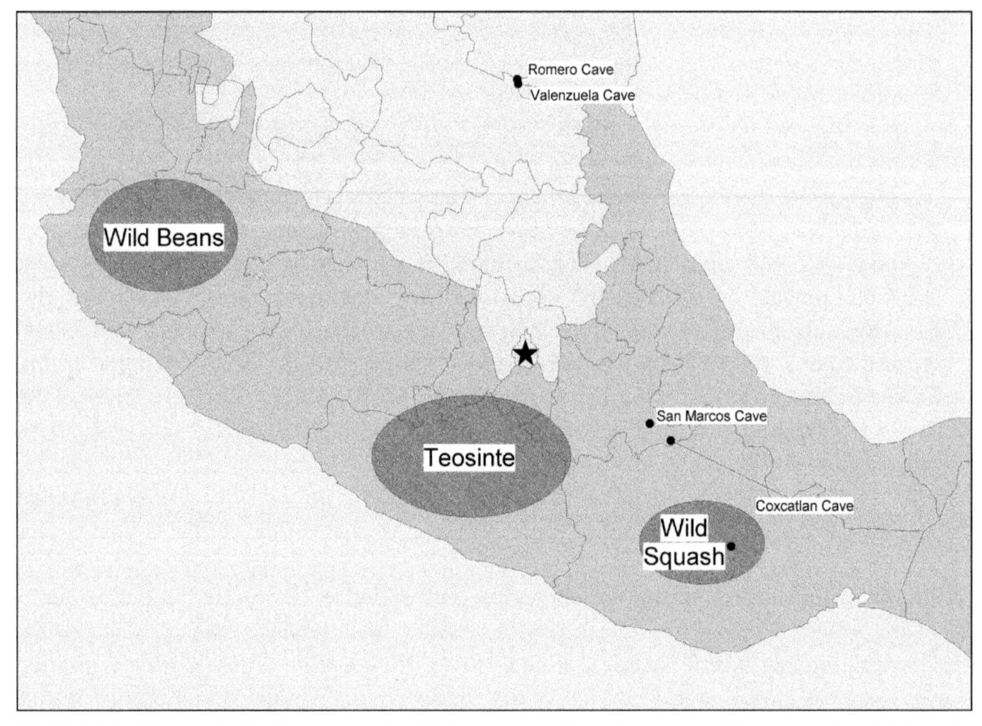

FIGURE 4.7 The probable locations of wild beans, squash, and teosinte. Five caves in which early domesticates have been found

long run. Their investments in new knowledge about local environments and new technology for extracting food from them led gradually to the domestication of a few plants and a shift from foraging and gathering to food production (Wolverton, 2005).

Architecture and Technology

There were numerous inventions made by Archaic peoples utilizing a wide range of materials. It is often only items made of the most durable materials, such as stone, that are preserved and recovered in the archaeological record. Most of what is known about early Archaic architecture is similar to the scanty information surviving from the Paleoindian era (later innovations are covered in the regional chapters of this textbook). Projectile points and other stone tools made by Archaic people and the debitage produced in the course of their manufacture are often the only obvious evidence found in the sites of the long period from 9000 to 3500 BCE. What were once tools for ancient hunter-gatherers become tools of a different sort for archaeologists. The points that tipped Archaic spears, darts, and knives come in a wide variety of forms that are often diagnostic for specific regions or time periods. This characteristic was more important prior to the advent of reliable radiocarbon dating than it is today, but people still use point typology for initial assessment of finds. Noel Justice (1987) has compiled an inventory of point types for the mid-continental United States. His inventory includes 41 types for just the period covered by this chapter in that region. To make that number more manageable, Justice has grouped them into 15 clusters, sets of types that hang together because they are similar and (sometimes or) occur together repeatedly in archaeological sites (Justice, 1987). Figure 4.8 shows four basic forms. Type descriptions might also indicate that a type is relatively large or small, thick or thin, biconvex or plano-convex in cross section, or typically made from some particular raw material.

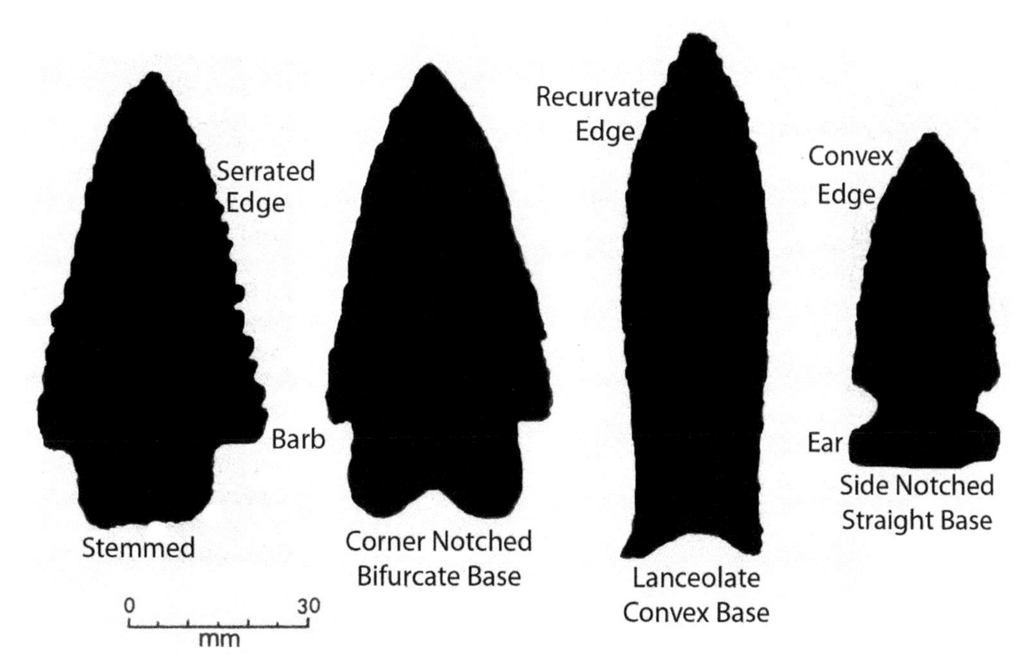

FIGURE 4.8 Basic projectile point forms. From left to right: stemmed, corner notched, lanceolate, and side notched

One purpose for continued interest in point typology is that it allows the archaeologist to define a tool or complex of tools as the hallmark(s) of a particular cultural adaptation. The regional context of such a tool type or complex can be examined once the time-space distribution of a set of known examples is worked out. Some tend to cluster in a particular ecological setting. Some prove to be older in one part of their range than across the rest of it and persist longer in one place as compared to others. It is often useful to use sets of specimens this way, as members of type populations (admittedly not breeding populations), for it is at the population level, rather than at the level of the individual artifact, that interesting archaeological problems more often reside.

In the analytical process it is important to be able to say whether two similar artifacts are **homolog**s or **analog**s. Two stemmed points, one from California and one from New Jersey, may look alike, but they are almost certainly analogs, similar points that originated independently. There are, after all, only a limited number of ways to make points that will serve the purpose of providing durable sharp tips for projectiles. In contrast, two stemmed points, both from Missouri, which are made from the same raw material, appear to have been produced by the same knapping techniques, and were found in the same area, are almost certainly homologs, specimens that have a common cultural origin. Because we are typically interested in sets of artifacts that were made by individual knappers in particular cultures, it is necessary to be reasonably certain that the specimens we study are homologous and not merely analogs of each other.

The development of a weighted flexible spear thrower was a clever technological advance in Archaic weaponry (Figure 4.9). Ground stone artifacts called "**bannerstone**s" have been turning up for many years all across the Eastern Woodlands. This type of artifact is often similar in shape and size to a computer mouse, but it has a 10- to 15-mm (0.4–0.6 in) hole drilled from side to side. Early archaeologists could not imagine for what they were used, so these objects were often classified as "ceremonial."

Fortunately, the low acidity of soils containing shell promotes preservation. Examples of bannerstones found with burials in the shell mounds of Kentucky were often similarly arranged with bone hooks and loops that made them all appear to be parts of complex spear throwers. The shafts had disappeared even in the relatively benign shell deposits, but the other parts survived, often in the same telltale arrangements, handle or finger loops at one end, bannerstone in the middle, and hook at the other end (Webb, 1974). Dry caves in the West also preserved composite

FIGURE 4.9 Two spear throwers. Composite weighted spear thrower in the Mathers Museum, Indiana (above) and a simple one-piece spear thrower in the Nevada State Museum, Las Vegas (below). One has a bannerstone as a counterweight

spear throwers with weights. Figure 4.9 shows one such composite spear thrower compared to a simple one-piece spear thrower.

The composite spear thrower is more complicated. The handle or finger loops provide the hunter with a good grip, and the bone hook would have fit well into the socket at the base of a spear shaft. But the bannerstone at first seemed unnecessary, at best, and dysfunctional, at worst. A weight at the middle of the spear thrower shaft confers no practical advantage, assuming that the shaft is rigid. Furthermore, the hole in the bannerstone is usually so narrow that experimentally any rigid wooden shaft small enough to fit through it would snap on the first throw. The answer must be that the shafts of the complex spear throwers were flexible. Green ironwood (*Carpinus caroliniana*) would be a perfect material for this purpose, and it might also explain why shafts are not preserved in eastern sites. Ironwood decays more rapidly in the ground than most woods, despite its supple hardness. Experiments with flexible spear throwers show that Archaic hunters probably discovered the benefits of flexibility, which fiberglass has brought to modern golf, pole vaulting, and other sports. The added weight flexes the spear thrower at the beginning of the throw, loading force and releasing it at the end of the throw. This results in greater velocity than would be possible with a rigid spear thrower (Palter, 1976).

Unlike the durable stone points or bannerstones, sometimes evidence exists for materials made of more fragile materials. Archaic people devised innovative clothing technology. For example, in the Midwest, the Arnold Research Cave in Missouri has produced among other things a long sequence of Archaic footwear. Sandals and slip-ons made from fiber and leather date to as early as 6205 BCE (Kuttruff et al., 1998).

As significant as the typology of projectile points is, the development of advanced radiocarbon dating techniques has changed archaeological practice. It has reversed the relationships between what we can observe and what we can infer from those observations. Radiocarbon dating is expensive, but we can usually directly date sites and strata within sites, making it unnecessary (and sometimes misleading) to assume that their ages correspond to those defined for similar artifact homologs of known age at other sites. Many archaeologists still use index types to get a first approximation for recently discovered artifacts or sites, but precision requires independent dating using radiocarbon or some other independent technique for any serious analysis. There are regional guides and state guides to point types, usually available from state museums or state or provincial archaeological societies. These guides can be found online or in published catalogs.

Archaic Indians used fire as an essential tool. The use of this ancient technology has many implications. In the absence of people and fires, pioneer species like grass, birches, tamaracks, pines, and aspens are the first to occupy disturbed ground. They grow rapidly and live relatively short lives. Some are well adapted for growth on recently deglaciated soils having few nutrients. Settler species like maples, beeches, hemlocks, and firs expand by infiltrating into stands of pioneer species, where they appear later, grow more slowly, but eventually replace the smaller, short-lived trees. Native Americans redirected this natural process with fire. Human firing changed the character of forest environments because it selected out mature settler tree species and repeatedly encouraged pioneer species, even as general climate change was reworking the makeups of shifting Holocene forests. The landscape of America has been in large part anthropogenic for thousands of years.

Culture, Language, and Identity

The ethnographic study of people who were still living by hunting and gathering in the last two centuries has allowed archaeologists to make general statements about their way of life that are

TABLE 4.2 Trends of change from Paleoindian through Archaic cultures (after Hayden, 1981)

	Paleoindian		*Archaic*
1.	High mobility and nonpermanent habitations.	1.	Seasonal sedentism and scheduling of annual movements.
2.	Little midden accumulation around sites.	2.	Midden accumulation due to specialization in resource rich areas.
3.	Relatively simple technology.	3.	Relatively complex technology with ground stone tools, fishing equipment, bow and arrow, and food boiling.
4.	Limited resource base of medium to large game.	4.	Resource diversification to more and smaller game species.
5.	Low population density with marginal habitats unpopulated.	5.	Increased population density with expansion into marginal areas.
6.	Egalitarian social organization.	6.	Competition and ranking in social organizations.
7.	Exchange of high-grade exotic lithic materials.	7.	Use of local lithic materials.
8.	Little environmental modification.	8.	Increased environmental modification through burning.
9.	Relatively large band ranges.	9.	Reduced band ranges.
10.	Little food storage.	10.	Increased importance of food storage.

relevant to our understanding of long-extinct Archaic cultures. Archaeological theory depends upon such ethnographic research and the use of analogy.

Many groups lived in parts of North America where natural abundance was exploited, resulting in larger tribal groups (100–1,000 people) than the previous hunter-gatherer bands. They eventually passed the threshold size of ±500 where it was no longer as important for them to share with nearby tribes in exchange for possible future reciprocity when their own circumstances turned to misfortune. Self-reliance meant that long-distance relationships were no longer needed for insurance against hard times or for the acquisition of marriage mates. Thus, for the emerging tribal societies of the Archaic world, settling in turned more inward looking and **endogamous** (in-marrying). Tribal boundaries, language barriers, and mutual intergroup estrangement were inevitable features of this process, and archaeologists see the vast diversity as reflected in the multiplicity of Archaic projectile point styles. Long-distance trade in rare desirable materials now required new formalities to overcome boundaries.

Despite the fickle and sometimes brutal effects of the environment, Archaic people were not simply at the mercy of the elements. General trends in cultural evolution relate to the dynamics of humans interacting with and modifying an evolving environment (Table 4.2). Brian Hayden long ago outlined these trends, which are still relevant (Hayden, 1981).

Art and Symbolism

As is the case for Paleoindian cultures, little art or symbolism has survived from Archaic cultures. It is possible that some of the rock art found across the continent, particularly petroglyphs, might be old enough to be associated with Archaic cultures. Pictographs, which are painted rather than incised, do not last as long on exposed rock faces, and it is unlikely that any have survived from Archaic times. However, there are a few candidates from protected cave sites that might be old enough to qualify

(Dye, 2008). Unfortunately, rock art of both types is notoriously difficult to date given current dating techniques. New techniques are allowing archaeologists to improve on this situation.

Sporadic findings across North America reveal early evidence of symbolic behavior that was elaborated upon by later descendant cultures. For example, in the Northeast some Archaic people began to bury their dead with offerings of bright red **hematite**. In some cases they used natural glacial **kame**s as burial monuments. Both practices presaged a later elaboration of burial ceremonialism. The use of natural mounds evolved into the construction of artificial earthen mounds, a practice that spread until there were thousands of such monuments scattered across parts of the Eastern Woodlands.

We know very little about the games played by Archaic peoples. As in the case of Paleoindians, we can guess at the likely activities of people confined to shelters in cold or rainy weather based on our general knowledge of hunter-gatherers. Some dry caves of the American West have produced what appear to be gaming pieces (see Chapter 9). Arctic analogs are also informative (Chapter 5).

Resilience and Collapse

Both the changing climatic conditions and the use of fire by early American Indians drove the complicated evolution of North American forests through the course of the Holocene. Horticulture emerged gradually in several world regions, two of which are in North America, where ethnobotanically useful plants occurred naturally. Populations grew well above the threshold of 500 as well as the density of humans across the landscape. Communities became more self-sufficient to outsiders and stored food for future consumption. The emergence of more bounded cultures was materialized by the production of hundreds of locally and regionally diagnostic types of projectile points.

Decreased mobility, a shift to smaller food resources, and increased competition were only three of several trends that characterized Archaic cultural evolution. Some Archaic cultures persisted in the Interior West, particularly the Great Basin, where hunter-gatherer cultures survived as recently as a century ago. In that sense, successful Archaic adaptations persisted until the late Holocene in some parts of the continent. In most regions, Archaic adaptations evolved into derivative traditions that came to be modified by the spread of plant domesticates and technological innovations that no Archaic hunter-gatherer could have imagined.

The list of ten Holocene trends in Table 4.2 summarizes a settling in process that took centuries to unfold. Hunter-gatherers live on what they can find and manipulate in their environments. Those who live in poor environments tend to practice conservation and hunt communally more often than those who live in naturally rich environments. In all cases the availability of dietary fat is important. There are other limiting factors too, some of which are not obvious. As a result it is not easy to assess the carrying capacity of any particular landscape for hunter-gatherers. What may appear at first glance to be a very productive environment might be short of some critical resource for a brief period each year, and even short-term starvation can keep numbers low over the long run. Seemingly unproductive environments can be made productive by a combination of human ingenuity and knowledge, imported plants, and irrigation technology. Examples of both are discussed in the chapters that follow.

Glossary

analog Forms that are similar but do not share a common origin.

bannerstone A ground stone artifact usually having a cylindrical hole for the insertion of a wood shaft that provides balance to a spear thrower.

collecting The gathering of edible species that involves no residential relocation.
cultivation The protection of a plant species to ensure its reproduction. The species may be either wild or domesticated.
debitage Waste flakes and chips from the manufacture of stone tools.
endogamy Marriage within the local group; contrasting with **exogamy**.
foraging Food collecting that involves residential relocation.
hectare A unit of area equal to a square 100 meters on a side or 2.471 acres.
hematite Iron oxide, a bright red naturally occurring mineral.
homolog Similar forms that share a common origin and may have similar functions.
horticulture A mode of subsistence that is dependent upon domesticated plant species.
kame A natural gravel mound left behind by melting glacial ice.
logistical mobility The temporary dispatch of task groups to specific field camps, usually for purposes of specialized hunting, fishing, or gathering activities.
migration For humans, the permanent relocation of an individual or group.
residential mobility The relocation of the local band within a known territory.
stochastic A sequence of events due to random chance.
territorial mobility The long-term shifting of a group's range due to the cumulative shifting of its constituent parts.
weir A stake or stone fence constructed underwater to catch fish, usually in a river.
wet site A site situated in swampy ground, requiring special excavation techniques.

References

Abrams, M.D., and Nowacki, G.J. (2008). Native Americans as Active and Passive Promoters of Mast and Fruit Trees in the Eastern USA. *The Holocene*, 18, pp. 1123–1137.

Alley, R.B., Marotzke, J., Nordhaus, W.D., Overpeck, J.T., Peteet, D.M., Pielke Jr., R.A., Pierrehumbert, R.T., Rhines, P.B., Stocker, T.F., Talley, L.D., and Wallace, J.M. (2003). Abrupt Climate Change. *Science*, 299, pp. 2005–2010.

Anderson, D.G. (2001). Climate and Culture Change in Prehistoric and Early Historic Eastern North America. *Archaeology of Eastern North America*, 29, pp. 143–186.

Anderson, D.G., and Sassaman, K.E. (2004). Early and Middle Holocene Periods, 9500 to 3750 B.C. In: R. Fogelson and W.C. Sturtevant, eds. *Handbook of North American Indians*. Washington, DC: Smithsonian Institution.

Anonymous. (2018). Russell Cave National Monument. Available: www.nps.gov/ (Accessed May 16, 2018).

Bayliss-Smith, T. (1978). Maximum Populations and Standard Populations: The Carrying Capacity Question. In: D. Green, C. Haselgrove, and M. Spriggs, eds. *Social Organization and Settlement*. Oxford: Archaeopress.

Binford, L.R. (1978). *Nunamiut Ethnoarchaeology*. New York: Academic Press.

Bonnicksen, T.M. (2000). *America's Ancient Forests: From the Ice Age to the Age of Discovery*. New York: John Wiley.

Bousman, C.B., Collins, M.B., Goldberg, P., Stafford, T., Guy, J., Baker, B.W., Steele, D.G., Kay, M., Kerr, A., Fredlund, G., Dering, P., Holliday, V., Wilson, D., Gose, W., Dial, S., Takac, P., Balinsky, R., Masson, M., and Powell, J.F. (2002). The Palaeoindian–Archaic Transition in North America: New Evidence from Texas. *Antiquity*, 76, pp. 980–990.

Britton, N.L., and Brown, A. (1923). *An Illustrated Flora of the Northern United States, Canada and the British Possessions*. New York: New York Botanical Garden.

Doran, G.H., Dickel, D.N., and Newsom, L.A. (1990). A 7,290-Year-Old Bottle Gourd from the Windover Site, Florida. *American Antiquity*, 55: 354–359.

Doran, G.H., ed. (2002). *Windover: Multidisciplinary Investigations of an Early Archaic Florida Cemetery*. Gainesville: University Press of Florida.

Duarte, C.M., Marbá, N., and Holmer, M. (2007). Rapid Domestication of Marine Species. *Science*, 316, pp. 382–383.

Dye, D.H., ed. (2008). *Cave Archaeology of the Eastern Woodlands: Essays in Honor of Patty Jo Watson*. Knoxville: University of Tennessee Press.

Fix, A. (1999). *Migration and Colonization in Human Microevolution*. New York: Cambridge University Press.

Griffin, J.W. (1974). *Investigations in Russell Cave*. Publications in Archaeology. Washington: National Park Service.

Hayden, B. (1981). Research and Development in the Stone Age: Technological Transitions among Hunter-Gatherers. *Current Anthropology*, 55, pp. 519–548.

Highsmith, H. (1997). *The Mounds of Kashkonong and Rock River*. Fort Atkinson, WI: Fort Atkinson Historical Society and Highsmith Press.

Homsey-Messer, L. (2015). Revisiting the Role of Caves and Rockshelters in the Hunter-Gatherer Taskscape of the Archaic Midsouth. *American Antiquity*, 80, pp. 332–352.

Janetski, J.C., Bodily, M.L., Newbold, B.A., and Yoder, D.T. (2012). The Paleoarchaic to Early Archaic Transition on the Colorado Plateau: The Archaeology of North Creek Shelter. *American Antiquity*, 77, pp. 125–159.

Justice, N.D. (1987). *Stone Age Spear and Arrow Points of the Midcontinental and Eastern United States*. Bloomington: Indiana University Press.

Kennett, D.J., and Winterhalder, B., eds. (2006). *Behavioral Ecology and the Transition to Agriculture*. Berkeley: University of California Press.

Kuttruff, J.T., Dehart, S.G., and O'Brien, M.J. (1998). 7500 Years of Prehistoric Footwear from Arnold Research Cave, Missouri. *Science*, 281, pp. 72–75.

Palter, J.L. (1976). A New Approach to the Significance of the "Weighted" Spear Thrower. *American Antiquity*, 41: 500–510.

Peterson, L. (1978). *A Field Guide to Edible Wild Plants*. Boston, MA: Houghton Mifflin.

Richerson, P.J., Boyd, R., and Bettinger, R.L. (2001). Was Agriculture Impossible During the Pleistocene but Mandatory During the Holocene? A Climate Change Hypothesis. *American Antiquity*, 66, pp. 387–411.

Ritchie, W.A. (1932). The Lamoka Lake Site. *New York State Archaeological Association Research Transactions* 7, no. 4.

Ritchie, W.A. (1965). *The Archaeology of New York State*. Garden City: Natural History Press.

Smith, B.D. (2001). Documenting Plant Domestication: The Consilience of Biological and Archaeological Approaches. *Proceedings of the National Academy of Sciences*, 98, pp. 1324–1326.

Smith, B.D. (2007a). Niche Construction and the Behavioral Context of Plant and Animal Domestication. *Evolutionary Anthropology*, 16, pp. 188–199.

Smith, B.D. (2007b). The Ultimate Ecosystem Engineers. *Science*, 315, pp. 1797–1798.

Tomczak, P.D., and Powell, J.F. (2003). Postmarital Residence Practices in the Windover Population: Sex-based Dental Variation as an Indicator of Patrilocality. *American Antiquity*, 68**,** pp. 93-108.

Walthall, J.A. (1998). Rockshelters and Hunter-Gatherer Adaptation to the Pleistocene-Holocene Transition. *American Antiquity*, 63: 223–238.

Watson, P.J. (1969). *The Prehistory of Salts Cave, Kentucky*. Springfield: Illinois State Museum.

Watson, P.J., ed. (1997). *Archeology of the Mammoth Cave Area*. St. Louis, MO: Cave Books.

Webb, W.S. (1974). *Indian Knoll*. Knoxville: University of Tennessee Press.

Wheeler, R.J., Miller, J.J., Mcgee, R.M., Ruhl, D., Swann, B., and Memory, M. (2003). Archaic Period Canoes from Newnans Lake, Florida. *American Antiquity*, 68, pp. 533–551.

Willey, G.R., and Phillips, P. (1958). *Method and Theory in American Archaeology*. Chicago: University of Chicago Press.

Wolverton, S. (2005). The Effects of the Hypsithermal on Prehistoric Foraging Efficiency in Missouri. *American Antiquity*, 70, pp. 91–106.

Zeder, M.A., Bradley, D.G., Emshwiller, E., and Smith, B.D. (2006). *Documenting Domestication: New Genetic and Archaeological Paradigms*. Berkeley: University of California Press.

5

THE ARCTIC AND SUBARCTIC

The Polar region conjures up images of a frozen uninhabitable landscape, yet Native North Americans were able to adapt and flourish in this harsh environment for thousands of years. This chapter is the first one to focus on the archaeology of a particular region of North America, even though the Polar region was the last area to be settled. It is appropriate to discuss at this point in the textbook rather than later because most of the societies of the North were organized at the band level. Only rarely did communities grow large enough to be considered tribal institutions with fixed villages dominated by leaders. Thus, as recently as the twentieth century, many Arctic and Subarctic people were living in hunter-gatherer bands that were functionally similar to those of the earliest inhabitants. Archaeologists have studied the modern communities partly as a means to understand their analogs of a dozen millennia ago (Binford, 1978).

The Arctic and Subarctic zones of North America extend from Alaska, across northern Canada to Greenland (Figure 5.1). Canada is the third largest country in the world, trailing only Russia and China. This vast northern area is almost twice the size of the rest of the continent. It has always been North America's coldest and most thinly populated region, an immense archaeological venue explored by a small number of hardy researchers.

Arctic Environment and Adaptation

Arctic archaeology has revealed broad changes in adaptation over time. Groups restricted their occupation to the productive fringes of the continent and its northern islands offshore. Despite disagreements over how to interpret the evidence, Arctic archaeologists from Russia, the United States, Canada, and Denmark have found ways to link their perspectives (Dumond, 1984).

Alaska was the source area for waves of northerners that repeatedly spread eastward across Arctic Canada to as far as coastal Greenland. Alaska was a center of innovation because of its environmental variability compared to the rest of the Far North, and its proximity to influences from both the Northwest Coast and Asia. Each new wave of migrants originated in the western Arctic. These waves were carried by multiplying bands moving eastward and displacing or absorbing older communities they encountered, each one penetrating farther than the previous one.

Through all five periods of Arctic prehistory (Table 5.1), we see a constant theme of clever innovation and cultural elaboration to cope with a hostile environment and incrementally

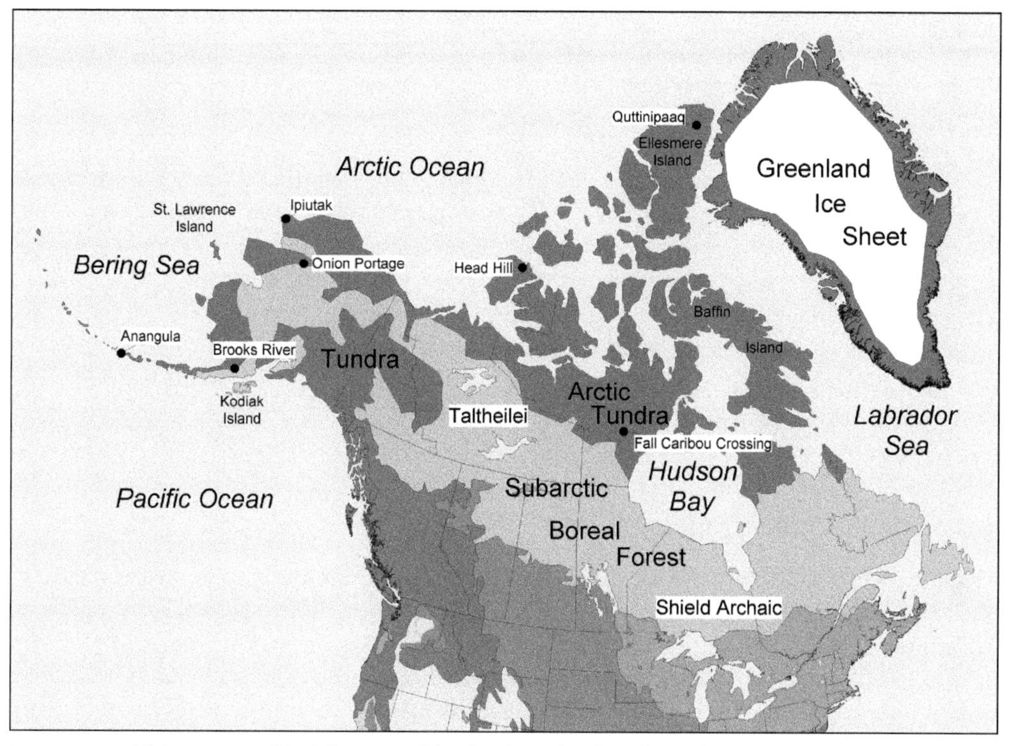

FIGURE 5.1 Major geographical features of the Arctic and archaeological sites mentioned in this chapter

TABLE 5.1 Basic Arctic chronology

Stage	*Cultures*	*Time Span*
1	Northern Paleoindian and Paleo-Arctic	15,000–5000 BCE
2	Northern Archaic	5000–2200 (±300) BCE
3	Arctic Small Tool Tradition	2200 (±300)–1200 (±400) BCE
4	Dorset and others	1200 (±400) BCE–600 (±500) CE
5	Thule	600 (±500)–1850 CE

improve and expand human adaptations to it (Potter, 2007). The Arctic is an environment in which small climatic changes can produce widespread consequences for human adaptation (Murray, 2005), which small-scale hunter-gatherer bands were able to accomplish (Gerlach and Murray, 2001).

Northern Paleoindian and Paleo-Arctic

Human occupation increased in the Arctic after the end of the Younger Dryas and the passing of Northern Paleoindian culture (Chapter 3). The dominant culture from then until 5000 BCE was the American Paleo-Arctic tradition, a culture whose hallmarks included microblades, cores, bifaces, and burins. This tradition had origins in Northern Paleoindian, with some roots extending back to Siberia. Another similar early tradition is the Northwest Microblade tradition (see Chapter 8) on the mainland and the Anangula complex of the Aleutian Islands. These are variations on a widespread theme that often emphasized microblades.

Northern Archaic and Related Adaptations

Archaeological evidence for Period 2 is widespread but poorly defined. This time period spanned 5000–2200(±300) BCE, the ending date varying from place to place over three centuries. People lived in the interior and along the coast. In the Aleutian Islands, near the Anangula site, people crafted chipped-stone tools and an elaborate bone industry, but they did not use slate. They made a living from the hunting of marine mammals and ocean fishing.

Interior adaptations appear to be more similar to some of the later Archaic cultures found farther south (Chapter 4) than to contemporaneous coastal cultures, prompting archaeologists to refer to them together as "Northern Archaic." Onion Portage is a key archaeological site among the many that include components falling into this broad category (Anderson, 1968).

The Arctic Small Tool Tradition

The Arctic's first widespread culture is called the Arctic Small Tool tradition by archaeologists. Its miniature tools were first discovered by Alaskan Iñupiaq, who are descendants of the people who made these implements. The tiny stone tools led to jokes about a race of little people. However, the small blades were used to edge clever compound tools of normal size. A bone or ivory point needed only a slot along its edge to receive a bifacial sliver of chert to serve as the hard, sharp cutting edge the tool required. Thus, the technological elaboration of compound tools presaged further inventiveness that would drive the efforts of northern peoples to penetrate ever deeper into the world's most hostile environment.

The adaptation of the early people who carried the Arctic Small Tool tradition was mainly terrestrial. Their technology was not yet sufficient to allow them to move permanently beyond the security of land and forest. Although they did some seal hunting along the seasonally open coast, they did not yet have the technology for seal hunting through the sea ice, a pursuit that was common much later on (Murray, 2005). Consequently, they did not yet have a reliable source of seal or whale oil fuel that would have allowed them to move permanently away from supplies of firewood.

BROOKS RIVER, KATMAI NATIONAL PARK AND PRESERVE, ALASKA

Brooks River is part of the northward flowing Naknek River and Lake system, largely within Katmai National Park and Preserve on the Alaskan Peninsula. The mile-and-a-half-long Brooks River flows from Brooks Lake to Naknek Lake. Beginning 3000 BCE, the banks of Brooks River were clustered with archaeological sites: first with the appearance of temporary campsites of hunters of two dissimilar cultural groups, one reflecting connections to the Northern Archaic to the north, the other to the Ocean Bay tradition known from Kodiak Island to the south. Sites became substantially larger after 1950 BCE, with clusters of houses, each dwelling of a single square room somewhat excavated into the earth and entered by a sunken pathway (Dumond, 1981: 120–131).

Three of the nine Brooks River volcanic ashes (tephras) of prehistoric age (those labeled G, F, and C) are especially heavy and consistently recognizable in sites. They probably originated from eruptions on the Peninsula more than 160 miles (240 km) west of Brooks River. Ash F may have been at least partially responsible for a lengthy period of abandonment. Following arrival of the Norton tradition from the north around 500 BCE, people continued the regular harvest of fish from Brooks River and also began to show increasing parallels with the culture of Kodiak Island.

The appearance of the first representatives of the Thule tradition represented a more radical change, but with continued reliance on houses of single rooms, now with more deeply sunken entries. This was also the time of deposit of Volcanic Ash C, which led to another temporary abandonment of Brooks River. Evidence indicates that reoccupation came from Kodiak Island (Dumond, 2011: 46–65). Finally, the aboriginal situation changed substantially with the Pavik phase, reflecting both a modest influx of Eskimoan people from farther north in western Alaska and the arrival of the Russians sometime after 1800 CE.

Don E. Dumond

Dorset, Kachemak, Norton, Choris, Ipiutak, and Old Bering Sea

During Period 4, several cultures emerged from the Arctic Small Tool tradition. By the last few centuries BCE, Norton culture predominated as the most widespread and successful of these adaptations. The Canadian variant of the Arctic Small Tool tradition is often referred to as Pre-Dorset (2500–500 BCE), a term that anticipates the later spread of Dorset culture across the region. Pre-Dorset people eventually spread along the coast all the way to Newfoundland. Derivative remnants of the tradition have been found in Greenland, labeled Independence I or Sarqaq by archaeologists.

Dorset culture emerged across northern Canada around 500 BCE after a drastic contraction of Pre-Dorset populations. Dorset people eventually reoccupied areas across Canada and Greenland that had been abandoned by their ancestors in the face of difficult conditions during one of the prolonged cold spells of the later Holocene. Dorset expansion coincided with a climatic improvement with a greater emphasis on sea resources than previously.

The people living in the Aleutian Island chain developed a culture apart from the rest. But on the Alaskan mainland there were clear breaks between the earlier Arctic Small Tool tradition communities and later ones. After 1200 BCE (±400), there were several derivative cultures in Alaska, each adapting to a different regional environment. Kachemak culture emerged in the Kodiak region while Norton culture developed along the coast of the Bering Sea. In northern Alaska the period saw an evolution from Choris to Norton and then to Ipiutak culture. Thus, the passing of the Arctic Small Tool tradition appears to have been followed by a variety of new adaptations as descendants undertook alternative adaptive strategies.

Old Bering Sea culture is the earliest example of a maritime adaptation, which characterizes later cultures across the Arctic. The technology for hunting seals, walruses, and whales from the ice and from boats was present in Old Bering Sea sites as early as 150 BCE. These people also exploited caribou and other land mammals, as well as birds and fish. The origins of Old Bering Sea, and closely related Okvik culture, appear to have been in northeast Siberia where most sites are located. But it extended to St. Lawrence Island and there are traces of it on the western coast of the Alaskan mainland (Dumond and Bland, 2002; Gibbon, 1998: 605–606).

Thule

Thule culture probably originated on the northwest coast of Alaska around 900–1000 CE, then spread eastward across the Arctic. Thule spread eastward rapidly from Alaska across northern Canada after 1000 CE, carried by a thin but expanding population of bands equipped with new technology (Friesen and Arnold, 2008).

HEAD HILL, BANKS ISLAND, CANADA

Head Hill (PlPx-1) is a muskox hunting site on Banks Island in Canada's western Arctic (Figure 5.2). It is the largest archaeological site in Aulavik National Park. Thousands of muskox bones, including over 500 skulls, litter a hillside above the confluence of two major rivers. Pieces of bows, arrows, and spears have been recovered from the site's surface. The locations where people erected skin tents are visible as tent rings, circles of stone used to hold down the outer edges. People made pavements of flat stones, where they laid out meat to dry and piled up small boulders to form caches for storing it. They also prepared animal skins at the site, stretching them by sticking muskox ribs vertically into the ground in alignments that are still visible today.

For years, the site was thought to date from the second half of the nineteenth century. In 1853, the crew of the British naval vessel H.M.S. *Investigator* abandoned their ship in the ice of Mercy Bay near the north coast of Banks Island, roughly 30 km northeast of Head Hill. Wood and metal from the ship were valuable resources for local Inuit, and they are found on many of the island's archaeological sites, including Head Hill. Vilhjalmur Stefansson heard oral accounts from Inuit of their discovery of *Investigator* shortly after it was abandoned and of seasonal travel to Mercy Bay to collect wood and iron until roughly 1895. Stefansson and others assumed that Head Hill was occupied only during this brief period. Recent radiocarbon

FIGURE 5.2 Muskoxen skulls on Head Hill. Photo by Lisa Hodgetts

dating of muskox bones from Head Hill suggests that many generations of Inuit utilized the site over a much longer period, between roughly 1650 and 1920 CE (Hickey, 1979; Stefansson, 1921).

Lisa M. Hodgetts

FALL CARIBOU CROSSING

Fall Caribou Crossing National Historic Site is a 40-km-long reach of the lower Kazan River and adjacent hinterland (Figure 5.3), located in subarctic tundra west of Hudson Bay, 75 km south of the Hamlet of Baker Lake (Qamani'tuaq) in the Kivalliq region of Nunavut Territory, Canada. During the 1990s, more than 1,500 surface archaeological features were recorded there for Parks Canada with Differential GPS (Stewart et al., 2000). They represent evidence of year-round interior settlement by the hunting-fishing-trapping Caribou Inuit during the nineteenth and twentieth centuries, part of the historic Inuit tradition that emerged from a pre-contact Thule ancestry in the central Canadian Arctic (Dawson, 2016). Their descendants, who continue to hunt caribou to supplement subsistence, today live in Baker Lake and in settlements along the Hudson Bay coast.

The recognition of this site as nationally significant is based on the integrity of the cultural landscape and the continuing presence of the Qamanirjuaq migratory barren ground caribou herd there (Friesen and Stewart, 2013). The Kazan River, a Canadian Heritage River, is managed jointly by community partners, coordinated by Nunavut Parks and Special Places, a division of the government of Nunavut.

FIGURE 5.3 A group of *inuksuit* overlooking the Lower Kazan River in Fall Caribou Crossing National Historic Site. Photo by Andrew Stewart

The east-west orientation of the river where the site is located, cross-cutting the annual (approximately north-south) migration of the Qamanirjuaq herd, afforded it strategic importance for interception of herds in spring and fall. Archaeological features such as tent rings, meat caches, hunting blinds and *inuksuit* (standing stones) are distributed widely across this region and concentrated at places where caribou crossed the river. The range of feature types and their distribution reflect, in part, temporal (seasonal and inter-annual) and spatial patterning of caribou. In this way, their spatial analysis contributes to understanding resource variability in a foraging society that was also integrated with the fur trade.

Andrew M. Stewart

Thule people hunted sea mammals of all kinds, large and small, including seals and walrus. Even the bowhead whale was fair game to these skilled marine hunters, which may have been the primary attraction for Thule hunters into and through the Canadian Arctic. Despite their focus on maritime resources, the Thule people also pushed up rivers as far as the interior forests to fish and hunt caribou as the seasons permitted. This flexibility and breadth of adaptation served them well when the Medieval Maximum waned and the climate slid towards the Little Ice Age. The onset of colder conditions around 1400 CE rendered life in parts of the Thule range no longer viable. Even where they could still make a living, Thule hunters were forced to shift emphasis away from the summertime open-water hunting of sea mammals to wintertime hunting through the sea ice. Whales disappeared and ringed seals became much more important. Some bands gave up the building and use of **umiak**s and large sea **kayak**s.

Arctic Demography and Conflict

Waves of migratory expansion are particularly apparent after 2200 BCE. During Period 3, people spread eastward across the Arctic to as far as Greenland and settled in wherever human adaptations were possible. This kind of expansion takes a long time, and it leaves later generations with no knowledge of their geographical origins. When the Arctic climate became more difficult for humans after the initial spread of the Arctic Small Tool tradition, descendant bands did not have the option of retreating back to some less hostile environment. They had no option but to readapt in place as best they could. Some survived in culturally modified form, but many bands must have simply shrunk and died out. There may have been little if any serious conflict involved in this process. Conflict in these band societies, when it occurred, probably tended to be interpersonal rather than across bands.

Later Dorset bands also experienced demographic oscillations as environmental conditions or simple luck caused cycles of expansion out of core areas followed by contraction back into them over time (Savelle and Dyke, 2009, 2014). The Dorset people were forced southward to as far as Newfoundland on Canada's east coast when a period of extended cold weather set in after 100 CE. They recovered and expanded once again during the warmer Medieval Maximum around 1000 CE, but by that time, the Thule people were expanding eastward out of Alaska. Thule people had technology that Dorset people lacked, tools that gave them an adaptive advantage. Just as important, Thule culture emerged amidst the improved climate of the Medieval Maximum, which facilitated their own adaptive expansion across the Arctic. As a result, bands of Thule people multiplied and spread rapidly eastward along the northern coasts of Alaska, Canada, and Greenland.

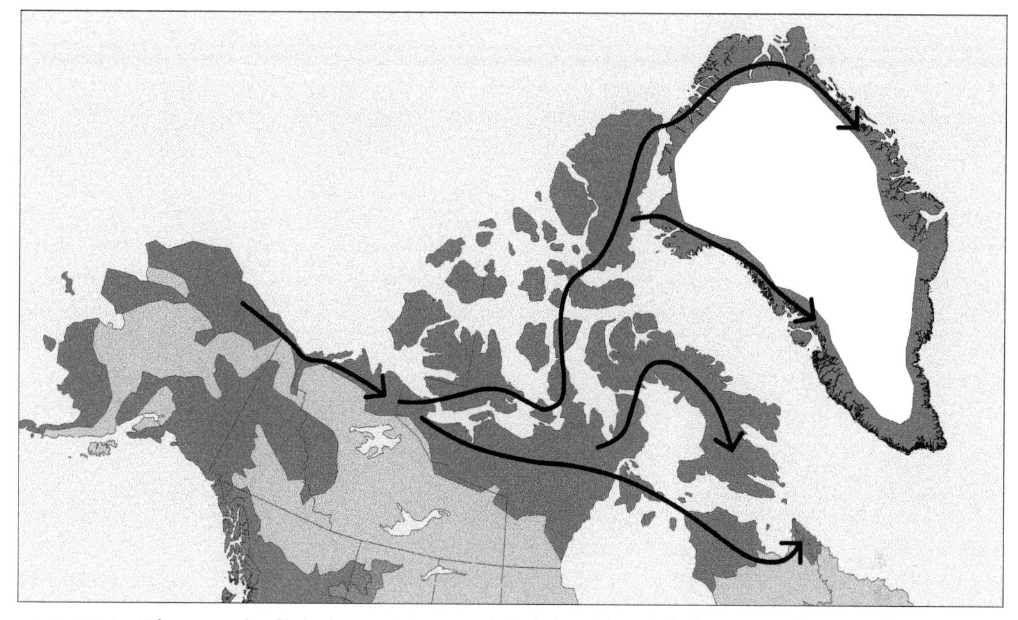

FIGURE 5.4 The spread of Thule people around 1000 CE from Alaska eastward across the Arctic to Greenland and Newfoundland

Dorset people collided with the rapidly expanding Thule people, and by 1100 CE, Dorset culture was overwhelmed and absorbed. Dorset culture dwindled in the face of this competition, and it disappeared as individual Dorset people were either recruited into Thule culture or slowly died off. Thule spread at a rate of at least 15 km (10 mi) per year, expanding as much as 3,200 km (2,000 mi) in only a century and a half (Figure 5.4).

Evidence for pre-Dorset, Dorset, and Thule expansions across the Far North has been found in Quttinirpaaq National Park on Ellesmere Island, the northernmost point in Canada. Stone tent rings and food caches show that the ancestors of the Inuit penetrated even to this remote and hostile corner of modern Nunavut. Inuits manage this and other parks in the province.

Colder conditions and more restricted hunting forced many later Thule bands to retreat into isolated pockets and to abandon parts of their former range. Some bands probably died out completely, whereas others survived in reduced circumstances. The Polar people, who lived in Greenland, farther north than anyone else, were isolated so long, they had no contact with other groups. European explorers first encountered the Polar people in the nineteenth century, to the astonishment of both groups. Environmental conditions were less rigorous south of the High Arctic and Thule adaptations have persisted in those areas into modern times.

Arctic Subsistence and Economy

Northern peoples became more adept through time at exploiting marine resources, particularly sea mammals, although terrestrial game remained important to them as well (Betts et al., 2015). Archaeological evidence shows increasing technological sophistication through time. The Thule people were particularly successful at exploiting this harsh environment that their lifeway existed into the twentieth century.

Arctic Architecture and Technology

People of the northern Archaic and related adaptations lived in semisubterranean **pithouse**s that were entered from the top (Figure 5.5). This basic architectural form persisted through Period 3. The permanent habitations of the Arctic Small Tool tradition were generally located near the interior forest edge of the tundra, where caribou and migratory fish would have been plentiful. Most or all of their sites lacked stone lamps for burning sea mammal oil rendered from blubber, so perhaps groups maintained camps near forests for fuel wood (Dumond, 2005: 25). **Oil lamp**s were among the innovations their descendants would need to move into the treeless High Arctic.

Pithouses were often constructed in lines just above the beaches of coastal sites in northwestern Alaska. As sea levels fell and new beaches were created by the tides, lines of later houses were built at lower levels as older houses were abandoned. Over time this pattern created the appearance of large villages with houses laid out along what might at first impression look like streets. The pattern was produced by cumulative effects over the long term. The native people of the region did not build large towns (Darwent et al., 2013).

Later Dorset people tended to live near the shore in smaller circular semisubterranean pithouses. They built these structures and paved the floors of whatever materials were available: stone, drift-wood, whale bones, sod blocks, or some combination of these (Dawson and Levy, 2005). An earthen bench built around the interior wall was for sleeping and sitting. Short entrance tunnels were often built to provide insulation from the cold outside.

Dorset people had many inventions, such as umiaks for transportation. However, they lacked pottery and complex dogsleds. Pottery, which had been made and used earlier by Norton people,

FIGURE 5.5 View from above of a semisubterranean house in Katmai National Park that dates to around 2000–1300 BCE. The house diameter is approximately 4 m (13 ft). Note the narrow foot trench to the left

was not part of Dorset technology, perhaps due to the lack of suitable clays. Dogsleds, part of all later human adaptations, were not yet utilized.

The classic snow house (igloo), which historically provided winter shelter when other building materials were scarce, might have been a Dorset invention, as evidenced by large specialized snow knives used to build them. From their houses and their internal layouts, we can infer that the Dorset people bands were egalitarian (Friesen, 2007).

Thule houses were highly variable, reflecting both the constraints and opportunities, on the one hand, and the cleverness of people, on the other (Dawson, 2001; Dawson and Levy, 2005). Thule people could build houses of whatever materials came to hand. To heat house interiors, soapstone (steatite) oil lamps were used and were less likely to break than the cruder pottery ones sometimes used by their predecessors. The lamps provided light and enough heat to drive away the chill even in igloos during the winter. Light generated from such lamps, though low, was essential for indoor tasks of carving and sewing during the long winter nights.

Earlier Arctic cultures were technologically generalized compared to the Period 3 Arctic Small Tool tradition and later cultures. Norton hunters took small sea mammals, possibly both through holes in sea ice and from kayaks. The closed kayak provided hunters with an ideal craft from which to hunt sea mammals with their toggling harpoons, lines, and sealskin floats. They also hunted caribou seasonally in the interior, but by this time terrestrial hunting was becoming less important than maritime hunting. Dorset people used umiaks for the transportation of whole families, food, equipment, and other supplies in months when the seas were open.

Dorset men and women made and used their own knives. **Semilunar** implements called "**ulu**s" (Figure 5.6) were used by women for tailoring and food preparation. Other important parts of their kits were tools that they had invented themselves or picked up from Norton and other related cultures west of them included toggling harpoons, oil lamps, stone cooking pots, bows and arrows, fish spears, kayaks, small sleds, **ice creepers**, **snow goggles**, and copper tools. Norton people even made pottery, the earliest known in the Arctic. It was often coarse and crude, but functional (Frink and Harry, 2008).

From sites that date to Period 4 and belong to the Ipiutak culture, neither microblades, pottery, slate tools, or oil lamps have been recovered, despite the derivation of this culture from Norton, which had these traits. This is all further evidence of growing technological diversity as people

FIGURE 5.6 Ulu, a typical woman's knife. The tool is grasped or hafted along the flat top and the long, sharp curved edge is used in a rocking or slicing motion

found solutions to varying ecological circumstances. The Ipiutak weapon of choice appears to have been the bow and arrow, which already had been a feature of Arctic technology for centuries.

All later Arctic cultures were known for their many gadgets made of bone, walrus ivory, whale baleen, copper, leather, fiber, and stone. They used virtually any material they could get their hands on, and the origins of all this gadgetry lie in the Arctic Small Tool tradition. Ground slate tools and ground-stone adzes made from basalt and other fine-grained stone increased in prevalence in Period 4. Chipped-stone implements continued to be made as well, but styles and proportions varied.

Advances in Thule (Period 5) harpoon technology that might have originated in the previous Period 4 along with the kayak made maritime hunting a very successful strategy for Thule hunters. The toggling harpoon point was attached to a long tether, and it was designed to turn sideways in the animal after it detached from the harpoon and foreshaft (Figure 5.7). The wounded animal could not pull free, but if the tether had been simply tied to the gunwale of a delicate kayak,

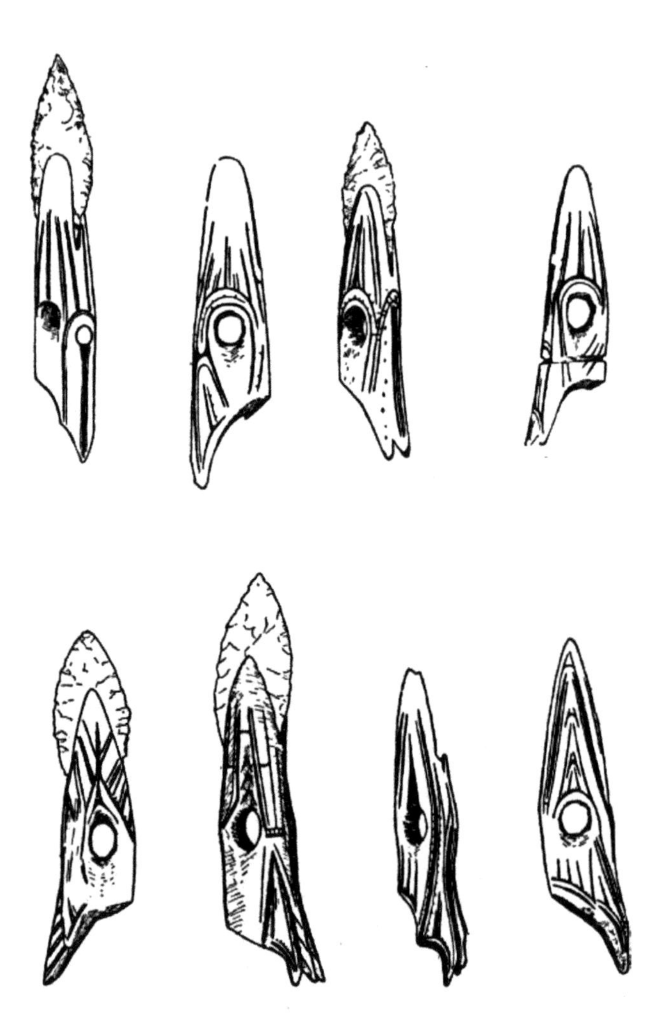

FIGURE 5.7 Eight antler toggling harpoon heads, four with intact stone points. All eight have basal foreshaft sockets (not visible) and holes for tethering lines to prevent a sea mammal from escaping once the tail of the head caught and turned the head sideways (toggling) inside the wound. *Source:* Larsen and Rainey (1948:71)

FIGURE 5.8 Inuit dog sleds at Tree River near Coronation Gulf, Nunavut. *Source:* Nunavut Photo © Canadian Museum of Civilization, photo O'Neill, 1915, image 38571LS

chances were that a seal would destroy the fragile craft in its frantic attempt to escape. The answer was yet another innovative Thule gadget. They made large floats from sealskin and tied them midway along the harpoon point tether line. A wounded seal or walrus was thus forced to pull against the float rather than against the kayak, and the hunter could simply wait for exhaustion and blood loss to take effect.

The Thule people carved soapstone lamps and designed numerous specialized forms of the toggling harpoons, but they also had swift new built-up dogsleds of an efficient design that is still used today (Figure 5.8). The light frameworks of standard sleds ran on iced runners of bone or ivory. Dogs were harnessed in a fanlike arc for travel across the great expanses of open sea ice, but they were paired in tandem for travel along narrow trails where rocks or shrubs were potential obstacles. The sled and the latter style of harnessing are still the rule for teams that compete in modern dogsled races. Thus, the success of Thule adaptation depended upon a broad range of gadgetry that included nearly everything made and used by their ancestors along with a few crucial new innovations.

Even the simplest tools often had clever twists or beautiful decoration. Harness toggles, needle cases, wrist guards, wound plugs to stop the loss of valuable blood from dead game animals, harpoon heads, snow goggles, and the like all were made from ingenious combinations of materials and often elaborately decorated. Bone, antler, fiber, feathers, gut, skin, copper, wood, baleen, chert, and even meteoric iron were used. The long Arctic winter nights provided the time for the work that went into the production of these items, and native ingenuity provided the inspiration.

Arctic Culture, Language, and Identity

During Period 5, each Thule house was typically built for a nuclear family or a small extended one. Males and females had significant complementary roles in this hunter-gatherer society. Proper roles were also assigned by custom according to age, and survival of the band was difficult if any of

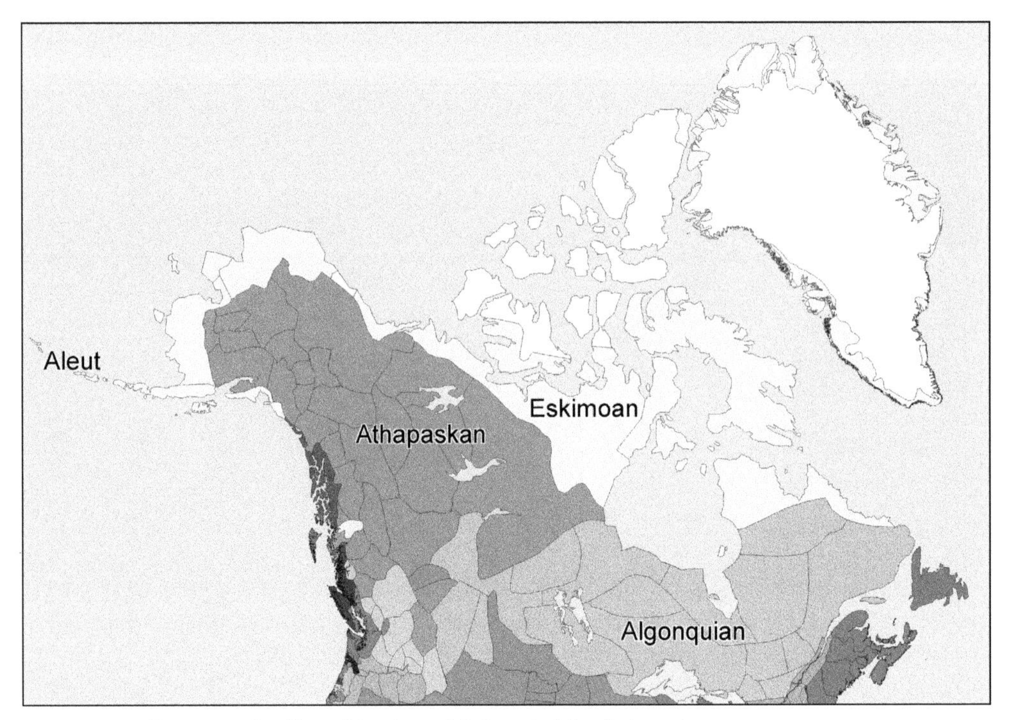

FIGURE 5.9 Language families of Arctic and Subarctic North America

these components were missing. Like band organizations in other times and places, Thule bands depended upon mutual support for insurance, marriage partners, and occasional cooperative undertakings. Memberships were fluid so that a band that had too many or too few males or females could split, shrink, or grow as circumstances required.

People living in the Aleutian Islands began their long separate evolution toward modern Unangax/Aleut culture, and the split between their language and the various Eskimo-Aleut family languages must date to the early periods of Arctic prehistory (Dumond, 1965, 2001). Speakers of the Yup'ic branch of Eskimo-Aleut languages still live in southwestern Alaska. Northwestern Alaska is home to the Iñupiaq. It is not surprising that Alaska is home to distinct branches of the Eskimo-Aleut language family that have relatively deep roots in time. Furthermore, given the rapid spread of Thule culture from west to east across the Arctic, a string of more closely related modern dialects, Inuit–Iñupiaq (Figure 5.9), is spoken by people from the Bering Sea to the east coast of Greenland. There are several Inuit–Iñupiaq dialects arrayed between the two at the extreme ends of the Thule continuum, and while the divisions between them are rather arbitrarily defined, and communication is relatively easy between any two adjacent bands, they are not a single speech community.

Arctic Art and Symbolism

People are often surprised to discover that hunter-gatherers can have time on their hands. For Arctic hunter-gatherers, this could involve long periods of confinement to cramped quarters when deep winter cold and darkness prevailed outside. Such confinement had its benefits, not the least of which was the flourishing of artistic expression on what otherwise would have been

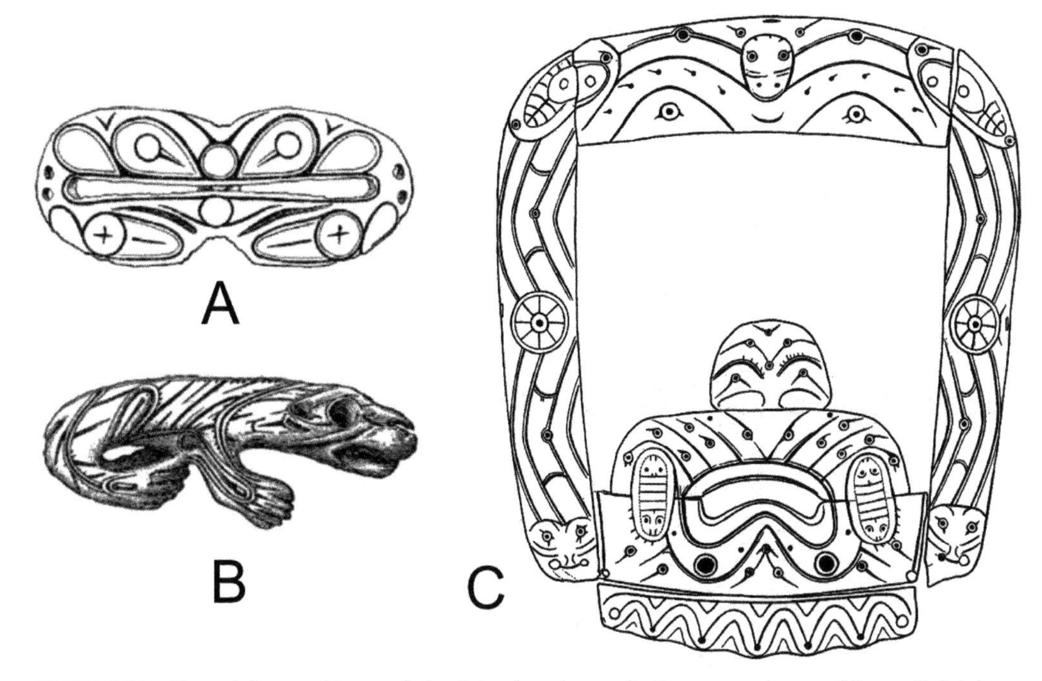

FIGURE 5.10 Carved ivory objects of the Ipiutak culture: A. Snow goggles, ca. 13 cm (5 in) long; B. Figure of a young walrus with skeletal decoration; C. Mask with labrets on either side of the mouth opening (Larsen and Rainey, 1948: 113, 125, 138)

mundane gadgetry. Tools made from difficult materials were often beautifully decorated in ways reflecting northern mythology and the natural world.

Period 4 Ipiutak artisans produced beautifully carved bone and ivory artifacts, which are often found as grave offerings. Carved compound human masks, which were probably attached to wooden or leather backings, were typically buried with their owners (Figure 5.10).

Later Dorset and Thule artisans continued and elaborated this tradition, producing tools that were also works of art. **Labrets**, some of them large lip plugs, and other ornaments became fashionable as well in the later periods, and it is clear from such ornamentation that there was much more to these cultures than mere survival. Clothing was used for more than just protection. The use of feathered bird skins as well as furs for insulation also involved fine stitching and treatment to make the garments waterproof. They typically decorated the garments with dyes, threads, and other ornamentation.

Long winter confinements also promoted the development of games and pastimes for both adults and children. Cat's cradle, cup-and-ball, games, and the like provided entertainment. Singing, storytelling, dancing, and male wrestling were the kinds of activities that made life in the winter darkness bearable. When the weather allowed, larger group recreation, such as the blanket toss, were and still are popular.

Arctic Resilience and Collapse

The five broad periods defined by archaeologists for peoples of the Arctic saw several episodes of resilience and collapse at a variety of scales. At one end of that scale, a single band could thrive or die out depending sometimes on the availability of critical resources, and at other times, on the random accidents of birth and death. At the other end of the scale, whole regions could be rendered uninhabitable by climatic cycling. The overall trend was for accumulated innovations to increase opportunities for survival and persistence in the long run. The Medieval Climate Optimum prompted demographic expansion in many parts of the world's Arctic and Subarctic. This included Norse expansion across the North Atlantic to Greenland. The Inuit descendants of the Thule persist today. In 1999 the Canadian government separated the mostly Inuit part of the Northwest Territories by creating the Nunavut Territory, a huge native homeland 1,877,787 km^2 (725,018 sq. mi) in size.

Subarctic Environment and Adaptation

The North American Subarctic, divided into two main areas, is a vast region covered largely by boreal forest. The western Subarctic is a mostly interior region dominated by the Rocky Mountains, and the eastern Subarctic is drained by Hudson Bay which dominates this landscape. Despite the differences of mountains and sea, people living in each area faced similar environmental challenges and opportunities but overcame them with different adaptations.

Peoples of the western and eastern portions of the American Subarctic spoke different languages and left behind different material remains. The prehistory of the western Subarctic is more directly connected to the earliest peoples of the Arctic and the Northwest Coast, but the prehistory of the eastern Subarctic is less ancient and further removed from the earliest archaeology, both in time and in space.

Like their Arctic neighbors, the native people of the Subarctic were hunter-gatherers. Theirs was a forest environment, and few bands had access to marine resources. Thus, their adaptations focused on terrestrial game, such as moose, caribou, and bears when possible, but more frequently on hares and fish. Due to the forested environment and the paucity of archaeological research, the early prehistory of these people is not yet well understood.

At least some of the early people who spread into North America probably moved southeastward between retreating ice sheets, as opposed to migrating southward along the Pacific Coast. However, there is only the scantiest archaeological evidence for this expansion in western Canada (see Chapter 3). This corridor was also the one by which the Clovis fluting technique probably spread back northwestward through Paleoindian bands to Alaska. Surely, the western Subarctic must hold some of the most interesting early remains of ancient America, but most of what should logically be there still waits to be found.

More certain is the arrival of microblade technology in the western Subarctic, which was the hallmark of a population that postdated the Paleoindians. The basic technology of the expanding Paleo-Arctic tradition, was well established in interior Alaska by 9000 BCE. Microblades disappeared from the archaeological record of the western Subarctic over the course of two and a half millennia. They were often replaced in local assemblages by side-notched bifaces that probably were inspired by prototypes in the tool inventories of contemporaneous Archaic cultures located farther to the south. The transition away from microblade technology occurred as early as 2500 BCE in some places in the western Subarctic, and as late as 1 CE in others (Clark, 1981:128).

The Taltheilei Shale tradition developed in the forests around Great Slave Lake and Great Bear Lake in western Canada around 500 BCE. This tradition was directly ancestral to the modern Athabascan cultures of the same region, but it contained no vestige of microblades (Clark, 1981:118; Noble, 1981:102). Most archaeologists conclude that there is no evidence for population replacement and that the slow loss of microblades from the Athabascan tool inventories was simply a matter of technological evolution over time.

The eastern portion of the Subarctic lies almost entirely in Canada, much of it drained by Hudson Bay. The region is underlain by ancient bedrock that is often referred to as the Canadian Shield, and the soils of the conifer forest are both thin and acidic. The Canadian Shield is bounded on the south by the Great Lakes and on the east by the Gulf of St. Lawrence and the Atlantic Ocean.

The first human inhabitants of the eastern Subarctic probably moved into the region no earlier than 7500 BCE, as it had lain frozen under the Laurentian ice sheet while Paleoindians spread across the rest of North America. By the time the eastern Subarctic became habitable, only unfluted lanceolate points were still being made and used, and these are the earliest artifacts found in the region. The late Paleoindian culture of these first arrivals evolved into what archaeologists term the Shield Archaic (Wright, 1981:88), which is known mainly from three artifact classes: side-notched points, knives, and scrapers. Thin acidic soils in the region allow little or no preservation of bone, wood, or other organic remains, so archaeologists must infer much from small inventories of durable artifacts.

Climate sometimes drove Archaic people southward from more northerly areas and facilitated their replacement by early People. They abandoned the area northwest of Hudson Bay sometime after 1500 BCE and were replaced there by pioneering people of the Arctic Small Tool culture. There is no evidence of contact between the two cultures, although the possibility cannot be excluded. Overall, it was a matter of one adaptation retreating from areas where changing conditions made their lifeway less adaptive, while other people whose culture was better adapted to the new conditions were drawn into the same areas (Noble, 1981:100; Wright, 1981:89).

Sometime in the last millennium BCE, the people of the Shield Archaic began making and using pottery similar to pottery found in contemporaneous sites around the Great Lakes. The rest of Shield Archaic culture did not change when pottery was added suggesting that the new ceramic technology was adopted by these people rather than carried in by a new replacement population.

There are two late-named ceramic complexes that occur in sites scattered across the western part of the eastern Subarctic. Selkirk ceramics are found in sites in northern Manitoba and Blackduck ceramics are found across southern Manitoba, northern Minnesota, and western Ontario. Selkirk pottery was made by the historic Cree Indians and Blackduck pottery by the Ojibwas. Pottery recovered from sites in the eastern part of the region appears to have been derived mainly from Iroquoian sources around the lower Great Lakes (Wright 1981: 94–96).

Subarctic Demography and Conflict

Before modern times the human population in this vast region never averaged more than about two people per 100 km^2, or about one person to every 20 mi^2. Travel in the Subarctic woodlands was by ancient trails or by canoe. Where the landscape was neither too rugged nor too swampy, people used well-worn trails that were probably first blazed thousands of years ago. Many of the trails that are still known are associated with dated archaeological sites (Magne and Matson, 2010; Meyer and Russell, 2007).

There was a tendency for bands to congregate at traditional locations during the warm months, where they could take advantage of cooperative fishing, food processing, and storage for future use. Winter conditions typically required dispersal by smaller groups to small camps where hunting of moose and other game was seasonally productive. Fish runs were important in the spring, when large numbers could be harvested, processed, and stored for future consumption. People used forest fibers to make nets and build rock weirs to trap fish at key places where stream topography concentrated the runs.

The southeastward expansion of Athabascans from Canada's Northwest Territories began as early as 400 BCE, and it continued into the historic era (Wright, 1981: 91–92). After 1600 CE, the movement became one of the features of the fur trade. The western Subarctic was a primary source for furs that were shipped eastward in large freight canoes. French-speaking traders penetrated increasingly farther westward from Quebec in search of furs, and the Hudson Bay Company established trading posts across western Canada to facilitate the trade.

Algonquians apparently expanded out of the eastern Subarctic with their adoption of the bow and arrow after 600 CE (Blitz, 1988; Fiedel, 1994). Some of them expanded south of the Great Lakes while the Eastern Algonquian branch spread down the Atlantic seaboard, some eventually reaching coastal North Carolina (Chapter 8).

Like the Algonquians in the East, the Athabascans expanded southward relatively late in prehistory, but in this case, some moved huge distances. A few bands ended up in northern California, where they flourished amidst other small nations in that region (Chapter 11). Others migrated slowly along the eastern foothills of the Rockies, eventually reaching the Southwest. They flourished there as well, moving into areas abandoned by the Ancestral Pueblo Indians in the face of warming and drying conditions. Athabascan migrants to the Southwest were ancestral to the modern Navajo and Apache nations (Chapter 10).

Subarctic Subsistence and Economy

The hunter-gatherer bands of the Subarctic subsisted on large and small game. Fur-bearing animals, particularly beavers, were trapped or hunted for food and clothing. Beavers became even more vital after contact with Europeans, when their pelts were traded by the Athabascans for such items as metal tools, cloth, and firearms.

Game animals and gathered foods varied seasonally. Wild plants providing edible tubers and berries could be exploited only during warm months. Runs of fish were more easily caught or netted in the warms months as well. In winter, hunting typically forced people to move to small, scattered isolated family camps.

The environment was and still is subject to periodic forest fires which forced hunter-gatherer bands to relocate and adapt to new conditions (Noble, 1981: 100). Thus, the Algonquians were adapted to a dynamic environment, characterized by periodic burning and subsequent renewal as a succession of plants and animals reappeared in the course of reforestation.

Subarctic Architecture and Technology

Archaeologists have found an 8,000-year-old stone burial mound on a stretch of the Labrador coast north of the Northeast region, which might presage later moundbuilders in the Eastern Woodlands (Chapter 6). The L'Anse Amour site contains the face-down burial of a 12-year-old, accompanied by an antler toggle-head harpoon, a walrus tusk, three quartzite knives, a bone whistle, and socketed bone points. A radiocarbon date indicates that the mound was constructed at least 8,000 years ago (McGhee, 1976).

Most Subarctic technology involved the use of bark, wood, bone, and fiber, all materials that do not preserve well in the absence of permafrost in the acidic soils of the boreal forest. The archaeological evidence of these people is thus often confined to post molds, hearths, and chipped-stone artifacts. Summer residences could feature congregations of extended-family houses at traditional sites, while dispersed winter camps featured smaller single-family shelters.

"Toboggan" and "wigwam" are both Algonquian words that were incorporated into English. Eastern Subarctic wigwams had circular or elongated floorplans, depending on the associated family sizes, circular for smaller and elongated for larger ones. Arched saplings were used to build domed frames, which were usually roofed and sided with slabs of bark. The only archaeological traces of these structures are usually confined to post molds left by the frames and stone-ringed fireplaces inside them. Historic wigwams show that smoke holes were left open above the hearths.

Like toboggans and wigwams, canoes were a large part of Subarctic technology. Birch bark canoes were built with creative designs that had evolved over millennia. Frames were made from carefully selected tree species such as cedar (*Thuja occidentalis*), and sheathing was made from the bark of the paper birch (*Betula papyrifera*).

In the western Subarctic, winter houses were more often small **tepee**s covered with bark or hides. Larger structures were constructed of logs and had oblong floorplans. More permanent materials could be used in traditional summer camps where families reunited into larger units. Their technology was different than the specialized gadgetry of the Arctic, but bark canoes, snowshoes, and toboggans of the Subarctic reveal that people found ways to effectively use local materials to manufacture efficient devices for travel and transportation. The bow and arrow slowly replaced spear throwers over the course of two centuries, 700–900 CE (Grund and Huzurbazar, 2018).

People in several cultures of southeastern Alaska and southwestern Yukon used native copper from late prehistory into the early historic period. While native copper was generally used for practical technological purposes rather than as overtly prestige objects, the metal was culturally charged with supernatural meanings. The production, trade, and exchange of objects made from native copper thus enabled the acquisition of prestige by the people who controlled it (Cooper, 2012).

Subarctic Culture, Language, and Identity

The interior portions of the western Subarctic in Alaska and Canada were occupied by bands of Athabascan-speaking Indians when Europeans first arrived, and today, they are still a major percentage of the regional population. The native peoples of the eastern Subarctic all spoke one or another of the languages of the Algonquian branch of the Algic language family. The region appears to have been the source of Algonquian-speaking nations that expanded southward through the Great Lakes region and down the East Coast over the preceding 1,400 years. Many of the Algonquian languages are still spoken across the eastern Subarctic, and there is no clear evidence for any other language family in the region.

Marriage and postmarital residence were very flexible, although women historically tended to move to their husbands' bands than the reverse. Communication, trade, and marriage between band members in the overlapping connubia fostered widespread continuity that is manifested archaeologically with similar remains across the entire eastern Subarctic (Wright, 1981: 86). Eastern Subarctic people spoke a single widespread Algonquian language, but one that was so diverse that while members of a given band could communicate easily with their nearest neighbors, their speech was unintelligible to those living a thousand kilometers away.

Subarctic Art and Symbolism

The arts and crafts of the Subarctic, like the technology that ensured their survival, featured materials that do not preserve well in the ground. Bark containers, fiber belts, and clothing made mainly from animal hides must have been the standard for thousands of years, but the chances of finding any examples archaeologically are slim. Modern Subarctic artisans still decorate bark containers with dyed porcupine quills and incised designs. Skins stretched on wooden hoops are still drummed. Fringes and floral designs decorate clothing, although colorful glass trade beads are today used more frequently than traditional quilling.

Petroglyphs and pictographs survive here and there in the archaeological record. Many of these symbols appear to relate to shamanism, which has been historically important in the Subarctic and which must have ancient roots linking to analogous practices in Siberia.

Like the people of the Arctic, Subarctic bands filled long hours of winter confinement with games and socializing. Stick and ball games, team games of chance, and similar activities can sometimes be noted with the archaeological discovery of items such as wood or bone gaming pieces.

Subarctic Resilience and Collapse

Most of the Central Algonquians died out or were pushed westward and eventually on to reservations in the United States and reserves in Canada. Remarkably, several of the Eastern Algonquian nations survive today in their homelands, despite the fact that they bore the brunt of initial European colonization and were in the middle of many of the colonial conflicts leading up to and including the American Revolution.

The Athabascans of central Alaska and western Canada were more fortunate in remaining in their traditional homelands. Intermarriage with European fur traders, most of whom were operating out of eastern Canada, led to emergence of a hybrid culture in the western Subarctic. Communities of mixed native and European descent are typically known as "Métis" (Slobodin, 1981). While they are an important component of Subarctic history, their archaeological presence is largely uninvestigated.

The native residents of Newfoundland were known later as the Beothuks. These people, the "Red Indians" of some later historical documents, were the easternmost of the thin populations scattered through the boreal forests of the Canadian Subarctic. So few words of the Beothuk language survive that linguists still debate its connections with other North American Indian languages. Genetic research has shown that Beothuk, Algonquian, and Inuit populations were biologically distinct (Duggan et al., 2017). It was the Beothuks who, like the Inuits, bore the brunt of initial contact with Europeans, first the Norse around 950 CE, then centuries later, English, French, and Basque fishermen.

Glossary

ice creepers Footwear designed to facilitate walking on ice, like modern crampons.
kayak A closed one-person skin boat used by Arctic sea hunters.
oil lamp Typically, a stone dish having a nipple to hold a wick above a small pool of oil fuel.
labret A decorative object designed to be worn in or near a pierced lip.
pithouse A snug, semi-subterranean house entered through a smoke hole in the roof or by way of an entry tunnel.
semilunar Having the shape of a half moon.
snow goggles Goggles carved from bone, wood, or ivory, having narrow viewing slits to protect the eyes from snow blindness.
tepee A conical house covered by bark, matts, or hides.
ulu A semilunar knife, often with a handle, sometimes called a "woman's" knife.
umiak A large open skin boat used for transporting several people and their belongings.

References

Anderson, D.D. (1968). A Stone Age Campsite at the Gateway to America. *Scientific American*, 218, pp. 24–33.

Betts, M.W., Hardenberg, M., and Stirling, I. (2015). How Animals Create Human History: Relational Ecology and the Dorest-Polar Bear Connection. *American Antiquity*, 80, pp. 89–112.

Binford, L.R. (1978). *Nunamiut Ethnoarchaeology*. New York: Academic Press.

Blitz, J.H. (1988). Adoption of the Bow in Prehistoric North America. *North American Archaeologist*, 9, pp. 123–145.

Clark, D.W. (1981). Prehistory of the Western Subarctic. In: J. Helm, ed. *Subarctic*. Washington, DC: Smithsonian Institution.

Cooper, H.C. (2012). Innovation and Prestige among Northern Hunter-Gatherers: Late Prehistoric Native Copper Use in Alaska and Yukon. *American Antiquity*, 77, pp. 565–590.

Darwent, J., Mason, O.K., Hoffecker, J.F., and Darwent, C.M. (2013). 1,000 Years of House Change at Cape Espenberg, Alaska: A Case Study in Horizontal Stratigraphy. *American Antiquity*, 78, pp. 433–455.

Dawson, P.C. (2001). Interpreting Variability in Thule Inuit Architecture: A Case Study from the Canadian High Arctic. *American Antiquity*, 66, pp. 453–470.

Dawson, P.C. (2016). The Thule-Inuit Succession in the Central Arctic. In: T.M. Friesen and O.K. Mason, eds. *The Oxford Handbook of The Prehistoric Arctic*. Oxford: Oxford University Press.

Dawson, P.C., and Levy, R.M. (2005). A Three-Dimensional Model of a Thule Inuit Whale Bone House. *Journal of Field Archaeology*, 30, pp. 443–455.

Duggan, A.T., Harris, A.J.T., Marciniak, S., Marshall, I., Kuch, M., Kitchen, A., Renaud, G., Southon, J., Fuller, B., Young, J., Fiedel, S., Golding, G.B., Grimes, V., and Poinar, H. (2017). Genetic Discontinuity between the Maritime Archaic and Beothuk Populations in Newfoundland, Canada. *Current Biology*, 27, pp. 3149–3156.

Dumond, D.E. (1965). On Eskaleutian Linguistics, Archaeology, and Prehistory. *American Anthropologist*, 67, pp. 1231–1257.

Dumond, D.E. (1981). *Archaeology on the Alaska Peninsula: The Naknek Region, 1960–1975*. Eugene: University of Oregon.

Dumond, D.E. (1984). Prehistory: Summary. In: D. Damas, ed. *Arctic*. Washington, DC: Smithsonian Institution.

Dumond, D.E., ed. (2001). *Archaeology in the Aleut Zone of Alaska: Some Recent Research*. Eugene: University of Oregon.

Dumond, D.E. (2005). *A Naknek Chronicle: Ten Thousand Years in a Land of Lakes and Rivers and Mountains of Fire*. Washington, DC: National Park Service.

Dumond, D.E. (2011). *Archaeology on the Alaska Peninsula: The Northern Section, Fifty Years Onward*. Eugene: University of Oregon.

Dumond, D.E., and Bland, R.L., eds. (2002). *Archaeology in the Bering Strait Region: Research on Two Continents*. Eugene: University of Oregon.

Fiedel, S.J. (1994). Some Inferences Concerning Proto-Algonquian Economy and Society. *Northeast Anthropology*, 48, pp. 1–11.

Friesen, T.M. (2007). Hearth Rows, Hierarchies and Arctic Hunter-Gatherers: The Construction of Equality in the Late Dorset Period. *World Archaeology*, 39, pp. 194–214.

Friesen, T.M., and Arnold, C.D. (2008). The Timing of the Thule Migration: New Dates from the Western Canadian Arctic. *American Antiquity*, 73, pp. 527–538.

Friesen, T.M., and Stewart, A.M. (2013). To Freeze or to Dry: Seasonal Variability in Caribou Processing and Storage in the Barrenlands of Northern Canada. *Anthropozoologica*, 48, pp. 89–109.

Frink, L., and Harry, K.G. (2008). The Beauty of "Ugly" Eskimo Cooking Pots. *American Antiquity*, 73, pp. 103–118.

Gerlach, S.C., and Murray, M.S., eds. (2001). *People and Wildlife in Northern North America*. Oxford: BAR Publishing.

Gibbon, G., ed. (1998). *Archaeology of Prehistoric Native America: An Encyclopedia*. New York: Garland Publishing.

Grund, B.S., and Huzurbazar, S.V. 2018. Radiocarbon Dating of Technological Transitions: The Late Holocene Shift from Atlatl to Bow in Northwestern Subarctic Canada. *American Antiquity*, 83, 148–162.

Hickey, C.G. (1979). Archaeological and Ethnohistorical Research on Banks Island. *Etudes/Inuit/Studies*, 3, pp. 132–133.

Larsen, H.E., and Rainey, F. (1948). *Ipiutak and the Arctic Whale Hunting Culture.* New York: American Museum of Natural History.

Magne, M.P.R., and Matson, R.G. (2010). Moving On: Expanding Perspectives on Athapaskan Migration. *Canadian Journal of Archaeology*, 34, pp. 212–239.

McGhee, R. (1976). *The Burial at L'Anse-Amour.* Ottawa: National Museum of Man, National Museums of Canada.

Meyer, D., and Russell, D. (2007). "Through the Woods Whare Thare Ware Now Track Ways": Kelsey, Henday and Trails in East Central Saskatchewan. *Canadian Journal of Archaeology*, 31, pp. 163–197.

Murray, M.S. (2005). Prehistoric Use of Ringed Seals: A Zooarchaeological Study from Arctic Canada. *Environmental Archaeology*, 10, pp. 19–38.

Noble, W.C. (1981). Prehistory of the Great Slave Lake and Great Bear Lake Region. In: J. Helm, ed. *Subarctic.* Washington, DC: Smithsonian Institution.

Potter, B.A. (2007). Models of Faunal Processing and Economy in Early Holocene Interior Alaska. *Environmental Archaeology*, 12, pp. 3–23.

Savelle, J.M., and Dyke, A.S. (2009). Palaeoeskimo Demography on Western Boothia Peninsula, Arctic Canada. *Journal of Field Archaeology*, 34, pp. 267–283.

Savelle, J.M., and Dyke, A.S. (2014). Paleoeskimo Occupation History of Foxe Basin, Arctic Canada: Implications for the Core Area Model and Dorset Origins. *American Antiquity*, 79, pp. 249–276.

Slobodin, R. (1981). Subarctic Métis. In: J. Helm, ed. *Subarctic.* Washington, DC: Smithsonian Institution.

Stefansson, V. (1921). *The Friendly Arctic: The Story of Five Years in Polar Regions.* New York: Macmillan.

Stewart, A.M., Friesen, T.M., Keith, D., and Henderson, L. (2000). Archaeology and Oral History of Inuit Land Use on the Kazan River, Nunavut: A Feature-Based Approach. *Arctic*, 53, pp. 260–278.

Wright, J.V. (1981). Prehistory of the Canadian Shield. In: J. Helm, ed. *Subarctic.* Washington, DC: Smithsonian Institution.

6

MOUNDBUILDERS OF THE EASTERN WOODLANDS

Dotted across the landscape of the woodlands of eastern North America are the remains of numerous mounds that were built by the Adena and Hopewell peoples and their Archaic-period ancestors. Most of these constructions ranged from circular-conical to elaborate geometric and animal-shaped earthworks that were formed over hundreds of years. A few had earthen platforms that presaged the flat-topped earthworks of the era that would follow (Chapter 7).

The Eastern Woodlands region is a temperate deciduous forest that lies south of the coniferous forests of central and eastern Canada, east of the Great Plains (Figure 6.1). The environment of the region varies due to differences in latitude, altitude, soils, and proximity to the ocean. Owing to subtle gradations across biozones of the Eastern Woodlands archaeologists consider the region as a cohesive unit.

Favorable climatic conditions, innovations in food production, and population reconfigurations resulted in new cultural formations after 5000 BCE. By 1000 BCE, the tribal societies of the region were enjoying unprecedented well-being, with newer technology in an environment that supported population growth and cultural elaboration. At the region's core, the domestication of native plants provided the subsistence base for the moundbuilder cultures. The florescence of these cultures spanned 14 centuries, beginning with Adena and concluding with Hopewell culture. These tribal societies came to be linked through a widespread network of trade and exchange. The hallmarks of both cultures include thousands of burial mounds and other earthworks scattered across much of the Eastern Woodlands. Eventually the mound building tradition evolved as new practices and purposes emerged (Case and Carr, 2008: 312–317). The construction of effigy burial mounds continued in the region's northwest, but earthworks were converted to new purposes elsewhere in the region (Chapter 7).

Environment and Adaptation

Each region of North America experienced its own series of vegetational changes over the course of the Holocene. Air masses moving west to east collide with others moving up from the south, producing the complex climatic conditions of most of the Eastern Woodlands, including

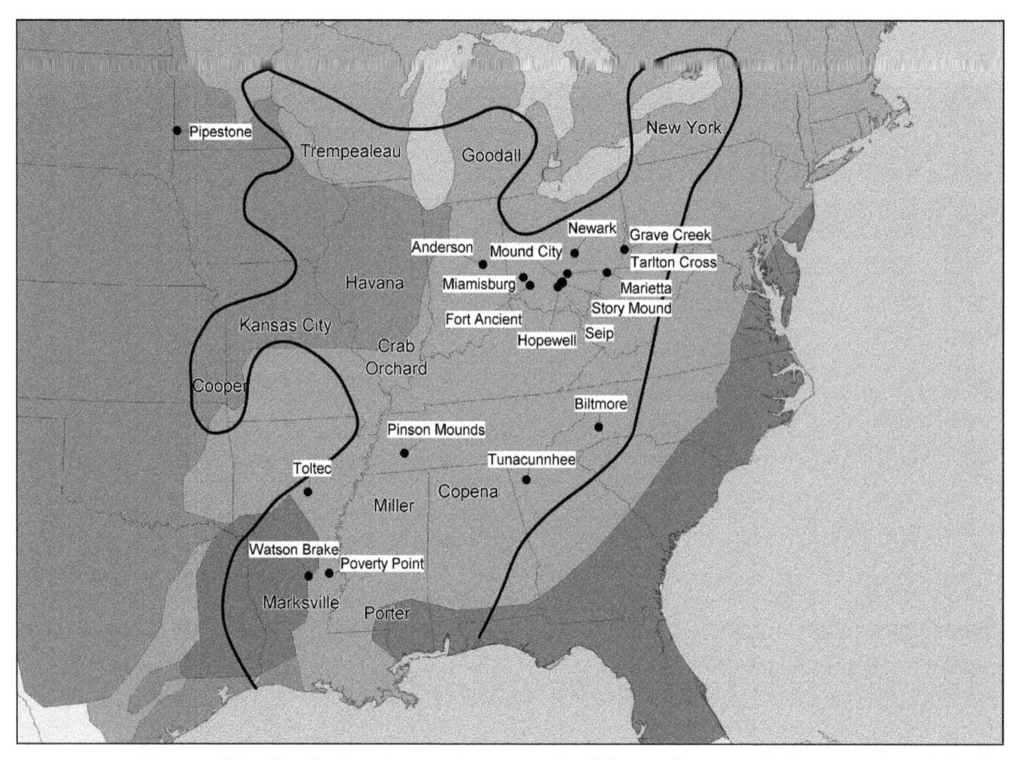

FIGURE 6.1 Eastern Woodlands showing major moundbuilding cultures and sites mentioned in the text. Many sites cluster in the Adena and Hopewell culture heartland

the ferocious "Noreaster" winter storms and deluges from exhausted summer hurricanes. Cold fronts advancing from the Great Plains spawn unpredictable tornados, especially in the absence of mountains.

The Appalachian Mountains, containing a mix of hardwood species, extend from southern New York to Alabama and Georgia. The northern forests were dominated by beech, maple, and elm trees, while oaks, chestnuts, and hickories prevailed in the south. Today, chestnuts and more recently elms have all but disappeared owing to twentieth-century blights.

The Great Lakes drain the northern interior of the Eastern Woodlands. The great ice sheets of the Pleistocene scoured the basins of these and thousands of smaller lakes. The Great Lakes were once surrounded by beech and maple forests. North of the lakes birch trees provided bark for canoes, the preferred mode of transportation in the streams and lakes of that region. Eventually, agricultural communities were established along the southern shores of the Great Lakes and north of the two southernmost lakes: Ontario and Erie. Elsewhere to the north, short growing seasons precluded farming as a reliable subsistence base.

The Southeastern Coastal Plain of eastern North America lies between the Appalachian Mountains and the Atlantic Coast, from New Jersey to the south. The coastal lowland fringe of the Eastern Woodlands was covered by Atlantic coniferous forest, dominated by southern pines and associated species. The lowland environment was fairly rich in natural resources, particularly on or near the coast, but it lacks effigy and burial mounds.

The Ohio River Valley and the other interior drainages of the heartland of the Eastern Woodlands was center stage during the Archaic. The vast hardwood forests of oak, hickory, chestnut, and other tree species provided abundant food. This zone was the core area of the Eastern Agricultural Complex, the set of locally domesticated plants that emerged during the Archaic period and underpinned the elaboration of mound building and burial ceremonialism after 1000 BCE (Smith, 1989).

People used fire to clear landscapes as they had for millennia, except now it was to clear patches in the forest where the plants they desired would flourish. The practice favored fire-tolerant oaks, chestnuts, and pines in the upland forests and reduced the frequency of other tree species (Delcourt et al., 1998).

Demography, Cooperation, and Conflict

The continent's human population had grown rapidly during the Paleoindian period, but it stabilized for about six millennia, through the better part of the Holocene. Population began increasing by about 5000 BCE and that lasted for 20 centuries or more. After a downturn, it resumed its upward trend again around 2000 BCE (Milner, 2004).

Farming led to larger and more permanent settlements, along with population growth and territorial expansion. Growing and spreading populations of farmers crowded out or overtook sparser populations of hunter-gatherers who happened to occupy regions where farming communities became established. Some languages must have disappeared as farming societies spread and multiplied. Others prospered as their speakers settled into new landscapes where diversification and local adaptations led to new mosaics of cultures sharing common origins and speaking related languages.

Geography conditioned many such expansions. Seas, mountain ranges, deserts, and cold latitudes all constrained the expansions of agriculturalists. Occasionally chance or technological advances allowed them to overcome such barriers. Farming based on local cultigens in the Eastern Woodlands expanded to the extent of the plants environmental limitations. Later, domesticates from Mesoamerica were introduced into the region, eventually dominating the subsistence economy (Chapter 7).

Subsistence and Economy

As early as 6000 BCE, people living in the Eastern Woodlands were foraging with considerable skill and a sophisticated knowledge of the native plant species. They used hundreds of plants to varying degrees of intensity. It was a logical step from intensive collecting and harvesting and the occasional firing of patches to selectively nurturing and tending of some plant taxa, given that groups had settled into predictable seasonal rounds. By harvesting stands of plants around their camps at the right times, people inadvertently reduced plant competitors and encouraged the synchronization of ripening. They were already focused on healthy stands, so the plants they were harvesting were those occurring in what for them were the most adaptive locations. It was not hard for people to take things a step further by suppressing competing plants.

Archaic people processed and stored food for future use, especially provisions like acorn and hickory nut meal, which preserved well. But the range of plants used in the Eastern Woodlands after 6000 BCE expanded significantly. Table 6.1 shows four species that evolved quickly through

TABLE 6.1 Domesticates and intensively used or managed plants in the Eastern Woodlands, 6000–2500 BCE

Scientific Name	*Common Name*	*Status*
Cucurbita texana	Squash	Domesticate
Lagenaria siceraria	Bottle gourd	Intensively used
Iva annua	Sumpweed/marshelder	Domesticate
Helianthus annuus	Sunflower	Domesticate
Chenopodium barlandieri	Goosefoot	Domesticate
Polygonum erectum	Erect knotweed	Intensively used
Phalaris caroliniana	Maygrass	Intensively used
Hordeum pusillum	Little barley	Intensively used

human selection to become true domesticates. Four more species were intensively used, but in those cases, there is not yet sufficient evidence to regard them as domesticates (Kay et al., 1980; Smith, 1989; Smith, 2001: 224).

Many other seeds and tubers were manipulated by people once they got to know the plants and understand how to prepare them. Groundnuts (*Apios apios*), tuckahoe (*Peltrandra virginica*), and wild calla (*Calla palustris*) are all edible, but the last must be thoroughly dried, and the second has to be first baked in an earthen oven. These examples show that across the Eastern Woodlands people were engaged in intensive plant utilization and in modifying landscapes. Unfortunately, there were only a few plant species that could become really productive domesticates.

Architecture and Technology

The origins of mound building are difficult to trace, as the origins of great traditions often are. Some of the ideas that led to mound building first appeared on the outskirts of the Eastern Woodlands. As elsewhere in North America, Archaic adjustments in the Eastern Woodlands focused on the intensification of local resources as the environment stabilized and people became increasingly familiar with their landscapes.

The upward bump in population after 5000 BCE appears to have been the result of favorable conditions for hunter-gatherers and their mastery of local resources, particularly in places where local plants could be domesticated or resources were abundant. It was in this context that the practice of building burial mounds began in the Northeast, around the Great Lakes, and in southern Illinois. Most consisted of earth, but occasionally they were heaps of stone. Glacial Kame culture people also used these geological features as cemeteries. Their descendants built artificial burial mounds, possibly inspired by the natural kames.

Other people began modifying landscapes with earthworks of another kind in the southwestern corner of the Eastern Woodlands. The Louisiana sites of Watson Brake and Poverty Point are very old and very large. Poverty Point was built later than Watson Break, around 1600 BCE. Older sites, which date to before the third millennium BCE, were not tentative first attempts but ambitious and impressive undertakings. There are 11 earthen mounds at Watson Brake, connected around a huge oval by a low meter-high (3.5-ft) earthwork ridge. The oval is about 280 m (919 ft) in diameter, and the highest mound stands 7.5 m (25 ft) high. The other mounds are lower, but as a whole the complex is imposing, all the more so because it dates to 3400 BCE (Saunders, 2012; Saunders et al., 1997; Saunders et al., 2005).

POVERTY POINT

Poverty Point is a residential and ceremonial site located in northeast Louisiana on a bluff overlooking the Mississippi River floodplain (Figure 6.2). Here, hunter-fisher-gatherers built monumental earthen architecture ca. 1700–1100 BCE. They moved as many as 100 million 22.7 kg (50 lb) basketloads of soil to level the landscape and create five mounds, six concentric C-shaped ridges, and a large plaza (Ellerbe and Greenlee, 2015). A later culture added a sixth mound in about 700 CE. The site is significant globally for its huge scale and unique design. The only U.S. earthworks site to surpass its size was the Cahokia site, which was built by later agriculturalists.

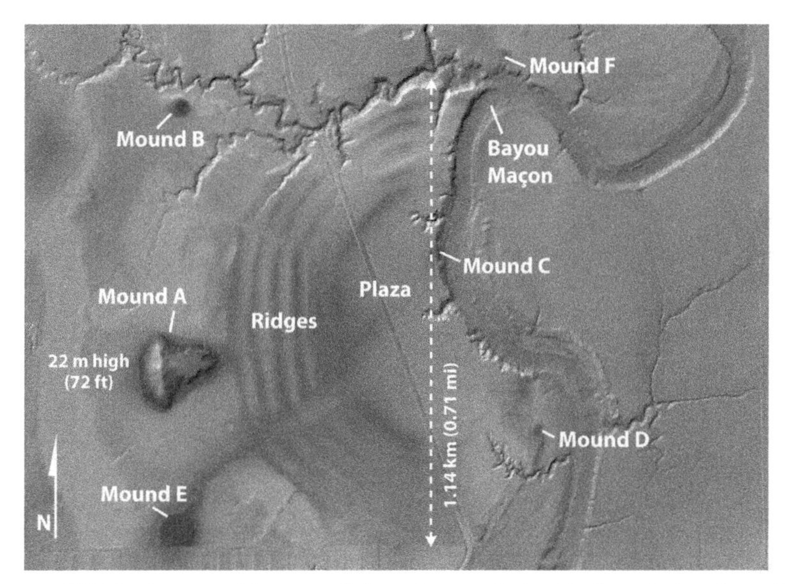

FIGURE 6.2 LiDAR image of Poverty Point. Poverty Point Station Archaeology Program. Data courtesy of FEMA and the state of Louisiana; data distribution courtesy of "ATLAS: The Louisiana Statewide GIOS," LSU CADGIS Research Laboratory, Baton Rouge, Louisiana

The people of Poverty Point did not grow crops—they ate wild foods such as fish, deer, nuts, and fruits. They used other resources to make a variety of characteristic artifacts (Webb, 1982). Earth was molded and fired to create cooking balls called "Poverty Point Objects," human figurines, pipes, and a small amount of pottery. Stone was the only critical raw material not found in the local area. Many tons of rock were brought to the site, some from hundreds of kilometers. The people used stone for tools, such as spear points, plummets, and celts, and for decorative items such as beads and gorgets.

For decades, archaeologists did not believe that hunter-gatherers were capable of long-distance trade and public construction projects on the scale seen at Poverty Point. One of Poverty Point's legacies will be its role in leading archaeologists to reevaluate their beliefs about what such groups could accomplish (Kidder, 2011). Continuing research aims to refine archaeological understanding of the Poverty Point community size and organization, earthwork construction, resource acquisition strategies, and the site's role within the surrounding cultural landscape. The Louisiana Office of State Parks manages this UNESCO World Heritage Site.

Diana M. Greenlee

The construction of earthworks at sites such as Watson Brake and Poverty Point did not necessarily require large labor forces or long-term efforts. Some mounds were built in single stages. Others grew as construction phases were carried out in brief episodes over centuries. These sites were clearly planned and constructed by members of tribal or perhaps chiefly societies (Anderson, 2002; 2004).

Adena Culture

While the earliest examples of moundbuilding around the margins of the Eastern Woodlands faded, the impulse for such construction did not. As people adapted to changing conditions, earthwork construction gradually became a major preoccupation across much of the region, and the center of it all came to be located in southern Ohio, heart of the Eastern Woodlands. Burial mounds became the visible hallmarks of the Adena cultures that arose from their Archaic ancestors.

The Adena culture (1000 BCE–400 CE) was centered in Ohio and Kentucky (Figure 6.1), whereas the heart of Hopewell was located in southern Ohio. Prior to the advent of radiocarbon dating, the Adena and Hopewell cultures were assigned to "Early Woodland" and "Middle Woodland" periods, respectively, but the relationship was not that simple. While they remain chronologically separate, it appears that some conservative Adena communities persisted into Hopewell times.

Adena people built simple mound earthworks in the early centuries, followed by more complex ones. Many were built over places where circular buildings had previously stood. The outward-leaning posts of some early examples once led archaeologists to reconstruct cupcake-shaped houses, but post mold patterns are also consistent with more familiar wigwam house styles of later times (Sturtevant, 1975).

Adena burial mounds sometimes featured simple clay-lined basins that were first excavated to hold the ashes of the cremated deceased, then mounds were built over the basins and their contents. At other times, elaborate log tombs were built for uncremated burials, covered up, but left accessible from the side of the mound for some duration. This construction was probably to make the mausoleum available for additional burials. Log tombs eventually decayed and collapsed, and their entrances were sealed.

Grave offerings included red ocher, graphite, and occasionally severed trophy heads. Many portable objects made of exotic materials such as copper, which had to have been obtained through a network of trade and exchange, were also included. Many Adena individuals exhibited deliberate cranial shaping. In other prehistoric and historical cultures, this cosmetic alteration was often a sign of beauty, high status, or both.

Many Adena mound sites have been destroyed and most of those that survive are characterized by simple shapes and attract little attention. Story Mound, for example, sits amidst residential properties in Chillicothe, Ohio. Others are more noticeable, mainly for their size. Grave Creek Mound still dominates a park in downtown Moundville, West Virginia. It was originally 20 m (66 ft) high and contained 70,000 m^3 (91,490 yd^3) of earth. Miamisburg Mound is an even larger conical Adena mound in southern Ohio.

Marietta holds a more complex set of earthworks near the Ohio River. The burial mound known as "Conus" is closely surrounded like a medieval castle by a berm or earthen wall and a ditch (Figure 6.3). However, an earthen wall that is *outside* the ditch defines a ceremonial precinct, not a fortification. A gap in the wall and an earthen ramp across the ditch provide access to the mound. The mound site is now preserved in a historic cemetery.

Artifacts traditionally used to identify Adena sites are largely beautiful portable items, many of them made from exotic materials obtained through large regional exchange networks. Barrel-shaped, effigy, and straight cylinder tubular pipes made from fine-grained stone (Figure 6.4) indicate

FIGURE 6.3 Marietta Mound, Ohio, from an 1840 engraving (Squier and Davis, 1848: 40)

FIGURE 6.4 Front and rear views of a human effigy tubular pipe from Adena Mound, 20 cm (8 in) tall. Courtesy of John Bigelow Taylor

FIGURE 6.5 Wilmington Adena tablet. The tablet is 12.8 cm (5 in) long. Courtesy of the Ohio History Connection

that tobacco had already spread to the Eastern Woodlands from South America. This was *Nicotiana rustica*, not the comparatively mild *Nicotiana tobacum* found in modern cigarettes. Other ingredients were probably added as well. Tobacco might have come into the Eastern Woodlands by way of the islands of the Caribbean. It was known in later Mesoamerica, perhaps a more logical route for the northward spread of tobacco, but smoking appears not to have been as widespread or as early there as it was elsewhere in North America, a circumstance that makes a route through the Caribbean Antilles a more attractive hypothesis.

Adena craftspeople made gorgets of stone, copper, and mica; freshwater pearl beads; mica cutouts; copper bracelets, rings, and beads; bird effigy atlatl weights; and engraved tablets. Tablets might have been used to apply dye patterns to textiles, but they might also have been used for body decoration and tattooing (Figure 6.5).

The Adena people were also early pottery manufacturers. Early examples of ceramics were crude, but later ones were better made and decorated by simple stamping. It is not clear what advantages spurred the adoption of pottery, for it represented a bigger time investment and was more cumbersome than existing bark or skin containers. It may have been related to a more-settled lifestyle and a trend toward slow cooking of porridges and similar foods. The durability of pottery would have offered a distinct advantage under those circumstances. Adena artisans also made a variety of woven cloth fabrics from fibers. Occasionally, fabrics have been preserved when deposited in contact with copper artifacts. Copper salts protect delicate fibers from decay.

Hopewell Culture

Hopewell culture appeared in Illinois after 100 BCE, later replacing Adena in southern Ohio perhaps a century later (Case and Carr, 2008; Lynott, 2015). Adena was not entirely replaced by Hopewell in some parts of Ohio and northern Kentucky, continuing and overlapping with Hopewell for two centuries. Hopewell sites continued to be constructed in southern Ohio as late as 400 CE. Hopewell subsistence and settlement patterns were new compared to those of Adena. Hopewell featured a more intensive use of the Eastern Agricultural Complex (Smith, 1989). Hopewell culture also produced more elaborate earthworks, its burial practices were geographically more extensive across the Eastern Woodlands, and its trade network was interregional in scope.

Hopewell people built burial mounds as the Adena had, again for a range of individuals, but they also built large earthen enclosures. These were often large square, circular, even octagonal earthen ridges. Some were as large as 500 m (1,640 ft) in diameter. Sometimes they included complexes of two or more shapes that were connected by avenues flanked by long earthen walls. In all cases the interiors of these sprawling figures were clearly intended to serve as ceremonial spaces, precincts specifically reserved for rituals. In some cases earthworks enclosed single burial mounds or clusters of them, monuments to the kin groups that built and maintained them, sometimes for centuries. In others, the interiors were large, open, and flat, singularly important theater-like spaces that were once the scenes of ceremonies with few archaeological traces other than the surrounding earthworks. The earthworks were built in a variety of ways. Earth could be scooped up from the loose forest floor or taken from borrow pits. In Illinois, Hopewell mounds were sometimes built at least in part by piling blocks of sod (Van Nest et al., 2001).

In many cases, individuals found in the central tombs of Hopewell mounds clearly enjoyed higher social standing than those buried in simple interments around the edges. Sometimes males dominated in the central tombs. At other times both males and females found in central tombs were taller than average, suggesting either that high-status individuals were better fed or that those naturally tall were accorded higher status.

Surviving Hopewell sites are today typically grassy knolls, often with mature trees growing on and around them. It is likely that the mounds were situated in cleared areas when initially constructed, and that periodic burning and general maintenance kept them bare and visible while in use. The purpose of monuments is to be seen, and the purpose of ceremonial precincts is to provide open ritual space. A few excellent examples of large complex Hopewell earthwork sites still exist, most often preserved in national, state, or local parks. Many are open to the public. As large and impressive as the earthworks are, they did not require great feats of engineering. A few clever people could have laid out even the largest of them using only sticks, cordage, and an understanding of basic geometry.

CORE HOPEWELL CULTURE SITES

Between 400 and 450 CE, three communities of several hundred people each, living in dispersed homesteads in three conjoining valleys in the Scioto drainage in south-central Ohio, formed a religious-social alliance (Carr and Case, 2005a). Together, they built in each valley a pair of massive earthen ceremonial centers that enclosed up to 120 acres, requiring millions of person-hours to sculpt millions of cubic feet of soil (Figure 6.6). Symbolizing the communities and their alliance, most of the centers were composed of three conjoined parts: a big square, a big circle, and a small circle. The earthworks were laid out to align precisely to 24 different solar and lunar events (e.g., winter solstice sunrise) and cardinal directions. Different centers incorporated different alignments, marking the schedule of a full calendar of religious and social ceremonies of many kinds that the communities performed together at different

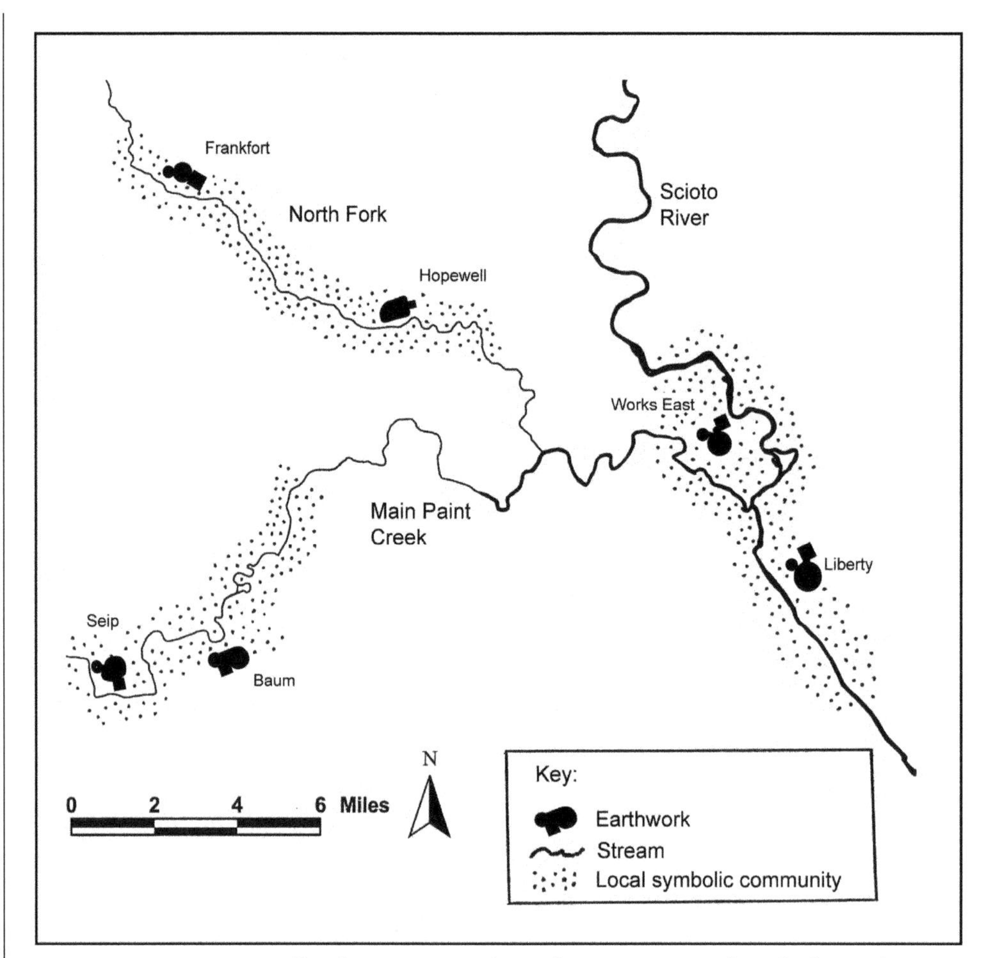

FIGURE 6.6 Core Hopewell Culture sites. Map by Katharine Rainey Kolb and Christopher Carr

centers in each other's lands. The three pairs of centers are Seip and Baum, Hopewell and Old Town, and Liberty and Works East. Seip and Hopewell are preserved within Hopewell Culture National Historical Park, along with the earlier, nearby centers of Mound City, Hopeton, High Bank, and Spruce Hill.

Among the ceremonies performed in the centers were funerary dramas that guided souls of the deceased to an afterlife. Some corpses were laid out with arms and legs spread in the form of flying birds, representing the soul's flight and serving as dramatic props (Carr and Novotny, 2015). The three communities anchored their alliance spiritually by burying their dead and the "body souls" within the remains together in three-room charnel houses up to half a football field long, similar to historic Huron Indian practices. Other rituals and feasts were orchestrated at huge circles of wood posts, recently discovered at Seip, Hopeton, and Hopewell (Ruby, 2018).

Christopher Carr and Bret J. Ruby

Some of the Hopewell mounds were topped by flat platforms rather than pointed or domed. A platform mound in the Anderson site, Indiana, has a sequence of clay platforms, each deliberately covered by a layer of ash. This architectural form presaged larger platform mounds that were later common in the Eastern Woodlands (Milner, 2004: 91–92). Tarlton Cross Mound is a symmetrical cross earthwork with a circular central depression. Its shape is reminiscent of the modern Blue Cross corporate symbol.

NEWARK EARTHWORKS

The Newark Earthworks are the largest connected series of geometric earthworks in North America. Built by the Hopewell culture around 2,000 years ago, they originally spread across more than 12 km^2 (4.5 mi^2) of a broad terrace along Raccoon Creek in the modern communities of Newark and Heath, Ohio (Figure 6.7). Surviving remnants include the Great Circle, a large circular enclosure 366 m (1,200 ft) in diameter with an interior ditch, and the Octagon Earthworks consisting of a circular enclosure 321 m (1,054 ft) in diameter connected by a short segment of parallel walls to an octagonal enclosure with walls approximately 168 m (550 ft) in length. Other earthworks at the site, which have been mostly destroyed by development, included a perfectly square enclosure 284 m (931 ft) on a side and an oval embankment with a maximum diameter of 549 m (1,800 ft) that enclosed 11 burial mounds. The burial mounds were leveled without any archaeological investigation, though some early accounts suggest these mounds contained offerings similar to what early archaeologists recovered from Hopewell burial mounds in the Scioto Valley (Lepper, 2016).

FIGURE 6.7 Newark Earthworks, Ohio. Courtesy of Steve Patricia

A network of parallel-walled avenues connected all the major enclosures to one another as well as to three streams that surrounded the earthworks. These corridors likely channeled the movements of pilgrims into and through the various earthworks in a prescribed sequence.

Careful surveys have revealed a sophisticated knowledge of geometry and astronomy in the design of the earthworks (Lepper, 2004). For example, the circumference of the Great Circle is equal to the perimeter of the large square enclosure; and the area of the square enclosure is equal to the area of the large circle connected to the octagon. In addition, the Octagon Earthworks incorporates alignments to points on the horizon marking the 18.6-year-long cycle of maximum and minimum moonrises and moonsets (Hively and Horn, 2016).

Brad Lepper

The Hopewell Trade Network

Hopewell architects took mound building to a new level, practices that were grafted on to a range of otherwise distinctive Eastern Woodlands cultures. Hopewell sites have produced an elaborate inventory of beautiful artifacts made from exotic raw materials that were imported from great distances. Luxury goods came to Hopewell centers through a far-flung exchange network that stretched far beyond the more limited reach of the earlier Adena trade network.

Copper nuggets came from the Keweenaw Peninsula of Upper Michigan and perhaps other sources. Silver probably came from Ontario. Meteoric iron came from wherever it landed. Mica came from quarries in the southern Appalachians, quartz crystal from eastern New York, aventurine and chlorite from the southern Appalachians, and galena cubes from Illinois or Missouri. Nodular flint came from deposits in Indiana and Illinois, and chalcedony from the Knife River region of North Dakota. Obsidian came from the Yellowstone region of the Rocky Mountains, and grizzly bear canines were probably also of western origin. **Catlinite** came from the Pipestone quarries in southwestern Minnesota and possibly Wisconsin. Cannel coal came from any of many coal deposits in Pennsylvania and elsewhere. *Cassis* shells came from the Florida east coast. *Busycon*, *Marginella*, *Oliva*, and *Olivella* shells were imported from the Gulf Coast, as were alligator teeth, barracuda jaws, and marine turtle shells. Shark teeth might have come from the Northeast Coast (Betts et al., 2012).

Copper nuggets were often beaten into sheets, then either embossed with designs or used as coverings for other objects, such as headdresses (Giles, 2013). Like earlier Old Copper craftspeople, Hopewell artisans used **anneal**ing to prevent the beaten copper from becoming brittle and cracking due to repeated pounding. Copper artifacts also included cutouts, breastplates, embossed sheets, artificial noses, beads, gorgets, celts, axes, and adzes. Copper-clad artifacts included ear spools, panpipes, and deer horns. Meteoric iron was also pounded into foil sheets. The foil was then used to cover ear spools, axes, adzes, and in one case a human arm bone. Sheets of mica were highly valued as blanks for cutouts that took the shapes of serpents, claws, human hands, human heads, swastikas, and other forms (Figure 6.8).

Culture, Language, and Identity

Adena and Hopewell are referred to here as cultures, even though the evidence for them is largely restricted to burial practices that could have been shared by several cultures that were otherwise quite different. Adena sites are concentrated in southern Ohio and parts of Kentucky and West Virginia, with a few outliers as far away as Vermont and New Jersey (Coe et al., 1986:51; Milner,

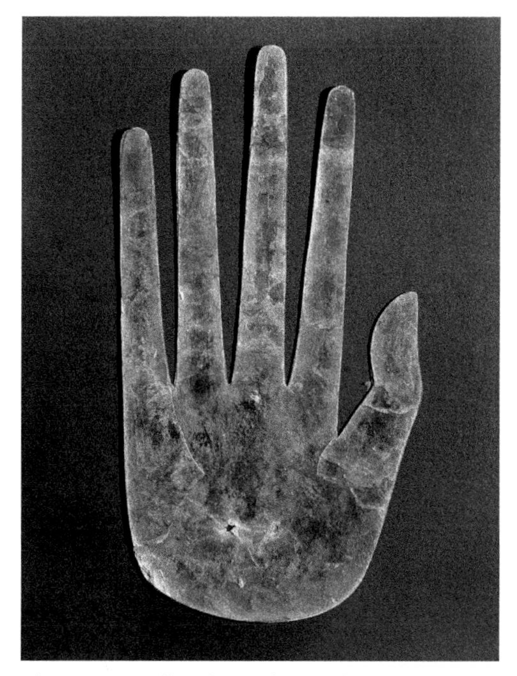

FIGURE 6.8 Mica hand, Ohio Hopewell culture, from Ohio, 300 BCE–500 CE. © Heritage Image Partnership Ltd / Alamy Stock Photo

2004). The earliest Adena settlements were constructed by around 1000 BCE, and they were still being built in northern Kentucky as late as 100 CE, two centuries after the appearance of Hopewell culture (Webb and Snow, 1974).

Burial mounds provided cultural centers for a dispersed society that did not have strong concepts of land tenure or political boundaries. However, the contents of Adena mounds often revealed differential social status among the dead, with the possessions of a few consisting of luxury goods imported from distant sources. It may seem contradictory, but this evidence of inequality is consistent with tribal organization. The most elaborate burials were probably reserved for local **clan** leaders, typically big men who had acquired their status through lifelong effort. Grave offerings of exotic imported materials imply a system of trade and exchange through which such things moved, which in turn was probably not much more than a network of friendships between widely scattered big men. Others afforded lavish burials might have been **shaman**s, religious practitioners who were probably among those who brought home exotic goods after long-distance pilgrimages to source locations (Carr and Case, 2005b). Burial ceremonialism was probably accompanied by feasting, the residues of which have sometimes been identified. Even people living at low population densities come together from time to time for large feasts (Wallis and Blessing, 2015).

The success of any clan leader brought benefits to the whole group, not just in terms of goods that were passed along to them, but also in terms of the status and prestige enjoyed by everyone in such a group. Lavish burials were the means through which clan or family members both signaled their respect for a deceased leader and made a statement about the relative status of their group as a whole. Thus all members of a leading clan or family benefited from strong leadership and the respect shown deceased leaders; prestige accrued to the whole group. That belief meant that the biggest mound and the most lavish burial probably went not to the most powerful or respected in a succession of leaders but rather to that person's immediate predecessor. In tribal society, the most elaborate treatment is typically organized *by* big men, not *for* them.

The same can be said for shamans, so long as they were perceived to be using their supernatural powers for the general good of the community. Traditional North American shamans often claimed the ability to transform themselves into animal forms while in trances, typically working their magic during states-of-transformation. Such power was as much feared as respected, thereby ensuring that powerful shamanic possessions accompanied a shaman in death and into the afterlife.

Art and Symbolism

Like their Adena predecessors, Hopewell artisans made use of a wide range of exotic materials when fashioning the finished artifacts that were the iconic hallmarks of their cultures (Griffin, 1967:184). The system was characterized by conspicuous consumption of valuable objects by acquiring them, giving them as gifts, and ultimately burying them rather than accumulating and bequeathing them to heirs as wealth. Funneling these items into burials and removing them from circulation maintained their high value. Some exotic raw materials were fashioned into a variety of finished products. Other exotic objects, such as galena cubes and grizzly bear canines, were only slightly modified treasures. By moving these objects through the system and into the archaeological record, Hopewell consumers maintained a steady demand for more of them.

People probably acquired both raw materials and finished artifacts through down-the-line trade, much of it couched as gift exchange between trading partners. Local leaders were nodes in widespread networks of trade and exchange that had the capacity to expand as new nodes became attached. The possessions of a **big man** thus fluctuated as items came and went. Ritual gift giving and trading partnerships was a pattern of friendship and cooperation that transcended social, political, and cultural boundaries that are frequently documented in historic American Indian tribes.

Trading partnerships across cultural and language boundaries were traditionally facilitated by bonds of fictive kinship. These were typically established in historic times by means of shared clan totems. Someone from the bear clan in one tribe was symbolically related to a person from the bear clan in a distant and unrelated tribe. Shared identities facilitated hospitality for travelers and fraternal reasons for ritual gift exchange (Tooker, 1971).

Shamans probably engaged in long-distance quests that took them to the magical sources of materials such as galena, obsidian, pipestone, quartz crystals, mica, and marine shell. Exotic materials from distant sources would have confirmed a successful quest and provided the shaman with a stock of powerful magic. Trace element analysis has shown that obsidian found in Ohio sites all came from Obsidian Cliff in what is now Yellowstone Park. Yellowstone obsidian was used to manufacture huge projectile points whose sizes and frequent odd shapes rendered them useless as projectiles or other kinds of tools.

Hopewell potters made elaborate "zoned" vessels with incised panel designs. They also made figurines in both clay and fossil mammoth ivory that tell us much about their hairstyles and clothing. Platform smoking pipes were made in simple monitor forms or more often to depict effigies of human heads, frogs, toads, water birds, raptors, ravens, bears, beavers, and the like (Figure 6.9).

Hopewell artisans also made items probably intended to be worn by shamans as parts of costumes. These objects include deer antlers, either real or made of copper, and masks made from the facial portions of human skulls. One buried individual, who had lost his front incisors years before his death, was equipped with the upper jaw of a wolf, carved to fit the gap in his mouth. It was probably part of a more elaborate costume.

FIGURE 6.9 Hopewell beaver effigy platform pipe from Bedford Mound, Illinois. Courtesy of Gilcrease Museum

Resilience and Collapse

Hopewell culture, and the trade network that sustained it, declined around 400 CE in the face of widespread social change. Circumstances caught up with the favorable environmental and technological conditions that had made the Hopewell golden age possible. Hopewell soon evolved into Fort Ancient culture, which was peripheral to the later Mississippian societies that later arose to its west and south. The historic descendants of Hopewell and later Fort Ancient culture, if they persisted past 1492, are uncertain.

Tennessee's Pinson site is one of several belonging to a secondary Hopewell development called the Miller Hopewellian, which was centered in northern Mississippi. The site is enclosed by a 365 m (1,200 ft) diameter earthwork. The central mound at Pinson, Sauls Mound, stands 22 m (72 ft) high. Unlike most mounds of the period, it is square and has four corners pointing to the cardinal directions. Ozier Mound is a 10 m (33 ft) high, flat-topped ceremonial platform, not a burial mound. These and a few other mounds in the Eastern Woodlands presaged a new architectural form that became widespread in the heyday of later Mississippian cultures (Chapter 7).

Elsewhere in the Eastern Woodlands, people continued to build burial mounds after 400 CE, albeit smaller and not accompanied by large earthwork enclosures or fancy artifacts made of exotic imported materials. Population growth continued, although in the absence of the Adena-Hopewell trade networks regional cultures became insular or inward-looking entities. The period from 400 to 1000 CE set the stage for major developments yet to come. Like many periods of human history that have not produced impressive artifacts for museum display, this one was long ignored by many archaeologists. Nevertheless, this was a time in which maize became adopted as a staple crop and large permanent towns became possible, setting the scene for dramatic developments described in Chapter 7.

The Toltec Mounds site in Arkansas is an excellent example of a thriving mound-building culture after Hopewell but before the rise of Mississippian cultures (Chapter 7). The site is also very inappropriately named. The mounds at Toltec were built between 600 and 1050 CE, and the later Toltecs of Mexico had nothing to do with them. Eventually at least 16 mounds were positioned within a high, curving 1,615 m (1 mi) embankment and exterior defensive ditch. A small lake, now called Mound Pond, protected the northwest side of the large D-shaped site.

The Toltec mounds were characterized by flat-topped rectangular platforms arranged around two plazas, a new architectural style in the Eastern Woodlands foreshadowed in some of the earlier-period sites of the region. Rather than burial mounds, these were structures designed to serve as elevated bases for imposing buildings. Two of the platform mounds had been 11–15 m (38–50 ft) high, and excavations in one of them revealed at least five construction stages. The new architectural form was similar to the larger Mesoamerican pyramids that had emerged earlier in highland Mexico (Chapter 13).

At least two low mounds at Toltec were apparently used for feasting. Deer were a favorite food, indicated by discarded bones. In addition, residential areas were identified within the fortified settlement. Villages and towns were now replacing nonresidential mortuary centers as central places in the Eastern Woodlands.

The transition from the kinds of exotic artifacts circulating in the Hopewell trade network to the new exotics associated with the rise in platform mound ceremonialism can also be tracked archaeologically here (Wright, 2014). It was a major shift in focus. Populations were growing, along with competition for the best farming land. The bow and arrow was introduced to the region by 600–700 CE, perhaps coincident with the rise in warfare, but too late to offer an easy explanation for the fading of Hopewell ceremonialism by around 440 CE. The days of sprawling ceremonial earthworks and friendly long-distance trade were over, and the scene was set for a new era in the Eastern Woodlands (Blitz, 1988; Erlandson et al., 2014; Walde, 2014).

The specific reasons for the decline of Hopewell remain uncertain and a continuing focus of archaeological research and debate. Generally population growth and tendency for societies to press the limits of carrying capacity had closed the gap between adaptive reality and adaptive potential, but the details are unclear.

Community organization changed such that earthworks were no longer highly valued. Perhaps villages became more important foci as food production and population density increased and settlements became more nucleated. Perhaps population growth approached regional capacity under the prevailing form of food production and competition reduced the general well-being.

It is likely that growing population sizes inititated competition for resources, and the availability of a new lethal weapon combined with those pressures produced a wave of intertribal conflict. Archaeologists have yet to find convincing ways to choose between these competing hypotheses. Whatever the causes, the importance of centralized earthwork complexes declined and people shifted to small family burial mounds on river bluffs. These featured a greater use of stone slab crypts, more frequent **bundle burials**, and a decline in the burial of cremated remains. Bundle burials result when bodies are exposed and the bones are later gathered for burial. Bundle burials and cremations are forms of deferred interment that might have been necessary initially in the absence of accessible tombs during the cold months when frozen ground precluded the ability to excavate burial pits. Once such tombs were no longer constructed and the public spectacle of cremations had waned as well, bundle burials probably became more common as a matter of convenience.

Fort Ancient culture (1000–1670 CE) followed Hopewell after a long time gap. The site of Fort Ancient in Ohio was long thought to be the type-site for later Fort Ancient culture. While Fort Ancient people used it in later times, the site now appears to date initially from the Hopewell period. It is located on a flat hilltop, and the earthen walls follow the natural topography in a manner suggesting a possible defensive and perhaps ceremonial purpose. There are numerous gaps in the walls at Fort Ancient, often partially blocked by mounds just inside, like those at many Hopewell sites.

FORT ANCIENT EARTHWORKS

Fort Ancient is the largest hilltop enclosure in North America. It was built by the Hopewell culture between about AD 1 and 400 (Figure 6.10). Around 600 years later, the Fort Ancient culture established a large village within the southern portion of the earthwork. Early archaeologists assumed, we now know incorrectly, that the village belonged to the builders of the earthwork and so named the culture after the site (Moorehead, 1890).

FIGURE 6.10 Oblique plan of Fort Ancient. Courtesy of the Center for the Electronic Reconstruction of Historic and Archaeological Sites at the University of Cincinnati

The walls of Fort Ancient surround a large, flat bluff 80 m (260 ft) above the Little Miami River. Originally, the earthwork was thought to have been an ancient fortification, which explains the misleading name of the site. It now is understood to have been primarily a place of ceremony though a wide range of activities have been documented at the site (Connolly and Lepper, 2004; Riordan, 2015).

Fort Ancient is composed of two primary enclosures, known as the North Fort and South Fort with a narrow connecting set of walls referred to as the Middle Fort. The earthwork follows the contours of the hilltop for 5.7 km (3.5 mi) with the walls ranging in height from 1–7 m (3–23 ft). There are more than 60 openings in the walls, a few of which appear to have served as primary gateways, whereas others may have allowed access to ancillary activity areas located outside of the enclosure (Connolly and Lepper, 2004). The most prominent of the gateways is located in the North Fort where the outer entrance is framed by two large mounds. Parallel walls frame an avenue that extended from this gateway 840 m (920 yds) to the northeast.

There are four small stone mounds in the North Fort arranged in a perfect square 156 m (512 ft) on a side. An observer standing at the westernmost mound can view the summer solstice sunrise as well as the maximum and minimum northern moonrise through three consecutive gateways.

Brad Lepper

Fort Ancient culture can be subdivided into at least eight chronological phases in different areas of southern Ohio and adjacent states. There was increasing similarity between Fort Ancient phases leading up to 1650 CE, characterized by the native artifacts and European trade goods found at the extraordinary Madisonville site.

Some archaeologists have equated Fort Ancient culture with the contemporary Mississippian cultures to the south. However, there is no evidence for an elite upper class on Fort Ancient sites. Fort Ancient leadership most likely continued the big man tribal forms of Hopewell culture. They may have had a system similar to the historic Iroquois, where obligations of generosity left leaders to be buried with no more than others of their ages. However, the Iroquois system based on matrilineal kinship – a special case involving large multifamily, female-dominated households – does not appear to have characterized Fort Ancient villages (Cook, 2008, 2012).

Glossary

anneal In the case of copper, a process to reduce brittleness by applying high heat and rapid cooling.

big man A male leader who emerges as a dominant figure through some combination of achievement and heredity and typically represents a large supportive kin group.

bundle burial A form of **secondary burial** in which disarticulated remains are gathered up and bundled before interment.

catlinite A dense red stone, found in Minnesota and Wisconsin, that was quarried and traded widely in the Hopewell and later exchange systems.

clan A type of social organization where members claim to be related to each other, though the actual ancestor may not be known.

primary burial An interment of an intact individual. Compare secondary burial.

secondary burial An interment of disarticulated, bundled, or cremated human remains. Compare with primary burial.

shaman A part-time religious practitioner (man or woman) who is perceived by others to have the power to contact the supernatural realm on a client's behalf.

References

Anderson, D.G. (2002). The Evolution of Tribal Social Organization in the Southeastern United States. In: W.A. Parkinson, ed. *The Archaeology of Tribal Societies*. Ann Arbor, MI: International Monographs in Prehistory.

Anderson, D.G. (2004). Archaic Mounds and the Archaeology of Southeastern Tribal Societies. In: J.L. Gibson and P.J. Carr, eds. *Signs of Power: The Rise of Cultural Complexity in the Southeast*. Tuscaloosa: University of Alabama Press.

Betts, M.W., Blair, S.E., and Black, D.W. (2012). Perspectivism, Mortuary Symbolism, and Human–Shark Relationships on the Maritime Peninsula. *American Antiquity*, 77, pp. 621–645.

Blitz, J.H. (1988). Adoption of the Bow in Prehistoric North America. *North American Archaeologist*, 9, pp. 123–145.

Carr, C., and Case, D.T., eds. (2005a). *Gathering Hopewell: Society, Ritual, and Ritual Interaction*. New York: Kluwer Academic/Plenum Publishers.

Carr, C., and Case, D.T. (2005b). The Nature of Leadership in Ohio Hopewellian Societies: Role Segregation and the Transformation from Shamanism. In: C. Carr and D.T. Case, eds. *Gathering Hopewell: Society, Ritual, and Ritual Interaction*. New York: Kluwer Academic/Plenum Publishers.

Carr, C., and Novotny, A. (2015). Arrangement of Human Remains and Artifacts in Scioto Hopewell Burials. In: E.A. Hargrave, S.J. Schermer, K.M. Headman, and R.M. Lillie, eds. *Transforming the Dead: Culturally Modified Bone in the Prehistoric Midwest*. Tuscaloosa: University of Alabama Press.

Case, D.T., and Carr, C. (2008). *The Scioto Hopewell and Their Neighbors: Bioarchaeological Documentation and Cultural Understanding*. New York: Springer Science+Business Media.

Coe, M., Snow, D.R., and Benson, E. (1986). *Atlas of Ancient America*. New York: Facts on File.

Connolly, T.J., and Lepper, B.T., eds. (2004). *The Fort Ancient Earthworks: Prehistoric Lifeways of the Hopewell Culture in Southwestern Ohio*. Columbus: Ohio Historical Society.

Cook, R.A. (2008). *SunWatch: Fort Ancient Development in the Mississippian World*. Tuscaloosa: University of Alabama Press.

Cook, R.A. (2012). Dogs of War: Potential Social Institutions of Conflict, Healing, and Death in a Fort Ancient Village. *American Antiquity*, 77, pp. 498–523.

Delcourt, P.A., Delcourt, H.R., Ison, C.R., Sharp, W.E., and Gremillion, K.J. (1998). Prehistoric Human Use of Fire, the Eastern Agricultural Complex, and Appalachian Oak-Chestnut Forests: Paleoecology of Cliff Palace Pond, Kentucky. *American Antiquity*, 63, pp. 263–278.

Ellerbe, J., and Greenlee, D.M. (2015). *Poverty Point: Revealing the Forgotten City*. Baton Rouge: Louisiana State University Press.

Erlandson, J.M., Watts, J.L., and Jew, N.P. (2014). Darts, Arrows, and Archaeologists: Distinguishing Dart and Arrow Points in the Archaeological Record. *American Antiquity*, 79, pp. 162–169.

Giles, B.T. (2013). A Contextual and Iconographic Reassessment of the Headdress on Burial 11 From Hopewell Mound 25. *American Antiquity*, 78, pp. 502–519.

Griffin, J.B. (1967). Eastern North American Archaeology: A Summary. *Science*, 156, pp. 175–191.

Hively, R., and Horn, R. (2016). The Newark Earthworks: A Grand Unification of Earth, Sky, and Mind. In: L. Jones and R.D. Shiels, eds. *The Newark Earthworks: Enduring Monuments, Contested Meanings*. Charlottesville: University of Virginia Press.

Kay, M., King, F.B., and Robinson, C.K. (1980). Cucurbits from Phillips Spring: New Evidence and Interpretations. *American Antiquity*, 45, pp. 806–822.

Kidder, T.R. (2011). Transforming Hunter-Gatherer History at Poverty Point. In: K.E. Sassaman and D.H. Holly, Jr., eds. *Hunter-Gatherer Archaeology as Historical Process*. Tucson: University of Arizona Press.

Lepper, B.T. (2004). The Newark Earthworks. In: R.V. Sharp, ed. *Hero, Hawk, and Open Hand*. New Haven, CT: Yale University Press.

Lepper, B.T. (2016). The Newark Earthworks: A Monumental Engine of World Renewal. In: L. Jones and R.D. Shiels, eds. *The Newark Earthworks: Enduring Monuments, Contested Meanings*. Charlottesville: University of Virginia Press.

Lynott, M.J. (2015). *Hopewell Ceremonial Landscapes of Ohio: More Than Mounds and Geometric Earthworks*. Oxford: Oxbow Books.

Milner, G.R. (2004). *The Moundbuilders: Ancient Peoples of Eastern North America*. New York: Thames and Hudson.

Moorehead, W.K. (1890). *Moorehead, Warren K. Fort Ancient: The Great Prehistoric Earthwork of Warren County, Ohio, Compiled by a Careful Survey, with an Account of Its Mounds and Graves*. Cincinnati, OH: R. Clarke.

Riordan, R. (2015). The End. In: B.G. Redmond and R.A. Genheimer, eds. *Building the Past: Prehistoric Wooden Architecture in the Ohio-Great Lakes*. Gainesville: University Press of Florida.

Ruby, B.J. (2018). Revealing Ritual Landscapes at the Hopewell Mound Group. In: B.G. Redmond, B.J. Ruby, and J. Burks, eds. *Encountering Hopewell in Ohio and Beyond*. Akron, OH: University of Akron Press.

Saunders, J.W. (2012). Early Mounds in the Lower Mississippi Valley. In: R.L. Burger and R.M. Rosenswig, eds. *Early New World Monumentality*. Gainesville: University Press of Florida.

Saunders, J.W., Mandel, R.D., Sacier, R.T., Allen, E.T., Hallmark, C.T., Johnson, J.K., Jackson, H.E., Allen, C.M., Stringer, G.L., Frink, D.S., Feathers, J.K., Williams, S., Gremillion, K.J., Vidrine, M.F., and Jones, R. (1997). A Mound Complex in Louisiana at 5400–5000 Years Before the Present. *Science*, 277, pp. 1796–1799.

Saunders, J.W., Mandel, R.D., Sampson, C.G., Allen, C.M., Allen, E.T., Bush, D.A., Feathers, J.K., Gremillion, K.J., Hallmark, C.T., Jackson, E.H., Johnson, J.K., Jones, R., Saucier, R.T., Stringer, G.L., and Vidrine, M.F. (2005). Watson Brake, A Middle Archaic Mound Complex in Northeast Louisiana. *American Antiquity*, 70, pp. 631–668.

Smith, B.D. (1989). Origins of Agriculture in Eastern North America. *Science*, 246, pp. 1566–1571.

Smith, B.D. (2001). The Transition to Food Production. In: G.M. Feinman and T.D. Price, eds. *Archaeology at the Millennium: A Sourcebook*. New York: Kluwer Academic/Plenum Publishers.

Squier, E.G., and Davis, E.H. (1848). *Ancient Monuments of the Mississippi Valley, Comprising the Results of Extensive Original Surveys and Explorations*, Washington, DC: Smithsonian Institution.

Sturtevant, W.C. (1975). Two 1761 Wigwams at Niantic, Connecticut. *American Antiquity*, 40, pp. 437–444.

Tooker, E. (1971). Clans and Moieties in North America. *Current Anthropology*, 12, pp. 357–376.

Van Nest, J., Charles, D.K., Buikstra, J.E., and Asch, D.L. (2001). Sod Blocks in Illinois Hopewell Mounds. *American Antiquity*, 66, pp. 633–650.

Walde, D. (2014). Concerning the Atlatl and the Bow: Further Observations Regarding Arrow and Dart Points in the Archaeological Record. *American Antiquity*, 79, pp. 156–161.

Wallis, N.J., and Blessing, M.E. (2015). Big Feasts and Small Scale Foragers: Pit Features as Feast Events in the American Southeast. *Journal of Anthropological Archaeology*, 39, pp. 1–18.

Webb, C.H. (1982). *The Poverty Point Culture*. Baton Rouge: Louisiana State University Department of Geography and Anthropology.

Webb, W.S., and Snow, C.E. (1974). *The Adena People*. Knoxville: University of Tennessee.

Wright, A.P. (2014). History, Monumentality, and Interaction in the Appalachian Summit Middle Woodland. *American Antiquity*, 79, pp. 277–294.

7

THE MISSISSIPPIANS

During the heyday of Adena and Hopewell cultures and their widespread networks of trade and exchange, people came to depend upon tubers and the starchy and oily seeds of various native plants. Through a process of selective nurturing, some of these important plants were gradually transformed from wild to domesticated varieties. Further cultural transformations occurred when maize spread from Mesoamerica to become a staple crop in the Eastern Woodlands. Evidence for chiefdoms as manifested in centers with large platform mounds appeared first along the rich bottomlands of the middle portion of the Mississippi River. Over the course of three centuries Mississippian peoples built centers elsewhere in the Southeast, from the edge of the Great Plains to the Atlantic and Gulf Coasts. The challenge to archaeologists has been to describe and explain the rise and spread of these Mississippian societies, which were still thriving at the time when the Spaniard Hernando de Soto made his **entrada** in 1539–1543. The ancient city of Cahokia is situated in the Mississippi Valley across from the modern city of St. Louis. It was the largest of all the Middle Mississippian sites.

The Mississippians built numerous towns, large and small, scattered across the Eastern Woodlands, but their heartland was centered on the "American Bottom" stretch of the Mississippi Valley. This area lies roughly between modern St. Louis and Memphis and is the region where Mississippian chiefdoms first arose. People of this Middle Mississippian area spawned colonies and other regional variants as social and political pressures resulted in chiefdom organizations throughout much of the Southeast. These secondary developments include Caddoan, Plaquemine, Moundville, and Savannah cultures, as well as smaller variants and some Gulf Coast cultures discussed in Chapter 12 (Figure 7.1). Each was home to a set of related chiefdoms. Archaeologically, each chiefdom is generally marked by a single major site surrounded by a constellation of smaller tributary sites (Ashley et al., 2015; Hudson, 1976; Pauketat et al., 2015).

Environment and Adaptation

The specific food plants varied from one region to another, but nearly everywhere south of the Great Lakes, people depended heavily on the collection, storage, and consumption of cultivars. This intensification of plant use accommodated the slow steady increase in population. Over time, and

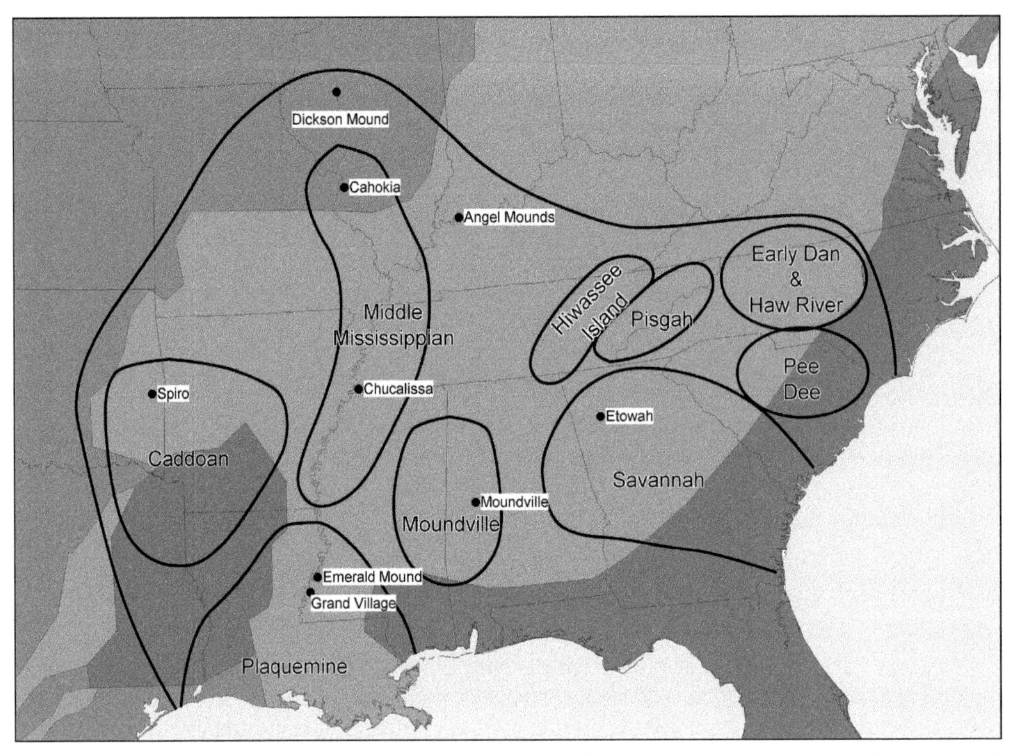

FIGURE 7.1 The extent of Mississippian culture, showing the locations of major regional variants and sites mentioned in the text

with the arrival of maize, populations reached a critical mass, whereby social and political innovations resulted in the replacement of tribal by chiefly formations. The Medieval Climate Anomaly (ca. 950–1250 CE) coincided with the adoption of intensive maize agriculture in the region. This event in turn facilitated the development of urban centers between 1000–1200 CE because increasingly dense concentrations of people could be sustained on a year-round basis (Bird et al., 2017).

Chiefdoms share elements that differentiate them from tribal societies. First, they maintain a subsistence economy sufficiently productive to support elites within a ranked organizational structure. Second, their population base is larger, more sedentary, and denser than what is typical for tribal formations.

Once this complex political structure developed in the Middle Mississippi region, it spread to other populations where similar conditions already existed or were emerging. Powerful and competitive Mississippian chiefdoms existed all along the great river from Illinois to Louisiana and the lower reaches of its major tributaries by approximately 1000 CE. By 1100 CE, chiefdom polities were flourishing in the Appalachians, eastern Texas, and along the Gulf Coast. By 1200 CE, they had spread as far east as the Atlantic Coast, on the northern prairies of Iowa, and in northern Florida (Anderson, 1999; Beck, 2003; Milanich, 1999).

Demography and Conflict

People brought the bow and arrow from northern sources to the Mississippi region around 600–800 CE. This innovation was marked archaeologically by a sudden increase in small projectile points used to tip arrows, commonly known as arrowheads. The new weapon allowed hunters to range widely from their homes in search of deer and smaller animals that were attracted to horticultural plots. Bows and arrows were also effective in warfare, which was on the increase. Rising population density resulted in competition for the best horticulturally productive land, which in turn made warfare more frequent (LeBlanc, 2006: 457–458).

The development of chiefdom societies appeared to be a natural outgrowth of the demands produced by increasing local population densities, competition for prime land, and the production of food surpluses. Stresses arose as people came to live in ever-larger communities. Challenges involved organizational requirements for the storage and redistribution of surplus food, the management of internal political problems, and the coordinated reaction to outside threats. These were problems that could not be addressed by consensus politics favored by segmental tribes, but they could be better accommodated by the formally structured leadership hierarchy of a chiefdom. Earlier small tribal communities could govern themselves by broad consensus, splitting and relocating when all else failed. But the burgeoning Mississippian communities were less easily moved due to **circumscription**, and factions within them were less willing to break away, tied as they all were to nearby rich riverine farming lands (Carniero, 1967).

Subsistence and Economy

Maize (*Zea mays*) is a plant well known to us today as corn. People in Mexico originally domesticated the wild ancestor, **teosinte** (see Chapter 13), and through numerous trading routes, maize was carried to the Mississippian area. Archaeologists are still determining the routes that it may have taken. Maize remained a minor crop for as much as seven centuries. Early varieties of maize needed up to 200 frost-free days to mature, a requirement that restricted its spread into higher latitudes. For many years maize appears to have been a minor crop, perhaps eaten green seasonally like modern sweet corn or reserved for special occasions. By 750 CE, maize varieties in the Mississippian region were sufficiently productive and had been elevated to the status of staple crop. Farming emerged from more generalized collecting over the centuries, a task that had long been largely the responsibility of women. Although both men and women were involved in provisioning the household, men typically took on the heavier work, such as clearing. But most of the labor of farming was borne mainly by women, and it remained so long after the arrival of Europeans. Thus the new adaptation was made possible largely by the labor of women (Milner, 2004: 118).

The point at which Mississippians consumed great quantities of maize can be detected through the remains of the people themselves. Human bone chemistry registers diet, thereby allowing researchers to gain insight into what people ate in the past. The bones of people who eat a lot of maize have slightly elevated levels of ^{13}C, which is an identifiable and measurable isotope of carbon. Archaeologists have been able to detect the shift to maize farming by observing the differences in the relative levels of ^{12}C (the normal form of carbon) and ^{13}C in skeletal assemblages. Dietary changes can also be detected in dental health. Diets higher in sticky carbohydrates led to more rapid tooth decay. In addition, the grinding of corn into meal using grinding stones introduced powdered stone that abraded molars into flat surfaces. After corn became a staple, all but the youngest people were plagued with dental problems including caries, lost and abraded teeth, and abscesses.

Even though farmers came to rely a great deal upon maize, the hunting of animals remained an important subsistence activity as a source of protein. A variety of other plants were cultivated to supplement their diets with much-needed nutrients. However, maize, as a new staple, seems to have been linked to higher populations, more villages, and the presence of food surpluses enabling people to make it through the lean winter months. The clearing and firing of fields had been going on for centuries, but now the practice began to transform large areas around towns into mosaics of cleared fields. Fields that were planted on the rich floodplains of the Mississippi and its major tributaries were virtually permanent, their fertility replenished by periodic spring flooding. Those opened in upland areas left patchworks of forest, new fields, and fields recently abandoned because of declining productivity. Upland **swidden** farming depended upon a ready supply of forestland to be cleared while old fields reverted to forest to regenerate their fertility. In both cases there were plenty of forest edges, where edible wild plants grew and animals (especially deer) were attracted.

The diets of farmers of the Eastern Woodlands would have been more nutritious had beans arrived from Mexico along with maize early in the first millennium, but they did not. Maize has the most essential amino acids, but when combined with beans, the two form a complete protein. Beans provide an excellent source of protein that reduced dependence on meat, but they did not arrive until centuries after maize. The evolution of the maturation mechanism of the bean plant was slow, making adoption of it perhaps not as convenient as that of maize. As a result, beans are common only in later Mississippian sites.

Rising population and the opportunities afforded by **oxbow lake**s in the broad Midwestern floodplains also led to intensification of fishing. Deer could not be domesticated to provide more meat protein, and beans were still not available as a plant source of protein; fish became a significant source of protein for Mississippian people whose diets were otherwise dominated by carbohydrates. Catfish and other species became impounded in the oxbow lakes that flanked major rivers when spring floods receded. The oxbows became natural holding ponds for the trapped fish, which Mississippians learned to exploit like fish farms (Figure 7.2).

Architecture and Technology

In the Southeast **chieftain**s signaled their ranks by living in fine houses on platform mounds (Figure 7.3). Other mounds served as platforms for council houses, **charnel house**s, or temples, where chieftains presided over public rituals. These constructions were typically arrayed around plazas that were probably the social and ritual centers of towns. Chieftains retained and exercised their power in part through the symbolic linkages between the mound structures. Some excavated mounds have been found to contain large deposits of animal bones and other food waste. This evidence indicates the importance of feasting by chieftains and other elites (Kidder, 2004).

The platform mounds that are the most prominent features of southeastern archaeological sites were often built in stages. What we see today is most commonly the final episode of mound construction over a long history. Successions of leaders enlarged and resurfaced earthworks that they inherited or took over. Colored or cleaned soils sometimes marked the construction episodes of later earthworks (Anderson, 2004: 282) finishing off a new building stage and giving it a fresh new look. Mississippians probably would not have thought much of the grassy knolls that their constructions have become in today's archaeological parks. Adding a new stage to a platform raised and validated the **rank** of the chieftain and called upon tradition through a physical connection with the earlier mound. Sometimes that historical connection can be traced archaeologically back to a single elite residential structure under the earliest mound platform and overlain by a succession of later ones. In other cases, such as at Etowah, Georgia, there is clear evidence of interruptions in the succession, as new groups took over the center after its abandonment by an earlier collapsed chiefdom (King, 2003). The Etowah site lies along the river of the same name in northwestern

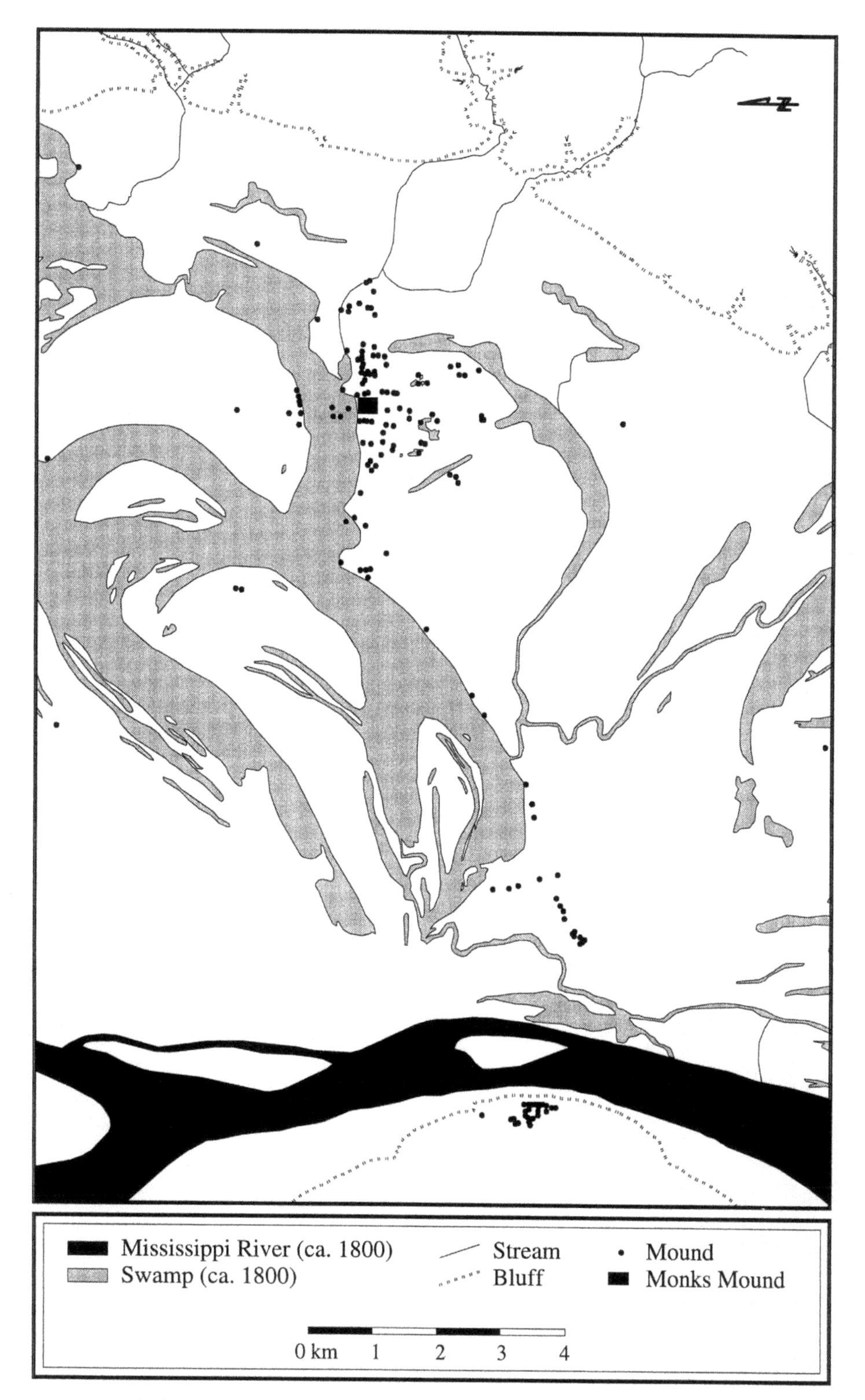

FIGURE 7.2 Cahokia mounds arrayed near oxbow lakes in the American Bottom just east of the Mississippi River. Courtesy of George Milner

FIGURE 7.3 Platform mound with reconstructed structure at Angel Mounds, Indiana

Georgia. It contains six platform mounds on 21 hectares (52 acres) inside a defensive ditch. The ditch originally had an inner **palisade** and **bastion**s, all designed to protect the sides of the site that were not facing the river. The Etowah site is well known for spectacular artifacts that had been cached in Mound C. These included chert swords, embossed copper plates, carved shell **gorget**s, and an exquisite pair of marble statues (Figure 7.4). The sculptures are male and female figures sitting with their lower legs tucked under them. They reveal much about Mississippian dress and hairstyles.

Etowah is an excellent example of a site that hosted a series of cycling chiefdoms over the course of five and a half centuries. The site was occupied around 1000 CE by the first of three chiefdoms. Etowah was a different community during each of its three occupations. Etowah was reoccupied, and its mounds refurbished for the last time around 1475 CE. This time it was occupied by a simple chiefdom, and it was no longer a regional center. The last occupation ended about a decade after Hernando de Soto's visit in 1540 CE (see box feature, Chapter 14).

Some platform mounds supported charnel houses. These buildings were specialized mortuary structures that were designed to contain the remains of distinguished ancestors. Charnel houses were cleaned out periodically and the accumulated human remains stored in them were taken elsewhere for burial. Such structures could hold only a small number of individuals, so it is clear that this honor and the ostentatious ritual surrounding it were reserved for elite families. The worst thing an enemy could do was to force entry to the town and defile the ancestral bones housed in the charnel house, as de Soto discovered during his entrada (Vega, 1962).

At least some chiefdoms were led by dynastic families that were strong enough to make human sacrifice part of their burial ritual. Examples are known from the Mississippian centers of Cahokia and Dickson Mounds in Illinois, as well as at some other major sites (Figure 7.5). These practices continued into the period following European colonization, and they were observed by French visitors among the Natchez, who were in turn part of the Plaquemine branch of the Mississippian phenomenon (Galloway, 2004).

Rare items, such as marine shell beads, were noted markers of high rank in Mississippian centers. A likely explanation for such large accumulations of marine shell is the same as that offered for peoples of the Southwest (Chapter 10), the association of marine shell with supernatural power

FIGURE 7.4 Marble statues from the Etowah site, 61 and 55.9 cm (24 and 22 in) tall. Etowah Indian Mounds State Historic Site, Georgia

FIGURE 7.5 The reconstructed site of Chucalisa in Memphis reproduces the clean, unvegetated appearance that Mississippians probably preferred

hoarding. Crafts were turned out in households and not manufactured centrally for general redistribution. Specialization was maintained at the household or family level. There is no evidence for either craft specialization or for markets in which crafts might have been bought and sold. These essential features of Mesoamerican state societies (Chapter 13) were lacking in Mississippian chiefdoms.

Cahokia grew to its large size by virtue of the people who knew how to exploit its rich farmlands and oxbow lakes and to establish trade routes for Mill Creek chert hoes and other goods. The hoes were in high demand by farmers around Cahokia as well as other more-distant agriculturalists living around Mississippian centers. Their manufacture and distribution was an important economic activity, and Cahokia's control of that trade probably contributed to its rise as the largest Mississippian urban center.

CAHOKIA

Cahokia, located in the Mississippi River floodplain in what is now Illinois, is by far the largest prehistoric settlement in the United States. It rose to prominence in the eleventh century CE, early in the Mississippian period, but within a few centuries, its occupants had started to abandon it. This once heavily populated part of the Mississippi Valley was all but abandoned when Europeans first passed through the area in the late seventeenth century.

Cahokia's mounds, once numbering over 100, cover an area of about 10 km^2 (Fowler, 1997; Milner, 1998). Interspersed among them were residential areas packed with pole-and-thatch houses, socially and ritually important precincts, fields for maize and other crops, and both seasonally inundated land and permanent bodies of water. An abandoned river channel ran from east to west across the site. Most of the occupation was on the south side of this oxbow lake on a natural levee of relatively high and well-drained ground.

The largest of the mounds, Monks Mound (Figure 7.6), covered about 7 ha, and with a height of around 30 m, it towered over all others (Fowler, 1997). It served as the central focus of the site, along with an elongated plaza extending to the south and a few other mounds, all enclosed by a wall made from stout posts.

Archaeologists debate about the population of Cahokia and the nature of its socio-political organization (Milner, 1998). At its peak, the site was probably occupied by 3,000 to 8,000 people, based on the most representative sample of excavated areas currently available, although some estimates are several times higher. Despite a relatively large population, the society seems to have been structured similarly to its locally powerful Mississippian counterparts elsewhere in eastern North America.

George R. Milner

FIGURE 7.6 Monks Mound, Cahokia

Cahokia's people constructed over 100 mounds from the ninth century until the city's abandonment around 1400 CE (Figure 7.2). About half of the entire fill used in these earthworks was used to construct Monks Mound, the largest earthen structure north of Mesoamerica. Increased periodic flooding might have led to the site's abandonment (Munoz et al., 2015).

Large towns like Cahokia were difficult to keep supplied with food in the absence of draft animals and wheeled vehicles. Waste disposal also presented a challenge in the absence of sanitary sewers and regular public garbage collection. Just like Cahokia, the absence of these services made colonial and early American cities unhealthy places until the cholera epidemics of the nineteenth century forced major reforms and improvements. Like all preindustrial urban centers, Cahokia probably depended upon its social and political attractions to attract a steady supply of immigrants. Without an influx of new inhabitants, such towns typically have death rates too high for them to sustain their populations by new births alone.

Some or all of many Mississippian towns were surrounded by log palisades that were often equipped with protective bastions. Fortifications were clearly intended to protect the cores of the towns from outside attack. In places the palisade at Cahokia passed through established neighborhoods, indicating that it was not initially part of the town plan but rather was added later in the occupational history of the community. Residential architecture for the great majority of people consisted of square or rectangular houses constructed with wattle-and-daub walls and thatch roofs. Subterranean storage pits and above-ground granaries provided food storage for most residents.

Culture, Language, and Identity

Chiefdoms are defined as sociopolitical organizations that feature minimally two or more levels of integration. A society with a permanent chieftain and two or more subordinate family heads would qualify under this definition. More complex chiefdoms are also known. Very complex ones exhibit attributes of states, and in some cases they are the simplified remnants of former states. Tribes can evolve into chiefdoms and states can collapse into chiefdoms (Earle, 1987).

Chiefdoms tend to be unstable social formations and subject to collapse, cycling in and out of existence, because of their tendency to break up when they experience internal conflict. This kind of cyclical fissioning is also common in segmentary tribes. While rarer among larger chiefdoms, the effects of collapse are greater in the context of larger investments in permanent villages and towns. In some circumstances chiefdoms may split into separate entities, spawning two or more smaller social units that might persist as segmentary tribes or eventually evolve into new chiefdoms, either through internal growth or merging with other similar polities (Anderson, 1990).

Mississippian chieftains were often charismatic leaders who held the allegiance of the people subordinate to them by force of their personalities as well as through whatever powers that custom and precedent accorded them and their immediate subordinates. They also typically served as religious leaders, managing and sometimes exploiting the shared ideology that helped hold together their polities. Successful chiefdoms were those in which succession was managed according to some formal process, so that they did not collapse when a charismatic leader died. Failure of that process was one of the key causes of the political collapse of chiefdoms. Individuals, families, and larger groups moved in and out of chiefdoms as circumstances changed, for while coercion made chiefdoms stronger than tribes, people could still occasionally vote with their feet (Boudreaux, 2013).

MOUNDVILLE

The Moundville site on the Black Warrior River near Tuscaloosa, Alabama, is one of the largest and best-known Mississippian sites, apart from Cahokia (Figure 7.7). The mound site was founded after 1000 CE and thrived from around 1100–1450 CE. Large platform mounds were built around a plaza at the town's center. Smaller mounds were constructed away from the center and diminish in size the further away they are from it. This size difference is probably a reflection of the relative ranks of the extended family groups that built and maintained them (Jackson and Scott, 2003).

In total, about 29 mounds are scattered across an area of 75 ha (185 acres). The large central mound eventually reached a height of 17.5 m (57 ft), and low spots around the center of the site were filled to produce a level surface. The life of the Moundville community extended from the eleventh century through the sixteenth century CE.

Moundville maintained a permanent population of around 1,000 people at its peak, ca. 1200 CE. Around a century later the site transitioned from a residential community to a center for the dead, a necropolis supported by outlying farming residential communities (Steponaitis and Scarry, 2016).

The Black Warrior River protected the center of the town on one side and a palisade was built around the three remaining sides, encompassing the principal mounds, the plaza, and central residential areas. The palisade was rebuilt at least six times through the course of the town's six-century life.

Hernando de Soto's expedition probably visited Moundville in late 1540 CE. The center was in decline at that time, a victim of the cycling rise and fall that affected so many chiefdoms. By the time of de Soto's visit, the town was a relatively small chiefdom, one of several in the region, and no longer a preeminent center. After a few more decades, it was deserted altogether, its final days perhaps shortened by the introduction of European diseases.

FIGURE 7.7 Platform mound with reconstructed structure at Moundville

Regional Variants

The Emerald Mound site is part of the Plaquemine variant, which grew out of Troyville-Coles Creek culture in the lower Mississippi Valley and surrounding territory around 1200 CE. It combined local elements with Mississippian influences to evolve into what has sometimes been characterized as a hybrid culture. This hybridization is a characteristic of all human cultures, which combine traditional elements with adaptive traits and practices borrowed from the outside. However one characterizes them, Plaquemine societies persisted until the late seventeenth century, well into a time when our knowledge of them is supplemented by detailed written descriptions. The best known historic Plaquemine culture is that of the Natchez, which was described by early French explorers (Du Pratz, 1972).

EMERALD MOUND

The Natchez people of the Plaquemine Mississippian tradition built Emerald Mound and its surrounding town between 1250 and 1600 CE. It is an enormous quadrilateral platform about 233 m long, 133 m wide, and 9 m high with two (of an original eight) secondary mounds atop it, one of which is another 9 m high. The mound's main axis lies east-west (Figure 7.8).

This construction was the ceremonial center of a large chiefdom community that had a powerful principal chief, whose line of succession was matrilineal. Eighteenth-century French explorers described Natchez society, the only chiefdom in the Mississippi Valley to survive earlier wars and epidemics relatively intact. They named the principal chief the Great Sun. The Great Sun was always the son of the current White Woman, and he was succeeded by the son of his sister, the next White Woman. This ensured that the chiefdom stayed under the control of the single matrilineal Sun line.

Natchez chiefdom society was stratified into four ranks, with rules governing intermarriage that served to perpetuate matrilineal lines of descent. Details remain controversial, but in a general way, the Natchez case illustrates the complexity typical of Mississippian chiefdoms.

Most Natchez people lived in hamlets on hilltops and along the banks of St. Catherine Creek and its tributaries. They traveled to Emerald to participate in annual rituals, ceremonies, and games and to trade. Natchez power shifted from Emerald to the Grand Village at the site of modern Natchez, Mississippi, around 1682 CE. By 1730 CE, they were dispersed by warfare with French colonists (Brown, 1985, 1989).

Ian W. Brown

FIGURE 7.8 Emerald Mound. Note two secondary mounds

Many Plaquemine towns were reoccupied and refurbished earlier Troyville-Coles Creek towns. Plaquemine people expanded existing platforms, layering them with thick new mantels of earth and constructing new secondary mounds around them. Most residents lived in small surrounding communities rather than at major centers. Elite families and their retainers occupied major towns, and such centers were heavily populated only during major ritual events, when people from smaller communities converged on them to take part in public events.

The Natchez Grand Village had a large open plaza with temple mounds located at each end, a typical Mississippian layout. A temple built of thick cypress logs stood atop the bigger of the two mounds, its door facing the plaza. Three large wooden bird effigies surmounted its ridged thatch roof, and a perpetual fire burned in the outer room of the temple. The temple's inner room contained a stone statue of the first chieftain, probably not unlike the one found at Etowah, Georgia. This and every subsequent leader were called the "Great Sun."

At the time of European contact, the man who served as the Great Sun lived in a house on the platform mound opposite the temple across the main plaza. When an individual who held the position of Great Sun died, his house was burned, the mound was expanded and refurbished with a new mantle of earth, and a new residence was built for his successor. This process was probably how many Mississippian platforms had grown for centuries.

Sociopolitically, the Natchez Indians were hierarchically organized in a ranked or chiefdom society, in which there was little ambiguity regarding rank. The chieftain (Great Sun) and his family occupied the topmost exclusive rank of Sun. Below the rank of Sun in decreasing order of power and authority were the Nobles, Honoreds, and Stinkards (commoners) (Table 7.1). Natchez society was strongly matrilineal, so inheritance of the Great Sun's office had to descend along female lines, thereby staying in the family. The solution was for leadership to pass from the Great Sun to his sister's son rather than his own son. Leadership was thereby maintained within the same **matrilineage** and at the same rank. Were leadership to pass to a man's own son in a matrilineal system, it would necessarily pass to the matrilineage of the younger man's mother, which for reasons of marriage restriction, would normally be a different matrilineage from that of his father.

People from the upper three ranks of Natchez society were all required to marry commoners (Stinkards). The children of these unions inherited the ranks of their mothers, if their mothers held the higher rank. If a child's father was the parent holding the higher rank, the child fell into the rank one step below that of the father. Table 7.1 reveals the other reason why a Great Sun could not pass his office on to his own son. The son of the Great Sun was a member of the Noble rank, a high rank but not high enough to be a legitimate Great Sun.

Ambitious Natchez people could earn their status through outstanding military accomplishments, the sacrifice of a child in a major ritual event, or some other notable act. Du Pratz (1972) documented some of this social mobility at the time of his visit, which coincided with the funeral of Tattooed Serpent, who was the Great War Chief and the brother of the Great Sun. The funeral

TABLE 7.1 Rank inheritance in Natchez society

Mother's rank	*Father's rank*	*Child's rank*
Sun	Stinkard	Sun
Noble	Stinkard	Noble
Honored	Stinkard	Honored
Stinkard	Stinkard	Stinkard
Stinkard	Sun	Noble
Stinkard	Noble	Honored
Stinkard	Honored	Stinkard

featured human sacrifices of several kinds. Tattooed Serpent's chancellor, physician, chief domestic servant, pipe bearer, two wives, and a volunteer noble woman were all among those who were drugged, strangled, and buried with the deceased man. The Great Sun himself was despondent over the loss of his brother and had to be dissuaded from committing suicide on the occasion.

Great Suns maintained their rank and power through a combination of fear and favoritism, techniques of chieftains everywhere. Each Great Sun filled about a dozen offices with key male supporters from the higher ranks. Such systems work well as long as there is a general sense of well-being and a belief that the chieftain is successfully managing things, ranging from everyday concerns to supernatural ones. But like all chiefdoms, this one was ultimately unstable and subject to catastrophic collapse. The Natchez offer just one example of how a Mississippian chiefdom was organized.

The Natchez were later decimated by epidemics and caught in colonial power struggles between the French and the English. This decline led to population losses that were eventually too great to be offset by the adoption of refugees from other groups. The remnants of the Natchez chiefdom were dispersed after a French attack in 1731, and the Natchez disappeared from history. Most survivors took refuge with the Chickasaws and other Southeastern nations and thus became integrated into their societies while losing their separate ethnic identity. Their descendants survive among those nations, which were largely relocated to Oklahoma in the nineteenth century.

The Spiro site in eastern Oklahoma is the centerpiece of the Caddoan Mississippian and a strategic entry port for trade goods and ideas coming northward out of Mesoamerica. This variant of Mississippian culture was borne by speakers of Caddoan languages, whose modern descendants include the Wichita and the Caddo Indians. Like other Mississippian regional variants, this one exhibits the ritual trappings of the Southeastern Ceremonial Complex, objects and symbols that were shared by the elite leaders of chiefdoms across the Southeast at this time.

SPIRO

Spiro is located along the Arkansas River in eastern Oklahoma and was most prominent from CE 1200–1400 (Rogers, 2011). The site has a tripartite spatial division. The western portion of the site consists of two platform mounds, house mounds containing specialized buildings, and midden mounds. The central section was likely residential because both long-term and temporary buildings have been found. The eastern division (Figure 7.9) was focused on mortuary activity and housed the Craig and two Ward mounds (Hammerstedt et al., 2017).

FIGURE 7.9 Craig Mound at the Spiro site. Courtesy of Scott Hammerstedt

Spiro first gained national prominence in 1935 when a group of looters calling themselves the Pocola Mining Company tunneled into the Craig Mound and found a hollow chamber (later called the Great Mortuary) that contained cedar litter burials and an unparalleled number of elaborate objects made from copper, shell, stone, wood, engraved marine shell, basketry, and textiles; much of this material had been transported great distances. Later work by **WPA** crews from the University of Oklahoma salvaged what was left of the Craig Mound and tested other areas of the site.

Previous models suggested that Spiro was the economic center of a chiefdom, based on the richness of burial goods within the Great Mortuary and the presumption that elites acquired these objects through trade prior to their interment. However, a recent reinterpretation suggests the artifacts might reflect a more cosmologically based system. The Great Mortuary was repeatedly cleaned out and re-used over several hundred years. Piles of intermingled bones removed from earlier graves were placed in it along with ritually smashed objects, suggesting an emphasis on the group rather than individual elites. This ossuary lay below the hollow chamber. The chamber contained unbroken objects laid out in a systematic pattern emphasizing the Caddoan cosmological structure (Brown, 2012). This spectacular display may have been an attempt to counter climate change that eventually led to the demise of Spiro as a polity (Rohrbaugh, 2012).

Scott W. Hammerstedt

Earthen pyramids, key domesticates, symbols, and other features of Mississippian sites have long suggested direct contacts with Mesoamerican cities. Some archaeologists have been skeptical, but trace element analyses of an obsidian artifact from Spiro and a couple of specimens from coastal Texas have shown that they came from the Pachuca source in the Mexican highlands of Mesoamerica (Barker et al., 2002; White and Weinstein, 2008).

Olivella shell beads were also recovered from Spiro and other Mississippian sites. Previously, these shells were assumed to have come from the Gulf of Mexico. Many did, but beads made from *Olivella dama* have also been found at Spiro, and this species is derived from the Gulf of California. This western source of shells means that in the years around 1400 CE, the people at Spiro were acquiring marine shells by way of traders along both the Gulf Coast and the Pueblo communities of the Southwest (Kozuch, 2002).

We still have much to learn about Mississippian societies, their origins, and the ways in which they were linked to each other and to distant centers to the West and South. Future research is likely to reveal more connections between the population centers of North America than we currently appreciate. Earlier Hopewell (Chapter 6) expeditions traveled from Ohio to Yellowstone and back long before Mississippian societies arose. Aztec traders traversed the length and breadth of Mesoamerica (and conceivably beyond) when Mississippians were enjoying their heyday. Spanish explorers de Soto and Coronado are unlikely to have been the first to undertake long-distance expeditions in the interior of North America.

Art and Symbolism

The earlier widespread trade networks of the Adena and Hopewell societies had collapsed by around 400 CE, but a new one emerged connecting Mississippian centers after 1000 CE. Archaeologists refer to the emergent complex of symbols and inferred ritual as the "Southeastern Ceremonial Complex." Some sources call it the "Southern Cult," or more rarely the "Buzzard Cult" (Pauketat and Alt, 2015).

Trade and exchange of luxury goods linked the elite leaders of major centers across the Southeast. The highest-ranking elites at Cahokia were consistently buried with symbolically charged artifacts. The symbols and the artifacts bearing them were widespread among the elite leaders of major centers across the Southeast. Mound 72 at Cahokia was found to contain clear evidence of human sacrifice. Two high-ranking people were buried there, accompanied by strings of thousands of marine shell beads. There were five pits nearby that contained the remains of a dozen sacrificed adults. Elsewhere nearby in the mound were four people laid out together. Their heads and hands were missing, and they too appear to have been sacrificed (Emerson et al., 2016).

Trade in symbolically charged luxury goods connected the elites of different Mississippian centers, promoting a shared set of beliefs. The principal mechanism by which these items moved was probably down-the-line exchange between chieftains and clan leaders. Distinctive figurines and pipes (Figure 7.10) produced at Cahokia have been found in many elite Caddoan Mississippian burials, indicating a direct trade link between the two regions. Perhaps chiefly delegations made long formal trips over the ancient trail systems of the Eastern Woodlands, as political leaders are wont to do. Such politically motivated travel would have entailed plenty of gift exchange. In other cases, objects probably passed through many hands from their points of origin to ultimate destinations (Emerson et al., 2003).

Shared symbolic themes permeated the Southeastern Ceremonial Complex (Figure 7.11). How these symbolic objects were interpreted and used probably varied from one part of the region to another, and not all of them are found together consistently. But it seems clear that there was a widely shared set of objects and symbols that had some standardized meanings and uses among the chiefly elites of the region. Those who were buried with these objects probably carried them in life, and the occurrence of very similar artifacts in widely scattered sites indicates that their meanings were widely understood.

Warfare and the importance of ancestors are primary themes in the artwork of the Southeastern Ceremonial Complex, themes that are also reflected in burial practices and defensive works at Cahokia and other Mississippian sites. Embossed copper plates and disks carved from large marine shells often

FIGURE 7.10 Large smoking pipe of a kneeling female figure in the Cahokia style, from Desha County, Arkansas. Courtesy of David H. Dye

FIGURE 7.11 The Rattlesnake Disk, a circular stone **palette** with the hand-and-eye motif inside intertwined rattlesnakes, 31.9 cm (12.5 in) diameter. Moundville. Courtesy of the University of Alabama Museums

depict warriors carrying trophy heads (Figure 7.12) or symbols of office. They are frequently dressed in costumes mimicking birds of prey, such as wooden, ceramic, or stone statues (Figure 7.4) of humans found in Mississippian sites, probably intended to represent ancestors. These objects are often found buried in prominent locations, typically inside platform mounds. Minerals, crystals, bird wing fans, and rattles were also highly charged symbolic artifacts and often found with burials.

Mississippian potters made vessels in the shapes of fish, ducks, beavers, turtles, and other wetland animals. These, too, were an essential component of funerary rituals. Pots made to look like trophy heads also have been found, but archaeologists do not agree whether these represent revered ancestors or unlucky opponents. These and other human and animal effigies were often decorated with "forked-eye" designs that might have been intended to mimic the eye pattern of falcons (Figure 7.12). In other cases, eyes have lines or dots descending from them, which archaeologists have interpreted as weeping eyes.

Probably connected to the symbolic objects of the ceremonial complex was the use of "Black drink." Historic Indians in the Southeast made the ritual concoction from a species of holly (*Ilex vomitoria*). The drink is loaded with caffeine, and it acts as a strong purgative, inducing vomiting, urination, and diarrhea. The Indians, particularly adult males, used it for ritual purification, often before battle (Hudson, 1976: 226–229; Miller, 2015).

Cahokia's Monks Mound still stands adjacent to a large plaza, which was the venue for games and public ritual. All Mississippian towns featured such plazas. The game of **chunky**, or some variant of it, was probably one of the most popular games. Chunky was later documented for historic societies in the region. It was played with a pill-shaped chunky stone that was rolled across a grassy field. Young people competed by throwing spears to mark the spot where they thought the chunky stone would stop. The game tested both their judgment and their aim.

Cahokians had other amusements besides chunky. In addition to chunky, Mississippian people and their descendants played a variety of other games. Some were team sports, while others were played by individual opponents. Cornstalk shooting, the corn game, the moccasin game, the

FIGURE 7.12 Marine shell gorget showing a warrior with forked-eye facial decoration holding a trophy head and a mace. Courtesy of National Museum of the American Indian, Smithsonian Institution (D150853)

peach pit game, foot racing, stickball, dice, string games, and the pole game are among those that continued to be played following the arrival of Europeans (Fogelson, 2004;Voorhies, 2017).

Clans probably originated to facilitate fictive kinship relationships, which in turn facilitated trading partnerships between tribes. Clans later often took on marriage regulation, as rules of exogamy were extended beyond the immediate family to lineages and clans. In many tribes and chiefdoms, clans were divided into two groups called **moieties.** These served mainly to determine the makeup of teams in ball games, whether they were local or intermural events. Games did not serve merely for recreation but strengthened the social and economic links between towns and regions (Walker, 2004: 382, 386).

Resilience and Collapse

Chieftains often earned their keep by managing food surpluses, external trade, and ideological frameworks. So long as stored foods were available and they were able to maintain surpluses, the temporarily needy could be supplied with critical resources. As long as religious observances were generally perceived to be working and external threats were kept at bay, chieftains were secure in their offices. Strong leaders clearly enjoyed perquisites, but modern readers often wonder what was in it for everybody else. The answer is that chieftains provided insurance for everyone except in the event of widespread catastrophe. Chiefdoms collapsed when rare events like warfare, drought, flooding, or the death of a leader shook public confidence. Towns were increasingly fortified during 1200–1400 CE (Krus, 2016), an indication of the increasing hostilities between competitive chiefly polities.

Ironically, political collapse might also have occurred when a long period of well-being led people to conclude that the expense of leadership was no longer justified. Thus chiefdoms were inherently unstable not only because of the rare natural disaster but because, like tribes, they were made up of smaller similar units. The leaders of secondary chiefdoms allied under a dominant chieftain undoubtedly looked for opportunities to further their own interests, break away, or seize power. The paramount seat of power could lose its political supremacy quickly if its chieftain became ill or lost his capacity to meet the demands of his constituents.

The climatic conditions that had been favorable for the development of maize horticulture and urban centers during the Medieval Climate Anomaly changed around 1250 CE, leading to political instability and an intensification of warfare in the following century. A particularly severe warm-season drought prevailed 1350–1450 CE, during which time many major urban centers were abandoned. Crop failures and dislocations prompted widespread demographic upheavals (Bird et al., 2017; Dye, 2006; LeBlanc, 2006).

The collapse of Middle Mississippian chiefdoms and the abandonment of many of their towns in the fifteenth century left a comparatively vacant quarter in the American Bottom portion of the Mississippi Valley and thinner populations around centers elsewhere across the Midwest (Cobb and Butler, 2002).

The inhabitants of the vacated Midwestern towns splintered into smaller political units and resettled, sometimes not far from their previous centers, but occasionally more distantly. These populations were mainly speakers of various Siouan languages, who later moved farther westward when they were pressured by European expansion from the east and attracted by the introduction of Spanish horses from the southwest. Nations including the historic Oto, Iowa, and Missouri were descendants of the Middle Mississippian chiefdoms, people who had adapted to changing climate and competition from European colonists. To the extent possible, people continued to farm, but incorporated additional survival strategies. Many reverted to more informal tribal social organization, and the construction of platform mounds became a thing of the past. After the arrival of Europeans, some eventually adopted horses and mounted nomadism for at least part of the year, taking advantage of the bounty of bison herds on the Great Plains until they were overhunted.

The Little Ice Age, which began around 1430 CE, did not affect the Southeast as much as it did the Midwest, but the southeastern chiefdoms collapsed and dispersed in the face of devastating epidemics introduced by the Spanish, beginning in 1539 with the entrada of de Soto. The historic Creek nation was comprised of refugees from various Muskogean-speaking nations that formed in the wake of these epidemics. Other Muskogean refugees moved to Florida with escaped African slaves and filled the vacuum left there by the declining fortunes of the Timucuas and Calusas. The Florida newcomers eventually came to be known as the Seminoles (Chapter 12). The Cherokees, distant relatives of the Northern Iroquoians, were a politically disconnected set of 30 or 40 related but independent chiefdoms until depopulation and external threat forced the formation of their confederation. By the time the United States was formed, the Creek and Cherokee nations, along with the Choctaws and Chickasaws, made up what European colonists referred to as the "civilized tribes" of the Southeast. Their civilized status did not prevent them from being subjected to forced relocation, a practice that is unfortunately common in expanding empires. Most of them were forcibly moved to Oklahoma following the federal Indian Removal Act of 1830 during the Jackson administration, and many of their descendants remain there today (Fogelson, 2004).

Glossary

bastion The part of a fortification that extends beyond its wall; built so that shooting can occur in numerous directions.

charnel house A building designed to hold the remains of the deceased.

chieftain Used in this context to distinguish the leader of a chiefdom from the less powerful chief or big man of a tribal society.

chunky An Eastern Woodlands game played with stone disks and javelins on a flat playing field. The object was to determine the landing place of the disk and mark it with one's javelin.
circumscription Constraint on population expansion imposed by surrounding populations of similar type or geographic/environmental barriers.
entrada A Spanish word used to describe an overland exploring and conquering expedition.
gorget An ornamental object worn around one's throat.
matrilineage A form of social organization where membership is based on a person's mother's line of descent. Compare with **patrilineage**.
moieties A fundamental division of a community into two sections. Each moiety is usually made up of a grouping of lineages or clans.
oxbow lake A lake formed from a segment of a river left isolated when the river changes course. It typically takes the form of a crescent.
palette A thin slab of stone, wood, shell, or some other material that is decorated.
palisade A defensive wall of large posts, also called a "stockade."
patrilineage A form of social organization where membership is based on a person's father's line of descent. Compare with matrilineage.
rank Ranking involves the definition of the relative status of individuals in a social organization.
swidden A form of shifting agriculture involving field rotation and long fallow periods.
teosinte A Nahuatl (Aztec) word for a wild grass from which maize developed.
WPA The federal Works Progress Administration program.

References

Anderson, D.G. (1990). Stability and Change in Chiefdom-Level Societies: An Examination of Mississippian Political Evolution on the South Atlantic Slope. In: M. Williams and G. Shapiro, eds. *Lamar Archaeology: Mississippian Chiefdoms in the Deep South*. Tuscaloosa: University of Alabama Press.

Anderson, D.G. (1999). Examining Chiefdoms in the Southeast: An Application of Multiscalar Analysis. In: J.E. Neitzel, ed. *Great Towns and Regional Polities in the Prehistoric American Southwest and Southeast*. Albuquerque: University of New Mexico Press.

Anderson, D.G. (2004). Archaic Mounds and the Archaeology of Southeastern Tribal Societies. In: J.L. Gibson and P.J. Carr, eds. *Signs of Power: The Rise of Cultural Complexity in the Southeast*. Tuscaloosa: University of Alabama Press.

Ashley, K., Wallis, N.J., and Glascock, M.D. (2015). Forager Interactions on the Edge of the Early Mississippian World: Neutron Activation Analysis of Ocmulgee and St. Johns Pottery. *American Antiquity*, 80, pp. 290–311.

Barker, A.W., Skinner, C.E., Shackley, M.S., Glascock, M.D., and Rogers, J.D. (2002). Mesoamerican Origin for an Obsidian Scraper from the Precolumbian Southeastern United States. *American Antiquity*, 67, pp. 103–108.

Beck, R.A., Jr. (2003). Consolidation and Hierarchy: Chiefdom Variability in the Mississippian Southeast. *American Antiquity*, 68, pp. 641–661.

Bird, B.W., Wilson, J.J., Gilhooly III, W.P., Steinman, B.A., and Stamps, L. (2017). Midcontinental Native American Population Dynamics and Late Holocene Hydroclimate Extremes. *Scientific Reports*, 7, issue 41628.

Boudreaux, E.A., III (2013). Community and Ritual within the Mississippian Center at Town Creek. *American Antiquity*, 78, pp. 483–501.

Brown, I.W. (1985). *Natchez Indian Archaeology: Culture Change and Stability in the Lower Mississippi Valley*. Jackson: Mississippi Department of Archives and History.

Brown, I.W. (1989). Natchez Indians and the Remains of a Proud Past. In: N. Polk, ed. *Natchez Before 1830*. Jackson: University Press of Mississippi.

Brown, J.A. (2012). Spiro Reconsidered: Sacred Economy at the Western Frontier of the Eastern Woodlands. In: T.K. Perttula and C.P. Walker, eds. *The Archaeology of the Caddo*. Lincoln: University of Nebraska Press.

Carniero, R. (1967). On the Relationship between Size of Population and Complexity of Social Organization. *Southwestern Journal of Anthropology*, 23, pp. 234–243.
Cobb, C.R., and Butler, B.M. (2002). The Vacant Quarter Revisited: Late Mississippian Abandonment of the Lower Ohio Valley. *American Antiquity*, 67, pp. 625–641.
Du Pratz, A.S.L.P. (1972). *[1774] The History of Louisiana.* Baton Rouge, LA: Claitor's Publishing.
Dye, D.H. (2006). The Transformation of Mississippian Warfare: Four Case Studies from the Mid-South. In: E.N. Arkush and M.W. Allen, eds. *The Archaeology of Warfare: Prehistories of Raiding and Conquest.* Gainesville: University Press of Florida.
Earle, T.K. (1987). Chiefdoms in Archaeological and Ethnohistorical Perspective. *Annual Review of Anthropology*, 16, pp. 279–308.
Emerson, T.E., Hedman, K.M., Hargrave, E.A., Cobb, D.E., and Thompson, A.R. (2016). Paradigms Lost: Configuring Cahokia's Mound 72 Beaded Burial. *American Antiquity*, 81, pp. 405–425.
Emerson, T.E., Hughes, R.E., Hynes, M.R., and Wisseman, S.U. (2003). The Sourcing and Interpretation of Cahokia-Style Figurines in the Trans-Mississippi South and Southeast. *American Antiquity*, 68, pp. 287–313.
Fogelson, R., ed. (2004). *Southeast.* Washington, DC: Smithsonian Institution.
Fowler, M.L. (1997). *The Cahokia Atlas: A Historical Atlas of Cahokia Archaeology.* Urbana: Illinois Transportation Archaeological Research Program, University of Illinois, Urbana.
Galloway, P. (2004). Natchez and Neighboring Tribes. In: R.D. Fogelson, ed. *Southeast.* Washington DC: Smithsonian Institution.
Hammerstedt, S.W., Lockhart, J.J., Livingood, P.C., Mulvihill, T., Regnier, A.L., Sabo, G.I., and Samuelsen, J.R. (2017). Multisensor Remote Sensing at Spiro: Discovering Intrasite Organization. In: D.P. McKinnon and B.S. Haley, eds. *Innovative Techniques for Anthropological Applications.* Tuscaloosa: University of Alabama Press.
Hudson, C. (1976). *The Southeastern Indians.* Knoxville: University of Tennessee Press.
Jackson, H.E., and Scott, S.L. (2003). Patterns of Elite Faunal Utilization at Moundville, Alabama. *American Antiquity*, 68, pp. 552–572.
Kidder, T.R. (2004). Plazas as Architecture: An Example from the Raffman Site, Northeast Louisiana. *American Antiquity*, 69, pp. 514–532.
King, A. (2003). *Etowah: The Political History of a Chiefdom Capital.* Tuscaloosa: University of Alabama Press.
Kozuch, L. (2002). *Olivella* Beads from Spiro and the Plains. *American Antiquity*, 67, pp. 697–709.
Krus, A.M. (2016). The Timing of Precolumbian Militarization in the U.S. Midwest and Southeast. *American Antiquity*, 81, pp. 375–388.
LeBlanc, S.A. (2006). Warfare and the Development of Social Complexity. In: E.N. Arkush and M.W. Allen, eds. *The Archaeology of Warfare: Prehistories of Raiding and Conquest.* Gainesville: University Press of Florida.
Milanich, J.T. (1999). *Famous Florida Sites: Mount Royal and Crystal River.* Gainesville: University Press of Florida.
Miller, J.R. (2015). Interior Carbonization Patterns as Evidence of Ritual Drink Preparation in Powell Plain and Ramey Incised Vessels. *American Antiquity*, 80, pp. 170–183.
Milner, G.R. (1998). *The Cahokia Chiefdom: The Archaeology of a Mississippian Society.* Washington, DC: Smithsonian Institution Press.
Milner, G.R. (2004). *The Moundbuilders: Ancient Peoples of Eastern North America.* New York: Thames and Hudson.
Munoz, S.E., Gruley, K.E., Massie, A., Fike, D.A., Schroeder, S., and Williams, J.W. (2015). Cahokia's Emergence and Decline Coincided with Shifts of Flood Frequency on the Mississippi River. *Proceedings of the National Academy of Sciences*, 112, pp. 6319–6324.
Pauketat, T.R., and Alt, S.M., eds. (2015). *Medieval Mississippians: The Cahokia World.* Santa Fe: School of American Research Press.
Pauketat, T.R., Boszhardt, R.F., and Benden, D.M. (2015). Trempealeau Entanglements: An Ancient Colony's Causes and Effects. *American Antiquity*, 80, pp. 260–289.
Rogers, J.D. (2011). Spiro and the Development of a Regional Social System. In: A.K. Sievert and J.D. Rogers, eds. *Artifacts from the Craig Mound at Spiro, Oklahoma.* Washington, DC: Smithsonian Institution Contributions to Anthropology.
Rohrbaugh, C.L. (2012). *Spiro and Fort Coffee Phases: Changing Cultural Complexes of the Caddoan Area.* Norman: Oklahoma Anthropological Society.

Steponaitis, V.P., and Scarry, C.M., eds. (2016). *Rethinking Moundville and Its Hinterland.* Gainesville: University Press of Florida.

Vega, G.D.L. (1962). *The Florida of The Inca.* Austin: University of Texas Press.

Voorhies, B., ed. (2017). *Prehistoric Games of North American Indians.* Salt Lake City: University of Utah Press.

Walker, W.B. (2004). Creek Confederacy Before Removal. In: R. Fogelson, ed. *Southeast.* Washington, DC: Smithsonian Institution.

White, N.M., and Weinstein, R.A. (2008). The Mexican Connection and the Far West of the U.S. Southeast. *American Antiquity*, 73, pp. 227–277.

8

THE NORTHEASTERN FORESTS

Archaic cultures constituted a theme with many variations. As in every other region of North America, the peoples of the northern portion of the Eastern Woodlands worked with the constraints and the potentials of their environments, their technology, and their ingenuity. The Eastern Woodlands held the center of burial mound building during the heyday of Adena and Hopewell cultures. However, the construction of burial mounds was absent or late to arrive around the Great Lakes and in the northeast (Figure 8.1).

A series of related Archaic cultures emerged across the Great Lakes region and along the Northeast coast after 5000 BCE. They are recognized by specific projectile point types, as well as spear thrower weights (bannerstones) and semilunar slate knives. In the upper Great Lakes craftspeople of this widespread culture learned to fashion points and other artifacts from nuggets of native copper, found mainly on the Keweenaw Peninsula of northern Michigan. This variant is often referred to as Old Copper culture. Working copper nuggets required the development of a whole new set of techniques that were not at all like those used to chip or grind stone tools. The same copper source was also important to later moundbuilder cultures discussed in Chapter 6.

The Maritime Archaic culture, which also emerged after 5000 BCE along the coast of northern New England, the Maritime Provinces, and the Atlantic Provinces of Canada, featured lavish burials. These were often placed in natural gravelly kames or **esker**s, glacial features that presaged artificial mound building (Tuck, 1984). Curiously the later artificial mounds described in Chapter 6 were never common here despite the early use of these natural mounds.

The Maritime Archaic people used red ocher (iron-rich hematite), causing them to be known as the "Red Paint People" in the popular literature of the last century (Figure 8.2). They used heavy ground stone **celt**s, axes, **gouge**s, and **adze**s as woodworking tools, probably to construct large dugout canoes and perhaps other things now long since decayed to dust. We infer that they were making substantial canoes because swordfish were one of their favorite targets. These large ocean fish do not come near shore, but occasionally bask on the surface of the Gulf of Maine, where they could only be hunted from boats at sea. Swordfish rostra (swords) were fashioned into engraved bayonet-like spears and daggers, then later left behind in shell middens along the coast (Bourque, 2001: 37–74).

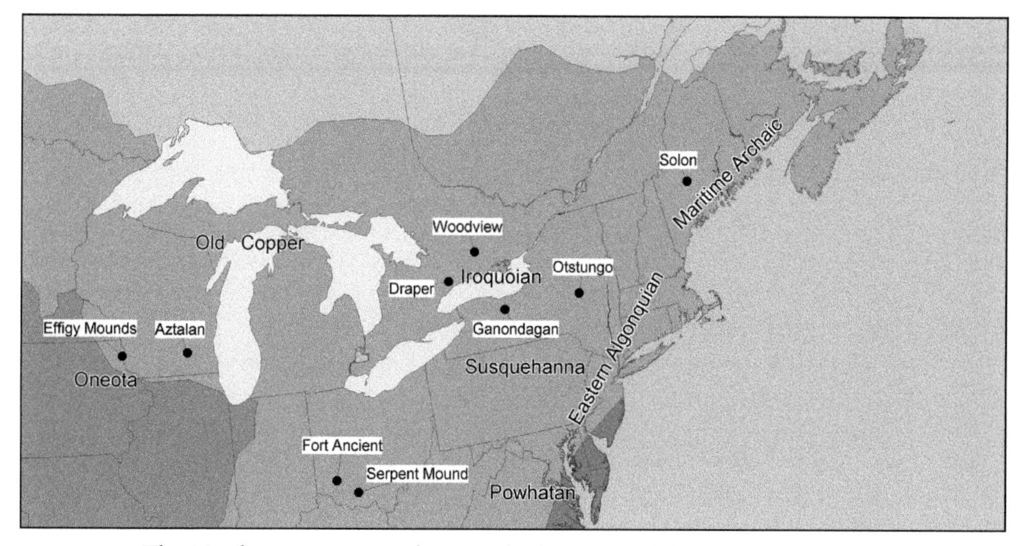

FIGURE 8.1 The Northeastern Forests, showing the locations of the sites and cultures mentioned in this chapter

FIGURE 8.2 Four Maritime Archaic gouges, ground stone tools used in heavy woodworking. The largest is 28 cm (11 in) long

Slate bayonets that mimicked the rostra were also made, but it is hard to say how these fragile artifacts might have been used. They turn up with woodworking tools, points, fishnet sinkers (plummets), and other distinctive artifacts in ocher-lined graves in cemeteries near estuaries and streams in Maine, the Maritimes, and Newfoundland (Snow, 1980: 187–222). There was also long-distance trade, as evidenced in Maine sites by elegant projectile points made from an exquisite smoky quartzite known as Ramah Chert, quarried in Labrador.

Environmental change and technological innovation brought a replacement of the Maritime Archaic and related adaptations by culture(s) from the Middle Atlantic region after 1700 BCE. Some made **steatite** containers that presaged pottery.

Environment and Adaptation

The weather systems that affect the Northeast tend to come from the west and northwest, bringing frigid air in the winters and fair skies in the summers. Winters can be very cold, and the snow deep. Areas downwind from any of the Great Lakes tend to get very heavy snowfalls, yet summers can be hot, humid, and productive for people reliant on plant foods.

The rugged landscape of New England is an ancient geological gift from another of the earth's great tectonic plates, long ago grafted on to the North American continent. The metamorphosed bedrocks of New England do not make agriculture easy even in the southern parts, where the growing season is generally adequate for it. Maize and other imported domesticates arrived late and did not always fare well. Northern New England and the Maritime provinces remained in the hands of hunter-gatherers until the arrival of European settlers. The spruce and fir forests of the northern part of the region were most easily traversed in swift birchbark canoes, whereas the more temperate forests of the southern part were laced with overland trails.

Demography and Conflict

The origins of the Maritime Archaic peoples of the Northeast Coast, and those of analog cultures in the Great Lakes basin, are uncertain. The replacement of these impressive cultures by Susquehanna and other traditions from the south were swift enough and pervasive enough to suggest population expansion and replacement, but the processes by which it all happened are uncertain.

Later change in the northeastern forests came from two directions. One of these was from the south. Fort Ancient culture developed after 1000 CE in southern Ohio (Chapter 6). Current evidence suggests that some of the Mississippians relocated up the Ohio River to land less subject to drought conditions. They made an important contribution to this emergent culture, probably including new strains of maize (Comstock and Cook, 2018).

Central and Eastern Algonquians

While the introduction of new domesticates from the south led to a northward expansion of farming, a second source of change arrived with the southward expansion of northerners into the region. This is the same time and area in which archaeologists have found Point Peninsula culture, which is identified mainly by its distinctive pottery. The evidence indicates that these people used wild rice, fishing gear, freshwater fish, and had tribal political organization, but that they lacked maize and did not take marine fish. These were probably the ancestors of the speakers of Algonquian languages.

Around 1600 CE, the Upper Great Lakes basin was inhabited primarily by speakers of Central Algonquian languages. Another branch of the family, the Eastern Algonquians, was distributed down the East Coast, from the Atlantic Provinces of Canada to coastal North Carolina. The latter distribution suggests a slow southward migratory expansion of Eastern Algonquians. This probably occurred sometime after 500 CE. Some of the Algonquians that settled along the middle Atlantic coast adopted maize horticulture more aggressively than those that retained more mixed economies. In those cases, horticulture in turn facilitated the rise of chiefdoms in a few places in the southern part of the Eastern Algonquian range. The best known of these is the historic Powhatan chiefdom of coastal Virginia (Potter, 1993).

Northern Iroquoians

The wedge-shaped distribution of Northern Iroquoian languages between the Central and Eastern Algonquian suggests that they expanded into the region from the south, along the axis of the Appalachian Mountains, and this hypothesis is supported by archaeological and genetic evidence (Snow, 1996). However, the timing remains controversial. Amidst this flow of innovations from both the south and the north, Iroquoian cultures pressed northward, probably encouraged by warming climate and carrying new strains of maize that grew well on upland glacial soils. By the sixteenth century CE, the northern forests were populated by a mix of farmers and hunter-gatherer cultures, some of whom later became major players in history of the colonial era, while others disappeared in the epidemics that followed settlement by Europeans.

The system of nucleated Northern Iroquoian villages and densely packed **matrilocal** houses suppressed internal competition between sets of related males and very effectively redirected their energies to the outside world. Smaller, less permanent, and more fractious groups of hunter-gatherers could not compete effectively with them, so it is no surprise that Northern Iroquoian villages propagated quickly across the interior Northeast after their first appearance (Divale, 1984). Smaller, more mobile hunter-gatherer communities were either displaced or absorbed by the proliferating Iroquoian farming communities.

The dense, compact, semi-permanent villages were possible because farming produced the necessary food. Maize and squash were staples early on, and beans were added later. Beans did not become an important dietary component in the Eastern Woodlands after 1200 CE, but beans in combination with maize eventually provided an important new source of protein that reduced dependence upon meat protein. This in turn allowed populations to grow even as changing climatic conditions began to compress village clusters into a shrinking array of suitable environments.

The way in which Northern Iroquoian villages propagated across the region led to the establishment of clusters of communities, which in turn differentiated into separate linguistic and political populations over time. The archaeological evidence of the growth and development of Northern Iroquoian **nation**s and confederacies can be tracked through large-scale demographic shifts. Hundreds of their village sites have been located, mapped, tested, and dated. A regional map that is redrawn for each decade from 1000 CE through the colonial period shows the appearance and disappearance of communities at those sites as they built and abandoned villages in quick succession. It is likely that few large villages have been missed by archaeologists, and it is rare that the same location was occupied more than once. The demands of swidden farming kept the communities moving every decade or two, so the regional maps show a constantly changing pattern over time.

Regional conflict caused Northern Iroquoian villages to aggregate into larger communities in the fifteenth century. These were typically palisaded and more frequently built on defensible sites than previously. This set the scene for the emergence of multivillage nations and confederacies, which came to dominate the region during the period of European colonization (Birch, 2012).

Subsistence and Economy

Wild rice (*Zizania aquatica*) is a tall, graceful, aquatic plant that became a staple food for people living in the Great Lakes region, from northern Minnesota to New Brunswick (Britton and Brown,

1923: 168). It is most abundant in Minnesota and Wisconsin, in precisely the zone where maize agriculture is possible but too risky to be relied upon as a dependable staple food.

Early farming in the Southeast produced maize varieties that could mature in significantly fewer than 200 days. Communities that farmed with the new varieties were able to hive off and establish themselves on suitable land farther north. Subsequently they spread to the ecological limits of the new varieties, far beyond the northern fringes of Mississippian societies. The new constraint became the line of 120 frost-free days, which today meanders through the Great Lakes region and across New England. Enterprising farming communities, or at least farming practices, spread northward to this new limit as domesticates adapted to shorter growing seasons emerged.

The expansion of northern farmers was further encouraged by the Medieval Maximum, a long-term warm spell that peaked around 1000 CE. Northern farming was a fortunate combination of environmental opportunity, the right plant domesticates, ingenuity, and enterprise. This led to population growth and competition for the best agricultural land. Over the course of a few centuries the landscape filled to near the maximum allowed by the prevailing adaptation. Deer were still a critical resource, hides were needed for clothing, and meat was needed for protein. But there was a limit to how many deer the forest could provide. Even at population densities far below those of today, the Indians of the northern forests were pressing the limits of sustainability, simply because a few such critical resources like deer could not be increased or replaced by substitutes (Milner, 2004: 121–123).

There is little or no macroscopic evidence (carbonized kernels or cobs) to indicate that maize was an important domesticate or even present in the region prior to 900 CE. The evidence of microscopic phytoliths is sometimes used to argue for an earlier presence of maize, but more basic research is needed. In the absence of carbonized kernels or cobs, the validity of the phytolith approach remains a subject of current debate. Evidence from the American Bottom and western Illinois shows that maize was not an important cultivated crop even there until about 900 CE, making its earlier presence in the Northeast very unlikely. Clarification may be provided by the continuing analysis of ^{13}C, a carbon isotope favored by maize, in cooking pot residues (Gates St-Pierre and Thompson, 2015; Hart et al., 2012; Simon, 2017).

New England and the Maritime Provinces

The historic Algonquian groups of northern New England, Quebec, and the Maritime Provinces of Canada lived beyond the limits of reliable maize agriculture. So did the Ojibwa (Chippewa) and other Central Algonquian peoples living just north of the Great Lakes to the west. These more northern Algonquian peoples were all mostly dependent upon hunting and gathering in the sixteenth century. Some traded for maize with the Northern Iroquoian farming communities living just south of them, supplying much-needed hides and furs in exchange. They were clearly familiar with maize and other domesticates, but the risk of crop failure was too great for them to adopt farming in this cool transitional region.

There were also reversals of fortune. The cycle of climate change eventually led to cooler conditions, and by 1430 CE, the cold episode known as the "Little Ice Age" was weighing heavily upon the northern farmers, just as it weighed upon the Mississippian polities to the south. Competition for land and other resources increased and villages increasingly relocated to defensible locations behind palisades. Shortened growing seasons forced the complete abandonment of some areas where farming had previously been possible. But for the most part the northern farmers were able to hang on. They remained scattered across the northern forests until the coming of Europeans. Some of them disappeared in the waves of epidemics that swept ahead of the newcomers in the sixteenth century, but others fared better, playing important roles in the political and military struggles of the colonial era and leaving communities of descendants that survive to this day.

Lower Great Lakes

The Northern Iroquoians practiced upland swidden farming techniques that required frequent moves. The farmers of the northern forests had to adopt this form of shifting agriculture because of the nature of their forest environment. They opened fields in the forest by girdling and killing trees to let the sun reach the forest floor and by burning off underbrush. There is no turf on the forest floor, so the newly opened fields had soils that were easy to work. Upland swidden farming was a successful strategy in a region where rich floodplains were in short supply. In contrast, Mississippian farmers in the Southeast often raised crops year after year on rich river bottom soils that were replenished annually by spring flooding (Ellis and Ferris, 1990).

The productivity of upland soil dwindles over time in the absence of animal fertilizer. As long as animal husbandry was not available to Indian farmers, fertilizer was in very short supply. Pests also built up in cleared fields as fertility fell, so the best solution was to clear additional fresh fields in the forest nearly every few years. This went on as older fields were abandoned to lie fallow and revert to forest. Swidden farmers thus constantly opened new fields and abandoned older ones in order to keep productivity high.

Crops were planted in small hills mounded by hand between the skeletal trees of the dead and partially cleared forest. Men did most of the heavy clearing, and women were responsible for the planting, tending, and harvesting of crops. This was probably an outgrowth of a very ancient division of labor between hunting and gathering. More importantly, we know from ethnology that Iroquoian women also ran the affairs of the village, while the domain of men was the forest beyond the edges of the woods outside their villages.

Swidden farming entailed periodic village relocations because new active fields tended to be opened farther and farther away from the settlements. This periodic shifting of fields and settlements forestalled the development of strong systems of land tenure and permanent architecture. So long as there was a vast forest of uncleared upland available people did not have to fight over farmland. While Mississippian farmers vied with each other for permanent use of rich river bottomlands, the northern swidden farmers competed mainly for much larger and more vaguely defined tracts of hunting territory.

Upper Great Lakes and Upper Mississippi River

The peoples of the Upper Great Lakes region also adopted swidden farming techniques, and they never gave up their hunting and gathering strategies. They lived near the northern limits of farming, and climatic cycles occasionally pushed those limits southward, forcing them to fall back on ancient food-getting practices. The expansion of displaced eastern Indians into and through this region after 1600 CE disrupted and displaced many of these cultures, making it difficult to connect them with the archaeological traditions that came before.

Serpent Mound is a unique large effigy in southern Ohio, but many more animal effigy mounds are found in southern Wisconsin and parts of adjacent states. Effigy mounds range in frequency from at least 10,000 to as many as 30,000, mostly located in the largely unglaciated "driftless" region of southern Wisconsin and nearby portions of Minnesota, Iowa, and Illinois (Theler and Boszhardt, 2006). With some modifications, people in the region continued the tradition of building small family burial mounds. Many of their mounds were laid out in the shapes of animals. Although the dating is uneven, many of the effigy mound sites date from approximately 650 to 1300 CE (Milner, 2004: 106–109).

SERPENT MOUND

Serpent Mound is one of the largest and most iconic effigy mounds in North America. Situated on a narrow bluff overlooking Ohio Brush Creek, the entire effigy is 427 m (1,400 ft) long and 1.5 m (5 ft) high at its highest point (Figure 8.3).

At the head of the serpent, there is a large, oval embankment 49 m (160 ft) in longest diameter, which has been variously interpreted as the serpent's eye, its gaping mouth, or a separate object, such as an egg clutched in the serpent's open jaws. There also is a wishbone-shaped earthwork that partially surrounds the oval earthwork. It may be part of the serpent's head or a separate effigy, such as a frog.

Frederic Ward Putnam (1890) investigated Serpent Mound and much of the surrounding landscape between 1887 and 1889. He explored the serpent effigy as well as two Adena culture burial mounds (circa 800 BC to AD 100), one Fort Ancient culture burial mound (circa AD 1000 to 1650), and an extensive Fort Ancient habitation site that was built upon an earlier occupation by the Adena culture (Putnam, 1890).

Initially, Serpent Mound was assumed to have been built by the Adena culture simply due to the proximity of the two Adena burial mounds. Radiocarbon dates published in 1996 indicated a Fort Ancient age for Serpent Mound, while dates reported in 2014 suggested it was built originally by the Adena culture and later refurbished by the Fort Ancient culture, but the Adena dates have been questioned (Lepper, 2018; Lepper et al., 2018; Romain and Herrmann, 2018; Romain et al., 2017).

FIGURE 8.3 Serpent Mound, Ohio, from the air. Courtesy of the Ohio Historical Society

Serpent symbolism and effigy mounds were important in the Fort Ancient era and virtually absent in the Adena culture, which supports the argument that Serpent Mound fits more reasonably into this later time period. In the traditions of many American Indian tribes, the Great Serpent is the lord of the Beneath World, and it appears likely that Serpent Mound was a shrine devoted to this powerful spirit.

Brad Lepper

Effigy mound forms appear to have favored birds, serpents, wolves, birds, elk, bears, turtles, and panthers, or at least those are the taxa archaeologists have assigned them. Some of the bird effigies have enormous wingspans. Some mounds have been identified as lizards or other less likely creatures, although many of the identifications are more than a little speculative. Numerous mounds continued to be simple earthen domes or stretched-out linear mounds.

Most effigy mounds have dedicatory hearths, often where the hearts of the animals depicted would have been located. Many but not all contain primary and secondary burials, both extended and flexed in form. Grave offerings appear to have been confined to the personal possessions of the deceased.

Effigy mounds were typically constructed in single building episodes. Usually sod was first stripped from the ground to define the outline of the effigy, and then one or a few individuals were buried in the head or heart area of the effigy. Finally, earth was mounded up over the entire stripped area.

The people of the effigy mound culture were primarily hunter-gatherers with plant cultivation most likely providing a minor component of the diet. They did produce pottery, although population density seems to have been lower than that of the earlier Hopewell people. Clusters of effigy mounds were probably important seasonal sites where people not only gathered to bury the recently deceased but also conducted important ceremonies, renewed friendships, and arranged marriages.

EFFIGY MOUNDS

Effigy Mounds National Monument, managed by the National Park Service, is home to over 200 earthen funerary monuments built by Woodland Tradition communities between 0–1200 CE. The main monument, located on the Mississippi River bluffs just north of McGregor, Iowa, features an interpretive center and nearly 100 mounds arranged in linear "processions" typical of upland sites in the locality. The separate Sny Magill unit, 18 km (11 mi) south of McGregor, preserves a large lowland group of over 100 mounds.

Excavation and research in the monument has illuminated local evolution of mound ceremony from the period of Middle Woodland Hopewellian exchange (0–500 CE) to the peak of the Late Woodland Effigy Mound ceremonial complex (EMCC) when most mounds in the monument were erected. During that period, there was a shift from group burial to single or small-group burial, mounds were built more frequently, and status-related mortuary offerings were discarded in favor of elaboration of mound form. By 700 CE, conical, compound, linear, and effigy mounds were all being built, perhaps to commemorate deceased originating from different social strata or subgroups within Late Woodland society (Figure 8.4).

The monument is at the western periphery of the EMCC, within the geographic extent of the Keyes/Eastman phase (ca. 700–1200 CE), characterized by increased population density, seasonal upland–lowland movement within circumscribed territories, intensive collection of shellfish and tree nuts, and the cultivation of small amounts of maize. Locally, the monument falls within a cluster of effigy mound sites notable for the almost exclusive construction of bear and bird forms, suggesting that social power within the regional community may have been held by individuals or groups associated with bear and bird forms, in contrast to adjacent communities where fork-tailed bird, raptor, canine, and/or other effigy forms predominate (Alex, 2000; Birmingham and Rosebrough, 2017; Emerson et al., 2000).

Amy L. Rosebrough

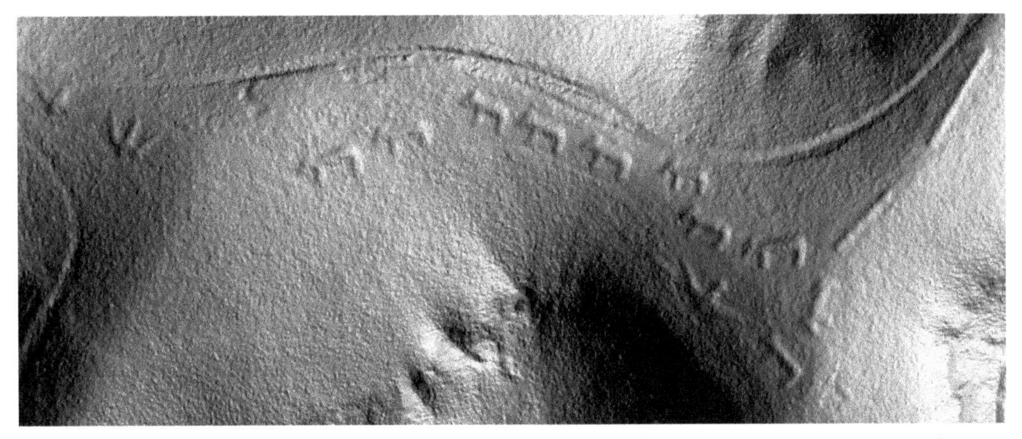

FIGURE 8.4 Marching bears and birds at Effigy Mounds National Monument, Iowa. Horizontal image distance ca. 600 m. NPS LiDAR image

The archaeology of Siouan-speaking cultures with connections to Mississippian centers is complicated. Speakers of Siouan languages pushed northward during the warm years of the Medieval Maximum, establishing what is known as Oneota culture. The previous occupants of the region, the builders of the effigy mound sites, withdrew northward. This might have been because their system collapsed when overhunting reduced critical deer populations, or it might have been more simply their inability to compete with better-adapted Oneota farmers (Theler and Boszhardt, 2006). Oneota eventually spread over Iowa, southern Wisconsin, and portions of adjoining states. Still later it gave rise to historic Siouan societies of the Upper Midwest, some of which subsequently took to mounted nomadic lives on the Great Plains. There are many archaeological phases in this region, most of which led one way or another to various historic tribes. However, the details of those lineages are very difficult to discern archaeologically.

Oneota economy was focused on maize agriculture combined with seasonal forays to the Great Plains for bison hunting. The early Oneota villagers built burial mounds but they later shifted to burying the dead in cemeteries, a change that ended construction of earthen burial mounds in the region. The region also saw the establishment of colonial settlements that originated from Middle Mississippian sources (Chapter 7). A well-known example of this is Aztalan, a palisaded Mississippian colonial site in southern Wisconsin.

AZTALAN

Aztalan is an ancient Native American palisaded town-and-mound site located in southern Wisconsin on a glacial lake terrace and recessional moraine along the west bank of the Crawfish River about a mile east of the modern town of Lake Mills (Birmingham and Goldstein, 2005). The site was designated as a National Historic Landmark in 1964, and today is a state park managed by the Wisconsin Department of Natural Resources and open to visitors year-round (Figure 8.5). Nearly a century of professional archaeological investigations has resulted in about 10% of the site being excavated. The accumulated data from these excavations have yielded grit-tempered cord-marked ceramics, which are associated with a Late Woodland occupation dating between roughly 800 and 1200 CE, and shell-tempered pottery that represents a Middle Mississippian occupation dating between about 1050 and 1200 CE (Richards, 2008).

FIGURE 8.5 One of two platform mounds inside a reconstructed palisade and four bastions at the Aztalan site, Wisconsin

Based on ceramic style, some of the Late Woodland residents likely migrated to Aztalan from Illinois, while others may have been local. Thin-section analyses of ceramics and strontium isotope studies of human skeletal remains indicate that at least some of the Mississippian settlers migrated directly from the Cahokia area, near present-day St. Louis, and joined the existing Late Woodland community. Following the influx of Mississippian migrants, this coalescent community was rapidly transformed by the construction of three earthen platform mounds and a sequence of substantial wooden walls studded with bastions – all highly visible hallmarks of the Middle Mississippian archaeological cultural tradition – as well as other efforts at landscape modification in nonresidential areas of the site. Plant and animal remains that have been recovered from the site indicate reliance on locally available foods, including numerous fish species, freshwater clams, other aquatic animals, waterfowl, deer, elk, various small mammals and birds, nuts, squash, corn, *Chenopodium*, and small amounts of other cultigens and wild plants. Although the site is often described as an isolated northern outpost of Cahokia, artifacts made from copper, pipestone, and silicified sandstone hint at connections across Wisconsin and the Upper Midwest (Schroeder and Goldstein, 2016).

Sissel Schroeder

Architecture and Technology

Historic Eastern Algonquians in the northern woodlands lived in bark-covered houses made with frameworks of bent saplings and often covered with flattened sheets of bark. Mats or hides were also used, depending upon what was available. These **wigwam** dwellings were designed to house nuclear families or modest extended families (Figure 8.6). In a few cases, people lived in elongated multifamily wigwams, structures designed to expand as needed to hold large extended families (Snow, 1980).

An important bit of linguistic evidence is that the partially reconstructed Proto-Algonquian language had terms for the bow and arrow. Archaeological evidence also indicates that they had this new weapon by at least 600 CE and probably earlier (Blitz, 1988; Fiedel, 1994). They probably acquired the bow and arrow from ancestral Inuits living far to the north in Arctic Canada, who had possessed the weapon for many centuries. The bow and arrow explain why projectile point sizes were much smaller in the first millennium CE, and they partially explain why the Algonquians had an adaptive advantage and were able to spread southward (Engelbrecht, 2014; Tomka, 2013).

FIGURE 8.6 A typical wigwam. Evidence is often limited to a stone hearth and post molds

The birchbark canoe was another of their technological advantages. This light and versatile craft is perfect for the chains of lakes, rivers, and streams that thread the dense forests on flat glaciated landscapes where the northern parts of the Eastern Woodlands slowly give way to the subarctic forests of eastern Canada. For at least the last 2,000 years, trails from this transitional zone northward have been mainly short portages between water routes, places where generations of people carrying canoes beat deep paths that are still used today. Once reliable birchbark canoes were available, they were the transportation mode of choice across this region, much better than dugouts.

The perishable nature of birchbark and the light wooden frames of the canoes has frustrated the attempts of archaeologists to determine when and how this craft was first developed. So far, the best approach has been the logical elimination of alternative possibilities. Dugouts were popular before 1500 BCE in northern New England. After that, influences and perhaps immigrants appear to have had more southern origins. If birchbark canoes were one of the adaptive advantages that propelled the Algonquian expansion in the first millennium CE, then we can infer their presence in the region by that time, even in the absence of clear archaeological evidence (Snow 1980).

Northern Iroquoians

The Northern Iroquoians reckoned descent and clan membership through female lines, and their longhouse architecture was designed to accommodate those practices. Residence after marriage was with the woman's family in a household managed by a senior woman. Accordingly, the Iroquoian longhouse was large, a multifamily household that could expand to accommodate more nuclear families as daughters brought home new husbands. The archaeological evidence for these social

FIGURE 8.7 The Draper site in Ontario shows the tight packing of multifamily longhouses in an unusually large village. Courtesy of the Museum of Ontario Archeology

arrangements is found in the layouts of tightly packed longhouse villages and the regular internal layouts of the longhouses (Figure 8.7).

The classic Iroquoian longhouse was a structure of variable length, about 3 **fathom**s (5.5 m or 18 ft) wide, and as long as it needed to be to house an extended family of related women, their husbands, and their children. Each longhouse had a central aisle a fathom wide with living areas on each site. A central fire in the aisle was shared by the nuclear families on either side of the aisle. Each family had a berth for sleeping and a set of work and storage areas. Because five was the average size of a nuclear family, each compartment of a longhouse was about as long as it was wide and contained about ten people on average. Some longhouses were very long, had many compartments, and housed dozens of people. Even recreated shorter longhouses seem immense when one enters them (Snow, 1997).

GANONDAGAN

The Onöndowa'ga:' are the westernmost nation of the Hodinöhsö:ni' (Iroquois) Confederacy. The archeological story, tells us that they emerged as a distinct people near the southern tip of Canandaigua Lake in New York, which is further confirmed by oral history (Doty, 1925). The Onöndowa'ga:' formed themselves into two branches: a western and eastern sequence of towns.

Ganöndagë:n, the "town surrounded by the color white" was part of the eastern town sequence that followed the Honeoye and Mud Creek Valleys north (Wray and Schoff,

FIGURE 8.8 Reconstructed longhouse at Ganondagan. Gabled roofs replaced arched roofs as architecture evolved through the seventeenth century. Courtesy of Michael Galban

1953:53–54). Construction of town began in the 1660s and, when complete, was widely regarded as the largest Onöndowa'ga:' community. Evidence of population and food production estimates are staggering. In 1677, Englishman, Wentworth Greenhalgh recorded 150 bark houses at Ganöndagë:n, and when the French invaded in 1687, they recorded 1.2 million bushels of corn destroyed while in Onöndowa'ga:' country alone (Greenhalgh, 1849–1851; Mt Pleasant and Burt, 2010).

Today, Ganöndagë:n is a center for Hodinöhsö:ni' studies and a NYS Historic Site open to the public. It encompasses 570+ acres, interpretive walking trails, and the newly founded Seneca Art & Culture Center, which houses hundreds of artifacts from the original town as well as contemporary Onöndowa'ga:' art in a large gallery setting.

Michael Galban

The longhouses were built with frameworks of saplings and covered with large sheets of bark, typically elm bark where that tree was abundant. The archaeological evidence for the longhouses consists of lines of hearths and rows of **post molds** left behind by the sapling frameworks (Figure 8.8). These were clearly designed to serve as residences for a decade or two, about the amount of time separating village relocations. More permanent houses would not have been worth the investment given the demands of swidden farming and the diminishing availability of firewood close by. But while they were occupied, some Northern Iroquoian villages grew to be large dense ceramic-producing communities containing dozens of longhouses (Figure 8.9).

Culture, Language, and Identity

Northern Iroquoians

Historic Northern Iroquoian communities were strongly matrilineal and matrilocal, similar to the Pueblos of the Greater Southwest (Chapter 10). However, Northern Iroquoian communities never had the equivalents of kivas, places for related men to come together. Instead, Northern Iroquoian

FIGURE 8.9 The contrasting shapes of traditional Iroquoian and Algonquian pottery relates to their uses and thermal properties. Iroquoian pots (left) are usually collared and round bottomed. Algonquian pots (right) more often have conical bottoms like this early Vinette 1 example from Milford, Connecticut. Left, 34 cm (13.5 in) tall, Walter Elwood Museum. Right, 24 cm (9.5 in) tall, American Indian Archaeological Institute. Resized for comparison

men were often away from the village hunting, on diplomatic missions, or at war, especially during the warm months.

The best known Northern Iroquois confederacy was known to the English as the League of the Iroquois. The confederacy is known as the Haudenosaunee (People of the Longhouse) to the Iroquois themselves, and descendant organizations still exist in New York and Ontario. The other three Northern Iroquoian confederacies probably had similar internal structures and ritual, so the League of the Iroquois is an instructive case study for understanding all of them.

Central and Eastern Algonquians

The Algonquian-speaking cultures of the Northeast were split between northern hunter-gathers and southern farmers at the time they were first contacted by expanding European settlers. The northerners in particular reflected cultural and religious beliefs that contrasted with those of their Iroquoian neighbors. Shamanism was important to the Algonquians, and it found expression in rock art, which is not at all common among Iroquoians.

Those Eastern Algonquians that pushed farthest south through coastal Virginia and into North Carolina lived in comparatively large farming communities. Some grew to be large, dense, sedentary communities that evolved from tribal polities into chiefdoms. The best known of these is the historic Powhatan chiefdom.

Like all chiefdoms, the Powhatan chiefdom was an unstable one. It depended upon a regular flow of both commodities and luxury goods to elite leaders. The production of these goods was managed by segmentary kin groups, and it was not so much surplus production as it was an obligatory provisioning of the political leadership by lower-ranking families. Disease spread through Powhatan villages after the establishment of a Spanish mission in the area in the sixteenth century. This caused a sudden decline in the local population, and the chiefdom fell apart politically (Barker, 1992).

Art and Symbolism

The engraved rostra and slate bayonets of the Maritime Archaic are only some of the artifacts that carry artistic decorations. Some of these artifacts could have had few if any practical uses, so it is possible that they were made for their symbolic values alone. Another class of artifacts found with them are long (±80 cm) stone cylinders that sometimes have holes for suspension at one end. These have long been labeled as whetstones or pestles, but they show no signs of wear that would be associated with those implied uses. These "Passadumkeag problematicals" were more likely stone bells, made for their acoustical qualities (Caldwell, 2013; Moorehead, 1922: 54, 72).

Central and Eastern Algonquians

Enigmatic pictographs are scattered on rock faces throughout the canoe country drained by the Great Lakes (Furtman, 2000). More are found in New England. Local archaeological sequences have revealed the details of early Algonquian adaptation to the environments of the Northeast, both interior and coastal, and this has been supplemented by their rock art, mainly petroglyphs, also found at many sites across the region. Fortunately, gaps in these lines of evidence have been partially filled by ethnographic knowledge from surviving Eastern and Central Algonquian cultures. We know that the Algonquians that lived beyond the limits of farming in southern Canada and northern New England had weak forms of tribal political organization in which leading men maintained their positions through the interconnected application of personal charisma, shamanistic power, and virility, all of which find expression in their rock art. As late as the nineteenth century, these elements were still combined in male chiefs of the Penobscot nation in Maine (Snow, 1976).

The Woodview petroglyphs in Ontario and the Solon petroglyphs in Maine are both excellent records of the themes of shamanistic transformation and sexuality in Algonquian cultures. One large female figure at Woodview was carved over a pocket in the rock face that contained a mineral that ran red whenever it rained, making it appear that the figure was menstruating. A modern museum structure over the site now protects the petroglyphs, but at the expense of ending the occasional display of its most dynamic feature.

The Solon petroglyphs, which were carved on a rock ledge that projects into the Kennebec River in Maine, represent houses, people in canoes, birds, and other animals. But there are also many phallic males, squatting females, and disembodied phalluses and vulvas, another instance of the close association of sexuality and shamanistic power in Algonquian cultures. These linkages were still apparent in the traditional leadership of Eastern Algonquian tribes living in Maine in the nineteenth century.

Northern Iroquoians

The historic Northern Iroquoian confederacies formed during the course of the late sixteenth and early seventeenth centuries, each consisting of three or more previously independent nations. Their formation was marked in the archaeological record by a new surge in trade and exchange between former enemies, particularly the exchange of ceramic effigy smoking pipes. Men made and carried

FIGURE 8.10 A human effigy smoking pipe, Otstungo site, New York. Collections of the New York State Museum. Drawing courtesy of Gene McKay

elaborate pipes for the smoking ritual that was so important for diplomacy and the maintenance of partnerships. It is not surprising that pipes often became gifts and found their way into deposits far from their places of manufacture (Kuhn and Sempowski, 2001; Wonderly, 2005).

Northern Iroquoians are also well known for the masks (false faces) they used in curing. They have prehistoric prototypes, as shown by some of their smoking pipes depicting them (Figure 8.10). But surviving examples are carved of wood and are decorated with horsehair and brass. Neither the decorations nor the metal tools needed to carve the masks were available before the arrival of Europeans, so it is likely that both the masks and associated curing ceremonies were greatly elaborated in the wake of the catastrophic epidemics that began in the seventeenth century (Fenton, 1987).

The currency of the historic Iroquoians and Algonquians, and many other political interactions of the colonial years, was marine shell **wampum** (Figure 8.11). Marine shell beads had been popular for centuries, but the availability of European metal tools after 1600 CE made it possible for New England Algonquian craftspeople to make small tubular beads in a standard size. As with the Mississippians, marine shell was apparently charged with supernatural power, and the desire for it was strong. Wampum came in two colors, white from whelk columns and purple from quahog valves. Strings of beads that combined the two colors in various ways quickly became popular as symbols and memory aids in Algonquian and Iroquoian communities. As wampum beads proliferated, people began weaving them into belts having politically and religiously significant functions. These became important for the conduct of seventeenth-century colonial politics, and they remain symbolically important to the Iroquois today. Wampum beads and a wide variety of glass trade beads are among the key artifacts used to date American Indian sites of the colonial era (Fenton, 1998: 224–239).

The peoples of this region all spent long hours indoors during long winters. Their games tended to be games of chance involving bowls or moccasins, along with marked counters. Gambling was often part of gaming.

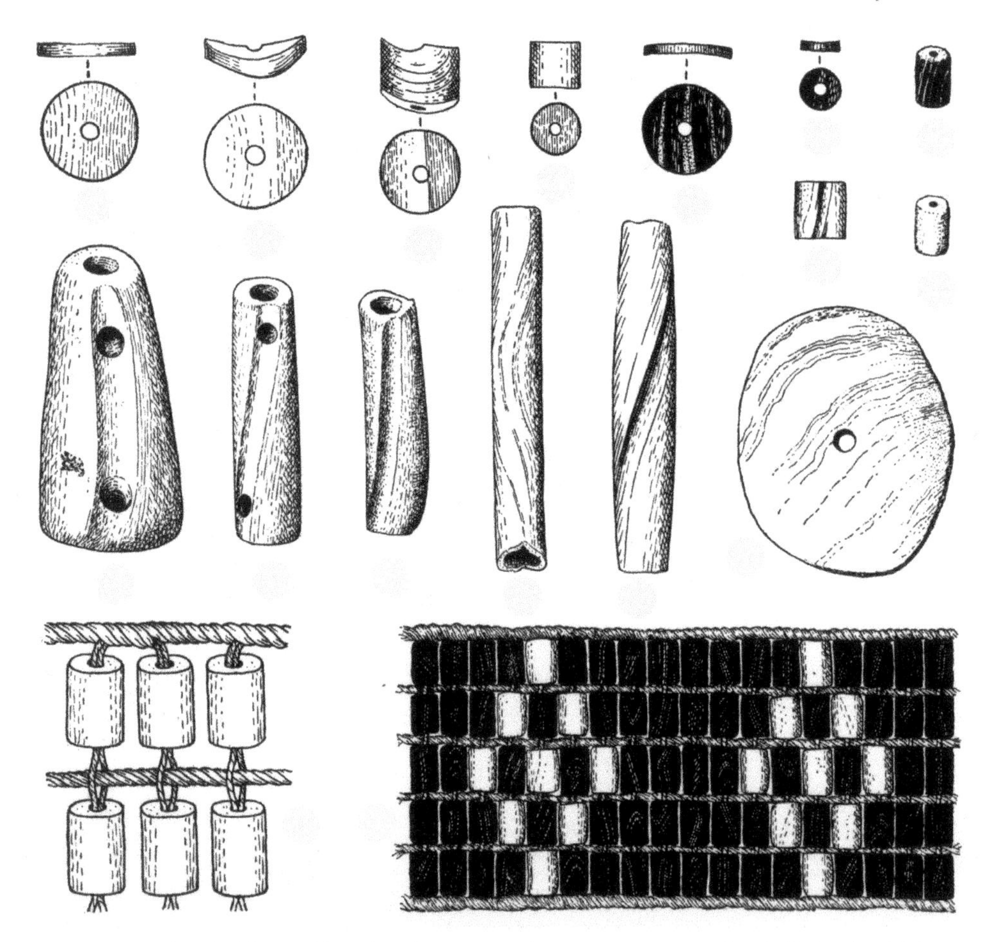

FIGURE 8.11 Marine shell beads (above) and seventeenth-century wampum beads (below), which were often used in strings or woven into symbolic belts (Willoughby, 1935: 267)

The Iroquoians are especially well-known lacrosse players, a team sport that pitted moieties against each other. The lacrosse stick and ball are still used in the modern game of lacrosse that the native game inspired, and the Iroquois National team is still competing. The Iroquoians played on the ice in winter, and modern ice hockey is its descendant sport. Although dictionaries often provide unlikely convoluted derivations of "hockey" from European languages, it is probably more significant that the word means "ouch" across Northern Iroquoia.

Snow snake is still played by Northern Iroquoians. In the modern version of the game a spear shaft is supplied with a lead head. The player then propels the spear down an icy trough by propelling it forward from the butt. The snow snake exits the trough, usually traveling across a frozen pond. The player throwing for the greatest distance wins.

Resilience and Collapse

Some of the Eastern Algonquian nations that dwindled in the face of European colonization hung on and survive today, whereas others disappeared from the East Coast. Communities descending from the Abenakis of northern New England persist there and in Quebec. A few, like the Penobscots of Maine, are vigorous and growing communities. Some groups in southern New England were so devastated by seventeenth-century epidemics that survivors tended to disappear into the rapidly growing immigrant communities from England. A few hung on as Native American communities, sometimes supplementing their populations by taking in former slaves of African descent.

Other Eastern Algonquian nations, such as the Delawares, moved westward during the colonial era, sometimes forming multiethnic communities with other displaced easterners, sometimes reconstituting themselves as nations in lands that were temporarily beyond the reach of expanding European settlement. Many Delawares eventually moved to Indian territory beyond the Mississippi, in what is today Oklahoma. Meanwhile, several small communities that remained behind have revived, in some cases developing casino operations that have given them new wealth and restored identity. The Pequot reservation in Connecticut now houses not only one of the world's largest casinos but also an excellent anthropology museum.

The effects of epidemic depopulation on many more western nations played out beyond the horizon and out of the view of literate observers, but the Northern Iroquoian experience is comparatively well documented. The crowd infections that were so devastating to American Indians had long since become common endemic diseases in Europe. Most had mutated and evolved from diseases carried by animal domesticates and other animal populations with which Old World peoples had long been in contact. Over the centuries European populations responded in part by increasing fertility to offset rising mortality from diseases such as influenza, measles, and smallpox. European social systems and subsistence practices allowed for larger numbers of children in anticipation of high childhood mortality because women were not heavily engaged in economic activities. But for Iroquoians and other northern farmers that was not a viable option. American Indian women did most of the farming, and they could not provide for their families while also tending to large numbers of children. Consequently, births were limited and carefully spaced by American Indian women. It was rare for an Indian woman to have more than three children and still more rare for her to have more than one at a time nursing. Had it been otherwise, average family size could have been larger, and the Northern Iroquoian longhouses necessarily would have had a very different architecture.

In Ohio, Fort Ancient culture survived into the era when European trade goods began to reach them. Unfortunately, lethal diseases were part of the exchange as well, and these were so disastrous that we cannot be sure which if any of the surviving tribes of the Eastern Woodlands are their descendants. The descendants of Fort Ancient were largely lost in the great dying that temporarily turned the core of the Eastern Woodlands into wilderness in the sixteenth century.

Some cultures probably dwindled to extinction, their survivors becoming refugees who were absorbed by luckier societies. Dynamic breakups and recombinations of all of these societies have often obscured their connections. The Algonquian-speaking Cheyennes provide an informative example from the western end of the Northeast, one that we would not be able to guess from archaeological evidence alone. Like some Dakota (Siouan) groups, the ancestral Cheyenne people were wild rice gatherers living in northern Minnesota in the seventeenth century. French fur trappers encountered them there at that time. The westward expansion of Ojibwas (Chippewas) prompted the Cheyennes to move south and to take up maize agriculture in southern Minnesota. Still later they became bison-hunting, horse-mounted nomads on the Great Plains (Chapter 9). This case and others like it illustrate the speed with which American Indian cultures could shift their adaptations and reinvent themselves. Neither the shift from wild rice to maize nor the conversion from farming to hunting appears to have been particularly traumatic for the adaptable ancestral Cheyennes, even though they involved profound cultural changes.

It should not be surprising that archaeologists often have difficulty tracing the ancestry of any particular culture. Migration was and is typically accompanied by cultural reinvention of the kind the Cheyennes illustrate, and the thread of continuity over time is elusive. However, that in itself produces a discernable pattern, one in which over the larger sweep of time and space the cultures of the region appear to be transitory and disconnected. Much of this is the result of our inability to detect episodes of rapid cultural evolution in the archaeological record. This is particularly a problem for the very rapid changes that occurred after the arrival of transformative introductions like horses. While it is comparatively easy to trace the ancestry of Northern Iroquoians, the later scramble of the northern farmers west of them on the edge of the Great Plains left trails much harder to follow.

The Shawnees appear to have come out of the Northeast region, but while they played an important role in the colonial era, the precise archaeological ancestry of these Algonquian speakers remains uncertain. There were several such survivors of the chaos of colonial wars and epidemics, whose origins are now difficult or impossible to trace back in time. On the other side of the archaeological ledger are late prehistoric cultures that are well known to archaeology but which have left no known living descendants. Some are known only from archaeology and possibly a few vague references in early documents. There are many others, in several cases cultures that would be anonymous had archaeologists not named them. Pennsylvania alone was home to the Monongahela, Clemson's Island, and Shenks Ferry cultures, all of which were real in their time, but unclear in their connections to either ancestral cultures or surviving cultures of the colonial era. They disappeared from history too early for them to get more than an occasional mention in surviving documents, too early for any survivors to be identified.

Glossary

adze A pecked and ground stone tool similar to a **celt**, but hafted with the cutting edge perpendicular to the implement handle.

celt A pecked and ground stone tool similar to an ax head.

esker A long sinuous ridge of gravel, once a river bed inside a glacier, deposited as a landscape feature when the glacier melted.

fathom A unit of measure equivalent to the arm span of a man.

gouge A pecked and ground stone tool similar to an **adze**, but having a concave face allowing the user to hollow out wood being worked.

matrilocal Postmarital residence in which men move in with their wives' families.

nation A polity or set of polities united by common language and customs.

post mold Typically, a line or circle of vertical cylinders of dark soil left behind by the frameworks of wigwams and longhouses.

steatite Soapstone, soft enough to be easily worked into stone bowls.

wampum Marine shell beads, specifically small cylindrical white and purple beads often combined as strings or belts.

wigwam A dome-shaped house having a framework of bent saplings and a covering of bark or mats.

References

Alex, L.M. (2000). *Iowa's Archaeological Past.* Iowa City: University of Iowa Press.

Barker, A.W. (1992). Powhatan's Pursestrings: On the Meaning of Surplus in a Seventeenth Century Algonkian Chiefdom. In: A.W. Barker and T.R. Pauketat, eds. *Lords of the Southeast: Social Inequality and the Native Elites of Southeastern North America.* Washington, DC: American Anthropological Association.

Birch, J. (2012). Coalescent Communities: Settlement Aggregation and Social Integration in Iroquoian Ontario. *American Antiquity,* 77, pp. 646–670.

Birmingham, R.A., and Goldstein, L.G. (2005). *Aztalan: Mysteries of an Ancient Indian Town.* Madison: Wisconsin Historical Society Press.
Birmingham, R.A., and Rosebrough, A.L. (2017). *Indian Mounds of Wisconsin.* Madison: University of Wisconsin Press.
Blitz, J.H. (1988). Adoption of the Bow in Prehistoric North America. *North American Archaeologist*, 9, pp. 123–145.
Bourque, B.J. (2001). *Twelve Thousand Years: American Indians in Maine.* Lincoln: University of Nebraska Press.
Britton, N.L., and Brown, A. (1923). *An Illustrated Flora of the Northern United States, Canada and the British Possessions.* New York: New York Botanical Garden.
Caldwell, D. (2013). A Possible New Class of Prehistoric Musical Instruments from New England: Portable Cylindrical Lithophones. *American Antiquity*, 78, pp. 520–535.
Comstock, A.R., and Cook, R.A. (2018). Climate Change and Migration Along a Mississippian Periphery: A Fort Ancient Example. *American Antiquity*, 83, pp. 91–108.
Divale, W. (1984). *Matrilocal Residence in Pre-Literate Society.* Ann Arbor, MI: UMI Research Press.
Doty, L.R. (1925). *History of the Genesee Country (Western New York).* Chicago, IL: Clarke.
Ellis, C.J., and Ferris, N. (1990). *The Archaeology of Southern Ontario to A.D. 1650.* London, Ontario: London Chapter, Ontario Archaeological Society.
Emerson, T.E., Mcelrath, D.L., and Fortier, A., eds. (2000). *Late Woodland Societies: Tradition and Transformation across the Midcontinent.* Lincoln: University of Nebraska Press.
Engelbrecht, W. (2014). Unnotched Triangular Points on Village Sites. *American Antiquity*, 79, pp. 353–367.
Fenton, W.N. (1987). *The False Faces of the Iroquois.* Norman: University of Oklahoma Press.
Fenton, W.N. (1998). *The Great Law of the Longhouse: A Political History of the Iroquois Confederacy.* Norman: University of Oklahoma Press.
Fiedel, S.J. (1994). Some Inferences Concerning Proto-Algonquian Economy and Society. *Northeast Anthropology*, 48, pp. 1–11.
Furtman, M. (2000). *Magic on the Rocks: Canoe Country Pictographs.* Duluth: Birch Portage Press.
Gates St-Pierre, C., and Thompson, R.C. (2015). Phytolith Evidence for the Early Presence of Maize in Southern Quebec. *American Antiquity*, 80, pp. 408–415.
Greenhalgh, W. (1849–1851). Observations of Wentworth Greenhalgh in a Journey from Albany to the Indians Westward begun 28th May and Ended 14th July 1677. *Documentary History of the State of New York.* Albany, NY: Weed, Parsons and Company.
Hart, J.P., Lovis, W.A., Jeske, R.J., and Richards, J.D. (2012). The Potential of Bulk Δ13c on Encrusted Cooking Residues as Independent Evidence for Regional Maize Histories. *American Antiquity*, 77, pp. 315–325.
Kuhn, R.D., and Sempowski, M.L. (2001). A New Approach to Dating the League of the Iroquois. *American Antiquity*, 66, pp. 310–314.
Lepper, B.T. (2018). On the Age of Serpent Mound: A Reply to Romain and Colleagues. *Midcontinental Journal of Archaeology*, 43, pp. 62–75.
Lepper, B.T., Duncan, J.R., Diaz-Granádos, C., and Frolking, T.A. (2018). Arguments for the Age of Serpent Mound. *Cambridge Archaeological Journal*, pp. 1–18.
Milner, G.R. (2004). *The Moundbuilders: Ancient Peoples of Eastern North America.* New York: Thames and Hudson.
Moorehead, W.K. (1922). *Archaeology of Maine.* Andover, MA: The Andover Press.
Mt Pleasant, J., and Burt, R.F. (2010). Estimating Productivity of Traditional Iroquoian Cropping Systems from Field Experiments and Historical Literature. *Journal of Ethnobiology*, 30, pp. 52–79.
Potter, S.R. (1993). *Commoners, Tribute, and Chiefs: The Development of Algonquian Culture in the Potomac Valley.* Charlottesville: University Press of Virginia.
Putnam, F.W. (1890). The Serpent Mound of Ohio. *The Century*, 39, pp. 871–888.
Richards, J.D. (2008). Viewing the Ruins: The Early Documentary History of the Aztalan Site. *The Wisconsin Magazine of History*, 91, pp. 28–39.
Romain, W.F., and Herrmann, E.W. (2018). Rejoinder to Lepper Concerning Serpent Mound. *Midcontinental Journal of Archaeology*, 43, pp. 76–88.
Romain, W.F., Herrmann, E.W., Monaghan, G.W., and Burks, J. (2017). Radiocarbon Dates Reveal Serpent Mound Is More Than Two Thousand Years Old. *Midcontinental Journal of Archaeology*, 42, pp. 201–222.

Schroeder, S., and Goldstein, L.G. (2016). Timelessness and the Legacy of Archaeological Cartography. In: A.P. Sullivan III and D.I. Olszewski, eds. *Archaeological Variability and Interpretation in Global Perspective.* Boulder: University Press of Colorado.

Simon, M.L. (2017). Reevaluating the Evidence for Middle Woodland Maize from the Holding Site. *American Antiquity*, 82, pp. 140–150.

Snow, D.R. (1975). The Passadumkeag Sequence. *Arctic Anthropology*, 12, pp. 46–59.

Snow, D.R. (1976). The Solon Petroglyphs and Eastern Abenaki Shamanism. In: W. Cowan, ed. *Papers of the Seventh Algonquian Conference, 1975.* Ottawa: Carleton University.

Snow, D.R. (1980). *The Archaeology of New England.* New York: Academic Press.

Snow, D.R. (1995). Microchronology and Demographic Evidence Relating to the Size of Pre-Columbian North American Indian Populations. *Science*, 268, pp. 1601–1604.

Snow, D.R. (1996). More on Migration in Prehistory: Accommodating New Evidence in the Northern Iroquoian Case. *American Antiquity*, 61, pp. 791–796.

Snow, D.R. (1997). The Architecture of Iroquois Longhouses. *Northeast Anthropology*, 53, pp. 61–84.

Theler, J.L., and Boszhardt, R.F. (2006). Collapse of Crucial Resources and Culture Change: A Model for the Woodland to Oneota Transformation in the Upper Midwest. *American Antiquity*, 71, pp. 433–472.

Tomka, S.A. (2013). The Adoption of the Bow and Arrow: A Model Based on Experimental Performance Characteristics. *American Antiquity*, 78, pp. 553–569.

Tuck, J.A. (1984). *Maritime Provinces Prehistory*. Ottawa: National Museums of Canada.

Willoughby, C.C. (1935). *Antiquities of the New England Indians*. Cambridge: Peabody Museum of Harvard University.

Wonderly, A. (2005). Effigy Pipes, Diplomacy, and Myth: Exploring Interaction Between St. Lawrence Iroquoians and Eastern Iroquois in New York State. *American Antiquity*, 70, pp. 211–240.

Wray, C.F., and Schoff, H.L. (1953). *A Preliminary Report on the Seneca Sequence in Western New York.* Harrisburg: Society for Pennsylvania Archaeology.

9

THE INTERIOR WEST

The western interior of North America contains large, arid and semiarid regions that challenge human adaptation (Figure 9.1). For most of human history American Indians in these regions had to rely mainly on hunting and gathering to make a living. A series of long fluctuating hot and dry climatic episodes scorched the Interior West from 7000 to 3500 BCE. Over the last two millennia favorable climatic conditions promoted the spread of farming into the Great Plains, up river valleys from the Eastern Woodlands. Climate change also allowed peoples of the Great Basin to adopt maize farming and pottery from the Pueblos of the Greater Southwest. Residents of the Plateau took on some of the cultural features of their distant relatives along the Northwest Coast. As is still the case today, the Interior West was made habitable over time to more than a light population of hunter-gatherers through the introduction of transplanted technologies and occasionally whole societies that had immigrated to the region.

Environment and Adaptation

Adaptive strategies across the Interior West varied over time in response to regional and local environmental shifts. Cultural solutions that people applied to these changing conditions were equally varied, which were often brought from other regions through migrations. This patchwork of circumstances resulted in a complex mosaic of archaeological cultures across the Interior West. Dramatic cultural changes occurred when horses became widely available in the eighteenth century. The image of the mounted Great Plains warrior in a feathered war bonnet was one that arose and disappeared quickly, an episode capping the long dynamic history of the American Indians in the western interior.

The Great Plains

The grasslands of the Great Plains, the iconic backdrop for the popular image of the American Indians, were all but nonexistent in the Late Pleistocene. White spruce forest covered most of what is now grassland. Two somewhat different islands of grassland survived the Pleistocene, one on the Llano Estacado of Texas and New Mexico and the other on the Edwards Plateau of central Texas. From these two islands of grass and smaller patches scattered around the mid-continent grew

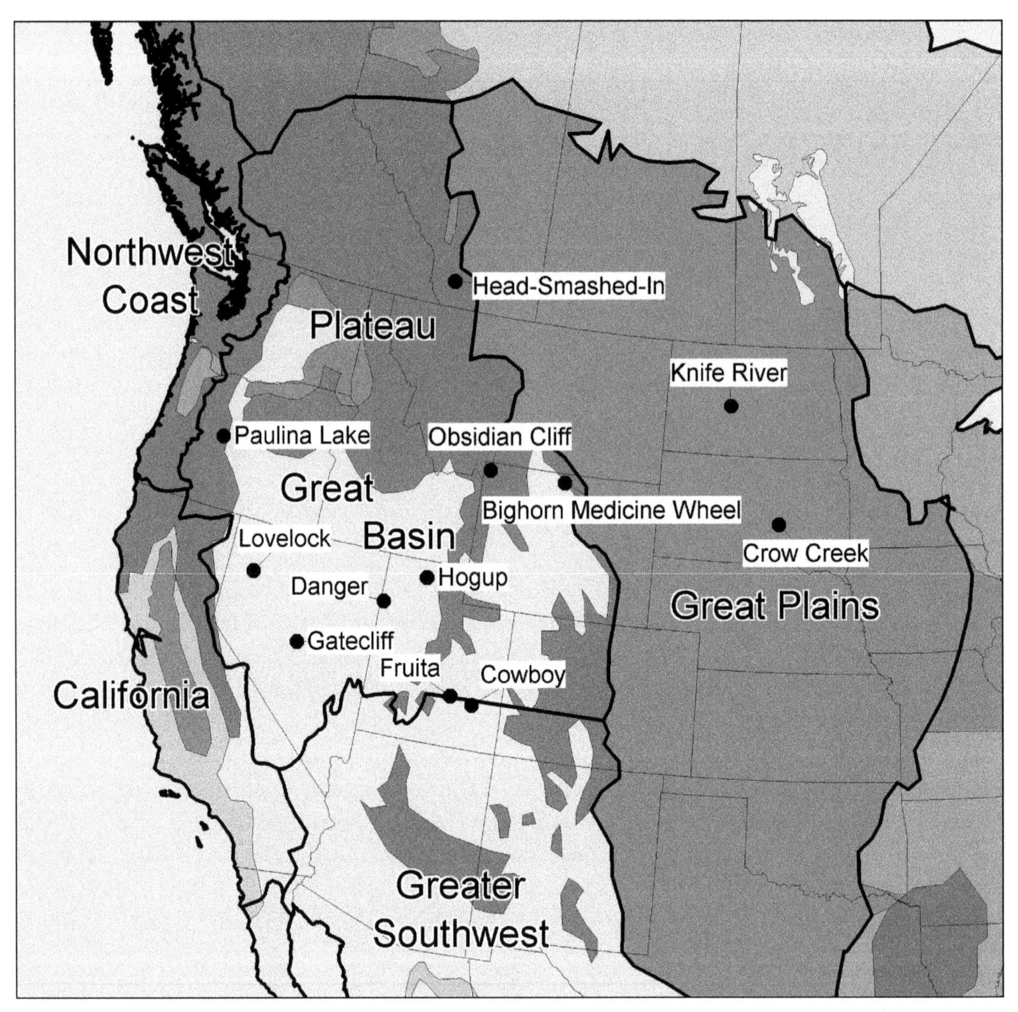

FIGURE 9.1 The Interior West, including the Great Plains, the Great Basin, and the Plateau regions, with sites mentioned in the text

the prairies and high plains familiar to us today. The spruce trees that dominated the Great Plains during the Pleistocene were gone from the central part of the region by 11,300 years ago, withered by the warmer drier conditions and blackened by more frequent fires. Some stands survive, most notably in northwestern Montana and the Black Hills of South Dakota (Bonnicksen, 2000: 9–40).

The western portions of the region are High Plains, hotter and drier in the summer than the moister eastern prairie. Short grass species predominate on the northern High Plains. The prairie is dominated by taller grasses. Grasses give way to mesquite, juniper, and oak savannas in central Texas.

There are not many plant foods for humans on the Great Plains, and herds of bison and pronghorn antelopes survived by their ability to digest tough grasses. Hunter-gatherers thus had to depend primarily on animals for food. This adaptation, difficult in the best of circumstances, was unpredictable because of erratic temperature fluctuations, rainfall patterns, and plant and animal resources. The summer rains on the Great Plains are spotty, randomly deluging some areas while missing others (Bamforth, 1988).

Bison herds came and went, moving more rapidly than hunters could. Until the Spanish arrived in New Mexico and introduced horses, Indians lacked the ability to efficiently pursue bison. Gear was limited to what they and their dogs could carry. Before the horse they depended on the chance appearance of herds and their ability to stampede them into gullies, box canyons, or over cliffs (buffalo jumps). It is not surprising that the archaeological evidence for Archaic adaptation to the Great Plains environment prior to 5,500 years ago is thin and discontinuous.

A fragmented pattern of adaptation continued to historic times, when the introduction of guns and horses led to even more radical cultural changes. The Cheyenne were wild rice gatherers in one century, maize farmers in the next, and mounted nomadic bison hunters in the subsequent century, moving great distances and reinventing themselves each time while maintaining their ethnic identity. Such patterns of frequent radical changes leave little consistency or continuity over space and time in the archaeological record. Cultures tended to disappear suddenly as conditions changed, making it difficult to trace them archaeologically. Great Plains archaeologists have paid close attention to the cycling of climate and regional ecology, which has helped them understand the timing of these adaptive episodes (Vehik, 2002).

The Great Basin

The Great Basin covers 408,600 km^2 (about 157,000 mi^2). Today it is a vast arid environment composed of mountain ranges and 150 basins. No rivers drain to the outside and only a few large brackish lakes exist. The largest of these is Great Salt Lake in northern Utah. During the Pleistocene, Great Salt Lake was much larger and higher than today, prompting scientists to refer to it as "Lake Bonneville." Smaller lakes were scattered about during the Pleistocene but have since disappeared.

The Pleistocene forests and lakes of the Great Basin diminished during the Holocene, and plant and animal species retreated up mountain slopes as warmer and drier conditions prevailed. Today rainfall is spotty and unpredictable. Desert plants can lie dormant for years until awakened by moisture. Then they flourish briefly before returning to dormancy when the soil dries out. Hunter-gatherers moved from one resource patch to another, as available, and from one cool productive mountain ridge to another when they could predict plant productivity.

The Great Basin was and still is more arid than the Great Plains, particularly during the extended period of hotter and drier conditions that prevailed, 7000–3500 BCE. What little rain falls there today concentrates in the winter months, in contrast to the pattern of predominantly summer rainfall on the Great Plains. The Great Basin is considered one of the deserts of the Interior West, a place where farming was difficult to impossible before modern irrigation.

GATECLIFF SHELTER

Gatecliff Shelter (Monitor Valley, Nevada) is the best-known archaeological site in the central Great Basin (Figure 9.1). Western Shoshone peoples occupied Monitor Valley during the historic period, and their foraging ancestors lived there for millennia. The valley floor lies at 2070 m (6,790 ft) and is covered by sagebrush flats and a shallow, sulfurous, alkaline desert lake. To the west is the Toquima Range, a mountain mass that tops out at 3,642 m (11,949 ft) on Mt. Jefferson.

Situated at 7,606 ft along the eastern flank of the Toquima Range, Gatecliff Shelter was first recorded and tested in 1970, with full-scale excavations in the summers throughout the 1970s (Figure 9.2). The 12 m (40 ft) of stacked-up sediments contained inside provide a deeply stratified

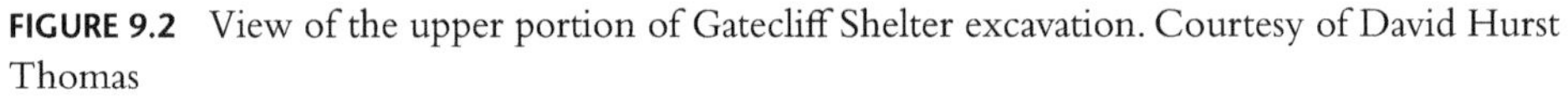

FIGURE 9.2 View of the upper portion of Gatecliff Shelter excavation. Courtesy of David Hurst Thomas

record of human–environment interaction in the Desert West spanning the last 7,000 years. The well-preserved deposits, sorted into 16 cultural horizons, serve as an important reference sequence for paleoenvironmental and cultural change in the Great Basin (Thomas, 1983).

During the earliest occupations (between 4100 and 1365 BCE), Gatecliff Shelter was a "Man Cave" – a temporary camp for bighorn hunters working the towering mountains nearby. Then, following abandonment during a dramatic thousand-year drought (1365 to 195 BCE), Gatecliff Shelter became a basecamp for entire families collecting plants and hunting bighorn in the surrounding piñon-juniper woodland (Kennett et al., 2014).

The Gatecliff Shelter sequence has been critical to a number of material culture studies, including more than 400 diagnostic projectile points (arrowheads and spear points), recovered in tight stratigraphic context and associated with more than 75 radiocarbon dates (Thomas, 2013). The Gatecliff sequence continues to provide the chronological backbone of the "short chronology" that characterizes much of the central and western Intermountain region. The Gatecliff shell artifact assemblage also provides the most sensitive sequence anchoring the Great Basin shell bead chronology. Gatecliff Shelter also contained 428 incised limestone slabs, one of the largest concentrations of such artifacts in the New World.

David Hurst Thomas

The Plateau

The Plateau region lies north of the Great Basin, between the Cascade Mountains on the west and the Rocky Mountains on the east. Much of the Plateau is drained by two great rivers: the Fraser and the Columbia. Archaeologists often extend discussion of the Northwest Coast into the Plateau (Chapter 11), and geographers have long referred to this larger region as "Cascadia." The Plateau is discussed separately here because human adaptations in the region have been oriented primarily to interior resources. Although Plateau cultures were influenced by surrounding more-complex societies, it remained a distinct archaeological region, like the Great Plains and the Great Basin.

The interior Plateau region is cold in winter and hot in the summer, an environment similar to the High Plains. The Cascade Mountains form a wall that keeps warmer moist air mostly to the west. Wintertime warm fronts known as Chinook winds occasionally spill across the mountains to bring sudden thaws to the Plateau region, but for the most part, the climate is unlike that of the West Coast.

Over the millennia following the Paleoindian period, adaptations for Native Americans living on the Plateau were based on migratory fish (mainly salmon), edible roots, and large game. The presence or absence of each of these major resource groups determined the specific adaptations possible in this region. The Plateau region has been geologically active. Dynamic environments can produce sudden changes in topography and biota that force humans to adjust rapidly or perish. American Indians on the Plateau adapted to an evolving landscape, sometimes featuring large dramatic events that forced sudden local or even regional readaptations. The Cascade Landslide and other similarly catastrophic events interrupted salmon runs, a vital food source, sometimes for long periods. The huge eruption of Mount St. Helens in 1980 was the most recent example of the Plateau's active geological history.

Demography and Conflict

The early hunter-gatherers of the region were probably not warlike, consistent with other simple hunter-gatherer societies. Complex hunter-gatherer societies tend to be more warlike, and some even keep slaves. Many of the nineteenth-century tribes and bands of the Interior West descended from earlier horticultural societies that had operated at the tribal or chiefdom levels. They brought with them traditions of warring that were probably lacking among earlier hunter-gatherers of the region and their direct descendants (Fry, 2005).

The Great Plains

The northern Great Plains Late period, 2000 BCE–1750 CE, followed the long cycling of extreme temperatures and drought that had prevailed earlier. Cooler and moister conditions brought about an increase in the bison herds and other game. Plains Indians continued to live in mobile **tepee** communities, but larger herds were linked to increases in mass butchering, exemplified in the buffalo jump site at Head-Smashed-In, Alberta.

Trade and exchange also increased and people once again began acquiring exotic materials from great distances. Cherts came from distant quarries and native copper from the Great Lakes region. All of this was probably related to the expansion of the Hopewell network of trade and exchange in the Eastern Woodlands. Hopewell traders pursued exotic raw materials through linkages that drew them farther from their Ohio homeland. At least a few came all the way to Obsidian Cliff in northwestern Wyoming to acquire volcanic glass (Chapter 6).

HEAD-SMASHED-IN BUFFALO JUMP

Located in southwestern Alberta, Canada, Head-Smashed-In Buffalo Jump (HSI) is the premier example of the site type where indigenous people drove large herds of bison over a cliff to their death (Brink, 2008; Thomas, 2000).

Five components of the site played a role in successful execution of a mass kill. First, a huge basin-shaped landform served as a collecting area from which to round-up the bison. Second, lines of stone **cairns**, some as much as 10 km long, snaked their way across the collecting basin, serving to guide the stampeding bison (Figure 9.3). Third, the jump-off was formed by a steep rock cliff, now some 10 m high, but which would have been higher in the past. Fourth, at the base of the cliff lies the kill site where animals not killed by the fall were dispatched and where the initial butchering of the carcasses was conducted. Finally, downslope from the kill site lies a rolling plain where animals were completely butchered for both immediate consumption and long-term storage. All told, the entire HSI site complex covers some 40 km^2 (25 mi^2).

The earliest use of HSI dates to 6400 BP, placing it among the oldest buffalo jumps known. It was used extensively after that time, although there were gaps when the site was abandoned. It is estimated that several hundred thousand bison met their death at HSI, perhaps more than any other site yet discovered on the Great Plains. The layers of butchered bison bones and stone killing/butchering weapons extend in stratified deposits more than 10 m (33 ft) below surface (Reeves, 1978).

HSI is among the best studied and best published bison kill sites. It is designated as a Provincial, National, and UNESCO heritage site and features a year-round visitor center open to the public with interpretive displays and walking tours.

Jack W. Brink

FIGURE 9.3 Head-Smashed-In buffalo jump, Alberta

The numerous ephemeral cultures that developed on the northern margin of the Great Plains produced a larger pattern over time and across space. Cycles of drought prevented the establishment of long-lived cultural traditions. Even after 1200 CE, when droughts settled into a less severe 160-year cycle, human adaptations waxed and waned with greater frequency than in most other parts of the continent. The region is complex archaeologically, expressed in the spotty and episodic nature of adaptations, cultural genesis, and abandonment.

Plains Woodland Cultures

Cultures that descended from the mound-building cultures of the Eastern Woodlands began to settle in the wooded valleys of the eastern Great Plains after 500 BCE. Sites of Kansas City Hopewell and Cooper cultures are both found west of the Eastern Woodlands. These were cultivators who made pottery, but like the Adena and Hopewell people who inspired them, they lacked the maize and bean crops that would later flourish in the Eastern Woodlands. There are at least 13 named and described derivative Plains Woodland archaeological cultures and variants that emerged around 500–1000 CE. The bow and arrow were universally adopted, and all of them depended upon a mixture of cultivating and gathering in the river valleys and periodic hunting on the treeless prairie away from the rivers (Figure 9.4).

The hunter-gatherers that the migrants from the Eastern Woodlands encountered probably had more meat than they could consume. Fat and carbohydrates were critical resources, which tended to be in particularly short supply in late winter and early spring. The hunter-gatherers rendered fat from bones and stored the grease with other ingredients as **pemmican**, which they made for future consumption after big hunts. But the arrival of farmers provided them with a new option. They could trade with the farmers for plant foods, solving their carbohydrate shortage and at the same time solving the farmers' meat protein shortage. The farmers had more options and consequently more security than did the hunter-gatherers, because they could either hunt for themselves or trade to supplement their diets. This economic relationship between hunters and farmers persisted until the coming of horses.

Plains Village Cultures

Cultures arose later as secondary developments from Mississippian culture in the Eastern Woodlands and the spread of maize agriculture. The circumstances that made the new human expansion possible were warmer climate, new crops, the bow and arrow, and the growth and eastward expansion of bison herds. This second expansion of farmers up the rivers of the eastern Great Plains began as early as 850 CE. Some of them probably developed locally out of earlier Plains Woodland cultures while others were established by migrants from the east. New villagers farmed small plots with maize, squash, sunflower, and a mix of other regional crops and tropical imports. They also hunted on the prairie, with pronghorn and bison being their preferred game (Henning, 2005; Steinacher and Carlson, 1998; Wedel, 2001; Wilson and Perttula, 2013).

The arrival of Europeans eventually added another, arguably the biggest, factor to the complex and dynamic adaptive system of Plains villagers. How they eventually evolved into the historic tribes of the eastern Great Plains consequently remains uncertain and the subject of continuing archaeological study and debate (Steinacher and Carlson, 1998).

Southern Plains villagers also penetrated upstream from the Eastern Woodlands on the southern Great Plains by 800 CE. Some reached the Texas Panhandle and southeastern Colorado (Bell and Brooks, 2001; Drass, 1998). Like others north of them, these southern Plains Village people depended upon cultivation, with seasonal trips onto the plains to hunt bison and other game (Bell and Brooks, 2001; Drass, 1998).

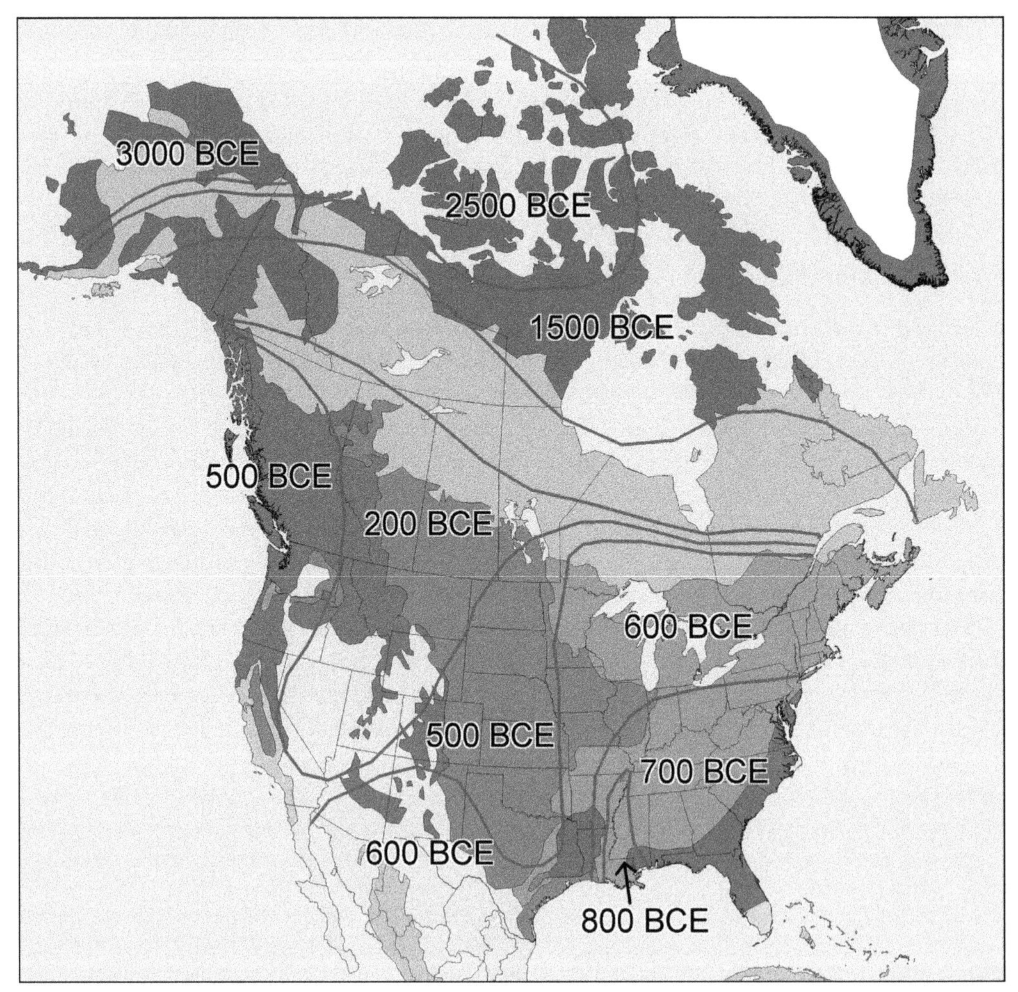

FIGURE 9.4 Introduction of the bow and arrow (after Blitz, 1988)

Middle Missouri Cultures

A branch of Late Woodland farming cultures called Great Oasis appeared after 850 CE in the Missouri basin in Nebraska and Iowa, as well as in southwestern Minnesota (Tiffany and Alex, 2001). Its development was influenced primarily by maize farming and initial contact with the Middle Mississippian cultures downstream. Related groups established villages along the river in North and South Dakota (Henning, 2001; Henning, 2005). The appearance of these Middle Missouri tradition villages coincided with the onset of warmer and drier climate, probably the major factor that prompted them to move up the Missouri. Scapula hoes, **manos**, and **metates** all point to the importance of farming. The earliest villages (970–1300 CE) were confined to the Missouri trench and western tributary valleys in South Dakota, Iowa, and western Minnesota. The subsistence base was agriculture, with hunting and gathering on the prairie away from the village making a nearly equal contribution. The Middle Missouri tradition evolved into the historic Siouan-speaking Mandan and Hidatsa nations.

KNIFE RIVER INDIAN VILLAGES

Knife River Indian Villages National Historic Site (KNRI) is administered by the National Park Service. Three prominent Hidatsa earth lodge villages – Big Hidatsa, Lower Hidatsa, and Sakakawea – each associated with an Hidatsa subgroup, are among the significant archaeological resources found on the property in north-central North Dakota. Karl Bodmer and George Catlin painted now-famous portraits and landscapes of prominent Hidatsas and their earth lodge settlements (Figure 9.5).

KNRI is considered homeland to the Hidatsa. The three subgroups or divisions (Hidatsa proper, Awatixa, and Awaxawi) spoke distinct dialects and characteristically occupied separate village settlements. Big Hidatsa Village (1600–1845 CE) was the largest community and home to the Hidatsa proper who according to archaeological data and oral tradition were the last to arrive in the area. Second was Lower Hidatsa and subsequently Sakakawea and Taylor Bluff Villages (1525–1845 CE), home to the Awatixa division whose oral traditions link their genesis to the Missouri River Valley. Amahami Village was an Awaxawi settlement (1786–1834 CE), the Hidatsa subgroup whose earlier community is thought to be the downriver Molander Indian Village State Historic Site. Following their departure from KNRI in 1845, the Hidatsas founded Like-A-Fishhook Village, which they occupied with the Mandans and Arikaras until 1886. Currently, their descendants reside on the Fort Berthold Indian Reservation as members of the Mandan, Hidatsa, and Arikara Nation (Ahler et al., 1991; Stewart, 2001).

FIGURE 9.5 Reconstructed Hidatsa Earth Lodge at Knife River Indian Villages National Historic Site. Courtesy of P.R. Picha

Beginning with publications in *Scientific Research in the National Parks* series in 1980, and continuing to the present, KNRI has sought meaningful and innovative ways to incorporate scientific knowledge and humanistic perspectives that are respectful of Hidatsa traditions to the public (Thiessen, 1993). Remote-sensing and fire-management research commonplace to archaeology and landscape studies today were pioneered at KNRI. Finally, the commemorative 2016 ArcheoBlitz program held in celebration of the National Park Service Centennial is an example of this continuing educational and cooperative dedication.

Paul R. Picha

The Coalescent Tradition

A new tradition appeared along the Missouri in northern Nebraska around 1250 CE, replacing the Middle Missouri communities that had lived there previously before expanding into South Dakota. These villagers were immigrants from the central Great Plains who lived in clusters of oval or squarish earth lodges (Johnson, 1998). In South Dakota they built ditch and palisade fortifications around their villages, an idea borrowed from the Middle Missouri villagers that lived north of them. Even those villages lacking palisades were made up of earth lodges that appear to have been clustered for defensive purposes. Endemic warfare in the region resulted in the establishment of fortified villages belonging to the Coalescent tradition. The Crow Creek site yielded skeletal evidence that at least 500 villagers were killed and mutilated by unknown assailants sometime around 1300 CE.

Oneota was an Upper Midwest culture centered on southern Wisconsin and Iowa, and like others in the region was related to Middle Mississippian culture (Chapter 7). The primary carriers of Oneota culture were probably speakers of various Siouan languages (Henning and Thiessen, 2004). Oneota and Plains Villagers also dispersed around 1400 CE, and their descendants are most probably several historic Siouan cultures. The late prehistoric or protohistoric agricultural societies on the prairies were rooted in the chiefdom societies of Middle Mississippian, and at least some of them later converted to nomadic lives centered on horses and bison (Ritterbush and Logan, 2000; Tiffany, 2003).

The Great Basin

Archaeologists use multiple lines of evidence to test hypotheses about how variable mobility strategies were deployed by Archaic hunter-gatherers. Trace element analysis was employed to identify quarry sources of finished obsidian tools found across the Great Basin. Quarry-source data were used to define band territories. Linking tools in camp sites to quarries enabled the identification of large band territories, each with its own distinctive set of obsidian types. The territories were mostly large oblong regions as much as 400 km (250 mi) across (Jones et al., 2003; Jones et al., 2012).

Fremont Culture

Fremont was comprised of at least five local farming cultures located in what is now Utah from about 400 CE to 1300 CE. These part-time farmers lived in scattered semisedentary farmsteads and small villages. Some switched to full-time farming when conditions were right, while others were full-time foragers. They made pottery, occupied permanent houses, and subsisted in part on maize farming (Adovasio, 1979; Madsen and Simms, 1998; Morss, 1931).

Some Fremont people probably descended from migrants originating in the South. A few appear to have descended from earlier Great Plains hunter-gatherers. Most were probably local hunter-gatherers who picked up agriculture and other southwestern traits. There is great archaeological variability among Fremont sites, likely the consequence of their different origins. Despite their marginality, the earliest Fremont sites are five centuries older than early Ancestral Puebloans. Therefore, Ancestral Puebloans could not have been the initial inspiration for the development of Fremont culture. Fremont culture most likely arose from early Mogollon influences on Great Basin hunter-gatherers, as did Ancestral Pueblo culture. Initially, Fremont and Ancestral Pueblo cultures were parallel developments.

The Numic Expansion

For the most part, Fremont farmers did not successfully revert to the hunting and gathering adaptation of their ancestors when climate change forced the abandonment of farming. Instead the region was overspread by Numic speakers of the Uto-Aztecan language family. The native people encountered by the first Europeans to enter the Great Basin were not the descendants of Fremont culture but rather the descendants of Numic migrants who spread northward and eastward across the region, at least partly after the demise of Fremont cultures (Madsen and Rhode, 1994; Wright, 1978). Their hunter-gatherer adaptation was better suited to the Great Basin during and after the onset of hotter and drier conditions of the Medieval Maximum. They probably expanded across the Great Basin sometime after 1000 CE, but there is disagreement about the timing of the process. The Numic peoples excelled in exploiting very small seeds and small animals.

The Plateau

On their expedition through the west in 1805, Lewis and Clark documented abundant game animals in western Montana but very few in the Columbia Basin. Their observations coincided with the impact of human predation on animal populations; human population density was higher west of the Rockies than to the east of the mountains. Game animals were relatively numerous in buffer zones between warring tribes, areas too risky for hunters. Areas close to human settlements were less rich in game (Martin, 1999a; Martin, 1999b).

Speakers of the Athapaskan languages of the Nadene family moved on to the northern Plateau. The timing of their arrival is debated, but it was linked to the general drift of Athapaskans southward out of western Canada. Some Athapaskans continued south along the eastern front of the Rocky Mountains, reaching the Southwest around 1500 CE (Matson and Coupland, 1995; Matson and Magne, 2006; Pokotylo and Mitchell, 1998: 99).

The Horse Nomads

The mounted nomads of the Interior West are popularly the best known of all American Indian nations, but they were in fact a widespread and short-lived historical phenomenon. Hunter-gatherers in the region had long used dogs to drag **travois** and carry packs for their owners. Some were nomadic groups who acquired horses from the Spanish as early as 1660. Native Americans quickly learned how to tame and ride the horses, adapting the travois to them as well. The adoption of horses dramatically altered the mobility patterns and hunting strategies of nomadic peoples in the Interior West. When the Pueblos revolted against the Spanish in 1680, they confiscated thousands of Spanish horses and redistributed them to tribes living around them. Some, like the Utes and Shoshones, became major horse breeders and traders, who in turn distributed horses to people living on or around the Great Basin and the Great Plains (Swagerty, 2001).

Western Indians quickly became skilled riders, using simplified equipment to hunt bison and fight from horseback. Stealing horses from neighboring tribes soon became a favorite activity of young men and a way to gain social standing. Horses multiplied and spread so rapidly that French-speaking fur traders from Quebec in the later 1600s observed horses with Spanish brands on the northern fringes of the western Canadian Great Plains (Driver and Massey, 1957: 284–287).

Nearly everyone in the Interior West had horses by the end of the eighteenth century, and many nations living in the western portions of the Eastern Woodlands moved on to the Great Plains to take up seasonal bison hunting. Pressure from European settlers moving westward from the East Coast combined with the attractions of horse nomadism prompted whole nations to shift their residences and lifestyles. Guns and other trade goods added to the mix of innovations, shifting the local balance of power here and there as tribes vied to acquire weapons and mobility while denying them to their enemies.

In short, the early historical archaeology of the Interior West is very complex, especially on the Great Plains. The mosaic of shifting opportunities afforded by climate, bison, crops, horses, and technology caused cultures to come and go across the region with dizzying speed. This pattern continued through the first century after the formation of the United States. The adaptation of the mounted Great Plains nomads could not last in the form that prevailed during the nineteenth century. The vast bison herds could not sustain the predation pressure of numerous hunters, particularly after Europeans joined in. In the end, and like so many earlier cultures, the phenomenon of mounted nomadic Indians came and went in two centuries.

Subsistence and Economy

Bison bones dominate the faunal remains of archaeological assemblages. These were probably the bones of *Bison bison occidentalis*, a now extinct subspecies or variety of bison that was slightly larger than modern bison (*Bison bison*). The bones often show butchering marks and breaks indicating that early Plains Indians were adept at extracting marrow from long bones.

By 3700 BCE, hunters were also skilled at stalking solitary animals such as mountain sheep and moose. Such skills are extraordinary given the wariness of these animals. People appear to have chosen settlement locations to maximize the range of plants and animals available to them, resources that often pattern differently on the modern landscape. Manos and metates found in many sites indicate that people had discovered ways to process available plants. Wood and antler digging tools were probably used to harvest bulbs and roots such as sego lily and bitterroot.

For thousands of years circumstances forced the various Archaic cultures of the Great Plains to depend upon individual skill and communal bison drives. Some participants enticed or chased bison into these funnels while others, including children, waved hides or set fires to steer them. The stampeding animals were run off cliffs known as "buffalo jumps." People came together under temporary leadership to plan and carry out bison drives and in the huge butchering task that followed. Communal hunts required leadership and organization, but these leadership positions were not carried over as permanent features of the sociopolitical system. Willingness to obey leaders lasted only so long as it was made necessary by the demands of the communal work. Whole bison herds could be dispatched quickly, and strips of dried (jerked) meat could feed families for weeks, even months. Meat loses most of its mass but none of its protein during drying, allowing it to be carried easily. When the drive and distribution of dried meat was over, the need for leadership relaxed and informal band organization prevailed.

Architecture and Technology

For most of prehistory, peoples of the Interior West lived in temporary shelters. Historic Shoshone bands lived in **wickiup**s that resembled earlier housing (Figure 9.6). Remnants of large rocky earthen ovens are more substantial than the remains of dwellings in some areas (Black and Thoms,

2014). Summer houses on the Great Plains were simple portable structures, probably skin-covered tents that could be packed up and moved. The northern Great Plains is a region where winters are long and very cold, and survival there would have been much more difficult without warm housing (Frison, 2001: 135).

Farmers, who arrived relatively late to the Great Plains and the Great Basin, lived in more substantial permanent houses. Pithouses became common on the Plateau even in the absence of farming.

Archaic adaptations followed the passing of Paleoindian cultures, and simple band-level hunter-gatherer societies persisted in the Great Basin until around 400 CE. Archaic hunter-gatherers made and used durable tools like projectile points and grinding stones, but they also produced a variety of items fabricated from more perishable materials. Fortunately, these are often preserved in dry caves, particularly in the Great Basin. Broadly defined, textiles included sandals, cordage, baskets, and bags. These items often exhibit sophisticated manufacturing techniques and since they are organic can be dated directly by radiocarbon (Connolly et al., 2016; Ollivier et al., 2017). The Paulina Lake site in the Newberry Crater of eastern Oregon holds the earliest house structure currently known for the Great Basin, a dwelling with several hearths that dates to at least 6000 BCE (Beck and Jones, 1997: 194).

The Plains Woodland people, derived from Hopewell antecedents, lived in dispersed villages of permanent circular or oval houses that were scattered along the forested courses of the western tributaries of the Mississippi (Johnson, 2001; Johnson and Johnson, 1998). Later Plains Village groups, descendants of the Mississippians, occupied fortified and more permanent settlements. Their communities first expanded westward up the river valleys of the Great Plains to the practical limit of maize horticulture, then remained there until the arrival of horses and Europeans.

The mounted nomads of the region left tepee ring sites across the landscape of the Interior West. While some of these sites date to before 2000 BCE, long before horses were available, most are later, an indication of increased population size and mobility in the Late period. Tepee diameters range widely, from as little as 1.2 m (4 ft) to as much as 7.3 m (24 ft). The average is probably around 4.6 m (15 ft), a substantial tepee.

Middle Missouri villages were typically fortified. Large, well-built semi-subterranean rectangular houses were at least banked if not entirely covered with earth for insulation. The later Coalescent tradition houses were just as substantial and often surrounded by fortifications. Later

FIGURE 9.6 Shoshone summer (left) and winter (right) houses (wickiups)

FIGURE 9.7 Reconstructed Plateau pithouse with one side left uncovered to expose the interior

communities were more spread out and lacked palisades. This suggests that warfare had decreased by these later times (Winham and Calabrese, 1998; Wood, 1998).

Most people today think of the Plains tepee as the iconic dwelling of the region's cultures. Hide tepees were used by many on summer hunting expeditions, but the tepee became a permanent feature of those who adopted horses and year-round nomadism.

The technology of the Plateau cultures was associated with the harvesting of migratory fish at narrow constrictions on major rivers. Weirs, dip nets, barbed spears, and toggling harpoons all became increasingly sophisticated over time. While fishing technology did not include much use of hooks and lures, fishermen knew from experience that salmon do not usually take bait while migrating. Their equipment was appropriate given the behavior of their prey. The bow and arrow was in use on the southern Plateau by 400–100 BCE, but it did not become popular elsewhere in the region until around 500 CE (Chatters and Pokotylo, 1998: 78; Hildebrandt and King, 2012).

The Plateau Pithouse tradition developed through several phases (Figure 9.7). House pits were initially small, 4–5 m (13–16.5 ft) in diameter and 30–40 cm (12–16 in) deep. Some later houses were deeper and up to 20 m (66 ft) in diameter. Pithouses were cool in the summer and warm in the winter, a good solution for people who could afford to live in permanent homes, despite being hunter-gatherers.

Culture, Language, and Identity

The Interior West has been a vast region of cultural diversity, chronologically and geographically. The challenges of adaptation described earlier in this chapter produced many ephemeral cultures, several of which have been mentioned. It was a region whereby **ethnogenesis** was complex and sometimes swift, often producing transient cultures that lasted for a few centuries then disappeared. Bands and tribes could flourish over time, then dwindle to a point where the individuals who constituted them had to reinvent themselves by innovating, migrating, or joining other groups. The drivers of cultural change were often environmental. In most cases, the threads of cultural continuity are difficult to follow archaeologically.

The languages of nations that moved on to the Great Plains after the introduction of horses derive from at least six major families. It is difficult to specify which, if any, of these families was spoken prior to the arrival of horses, but Kiowa-Tanoan is a possibility. Numic speakers, whose language belongs to the Uto-Aztecan family, overspread the Great Basin prehistorically, replacing Fremont and various hunter-gatherer cultures there.

Five language families of the Plateau portion of the Interior West appear to have been there longer. The languages of the adjacent Northwest Coast probably have similarly ancient histories. Despite the antiquity of these populations, they too were changed by innovations from outside over time. Trade frequently took place between coastal people downstream on the two great rivers that drain this part of the Interior West and those of the Plateau.

Variations in the sizes of pithouses in some late village clusters of the Plateau Pithouse tradition have been sometimes interpreted as indicating differentials in wealth and status. Social inequality in these communities may have been minor compared to what has been documented along the nearby Northwest Coast. If social inequality developed on the Plateau, it may have been the product of cultural imitation (Pokotylo and Mitchell, 1998: 99–100). Some Plateau tribes became very active participants in the transition to nomadism with the arrival of horses and associated innovations.

BIGHORN MEDICINE WHEEL

Bighorn Medicine Wheel, also known as Medicine Wheel/Medicine Mountain National Historical Landmark, is one among some 70 stone rings spread across the Plains Nation territory in the northern United States (15%) and southern Canada (85%). They are so-named because of the resemblance of their circular plans to the medicine lodge.

Situated near the summit of Medicine Mountain (elevation 3,000 m) in northwest Wyoming just south of the Montana border, Bighorn Medicine Wheel consists of a hollowed-out central cairn 4 m across made from unworked loaf-sized limestone boulders, from which 28 spokes, approximately 12 m in length, radiate to an outer ring (diameter 24 m). Six smaller cairns mark the termini of six of the spokes (Figure 9.8). Though there have been no indigenous claims regarding construction, oral histories relate the structure to native rites of fasting and vision quest (Cowell and Moss, 2003: 251–287). Crow youth still employ it for such purposes. The only radiocarbon date (ca. 1750 CE, *terminus ante quem*) comes from a piece of wood lodged in one of the cairns.

Based on alignments among the cairns, astronomer John Eddy proposed an astronomical/calendrical function for Bighorn. He discovered alignments corresponding to the rising positions of prominent stars that made their first annual appearance above the predawn horizon on dates set approximately one month apart following the summer solstice. He posited that these observations, occurring around the three "warmest" moons, could have been used, most effectively between 1200 and 1700 CE, to time rituals leading up to the

FIGURE 9.8 The Bighorn Medicine Wheel, Wyoming. Courtesy of Richard Collier, Wyoming Historic Preservation Office, Department of State Parks and Cultural Resources

annual abandonment of the site prior to the start of the winter season. A similar function fit alignments at the Moose Mountain Medicine Wheel in Saskatchewan and at the Ft. Smith, Montana, Medicine Wheel (Eddy, 1977), though the astronomical orientation hypothesis applied to all medicine wheels has been criticized on a statistical basis by Vogt (Eddy, 1977; Vogt, 1993).

Anthony F. Aveni

Art and Symbolism

The expanding Numic hunter-gatherers encountered rock art left by the previous Fremont inhabitants of the Great Basin and created some of their own (Figure 9.9). However, most of the art dates to earlier times, and thus the rock art of the region is largely unintelligible to historic Indian tribes. There is little in their oral traditions than can be used to interpret the rock art they inherited (Quinlan and Woody, 2003).

Like the Fraser River to the north in British Columbia, the Columbia River was an important route between the Pacific Coast and the interior Plateau region. Salmon and Indian traders moved up and down through the Columbia Gorge. Ancient lava flows used to constrain the Columbia for several kilometers, where it flows through a gap in the Cascade Mountains. The resulting Five Mile Rapids made migration difficult for fish, but accordingly, made fishing easy. The stretch is now a placid reservoir behind a modern dam.

Rock art at the upper end of the rapids marks the place where Indian traders met for thousands of years (Figure 9.10). Marine shell, candlefish (eulachon) oil, and other coastal goods moved upstream. In exchange, obsidian, hides, and other interior resources moved downstream to coastal communities (Ames et al., 1998).

FIGURE 9.9 Fremont petroglyphs at the Fruita site

FIGURE 9.10 *Tsagagalal*, "She Who Watches," is the most prominent of many examples of rock art that adorn the jagged basalt cliffs at the upper end of the narrows of the Columbia River

Bands living in the northern Great Basin of eastern Oregon acquired marine shell (*Olivella*) beads from the Pacific Coast through exchange networks. Artistic influences from coastal sources also influenced the nations of the Plateau, and archaeologists can detect these styles in attenuated form on artifacts (Smith et al., 2016).

The widespread cultural reinventions occasioned by the introduction of horses created a whole new mosaic of cultures across much of the Interior West. Traditional crafts based on leather, wood, horn, porcupine quills, catlinite, chert, paint, and feathers eventually incorporated such European trade items as glass beads, brass, lead, and broadcloth. The symbolism expressed in the crafts that included traditional and European materials tend to be specific to the histories of the dozens of participating cultures.

Resilience and Collapse

Human resilience in the Interior West is most apparent at large scale. Collapse was frequent at the scale of vulnerable band communities. Hunting bands retreated or died out repeatedly over the long term, but they multiplied and expanded again when conditions allowed. Larger and more permanent farming communities were established after groups expanded from the east into the Great Plains or northward from the Southwest.

The Coalescent tradition of the Dakotas grew and expanded rapidly from about 1450 to 1650 CE. Villagers founded many new settlements, which were often occupied only for brief periods. People of the Coalescent tradition evolved into the historic-period Caddoan-speaking Arikara nation. The Arikaras and the Siouan-speaking Mandans and Hidatsas flourished along the Middle Missouri in North and South Dakota until they were all decimated by epidemics around 1750. Devastating smallpox epidemics came later in the nineteenth century, reducing the surviving villages even further (Betts, 2006; Lehmer, 2001).

Continuities between Fremont and earlier phases were documented at Hogup Cave and other sites, with the addition of maize, ceramics, and a few other associated traits over time. Fremont culture consequently was comprised of several variants scattered in clusters around the portion of Utah north of the Ancestral Pueblo sites. Common traits included ceramics, clay figurines, petroglyph styles, and settlement types. Despite its precarious adaptation to the Great Basin environment, Fremont was a resilient culture. Nevertheless, Fremont as a culture could not survive environmental changes in a region where all cultures were only temporary successes over the long term (Marwitt, 1986). Fremont persisted for another four centuries around the marshlands of northwest Utah, but it too eventually disappeared (Coltrain and Leavitt, 2002; Kloor, 2007).

The mounted nomads that flourished briefly over so much of the Interior West collapsed in the face of Euro-American westward expansion and the attendant near extinction of bison. The subjugation of the Plains Indians resulted in the reservation-based cultures of their modern descendants.

Glossary

cairn A stack of stones built up by humans.

ethnogenesis The set of processes by which new human cultures emerge.

mano A hand stone used on a **metate** to produce flour. A term borrowed from Spanish.

metate A grinding stone, used with a **mano** to convert seeds into flour. A term borrowed from Spanish.

pemmican Pounded dried meat, and sometimes dried fruits, mixed with an equal amount of melted fat, normally stored for future use.

tepee A mobile house form consisting of a conical pole frame and a hide or mat covering.
travois A simple framework of poles dragged by dogs or horses to assist western nomads in moving possessions.
wickiup A temporary shelter used by mobile hunter-gatherers.

References

Adovasio, J.M. (1979). The Fremont and the Sevier: Defining Prehistoric Agriculturalists North of the Anasazi, by David B. Madsen. *American Antiquity*, 44, pp. 723–731.
Ahler, S.A., Thiessen, T.D., and Trimble, M.K. (1991). *People of the Willows: The Prehistory and Early History of the Hidatsa Indians*. Grand Forks: University of North Dakota Press.
Ames, K.M., Dumond, D.E., Glam, J.R., and Minor, R. (1998). Prehistory of the Southern Plateau. In: D.E. Walker, Jr, ed. *Plateau*. Washington, DC: Smithsonian Institution.
Bamforth, D.B. (1988). *Ecology and Human Organization on the Great Plains*. New York: Plenum Press.
Beck, C., and Jones, G.T. (1997). The Terminal Pleistocene/Early Holocene Archaeology of the Great Basin. *Journal of World Prehistory*, 11, pp. 161–236.
Bell, R.E., and Brooks, R.L. (2001). Plains Village Tradition: Southern. In: R.J. Demallie, ed. *Plains*. Washington, DC: Smithsonian Institution.
Betts, C.M. (2006). Pots and Pox: The Identification of Protohistoric Epidemics in the Upper Mississippi Valley. *American Antiquity*, 71, pp. 233–259.
Black, S.L., and Thoms, A.V. (2014). Hunter-Gatherer Earth Ovens in the Archaeological Record: Fundamental Concepts. *American Antiquity*, 79, pp. 203–226.
Bonnicksen, T.M. (2000). *America's Ancient Forests: From the Ice Age to the Age of Discovery*. New York: John Wiley.
Brink, J.W. (2008). *Imagining Head-Smashed-In: Aboriginal Buffalo Hunting on the Northern Plains*. Edmonton: Athabasca University Press.
Chatters, J.C., and Pokotylo, D.L. (1998). Prehistory: Introduction. In: D.E. Walker, Jr, ed. *Plateau*. Washington, DC: Smithsonian Institution.
Coltrain, J.B., and Leavitt, S.W. (2002). Climate and Diet in Fremont Prehistory: Economic Variability and Abandonment of Maize Agriculture in the Great Salt Lake Basin. *American Antiquity*, 67, pp. 453–485.
Connolly, T.J., Barker, P., Fowler, C.S., Hattori, E.M., Jenkins, D.L., and Cannon, W.J. (2016). Getting Beyond the Point: Textiles of the Terminal Pleistocene/Early Holocene in the Northwestern Great Basin. *American Antiquity*, 81, pp. 490–514.
Cowell, A., and Moss, A., Sr. (2003). *Arapaho Historical Traditions*. Winnipeg: University of Manitoba Press.
Drass, R.R. (1998). The Southern Plains Villagers. In: W.R. Wood, ed. *Archaeology on the Great Plains*. Lawrence: University of Kansas Press.
Driver, H.E., and Massey, W.C. (1957). *Comparative Studies of North American Indians*. Philadelphia, PA: The American Philosophical Society.
Eddy, J. (1977). Medicine Wheels and Plains Indian Astronomy. In: A.F. Aveni, ed. *Native American Astronomy*. Austin: University of Texas Press.
Frison, G.C. (2001). Hunting and Gathering Tradition: Northwestern and Central Plains. In: R.J. Demallie, ed. *Plains*. Washington, DC: Smithsonian Institution.
Fry, D.P. (2005). *The Human Potential for Peace: An Anthropological Challenge to Assumptions about War and Violence*. New York: Oxford University Press.
Henning, D.R. (2001). Plains Village Tradition: Eastern Periphery and Oneota Tradition. In: R.J. Demallie, ed. *Plains*. Washington, DC: Smithsonian Institution.
Henning, D.R. (2005). The Evolution of the Plains Village Tradition. In: T.R. Pauketat and D.D. Loren, eds. *North American Archaeology*. Malden, MA: Blackwell.
Henning, D.R., and Thiessen, T.D., eds. (2004). Dhegihan and Chiwere Siouans in the Plains: Historical and Archaeological Perspectives, Part II. *Plains Anthropologist*, 49, pp. 345–625.
Hildebrandt, W.R., and King, J.H. (2012). Distinguishing Between Darts and Arrows in the Archaeological Record: Implications for Technological Change in the American West. *American Antiquity*, 77, pp. 789–799.

Johnson, A.E. (2001). Plains Woodland Tradition. In: R.J. Demallie, ed. *Plains*. Washington, DC: Smithsonian Institution.

Johnson, C.M. (1998). The Coalescent Tradition. In: W.R. Wood, ed. *Archaeology on the Great Plains*. Lawrence: University of Kansas Press.

Johnson, M.A., and Johnson, A.E. (1998). The Plains Woodland. In: W.R. Wood, ed. *Archaeology on the Great Plains*. Lawrence: University of Kansas Press.

Jones, G.T., Beck, C., Jones, E.E., and Hughes, R.E. (2003). Lithic Source Use and Paleoarchaic Foraging Territories in the Great Basin. *American Antiquity*, 68, pp. 5–38.

Jones, G.T., Fontes, L.M., Horowitz, R.A., Beck, C., and Bailey, D.G. (2012). Reconsidering Paleoarchaic Mobility in the Central Great Basin. *American Antiquity*, 77, pp. 351–367.

Kennett, D.K., Culleton, B., Dexter, J., Mensing, S., and Thomas, D.H. (2014). High Precision AMS 14C Chronology for Gatecliff Shelter, Nevada. *Journal of Archaeological Science*, 52, pp. 621–632.

Kloor, K. (2007). The Vanishing Fremont. *Science*, 318, pp. 1540–1543.

Lehmer, D.J. (2001). Plains Village Tradition: Postcontact. In: R.J. Demallie, ed. *Plains*. Washington, DC: Smithsonian Institution.

Madsen, D.B., and Rhode, D., eds. (1994). *Across the West: Human Population Movement and the Expansion of the Numa*. Salt Lake City: University of Utah Press.

Madsen, D.B., and Simms, S.R. (1998). The Fremont Complex: A Behavioral Perspective. *Journal of World Prehistory*, 12, pp. 255–336.

Martin, P.S. (1999a). Deep History and a Wilder West. In: R.H. Robichaux, ed. *Ecology of Sonoran Desert Plants and Plant Communities*. Tucson: University of Arizona Press.

Martin, P.S. (1999b). War Zones and Game Sinks in Lewis and Clark's West. *Conservation Biology*, 13, pp. 36–45.

Marwitt, J.P. (1986). Fremont Cultures. In: W.L. D'Azevedo, ed. *Great Basin*. Washington, DC: Smithsonian Institution.

Matson, R.G., and Coupland, G. (1995). *The Prehistory of the Northwest Coast*. New York: Academic Press.

Matson, R.G., and Magne, M.P.R. (2006). *Athapaskan Migrations*. Tucson: University of Arizona Press.

Morss, N.M. (1931). The Ancient Culture of the Fremont Sevier in Utah. *Papers of the Peabody Museum of American Archaeology and Ethnology*, vol. 12.

Ollivier, A.P., Smith, G.M., and Barker, P. (2017). A Collection of Fiber Sandals from Last Supper Cave, Nevada, and Its Implications for Cave and Rockshelter Abandonment During the Middle Holocene. *American Antiquity*, 82, pp. 325–340.

Pokotylo, D.L., and Mitchell, D. (1998). Prehistory of the Northern Plateau. In: D.E. Walker, Jr, ed. *Plateau*. Washington DC: Smithsonian Institution.

Quinlan, A.R., and Woody, A. (2003). Marks of Distinction: Rock Art and Ethnic Identification in the Great Basin. *American Antiquity*, 68, pp. 372–390.

Reeves, B.O.K. (1978). Head-Smashed-In: 5500 Years of Bison Jumping in the Alberta Plains. In: L.B. Davis and M.C. Wilson, eds. *Bison Procurement and Utilization: A Symposium*. Norman, OK: Plains Anthropological Society.

Ritterbush, L.W., and Logan, B. (2000). Late Prehistoric Oneota Population Movement into the Central Plains. *Plains Anthropologist*, 45, pp. 257–272.

Smith, G.M., Cherkinsky, A., Hadden, C., and Ollivier, A.P. (2016). The Age and Origin of Olivella Beads from Oregon's LSP-I Rockshelter: The Oldest Marine Shell Beads in the Northern Great Basin. *American Antiquity*, 81, pp. 550–561.

Steinacher, T.L., and Carlson, G.F. (1998). The Central Plains Tradition. In: W.R. Wood, ed. *Archaeology on the Great Plains*. Lawrence: University of Kansas Press.

Stewart, F.H. (2001). Hidatsa. In: R.J. Demallie, ed. *Plains*. Washington, DC: Smithsonian Institution Press.

Swagerty, W.R. (2001). History of the United States Plains Until 1850. In: R.J. Demallie, ed. *Plains*. Washington, DC: Smithsonian Institution.

Thiessen, T.D. ed. (1993). *The Phase I Archeological Research Program for the Knife River Indian Villages National Historic Site*. Four Volumes. National Park Service, Midwest Archeological Center, Occasional Studies in Anthropology No. 27. Lincoln, NE: National Park Service, Midwest Archeological Center.

Thomas, D.H. (1983). The Archaeology of Monitor Valley: 2. Gatecliff Shelter. *Anthropological Papers of the American Museum of Natural History*. New York: American Museum of Natural History.

Thomas, D.H. (2000). *Exploring Native North America.* Oxford: Oxford University Press.
Thomas, D.H. (2013). Great Basin Projectile Point Typology: Still Relevant? *Journal of California and Great Basin Anthropology*, 33, pp. 133–152.
Tiffany, J.A. (2003). Mississippian Connections with Mill Creek and Cambria. *Plains Anthropologist*, 48, pp. 21–34.
Tiffany, J.A., and Alex, L.M. (2001). Great Oasis Archaeology: New Perspectives from the DeCamp and West Des Moines Burial Sites in Central Iowa. *Plains Anthropologist*, 46, pp. 1–104.
Vehik, S.C. (2002). Conflict, Trade, and Political Development on the Southern Plains. *American Antiquity*, 67, pp. 37–64.
Vogt, D. (1993). Medicine Wheel Astronomy. In: C. Ruggles and N.J. Saunders, eds. *Astronomies and Cultures.* Niwot: University Press of Colorado.
Wedel, W.R. (2001). Plains Village Tradition: Central. In: R.J. Demallie, ed. *Plains.* Washington, DC: Smithsonian Institution.
Wilson, D., and Perttula, T.K. (2013). Reconstructing the Paleodiet of the Caddo through Stable Isotopes. *American Antiquity*, 78, pp. 702–723.
Winham, R.P., and Calabrese, F.A. (1998). The Middle Missouri Tradition. In: W.R. Wood, ed. *Archaeology on the Great Plains.* Lawrence: University of Kansas Press.
Wood, J.W. (1998). A Theory of Preindustrial Population Dynamics: Demography, Economy, and Well-Being in Malthusian Systems. *Current Anthropology*, 39, pp. 99–135.
Wright, G.A. (1978). The Shoshonean Migration Problem. *Plains Anthropologist*, 23, pp. 113–137.

10

THE GREATER SOUTHWEST

The Greater Southwest region straddles the continental divide, an international border, and zones of desert and mountain forests (Figure 10.1). The Colorado Plateau, where most of the landscape lies over 1,500 m (4,920 ft) above sea level, covers the northern part of the region. The region centers on Arizona and New Mexico but includes portions of adjoining states, both U.S. and Mexican.

No other archaeological region of the United States features more sites open to public visitation, more vibrant descendant communities, or a more pervasive native influence on modern American culture. The shared archaeological heritage of the Greater Southwest is an extraordinary treasure to this region, and like Mesoamerica (Chapter 13), it is a model to what might be possible in other regions of the continent.

Environment and Adaptation

The region is generally dry, but it has never been devoid of edible plants and game. What little rain falls on the western deserts comes from the Pacific, while the eastern part of the Southwest gets most of its summer rain from the Gulf of Mexico. Winter sometimes brings soaking rain, mostly to higher elevations, but most rain falls unpredictably as localized thundershowers. The deserts of the Greater Southwest come in three varieties, depending upon moisture and the amount of winter frost. The Mojave Desert includes Death Valley, seasonally one of the hottest and driest places on earth, but it is also subject to winter freezing. The Sonoran Desert is hottest and driest overall, home to the huge saguaro cactus. The Chihuahuan Desert is high, with altitudes generally above 1,000 m (3,300 ft).

Village farming spread northward from Mesoamerica over three millennia ago into the deserts of the U.S. Southwest and the Mexican Northwest. Three major cultural traditions, **Hohokam**, **Mogollon**, and **Ancestral Pueblo**, followed different adaptations to practice farming in this arid region. Secondary traditions, such as **Sinagua** and **Patayan**, developed between and around the margins of the major lifeways. The frontiers of farming expanded over time, but farming also spread beyond the margins of the major traditions, adopted by hunter-gatherers in even more unlikely environments. Much later, farming collapsed in many areas in the face of climate change, forcing

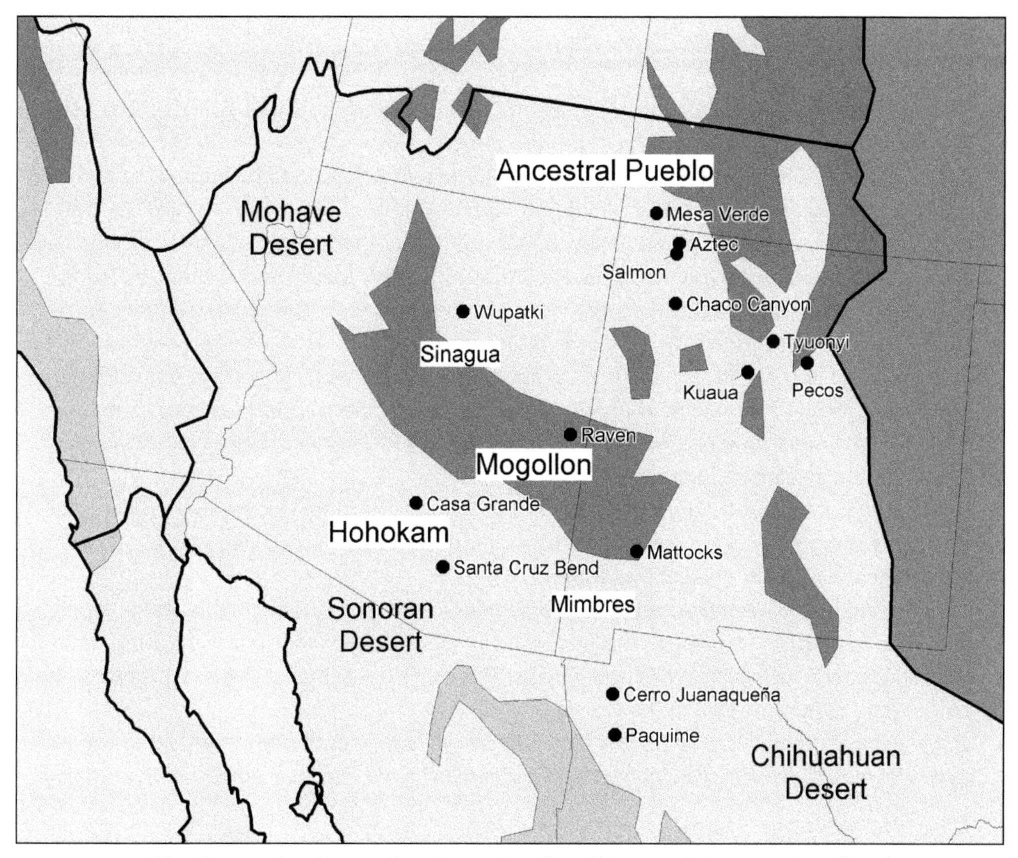

FIGURE 10.1 The Greater Southwest, showing regional traditions and sites mentioned in the text

widespread relocations and spawning new derivative cultures. Major tasks for archaeologists have been to determine when, how, and why farming was established in this environment, and why it was abandoned across so much of the region by 1200 CE (Kantner, 2005).

There are three early sites that pertain to this early farming period, Cerro Juanaqueña, the Santa Cruz Bend site, and Paquimé. The Cerro Juanaqueña site in the northwestern part of the state of Chihuahua, Mexico, not far from the New Mexico border, has produced several of the earliest maize specimens known for the region. They date to around 1000 BCE. Despite its age, the settlement was already a large terraced residential complex with 8 km (5 mi) of terraces and evidence of cultivation (Hard and Roney, 1998). The Santa Cruz Bend site was found buried under a meter of river alluvium in Tucson, Arizona. Researchers found hundreds of pithouses and storage pits containing maize kernels and other seeds dating to 800–200 BCE. Even these dates put the site into what was previously thought to have been a pre-agricultural Archaic phase. The site also produced early ceramics and the region's earliest known ceremonial structure (Muro, 1998).

The beginnings of the Hohokam tradition were in place in southern Arizona by the first millennium BCE. So too were the first residents of Paquimé, a community that would become a major trading center in Chihuahua. The Mogollon tradition developed a little later in the mountains of Arizona and New Mexico. The people called Basketmakers emerged on the Colorado Plateau to the north. They would eventually evolve into the communities of the Ancestral Pueblo tradition.

PAQUIMÉ

Since its description by European explorers in 1584, Paquimé (or Casas Grandes) has been recognized as one of the most important and unusual archaeological sites in the Southwest United States and Northwest Mexico (SW/NW). Its Pueblo domestic architecture is combined with Mesoamerican ceremonial facilities, iconography, and goods. Now a UNESCO World Heritage Site, Paquimé is administered by the Mexican government, has a world-class museum, and is easily accessible to visitors (Kelley and Phillips Jr., 2017; Minnis and Whalen, 2016).

Paquimé was a large, influential, and vibrant community during the Medio Period, 1200–1450 BCE. Its multistory adobe domestic structures contained 1,000 or more rooms that housed a large population (Figure 10.2). In addition, Paquimé was a political and ritual center with public architecture where important ceremonies took place. Large ball courts, massive ovens for communal food preparation, and many small platform mounds are present, some of which are in the shapes of animals.

Many imported, exotic goods were found at Paquimé, including over four million shell artifacts, a few copper items, and the remains of hundreds of macaws and parrots. Scholars still debate their uses in ritual and economy.

The community was favored by its excellent location, with a dependable water supply, abundant high-quality farmland, and a robust mix of nearby environments including mountain ranges, river valleys, and extensive plains. This natural wealth likely allowed Paquimé to become the dominant town in the region.

Many basic questions remain. How did Paquimé become so important? How extensive was its power over hundreds of neighboring communities? How was that power used, and why did it end?

Paul E. Minnis and Michael E. Whalen

FIGURE 10.2 Main building block at Paquimé

Early Hohokam settlers were Sonoran Desert farmers, who grew crops using irrigation. Their practices spread in modified forms to the Mogollon and Ancestral Pueblo peoples north and east of them. The earliest Mogollon sites are clusters of pithouses, often located on high ground in rugged eastern Arizona and western New Mexico where the Colorado Plateau gives way to lower deserts.

TABLE 10.1 The Pecos chronology of the Ancestral Pueblo (Anasazi) tradition. Dates vary from one area to another

Periods	*Approximate Dates*
Basketmaker II	0 to 400–500 CE
Basketmaker III	400–500 to 725–750 CE
Pueblo I	725–750 to 920 CE
Pueblo II	920 to 1100 CE
Pueblo III	1100 to 1300 CE
Pueblo IV	1300 to 1600 CE
Pueblo V	1600 CE to present

The first villages appeared around 200 BCE. Each had fewer than 20 houses on high ground, some on the ridges and bluffs of the Mogollon Rim, from which archaeologists have taken the name of the tradition.

Ancestral Pueblo emerged as the largest major cultural tradition of the region (Table 10.1). For decades, this tradition has been termed "Anasazi," a word that means "enemy ancestors" in Navajo. It is a term that is neither accurate nor appealing to modern Pueblo Indians, their living descendants. Some people argue that it should be abandoned, and for the most part it has been here. But "Anasazi" is so entrenched in the literature that avoiding it without explanation could be confusing (Cordell, 1984).

The Ancestral Pueblo solution to farming was a flexible form of dry farming, raising maize and other crops where rainfall and springs made productive cultivation possible. Seeps and springs along the cliffs of the plateau were used to supplement natural rainfall in many places. Small fields were laid out in those places, an intensive yet finely tuned approach to farming (Damp et al., 2002).

For Ancestral Pueblo farmers, a slight drop in rainfall or a slight rise in temperature could end the productivity of most fields around a village and force people to relocate. Despite the hazards of living on the edge, Ancestral Pueblo communities prospered and expanded over time, branches of the culture eventually spreading to portions of five modern states. Fluctuating environmental conditions forced the delicately adapted communities to abandon some areas even as they expanded into others, so no single map can accurately portray the history of this dynamic tradition (Malakoff, 2015).

Demography and Conflict

A major problem in archaeological reconstruction has long been to determine whether the prehistoric traditions of the Southwest arose from the spread of key Mesoamerican cultigens to local bands of Archaic hunter-gatherers or if they arose from the northward expansion of farmers who brought domesticates with them from Mexico. Accumulating evidence currently indicates that the latter reconstruction of Mexican influence, followed by secondary developments among local cultures, is more likely. People speaking Uto-Aztecan languages probably expanded northward, eventually reaching the Colorado Plateau by the first millennium BCE. Words for "maize" and other key agricultural terms were already present in the Uto-Aztecan protolanguage at that time, consistent with the archaeological evidence (Hill, 2001).

Hohokam people in southern Arizona established villages at key points, where they could tap into rivers of the Sonoran Desert. They depended upon human-made irrigation ditches, bringing

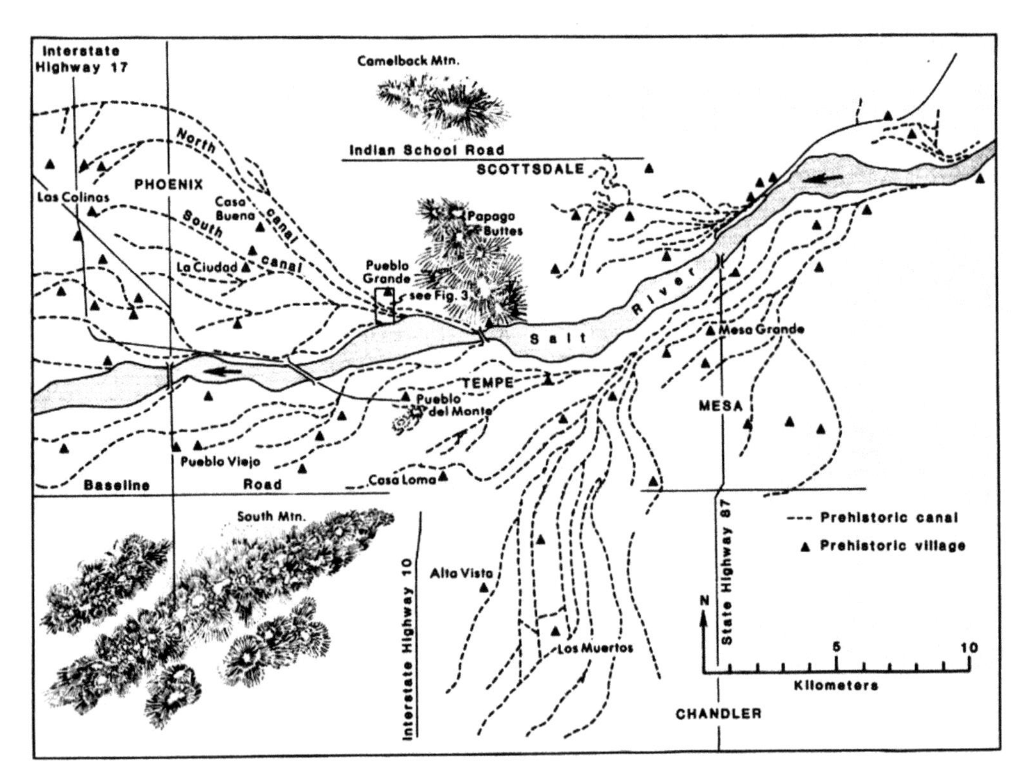

FIGURE 10.3 Hohokam canals in the Phoenix area. From Masse, 1981: 410

water to their fields as early as 800–200 BCE, but irrigation had already been practiced farther south for centuries, and maize had been in the region for even longer (Figure 10.3).

By 300 CE, Mogollon cultures were expanding and their influences can be found in Hohokam sites to the west in the southern Arizona desert and to the north in Ancestral Pueblo sites. They began making decorated pottery around 650 CE, often red-painted designs on brown backgrounds, their contribution to the vast range of pottery types that were produced across the Greater Southwest in the distant past and still manufactured today.

The **Mimbres** branch of Mogollon grew and aggregated into larger surface pueblo communities between 1000 and 1130 CE. Some larger villages had substantial ceremonial rooms, either above or below ground. Dependence on farming probably increased for a time, but construction of new pueblos and the manufacture of distinctive Classic Mimbres pottery came to an end when climate change affected the region (Powell-Marti and Gilman, 2006). A few older pueblos were remodeled and new adobe-walled ones were founded (Nelson and Gilman, 2017; Nelson and Hegmon, 2001).

Small band-sized communities formed the basis of early Ancestral Pueblo settlements. However, their sizes doubled by 600 CE. Despite the later start in farming, Ancestral Pueblo peoples of the Colorado Plateau expanded rapidly during the cooler and wetter conditions that prevailed across the region before 1150 CE. They reached their maximum geographic expansion to the west around then. After that, environmental conditions forced the western part of the range to contract. Later environmental change brought about population disruption, frequent migration, and the abandonment of many areas.

Ancestral Pueblo peoples spoke languages long resident in the region. The Navajos and Apaches are speakers of Athapaskan languages, a branch of the larger **Nadene** family of languages. These

FIGURE 10.4 Traditional Navajo house (*hogan*)

speakers moved into the region after 1500 CE; they had drifted southward from Canada, probably along the eastern edge of the Rocky Mountains. The Navajos and Apaches were not responsible for the contraction and dislocation of Ancestral Pueblo communities but rather moved into areas already largely abandoned by farmers. Their hunter-gatherer adaptation was well suited to conditions that emerged after the thirteenth century in the Southwest. Navajo and Apache communities remain scattered across the region today (Figure 10.4).

The Southwest was once widely considered to be a region of perpetual tranquility, but research in recent decades has shown that warfare was present, and its causes were as complicated as anywhere else. There were many contingencies. While drought might correlate with the construction of fortifications and other signatures of warfare in some cases, social and political factors might predominate in others. Some shrines related to warfare show evidence of persisting for centuries (Geib et al., 2017; Kohler et al., 2014; LeBlanc, 1999; LeBlanc, 2006; Lekson, 2002; McGuire and Villalpando, 2015; Solometo, 2006).

Subsistence and Economy

Farming practices are categorized as the Upper Sonoran Agricultural Complex: maize, bottle gourd, three kinds of beans (pinto, navy, and kidney), and squash (Ford, 1985). While the Hohokam depended on larger-scale irrigation, the early Mogollon people probably used simpler irrigation techniques. Hunting and gathering resources supplemented the diet in good years and served as a backup in years when crops failed. Like the Hohokam and Ancestral Pueblo farmers, crops probably included tobacco.

Subsistence practices of the early Ancestral Pueblos were rudimentary compared to the Mogollon and Hohokam around 100 BCE but quickly became more complex. Initially, the Ancestral Pueblos concentrated on maize and squash cultivation, adding beans and domesticated turkeys after 500 CE. Early houses had depressed clay floors, although pithouses were not yet features of Ancestral Pueblo settlements. Pottery, derived from Mogollon prototypes, was not adopted by Ancestral Pueblo people until around 450 CE (Lipe et al., 2016; Schollmeyer and Turner, 2004).

Pueblo culture did not emerge simultaneously across the Colorado Plateau, dating to 500 CE in the east and 700 CE in the west. Developments included greater emphases on farming and permanent housing, clustering of pithouses into hamlets and villages, and replacement of the spear thrower by the bow and arrow. Eastern Ancestral Pueblo villages were particularly large, and some came to feature large communal structures, great **kiva**s like those built by people of the Mogollon tradition. In tandem with these social and demographic changes, the use of pottery became widespread in Ancestral Pueblo communities.

Pottery provided early archaeologists with a means to define a series of ceramic phases for the Ancestral Pueblo tradition, known as the Pecos classification system (Table 10.1). The Pecos classification is a developmental scheme rather than a strictly chronological one. Before the availability of **dendrochronology** and radiocarbon dating techniques, archaeologists used ceramic styles for cross dating local sequences. Pueblo I ceramics in one area were assumed to be roughly the same age as Pueblo I ceramics found in another. The scheme is still referenced, but dating now relies on the newer techniques (Cordell, 1997: 164–167).

Architecture and Technology

With the introduction and development of farming, people in this region built permanent settlements of stone and adobe, which were found to be durable building materials. Residential architecture survived better here than in most other regions on the continent, and today, their ruins attract many visitors.

Hohokam

Hohokam houses were mostly above-ground structures of **wattle and daub**. Hohokam irrigation engineering may seem difficult and unlikely under premodern conditions, but it is not. Rivers with steep gradients run fast. Digging a ditch from the edge of a fast river toward the inland creates a more sluggish canal with less steep gradient. The ditch can be made to veer farther from the river by controlling its gradient, letting it wind along the lower slopes of bluffs adjacent to the river's floodplain. Even a short canal allows a farmer to water crops between the canal and the river by breaching the irrigation ditch slightly uphill from the fields. Water from the ditch then flows down across the fields. As the ditch is extended and it veers farther from the faster-flowing river, more fields can be opened for irrigation agriculture (Plog, 1997:75).

Digging irrigation canals was hard work, but feasible, despite the hardpan of the Sonoran Desert because water flowing in behind excavators softened the soil around the legs of diggers as they gradually worked their way across the floodplain, toward the flanking bluffs and away from the river. Digging sticks and baskets were the only tools needed for the job. Since water seeks its own level, excavators were guided from veering off track, either uphill or downhill. Additional digging every year eventually produced bigger irrigation systems with canals and secondary ditches many kilometers long, watering many hectares of land (Masse, 1981). Maintenance of these ditches was time consuming, but worth it.

Mogollon

Early Mogollon pithouses were circular, built into the ground to a height of knee or waist deep, and often built facing east. Their depths provided insulation in this cool part of the region. Excavated ramps that gave access on the east sides of the houses captured the morning sun, brightening and warming their interiors. Early pithouses were round and shallower than later ones. The change from round to square housing units was driven by the mechanical demands of surface rooms. Mogollon villagers lived mostly in pithouses before 1000 CE but in aboveground rooms after that time. Early dwellings were larger than later ones, but the significance of this architectural trend for Mogollon society is still debated. Ceremonial kivas appeared around the same time. In historic Pueblo villages kivas typically served as men's clubs and were modeled on older pithouses. They were exclusive places where male members of clan segments could gather, since residences were dominated by related females and married male clan brothers were scattered across matrilocal households. Good examples are found in the Raven site near Springerville, Arizona.

Large, square great kivas began to appear in some but not all Mogollon villages after 850 CE. These very large ceremonial structures were clearly designed to serve more than a few closely related males. Archaeologists infer that they must have served as ceremonial places for whole communities. Variations in architectural details over time and space suggest that local groups varied culturally (Gilman and Stone, 2013). The bow and arrow appeared before 1000 CE, although Mogollon hunters retained spear throwers as well for many years.

Mimbres was a culture of the Mogollon tradition best known for spectacularly decorated pottery bowls late in its history, 1000–1130 CE (Brody, 2004; Creel and Anyon, 2003). Settlements in the early phases were clusters of circular pithouses on the tops of steep hills and ridges.

Mimbres pottery reached its peak after 1000 CE. It is particularly appealing to modern tastes, with the consequence that many Mimbres sites have been irreparably damaged or destroyed through systematic looting, sometimes using bulldozers. Many vessels are bowls with stylized human, animal, and other designs on their interiors. Symbols range from figurative to nonfigurative and depicted in positive or negative views. Vessels used as burial offerings were often symbolically killed, with holes deliberately puncturing their bottoms. While they were very well made and exquisitely decorated, probably by craft specialists, there is no evidence that they were intended for use by an elite minority.

MATTOCKS SITE

Most large Mimbres Classic (1000–1130 CE) pueblos superimpose many earlier pit structures and great kivas (200–1000 CE). They also had pottery production and distribution during this Pithouse period and houses that were transitional between pit structures and pueblo rooms. During the Classic period, these large pueblos (more than 100 rooms) had room blocks inhabited by corporate extended families, and there was much imported marine shell on most sites (Nelson and Gilman, 2017; Shafer, 2003).

The Mattocks site was different. It was a large Classic site with six to eight pueblo room blocks and about 180 rooms, but there were only three earlier pithouses (Figure 10.5). Mattocks did have a great kiva, but there was only one pit structure contemporary with it on the site, suggesting that the people who built and owned the Great Kiva did not attract others to live with them at the site and to therefore help with the community ceremonies performed in that structure. Mattocks had no transitional houses and no pottery production during the Pithouse period. Single families that were not extended or corporate probably occupied each room block, with only one family through time per room block. There was little marine shell on the Mattocks site (Gilman and LeBlanc, 2017).

FIGURE 10.5 Mattocks site Classic period room block showing the contiguous rooms. Photograph courtesy of Patricia A. Gilman

The differences between the Mattocks and other Mimbres pueblos suggest that not many people, and perhaps just one family, lived at the Mattocks site until the Classic period. People during the Classic period had a different social structure and context than those at other sites, given the one family per room block. The paucity of marine shell hints that people at the Mattocks site did not have the social connections needed to obtain such shell, they did not want the shell, or they were kept from having this important item. They probably did produce chipped-stone hoes and ground stone axes for others in the Mimbres region, signifying a special, although relatively minor, role for them.

Located in the northern Mimbres Valley in southwestern New Mexico, the Mattocks site is part of the Mimbres Cultural Heritage site, which is owned and protected by the Imogen F. Wilson Education Foundation and Archaeology Southwest and which is open to the public.

Patricia A. Gilman

Ancestral Pueblo

Permanent Ancestral Pueblo architecture began as clusters of round semisubterranean pithouses. Early shallow pithouses had excavated side entrances and smoke holes above their central hearths. Later pithouses were deep, so much so that their cribwork roofs were at or slightly aboveground level. Smoke holes eventually doubled as entrances, and side entrances narrowed to become ventilator shafts. This modification ensured the inflow of fresh air and the outflow of smoke through the smoke hole.

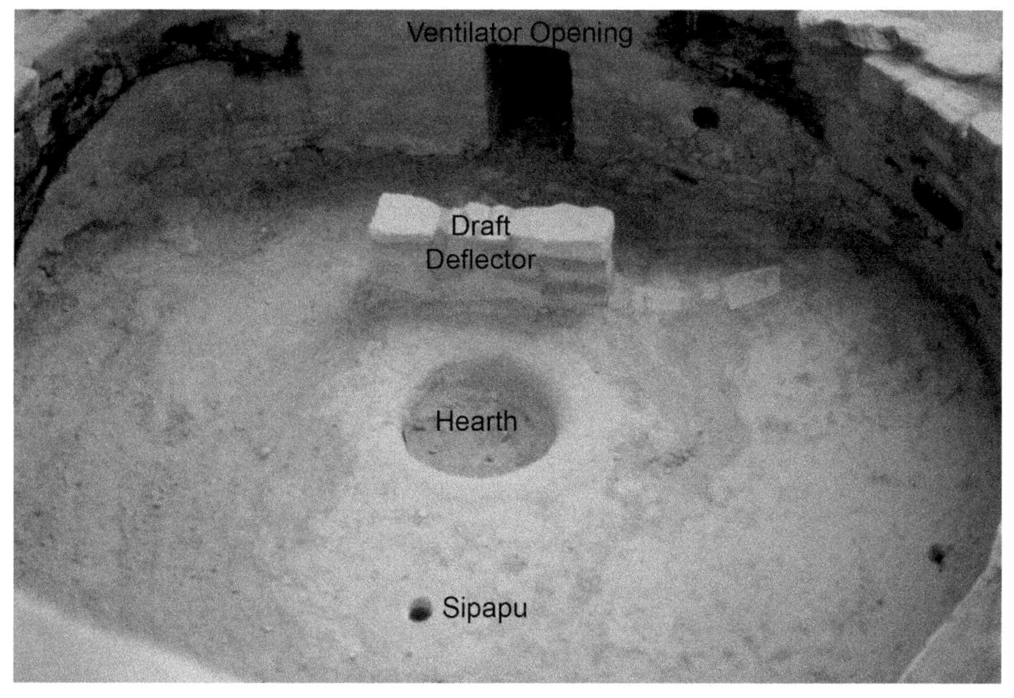

FIGURE 10.6 Kivas exhibit standard features. Pilasters to hold up cribwork roofs and niches to hold special objects are often present. Mesa Verde National Park

Later aboveground houses were constructed from laid masonry or adobe, with contiguous square or rectangular habitation and storage rooms often sharing common walls. Subterranean rooms continued to be built as ceremonial kivas. Larger communities eventually featured great kivas, plazas, and towers.

By 800 CE, villages often had both residential pithouses and surface residences. Kivas evolved out of earlier pithouse forms, which served as meeting places for related males in what were becoming strong matrilineal societies. Great kivas were being built as larger centers of community activity in eastern Ancestral Pueblo communities by this time, but they remained absent in the West, where villages were smaller and less numerous. Typically, kivas consist of four diagnostic features: a ventilator shaft, a deflector in front of it to prevent strong drafts, a hearth, and a **sipapu** (Figure 10.6). The last is the symbolic representation of the hole through which people emerged into the world in Pueblo myth.

The stone available in Chaco Canyon, New Mexico, worked well for masons, and perhaps it was for this reason that the **Chaco Phenomenon** arose where it did. The stone splits easily into tabular slabs, which are perfect for the walls of multistory buildings. Masonry techniques and materials evolved over time as Chacoan builders perfected their craft and came to depend less on thick mud mortar. Figure 10.7 shows a simplified succession of improving bonds over time.

Chacoan communities controlled regional turquoise trade by the ninth century. Chaco Canyon became a distribution hub for a system that imported turquoise from distant quarries and at least some of it was exported in exchange for a variety of goods. Residues in the cylindrical vessels (mentioned above) contain evidence of cacao, linking Chaco to the Mesoamerican chocolate drink and probably its associated ritual (Crown and Hurst, 2009). Copper bells, macaws, and conch shell

FIGURE 10.7 Masonry evolution in Chaco Canyon, from rough stone and thick mortar (left) to dressed stones and little mortar (right)

trumpets from Mexico have all been found in Chacoan sites. Chacoan roads linked great houses locally and linked the canyon to at least 30 more distant outliers (Figure 10.8). Archaeologists have mapped 400 km (250 mi) of roads so far, and there might be a total of 650 km (400 mi). Some predict that five times that total might eventually be found in the Chacoan road network (Watson et al., 2015).

Chacoan roads were built up to 12 m (40 ft) wide and very straight. One example is 95 km (59 mi) long. The Chacoans lacked wheeled vehicles but their roads ran straight because they overcame rock outcrops by cutting steps into them. Roads were occasionally discontinuous, and in places, there were sharp angles. Researchers have hypothesized that the roads were designed to facilitate pilgrimages to Chaco Canyon. This hypothesis accounts for several aspects of Chacoan society (Judge, 1989; Vivian, 1990). It explains how timbers were acquired and transported, why the roads were so well built, why there is a surplus of rooms in Chacoan great houses, and why turquoise was important. Other evidence is not always consistent with the pilgrimage hypothesis (Plog and Watson, 2012).

Cotton was brought to the area by 850 CE, an important introduction from Mexico. Cotton is difficult to transform into cloth, but it makes for more desirable fabrics than do native fibers. Cotton served well for clothing since animal hides were scarce. Some specimens of cotton cloth are so finely made that they can be mistaken for lace.

Ancestral Puebloans made pottery that ranged from plain and corrugated gray utility wares to a series of painted wares. The latter were often black-on-white, black-on-red, or polychrome painted types. All were traditionally made by the coil and scrape method. Vessels were varied and specialized after 1100 CE, and often traded between communities (Glowacki et al., 2015; Harry et al., 2013).

In some areas, influence from potters working in the Mogollon region led to the development of oxidized types of vessels with red, yellow, and orange designs. By firing the pots in ways that allow oxygen to circulate around the vessels thereby oxidizing the paints, potters learned how to produce the bright colors. A true glaze was developed by potters along the upper Rio Grande,

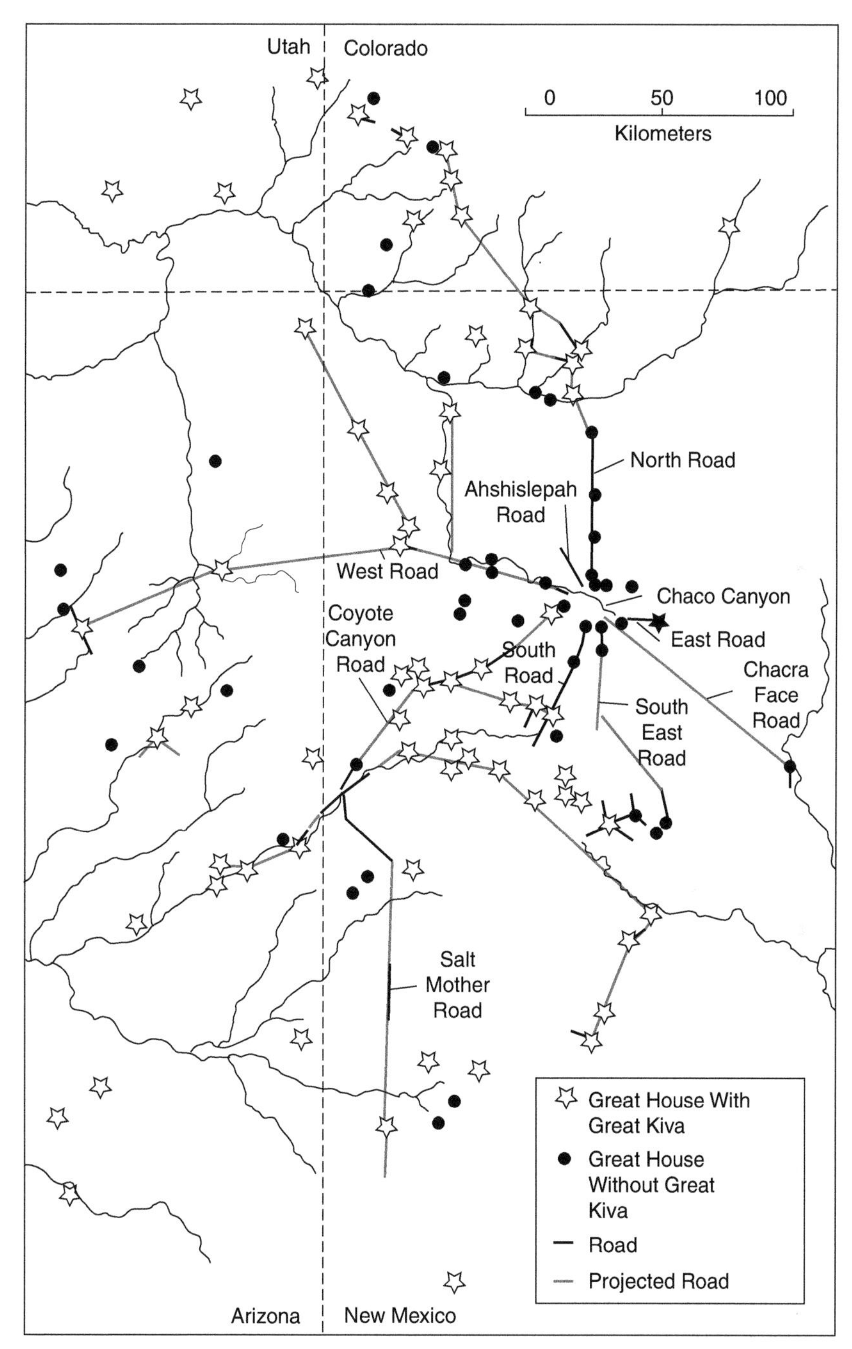

FIGURE 10.8 Chacoan regional roads

but it does not appear that the glaze was used to coat and waterproof whole vessels. Ancestral Puebloans preferred porous pottery, which kept liquids cooler by allowing vessels to sweat. Firing pots on top of fuel, but covered so that oxygen cannot reach them, leads to chemical reduction of the paints used in decoration, yielding a range of white, gray, and black shades. Modern Puebloan potters have retained these traditional techniques and painted designs.

Culture, Language, and Identity

Language Families

The distribution of the six native language families in the Southwest region reflects their long complex histories. Speakers of the Nadene languages arrived about five centuries ago, when climate change forced farmers to retreat, opening up vast areas for simpler hunter-gatherer societies. Uto-Aztecan is much older and the likely language family of the first immigrant farmers. Three other language families – Keresan, Kiowa-Tanoan, and Cochimí-Yuman – have ancient roots in the West. The Zuni language might be related to California Penutian, but its origins remain a topic of debate. All of these language families survive in the region, still being spoken by modern Native American descendants of the ancient traditions.

The Chaco Phenomenon

The Chaco Phenomenon was perhaps the most remarkable of all Ancestral Pueblo developments (Lekson, 2006; Noble, 2004; Sebastian, 1996; Vivian and Hilpert, 2002). Like some other archaeological centers, the center of the Chaco Phenomenon is hard to define. People settled Chaco Canyon around 490 CE, and initially it was little different from other Ancestral Pueblo areas. However, by 860 CE, there were many small communities in the canyon and a few larger ones. Larger communities held 100–120 households, and the total population in the early years was probably 1,000–1,500 people.

CHACO CANYON

In a small canyon in the arid and sparsely populated San Juan Basin of northwestern New Mexico lie the ruins of one of the most spectacular prehistoric cultures of the American Southwest. Now protected as Chaco Culture National Historical Park and honored by UNESCO as a World Heritage Site, the canyon contains 11 huge stone buildings or great houses, some of them four stories high and containing hundreds of rooms (Figure 10.9). Smaller stone buildings, mounds, large subterranean ceremonial structures (great kivas), roads, rock-cut stairways, and water-control and garden features combine to form a dense, symbolically ordered landscape.

By the eleventh century CE, Chaco Canyon was the central place for hundreds of culturally related sites and communities in present-day New Mexico, Utah, Arizona, and Colorado. These far-flung sites are related to Chaco Canyon not only by similarities in architectural and site layout but by a system of well-engineered roads and by elevated signaling stations.

Excavations in both the canyon and the outlying communities of the larger Chacoan world have yielded wealth items, such as turquoise and shell, and exotic goods, such as parrots, copper bells, and chocolate imported from Mesoamerica. The presence of highly formalized great kivas, mounds and shrines, and features believed to mark the solstices, equinoxes, and various lunar phenomena clearly indicate that the Chacoan people experienced rich ceremonial and spiritual lives as well.

After more than 120 years of archaeological research in Chaco Canyon and the larger Chaco World, researchers have amassed huge amounts of data and achieved much consensus about the nature of Chacoan life – architecture, artifacts, diet, technology, environment,

FIGURE 10.9 Pueblo Bonito, the largest great house in Chaco Canyon

chronology (Lekson, 2006; Mathien, 2005). But explaining the cultural elaboration and geographical extent of Chaco – was it a stratified society, a theocracy, a communal cooperative venture? – remains a subject of continuing controversy and ongoing research.

Lynne Sebastian

The heyday of Chaco was 900–1125 CE, sustained by cooler and wetter conditions that favored new strains of maize. Chacoan laborers gradually built a system of roads that radiated out to other Ancestral Pueblo centers, creating a regional web of trade and exchange between Chaco Canyon and an array of Chacoan outliers. Proximal sites tended to be on locations that shared intervisibility; a person could often see one or more neighboring sites in the network (Van Dyke et al., 2016).

Chaco Canyon villagers reached their maximum population of around 5,500 people by 1050 CE. There is no evidence of centralized government, so most archaeologists infer that it was probably organized around ritual, as is still the case among the Hopi. Despite this politically weak form of chiefdom organization, Chacoan builders accomplished great things, such as the importation of 200,000 timbers for construction projects, most of them from great distances (English et al., 2001).

The most striking D-shaped pueblo in Chaco Canyon is Pueblo Bonito. A few other smaller villages in the canyon include Wijiji, Tsin Kletzin, and Kin Kletso. All of these were rapidly built by 1100 CE. Roof beams were imported from great distances, many more rooms were built than needed by the resident population, and turquoise was an important material (Crown and Judge, 1991; Lekson, 1991).

In addition to the many large structures in Chaco Canyon, there were at least 70 outlier communities by 1115 CE, which include the sites known as Aztec and Salmon. They tended to be located at 32–40-km (20–25-mi) intervals, which is a hard one-day journey on foot. Not all of them were linked by Chacoan roads, but most were linked to each other and with Chaco Canyon by signal stations located on cliff tops. Many outliers mimicked the D-shaped structures of the great houses in Chaco Canyon. It appears that they might have supplied food to the central communities in the canyon, which were probably not self-sustaining if current population estimates are correct.

The cultures of the Southwest participated in interpersonal games and athletic competitions analogous to those described for other regions of North America. Recent work has shown that gambling was an important part of these activities, which was integrated with other social institutions (Weiner, 2018).

Art and Symbolism

Rock art is found throughout the region, sometimes in the vicinities of well-known residential sites as well as scattered in remote locations. They are the frequent subject of popular publications because they are at once visually captivating, mysterious, and at risk. The art found in the numerous canyons of southeastern Utah provide a good example (Repanshek, 2005).

Dating and symbolic interpretation of rock art continue to be challenging. There is an urgency to document the art owing to the risks from human activities, including vandalism, and from natural erosion. There has been recent progress in the direct dating of rock art, allowing those cases to be linked with known archaeological cultures in the region. The famous All American Man pictograph (Figure 10.10) in the Upper Salt Creek canyon of Canyonlands National Park has been dated to the fourteenth century CE, suggesting that the art is likely associated with one of the variants of Ancestral Pueblo or Fremont cultures that were thriving in the region at the time (Chaffee et al., 1994). The meaning(s) of the pictograph remains elusive.

FIGURE 10.10 All-American Man pictograph, Canyonlands National Park. Courtesy of Tom Till Photography

Mogollon

The Mimbres people of southwestern New Mexico participated in the use of great kivas until 1000 CE, but in the ensuing years, they ceased using them. The arrival of scarlet macaws and Mesoamerican symbolism in the same period suggest Mimbres began participating in long-distant networks linked to Mexican centers far to the south, with profound effects on their ritual culture (Gilman et al., 2014).

Farther east, people of the Jorada branch of the Mogollon tradition appear to have been responsible for the Hueco Tanks pictographs near El Paso. The more-than 200 human, bird, and other animal faces are often inferred to represent masks, the largest such collection in North America. The specific meanings of the symbols remain uncertain, but the site is regarded as sacred by several descendant communities in the region.

The earliest Mimbres pottery dates between 200 and 550 CE. It was brown and undecorated, standard for all early Mogollon phases. Later types were red-slipped, and then still later, decorated red-on-brown types. Around 750 CE Mimbres potters began applying a white slip to vessels before decorating them with red paint. Designs were more complex than previously. Still later, vessels were fired in reducing rather than oxidizing atmospheres, causing the red paint to turn black during firing (Figure 10.11). At this time too people in the Mimbres region were moving their villages from the ridge tops down to terraces near streams. Houses were square and burials accompanied by black-on-white painted vessels were often placed beneath the floors.

Ancestral Pueblo

The petroglyphs of Chaco Canyon attract interest and speculation, but are not easy to be linked with beliefs and rituals. Curiously, both burials and petroglyphs indicate that people with six-toed feet lived at Pueblo Bonito and may have held special status (Crown et al., 2016).

FIGURE 10.11 Late Mimbres bowls. Mesa Verde National Park

Fajada Butte is a solitary natural monument in Chaco Canyon with a small rock shelter containing an enigmatic spiral petroglyph. Three large stone slabs near its top enclose a small space, probably used by shamans (Plog, 1997: 100–101). The slabs lie at odd angles, but claims that they were deliberately moved there by humans are doubtful. Sunlight shining through cracks between the slabs casts slivers of light on the interior rock face. The positions of the "sun daggers" vary through the year.

The **Kachina Cult** flourished in the difficult years during which the Ancestral Pueblo villagers abandoned many of their settlements and moved to locations where farming was still possible. Kachinas remain an important part of Hopi culture and religion today, supplying inspiration for replicas that are carved from cottonwood and sold to collectors worldwide.

The major traditions of the Greater Southwest fared well before the climate changes that began around 1150 CE, and hunter-gatherers who lived at the margins of the region sometimes adopted farming, pottery, and the basics of settled life from them. One such cultural development is characterized by the Patayan tradition, which emerged among peoples living along the Colorado River on the western margin of the Southwest. The Patayan people adopted agriculture and settled life primarily from the Ancestral Pueblo and Hohokam traditions, but they never built the elaborate pueblo dwellings and ritual structures found at the region's core. Large enigmatic ground figures occur in Patayan territory. Those near Blythe, California, are particularly notable. It is not known whether they were made by the Patayan people or their ancestors. The figures were created by moving weathered rocks to the side, resulting in light figures on a darker background, which are best appreciated from the air. Like the large effigy mounds of the northern Midwest, they were invested with symbolic significance about which we can now only speculate.

Resilience and Collapse

Environmental changes after 1150 CE forced new strategies upon all peoples of the Greater Southwest. Dendrochronology allows for precise dating of this climatic episode. A severe drought from 1276 to 1299 CE resulted in widespread social and economic disruption across the region. Outermost villages collapsed first and refugees from them retreated to more centrally located surviving communities, thereby stressing the available resource base of increasingly larger population centers. Warfare broke out between Ancestral Pueblo communities as they competed for water and other increasingly scarce resources (Jones et al., 1999; LeBlanc, 1999; Polyak and Asmerom, 2001).

Hard times for the Hohokam (Akimel O'Odham) communities around modern Phoenix began as early as 1020–1160 CE, when they experienced widespread erosion of their irrigation canals. Larger towns were partially or entirely abandoned in the face of this breakdown of irrigation systems. Many Hohokam communities underwent significant change during the demographic disruptions that followed climate change (Ingram, 2008; Loendorf and Lewis, 2017; McClelland, 2015).

Some Mogollon communities dispersed as early as 1150 CE, while others persisted until 1450 CE. Mimbres pottery dwindled after 1130 CE and disappeared by 1150 CE, replaced by other forms. Gila Polychrome ceramics were added later as Mimbres people were included in the widespread **Salado** phenomenon. New Salado pottery styles resulted from the migration of Ancestral Pueblo people moving southward to areas where farming was still viable. Some of them took up residence in the Mimbres region, just as others did at Casa Grande. The spread of Salado pottery styles was linked to active processes of ethnogenesis during this time of turmoil. Salado styles were derived from older traditions as refugees and even whole communities relocated, merged, and adapted to new circumstances.

FIGURE 10.12 Gila Polychrome vessel, an example of Salado pottery

Salado pottery types spread rapidly in the thirteenth century across parts of the Hohokam and Mogollon ranges as well as some adjoining territory (Figure 10.12). The central pottery type is Gila Polychrome. Salado ceramics were particularly dominant in three branches of the Mogollon tradition during the thirteenth and early fourteenth century. The late great adobe house site of Casa Grande and the cliff dwelling at Tonto are two examples with evidence for this cultural transformation. After 1450 CE, the last of the Mimbres people including the refugees disappeared from the area, and the landscape became home to newcomers, Apache hunter-gatherers (Nelson et al., 2006).

MESA VERDE

Home to farming ancestors of contemporary Pueblo Indians for 700 years, Mesa Verde National Park today protects some of the best-preserved remains documenting their extraordinary growth and eventual departure under duress. On a sloping mesa highest along its northern edge, Mesa Verde's elevation helps ensure adequate precipitation, while the southern dip allows cold air to drain and catches additional sunshine. With fertile wind-deposited topsoil, Mesa Verde supported the region's densest populations, well situated to withstand drought and cold (Schwindt et al., 2016).

Pioneering Basketmaker III farmers colonized Mesa Verde shortly before 600 CE, and the sorts of pithouses they built and occupied can still be seen today. These farmers already relied heavily on maize although they grew squash and beans, gathered numerous wild plants, and hunted. By the middle ninth century, Pueblo I villages of 100 households, each consisting of a pit structure and adjacent surface rooms, were present.

Population declined markedly beginning around 900 CE, as poor growing conditions affected even Mesa Verde. Immigration resumed in the next century (Pueblo II), and Mesa Verde experienced its peak population in the late 1000s, including a number of sites with Chacoan characteristics (see Chaco Canyon). Some of these contain massive masonry Great Houses with very large, round great kivas partially excavated into the ground for dances and other ceremonies (Lipe, 2006).

FIGURE 10.13 Cliff Palace, a large community on Mesa Verde

Many of the park's most famous sites, such as Cliff Palace (Figure 10.13) and Spruce Tree House, were built in alcoves that helped preserve their structures. These Pueblo III sites mainly date to the last decades of occupation, 1250–1280 CE. Their defensive placement, and the fact that they were built as farmers elsewhere in the region were already starting to leave, suggest a pervasive feeling of apprehension. The inhabitants soon rejoined their relatives in the northern Rio Grande region of New Mexico and other refuges to the south (Kohler et al., 2008b).

Timothy A. Kohler

Ancestral Pueblo communities completely abandoned the San Juan River drainage around 1300 CE. People from Mesa Verde moved to the Rio Grande area, augmenting the village populations of that area (Kohler, 2004). Chacoan people dispersed and founded new villages to the south by the early 1200s, while other communities either merged with Pueblos in the area where their Hopi descendants still survive or relocated to join Mogollon communities, forming multiethnic communities. Another branch concentrated where their modern Zuni descendants still live. Some sites, such as Bandelier, Pecos, and Kuaua, have long prehistoric sequences and persisted into the Spanish colonial period. The Kachina Cult grew rapidly under these stressful conditions of population relocations as religious movements often do. It appeared in nearly all Pueblo religious systems after their relocations, and it may have served in part to integrate the amalgamating new communities (Cordell et al., 2007; Kohler et al., 2008a; Schwindt et al., 2016).

Navajo culture illustrates the speed and ease with which pervasive culture change can occur. The Navajos acquired weaving and pottery-making from Ancestral Pueblo teachers. At the same time, the Navajos acquired sheep and herding practices from the Spanish; wool rather than cotton or wild fibers became the favored material for weaving. The Navajos also learned to cast silver from the Spanish, and they combined this knowledge with the traditional use of turquoise in the region to produce the jewelry for which they, and many Pueblo communities, remain well known. The indigenous landscape of the Greater Southwest, familiar to many people today, is the outcome of adjustments to climate, demographic, and cultural changes over thousands of years.

Glossary

Ancestral Pueblo A comprehensive term for the prehistoric cultures of the Colorado Plateau of northern Arizona and New Mexico, whose descendants include the modern Pueblos. One of three major traditions of the Southwest, who emerged from Archaic cultures of the same region. Distinguish from "pueblo," which refers to a form of stone and adobe architecture.

Chaco Phenomenon A special case of one branch of the Ancestral Pueblo tradition. Centered at Chaco Canyon, New Mexico, but with widespread outliers.

dendrochronology A technique that uses tree rings to date samples of wooden timbers found in archaeological sites. Also known as tree-ring dating.

Hohokam One of the major prehistoric traditions of the Southwest, located in the Sonoran Desert of southern Arizona. Probably founded by Uto-Aztecan migrants from what is now Mexico.

Kachina Cult Alternatively, "Katsina" or "Katcina" Cult, is an Ancestral Pueblo cult focused on a series of over 200 supernatural beings that are often represented in the art of descendant Pueblos.

kiva A subterranean or semisubterranean room used for ceremonial purposes, often by related men, in the Greater Southwest. Great kivas accommodated larger groups, sometimes including whole communities.

Mimbres A branch of Mogollon popularly known for its ceramics.

Mogollon One of three major traditions of the Southwest. The tradition emerged from Archaic cultures in the mountains of Arizona and New Mexico.

Nadene The language family that includes the Athapaskan branch to which Navajo and Apache languages belong.

Patayan A minor tradition of western Arizona and adjacent California, ancestral to modern cultures whose members speak languages of the Cochimí–Yuman family.

Salado A derivative culture that arose through the amalgamation of refugee communities in the wake of demographic disruptions following climate change characterized by hotter and drier conditions.

Sinagua A secondary culture of the Verde Valley in central Arizona, located between the three major traditions of the region.

sipapu A symbolic hole found in the floor of an Ancestral Pueblo kiva.

wattle and daub A construction technique involving wood pole frames and adobe mud applied to smaller sticks woven into uprights.

References

Brody, J.J. (2004). *Mimbres Painted Pottery*. Santa Fe, NM: School of American Research Press.

Chaffee, S.D., Hyman, M., Rowe, M., Coullam, N., Schreodl, A., and Hogue, K. (1994). Radiocarbon Dates on the All American Man Pictograph. *American Antiquity*, 59, pp. 769–781.

Cordell, L.S. (1984). *Prehistory of the Southwest*. New York: Academic Press.

Cordell, L.S. (1997). *Archaeology of the Southwest*. New York: Academic Press.

Cordell, L.S., Van West, C.R., Dean, J.S., and Muenchrath, D.A. (2007). Climate Change, Social Networks, and Ancestral Pueblo Migration. *Kiva*, 72, pp. 391–417.

Creel, D., and Anyon, R. (2003). New Interpretations of Mimbres Public Architecture and Space: Implications for Cultural Change. *American Antiquity*, 68, pp. 67–92.

Crown, P. L., and Hurst, W. J. (2009). Evidence of Cacao Use in the Prehispanic American Southwest. *Proceedings of the National Academy of Sciences*, 106, 2110–2113.

Crown, P.L., and Judge, W.J., eds. (1991). *Chaco & Hohokam: Prehistoric Regional Systems in the American Southwest*. Santa Fe, NM: School of American Research Press.

Crown, P.L., Marden, K., and Mattson, H.V. (2016). Foot Notes: The Social Implications of Polydactyly and Foot-Related Imagery at Pueblo Bonito, Chaco Canyon. *American Antiquity*, 81, pp. 426–448.

Damp, J.E., Hall, S.A., and Smith, S.J. (2002). Early Irrigation on the Colorado Plateau near Zuni Pueblo, New Mexico. *American Antiquity*, 67, pp. 665–676.

English, N.B., Betancourt, J.L., Dean, J.S., and Quade, J. (2001). Strontium Isotopes Reveal Distant Sources of Architectural Timber in Chaco Canyon, New Mexico. *Proceedings of the National Academy of Sciences*, 98, pp. 11891–11896.

Ford, R.I. (1985). *Prehistoric Food Production in North America*. Ann Arbor: Museum of Anthropology, University of Michigan.

Geib, P.R., Heitman, C.C., and Fields, R.C.D. (2017). Continuity and Change in Puebloan Ritual Practice: 3,800 Years of Shrine Use in the North American Southwest. *American Antiquity*, 82, pp. 353–373.

Gilman, P.A., and LeBlanc, S.A. (2017). *Mimbres Life and Society: The Mattocks Site of Southwestern New Mexico*, Tucson: University of Arizona Press.

Gilman, P.A., and Stone, T. (2013). The Role of Ritual Variability in Social Negotiations of Early Communities: Great Kiva Homogeneity and Heterogeneity in the Mogollon Region of the North American Southwest. *American Antiquity*, 78, pp. 607–623.

Gilman, P.A., Thompson, M., and Wyckoff, K.C. (2014). Ritual Change and the Distant: Mesoamerican Iconography, Scarlet Macaws, and Great Kivas in the Mimbres Region of Southwestern New Mexico. *American Antiquity*, 79, pp. 90–107.

Glowacki, D.M., Ferguson, J.R., Hurst, W., and Cameron, C.M. (2015). Crossing Comb Ridge: Pottery Production and Procurement Among Southeast Utah Great House Communities. *American Antiquity*, 80, pp. 472–491.

Hard, R.J., and Roney, J.R. (1998). A Massive Terraced Village Complex in Chihuahua, Mexico, 3000 Years Before Present. *Science*, 279, pp. 1661–1664.

Harry, K.G., Ferguson, T.J., Allison, J.R., Mclaurin, B.T., Ferguson, J., and Lyneis, M. (2013). Examining the Production and Distribution of Shivwits Ware Pottery in the American Southwest. *American Antiquity*, 78, pp. 385–396.

Hill, J.H. (2001). Proto-Uto-Aztecan: A Community of Cultivators in Central Mexico? *American Anthropologist*, 103, pp. 913–934.

Ingram, S.E. (2008). Streamflow and Population Change in the Lower Salt River Valley of Central Arizona, ca. A.D. 775 to 1450. *American Antiquity*, 73, pp. 136–165.

Jones, T.L., Brown, G.M., Raab, L.M., Mcvickar, J.L., Spaulding, W. G., Kennett, D.J., York, A., and Walker, P.L. (1999). Environmental Imperatives Reconsidered: Demographic Crises in Western North America during the Medieval Climatic Anomaly. *Current Anthropology*, 40, pp. 137–170.

Judge, W.J. (1989). Chaco Canyon-San Juan Basin. In: L.S. Cordell and G.J. Gumerman, eds. *Dynamics of Southwest Prehistory*. Washington, DC: Smithsonian Institution Press.

Kantner, J. (2005). *Ancient Puebloan Southwest*. New York: Cambridge University Press.

Kelley, J.H., and Phillips, D.A. Jr. (2017). *Not So Far from Paquimé: Essays on the Archaeology of Chihuahua, Mexico*. Salt Lake City: University of Utah Press.

Kohler, T.A., ed. (2004). *Archaeology of Bandelier National Monument: Village Formation on the Pajarito Plateau, New Mexico*. Albuquerque: University of New Mexico Press.

Kohler, T.A., Glaude, M.P., Bocquet-Appel, J.-P., and Kemp, B.M. (2008a). The Neolithic demographic transition in the U.S. Southwest. *American Antiquity*, 73, pp. 645–669.

Kohler, T.A., Ortman, S.G., Grundtisch, K.E., Fitzpatrick, C.M., and Cole, S.M. (2014). The Better Angels of Their Nature: Declining Violence Through Time among Prehispanic Farmers of the Pueblo Southwest. *American Antiquity*, 79, pp. 444–464.

Kohler, T.A., Varien, M.D., Wright, A., and Kuckelman, K.A. (2008b). Mesa Verde Migrations: New Archaeological Research and Computer Simulation Suggest Why Ancestral Puebloans Deserted the Northern Southwest United States. *American Scientist*, 96, pp. 146–153.

LeBlanc, S.A. (1999). *Prehistoric Warfare in the American Southwest*. Salt Lake City: University of Utah Press.

LeBlanc, S.A. (2006). Warfare and the Development of Social Complexity. In: E.N. Arkush and M.W. Allen, eds. *The Archaeology of Warfare: Prehistories of Raiding and Conquest*. Gainesville: University Press of Florida.

Lekson, S.H. (1991). Settlement Pattern and the Chaco Region. In: P.L. Crown and W.J. Judge, eds. *Chaco & Hohokam: Prehistoric Regional Systems in the American Southwest*. Santa Fe, NM: School of American Research Press.

Lekson, S.H. (2002). War in the Southwest, War in the World. *American Antiquity*, 67, pp. 607–624.

Lekson, S.H., ed. (2006). *The Archaeology of Chaco Canyon: An Eleventh-Century Pueblo Regional Center*. Santa Fe, NM: School of American Research Press.

Lipe, W.D. (2006). The Mesa Verde Region during Chaco Times. In: D.G. Noble, ed. *The Mesa Verde World*. Santa Fe, NM: School of American Research Press.

Lipe, W.D., Bocinsky, R.K., Chisholm, B.S., Lyle, R., Dove, D.M., Matson, R.G., Jarvis, E., Judd, K., and Kemp, B.M. (2016). Cultural and Genetic Contexts for Early Turkey Domestication in the Northern Southwest. *American Antiquity*, 81, pp. 97–113.

Loendorf, C., and Lewis, B. (2017). Ancestral O'Odham: AkimelL O'Odham cultural traditions and the archaeological record. *American Antiquity*, 82, pp. 123–139.

Malakoff, D. (2015). Grappling with a Great Mystery. *American Archaeology*, 19, pp. 33–37.

Masse, W.B. (1981). Prehistoric Irrigation Systems in the Salt River Valley, Arizona. *Science*, 214, pp. 408–415.

Mathien, F.J. (2005). Culture and Ecology of Chaco Canyon and the San Juan Basin. Santa Fe, NM: National Park Service, U.S. Department of the Interior.

McClelland, J.A. (2015). Revisiting Hohokam Paleodemography. *American Antiquity*, 80, pp. 492–510.

McGuire, R.H., and Villalpando, M.E. (2015). War and Defense on *Cerros de Trincheras* in Sonora, México. *American Antiquity*, 80, pp. 429–450.

Minnis, P.E., and Whalen, M.E. (2016). *Discovering Paquimé* . Tucson: University of Arizona Press.

Muro, M. (1998). New Finds Explode Old Views of the American Southwest. *Science*, 279, pp. 653–654.

Nelson, M.C., and Gilman, P.A. (2017). Mimbres Archaeology. In: B. Mills and S. Fowles, eds. *The Oxford Handbook of Southwest Archaeology*. Oxford: Oxford University Press.

Nelson, M.C., and Hegmon, M. (2001). Abandonment Is Not as it Seems: An Approach to the Relationship between Site and Regional Abandonment. *American Antiquity*, 66, pp. 213–235.

Nelson, M.C., Hegmon, M., Kulow, S., and Schollmeyer, K.G. (2006). Archaeological and Ecological Perspectives on Reorganization: A Case Study from the Mimbres Region of the U. S. Southwest. *American Antiquity*, 71, pp. 403–432.

Noble, D.G., ed. (2004). *In Search of Chaco: New Approaches to an Archaeological Enigma*. Santa Fe, NM: School of American Research Press.

Plog, S. (1997). *Ancient Peoples of the American Southwest*. New York: Thames and Hudson.

Plog, S., and Watson, A.S. (2012). The Chaco Pilgrimage Model: Evaluating the Evidence from Pueblo Alto. *American Antiquity*, 77, pp. 449–477.

Polyak, V.J., and Asmerom, Y. (2001). Late Holocene Climate and Cultural Changes in the Southwestern United States. *Science*, 294, pp. 148–150.

Powell-Marti, V., and Gilman, P. (2006). *Mimbres Society*. Tucson: University of Arizona Press.

Repanshek, K. (2005). Traces of a Lost People. *Smithsonian*, 35, pp. 48–53.

Schollmeyer, K.G., and Turner, C.G., II (2004). Dental Caries, Prehistoric Diet, and the Pithouse-to-Pueblo Transition in Southwestern Colorado. *American Antiquity*, 69, pp. 569–582.

Schwindt, D.M., Bocinsky, R.K., Ortman, S.G., Glowacki, D.M., Varien, M.D., and Kohler, T.A. (2016). The Social Consequences of Climate Change in the Central Mesa Verde Region. *American Antiquity*, 81, pp. 74–96.

Sebastian, L. (1996). *The Chaco Anasazi: Sociopolitical Evolution in the Prehistoric Southwest*. New York: Cambridge University Press.

Shafer, H.J. (2003). *Mimbres Archaeology at the NAN Ranch Ruin*. Albuquerque: University of New Mexico Press.

Solometo, J. (2006). The Dimensions of War: Conflict and Culture Change in Central Arizona. In: E.N. Arkush and M.W. Allen, eds. *The Archaeology of Warfare: Prehistories of Raiding and Conquest*. Gainesville: University Press of Florida.

Van Dyke, R.M., Bocinsky, R.K., Windes, T.C., and Robinson, T.J. (2016). Great Houses, Shrines, and High Places: Intervisibility in the Chacoan World. *American Antiquity*, 81, pp. 205–230.

Vivian, R.G. (1990). *The Chacoan Prehistory of the San Juan Basin*. New York: Academic Press.

Vivian, R.G., and Hilpert, B. (2002). *The Chaco Handbook: An Encyclopedic Guide*. Salt Lake City: University of Utah Press.

Watson, A.S., Plog, S., Culleton, B., Gilman, P.A., LeBlanc, S.A., Whiteley, P.M., Clarmunt, S., and Kennett, D.J. (2015). Early Procurement of Scarlet Macaws and the Emergence of Social Complexity in Chaco Canyon, NM. *Proceedings of the National Academy of Sciences*, 112, pp. 8238–8243.

Weiner, R.S. (2018). Sociopolitical, Ceremonial, and Economic Aspects of Gambling in Ancient North America: A Case Study of Chaco Canyon. *American Antiquity*, 83, pp. 34–53.

11

THE WEST COAST

North America's portion of the vast Pacific Rim arcs from the Aleutian Islands to the coast of Mexico. The Alaskan portion is properly part of the Arctic and Subarctic regions (Chapter 5), and the Mexican and Central American portions are part of Mesoamerica (Chapter 13). What lies between is the long West Coast from the Alaskan panhandle to Baja California, a rich and diverse maritime environment that produced unique cultural adaptations (Figure 11.1).

This was the coastal region peopled by the first American immigrants (Chapter 3). The range of environmental settings later hosted an array of native speakers whose languages belonged to more than two dozen ancient language families (Goddard, 1996).

Environment and Adaptation

Northwest Coast

The Northwest Coast extends 2,000 km (1,250 mi) from Yakutat Bay in southeastern Alaska to northwestern California. In many places, sites are confined to a long, narrow, twisting band of habitable land sandwiched between the sea on one side and mountainous terrain on the other. The maritime climate of the Northwest Coast is characterized by cool summers and wet, mild winters. The warm currents of the North Pacific buffer the effects of latitude, maintaining temperatures above freezing much of the time. The misty rain persists during the winter, but from mid-Vancouver Island south there are long dry spells in the summer. South of British Columbia, small coastal mountain ranges parallel the larger Cascade Range that separates the West Coast from the rest of the continent. Mountains force eastwardly weather systems to shed their rain, resulting in dramatically different environments between the Northwest Coast and the interior Plateau a short distance to the east.

The coastal environment is a temperate rain forest dominated by giant conifers, particularly western hemlocks, Sitka spruces, and Douglas firs. The western red cedar is less abundant but much more important to the adaptations of Northwest Coast cultures. The West Coast teems with a vast variety of fauna: deer, wapiti (elk), bears, mountain sheep, cougars, and mountain goats inhabit the forests; halibut, Pacific cod, and herring occupy the shallow seas of the continental shelf. Hunting extended seaward, while fishing was important along inland rivers. Marine hunting included sea

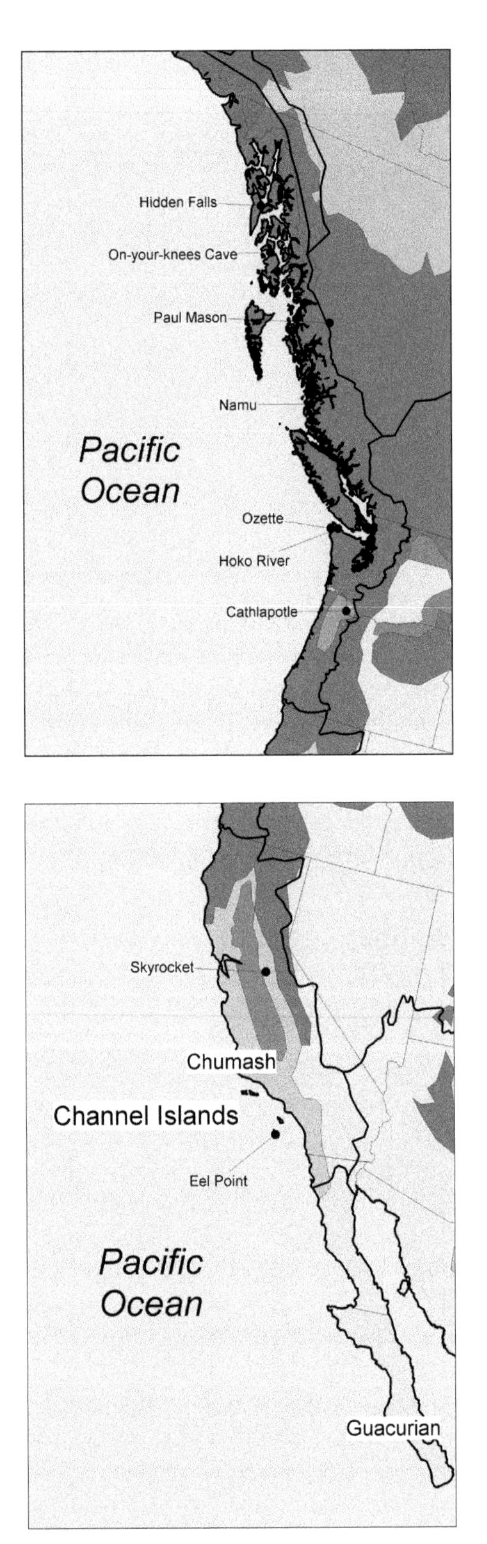

FIGURE 11.1 The West Coast, with sites mentioned in the text. Top: Northwest Coast, Bottom: California and Baja California

otters, seals, sea lions, and in some places porpoises and whales. Anadromous fish include six species of salmon that swim up rivers to spawn. Steelhead trout, smelt, and eulachon (candlefish) still push up main rivers and coastal streams in huge numbers every year. Once dried, eulachon (*Thaleichthys pacificus*) can be burned like candles or rendered for their rich oil, which has been an important food source for millennia.

The oldest human remains recovered from the Northwest Coast come from On-Your-Knees Cave on the northern tip of Prince of Wales Island in southeastern Alaska. These burials were dated to 9730–10,300 radiocarbon years BP (Fedje et al., 2004). Later cultural developments of the Northwest Coast included distinctive hunter-gatherer subsistence strategies, large settled villages, social stratification, and the art styles for which they are justifiably famous beginning in the Middle Holocene, 5000–1500 BCE. Marine shell middens appeared more frequently around 4400 BCE. Ocean levels and river estuaries were stabilizing around the same time (Bicho et al., 2011).

These simultaneous changes were ultimately driven by global climatic cycles. Average temperatures peaked in the northern hemisphere by 5000 BCE before cooling again. Cooler and wetter conditions prevailed until after 4000 BCE along the Northwest Coast, particularly in the summer, resulting in the unique temperate rain forest of the region. Wood does not generally preserve well, but the perpetually wet climate of the region has produced coastal bogs where preserved ancient wood has been recovered by archaeologists. Fine examples have been found along the Hoko River in Washington State (Erlandson and Moss, 2001).

Historic peoples of the region harvested shellfish in huge numbers, frequently leaving large shell middens near productive flats. Canoe transportation facilitated strategic harvesting of briefly abundant and distant seasonal resources for long-term storage (Hobler, 1990:300–301; Lepofsky et al., 2015).

California

The California coast and the Coast Range just east of it is characterized by a complex mosaic of small microenvironments. This patchiness prompted the indigenous inhabitants of the region to follow a variety of specialized local adaptations (Baumhoff, 1978). California's pattern of microenvironments resulted from the complex interplay of topography, latitude, altitude, prevailing winds, and ocean currents. Weather systems often move eastwardly across mountains and valleys. At times hot, dry winds blow in the opposite direction, from the interior deserts to scorch vegetation closer to the ocean. These factors produce an unusually complex mosaic of small ecozones, patches of distinct plant and animal communities. The first Californians learned how to exploit those variable resources and preserve them for future use by maximizing storage (Morgan, 2012).

The native people of California participated in the same process of adaptation as other early people after the beginning of the Holocene around 8050 BCE. These changes entailed the emergence of a regional version on an Archaic theme. The sight of a band of people harvesting seeds with only shallow basketry trays and sticks would have seemed deceptively simple to a modern observer, but underlying the simple techniques was a detailed knowledge about the environment and food processing. Scheduling optimal harvesting times, grinding seeds into flour, and special processing of acorns to remove toxins represented a complex adaptation to some of the arid regions of California.

The early Archaic peoples of coastal California appear to have subsisted primarily on seeds and shellfish. Their shell middens contain milling stones for the grinding of seeds, but no evidence for harpoons, fishing tackle, or other equipment needed to pursue sea mammals and large fish. They hunted seals, but these could have been taken on land. Deer bones indicate that they hunted terrestrial game too, so their coastal adaptation was not an entirely maritime economy (Erlandson, 1994; Erlandson and Glassow, 1997; Jones et al., 2002).

Baja California

Baja (lower) California is one of the ends of the earth, a peninsula that is a blind alley that trapped early American Indian migrants who maintained their Archaic lifestyle until the arrival of Spanish colonists (Laylander and Moore, 2006). The peninsula begins and ends as a desert, a 1,000 km (620 mi) long sliver of Mexico that is separated from northwestern Mexico by the Gulf of California. Its first inhabitants were apparently closely related to the Early Holocene hunter-gatherers of southern coastal California and the Channel Islands. The people who lived on the southern cape of Baja California hunted dolphins. They also took seals onshore, gathered shellfish, and hunted and gathered plants and small game away from the shore, but they had little or no equipment that indicated their reliance on fishing (Porcasi and Fujita, 2000).

Demography and Conflict

People have been present on the West Coast for a long time, evidenced by dozens of native languages documented historically. These belong to several language families so old that their common ancestry cannot be detected. Cultural traditions followed numerous developmental paths in this rich environment, resulting in a mosaic of many different cultures.

Northwest Coast

Archaeologists infer that Northwest Coast inhabitants developed simple ranked societies by 1800 BCE, which became more complexly organized over time. Ranked societies make distinctions between individuals with differential access to prestige, wealth, and power. Stratified societies are characterized by institutionalized social inequality with mutually exclusive classes (strata). In the Northwest, there were two societies with two classes: free people and slaves, the latter being war captives. Such social inequality and stratification typically do not arise in nonstate societies because kin-based societies generally lack the coercive mechanisms to maintain mutually exclusive strata. But on the Northwest Coast, communities were small enough and permanent enough for the custom to arise and persist in kin-based systems (Coupland et al., 2016; Prentiss et al., 2012).

Historic Northwest Coast warfare was conducted to capture slaves but also for revenge, to enhance prestige, or to secure critical food resources. Men also fought over women, whether to avenge infidelity or to capture wives. Quarrels could lead to the breakup of villages and the emigration of one or more factions, and warfare between former neighbors occasionally followed (Ames, 2001).

Warfare probably became more intense later in prehistory. Some villages were strategically placed on bluffs and defensive fortifications were constructed in places (Moss and Erlandson, 1992). Attacks could be launched from great distances, generally by sea. Attackers used clubs, spears, daggers, and bows and arrows and wore helmets and armor made of wooden slats and hide. The last were tough enough to stop even European musket balls. Chipped-stone tools nearly disappeared from the inventory in this late period and were increasingly replaced by bone and antler tools. Experimentation has shown that while chipped-stone and slate points could not penetrate native armor, bone points could. In some areas, village locations eventually shifted from places with easy access to resources to more defensible ones with better visibility of approaches from the sea. Subsistence strategies may have changed in the face of intensified warfare. Sea mammal hunting and other small-group activities declined, whereas salmon harvesting and activities that required whole communities increased. The vulnerability of smaller groups versus the security of numbers probably explains this shift, for there is no evidence that the abandoned resources were in decline (Maschner and Reedy-Maschner, 1998).

California and Baja California

Pinto Basin culture emerged after 8050 BCE around the shrinking playas (beaches) of the interior desert of southern California, just north of Baja California. This lifeway persisted for millennia and spread southward along the coasts of the slender Baja peninsula. A later Yuman-speaking culture spread from southern California part way down the Baja peninsula, absorbing or displacing the ancestors of the Guacuras southward sometime within the last two millennia. Other Yuman speakers expanded into the northern end of the peninsula and were living there in the sixteenth century. These people possessed dogs and pottery, unlike others south of them along the peninsula. Thus, at first contact with Europeans, Baja California held three sets of band cultures, the simplest at the end of the peninsula, more complex Yumans in the middle, and the most complex Californian Yumans in the North, the descendants of three waves of migration down the long peninsula (Des Lauriers, 2005; Rosales-López and Fujita, 2000).

Subsistence and Economy

The Northwest Coast is a maritime environment characterized by very productive but seasonally specific food resources. Technical innovations resulted in the intensification of resource harvesting as well as storage for future use (Ames, 2005a). These innovations included an array of weirs and traps. Later communities shifted from residential to logistical mobility strategies, which in turn led to more complex division of labor and larger households (Ames, 1985; Schalk, 1981: 62). This shift in mobility patterns promoted the storage of food surpluses for use at other times in the seasonal round.

California exhibits more environmental diversity than any other area of comparable size in North America, and the mosaic of subsistence strategies was equally variable (Jones and Klar, 2007). Viewing environmental diversity and variability in subsistence strategies against cultural institutions regionally and over time allows us to address multiple pathways to sociopolitical complexity. Further, the persistence of hunter-gatherer cultures into post-European contact times has enabled historians, cultural anthropologists, and archaeologists to assess directly underlying processes of change (Anderson, 2005).

Architecture and Technology

Northwest Coast

The Archaic peoples of the Northwest Coast were generalists who took full advantage of marine, coastal, and interior forest resources (Ames, 2002; Ames and Maschner, 1999: 126). The manufacture and use of microblades spread to the northern part of the Northwest Coast from Alaska during the Early Holocene, around 7000 BCE. Elements of this more southerly Pebble Tool tradition appear at Namu, an important Archaic site on the central Northwest Coast in British Columbia. Namu appears to have been situated at the interface of these two technological traditions. Microblades largely disappeared from tool assemblages on the Northwest Coast by 4000 BCE except in a few places where they persisted along the coast of southeastern Alaska and British Columbia. Microblades were replaced by other kinds of chipped-stone, bone, antler, and ground slate tools (Ames and Maschner, 1999).

Barbed harpoons later became numerous, evidence that large marine mammals and fish were hunted. Detachable harpoon heads were connected to shafts by lines, allowing hunters to tether wounded animals until they died or could be drawn near enough to the boat to be dispatched by clubs or lances. Slate, bone, and antler points were all manufactured by similar grinding techniques.

Slate implements appeared in coastal sites all around the Northern Hemisphere. Slate can be worked using the same techniques that work well on bone and ivory. Slate points are brittle and break easily, but they are also very sharp and can penetrate the thick blubber of marine mammals. Slate tools of the Northwest Coast are similar to those found elsewhere but do not necessarily share a common origin. Ground-stone technology was also used to produce beads, pendants, and labrets, all objects that might have been used to symbolize social rank. It is likely that we are seeing the evidence. These message-laden items appear in the archaeological record during a time of increasing social inequality, establishment of more permanent settlements, and greater food surpluses.

Two other key sites in the North are Hidden Falls and Paul Mason. The latter is an interior site with 12 rectangular houses dating to around 1200 BCE. Despite evidence of economic intensification and year-round use, the Namu and Boardwalk sites produced little evidence of large permanent houses (Cannon and Yang, 2006).

The bow and arrow reached the region between approximately 500 and 100 BCE. The new weapon eventually replaced the spear thrower, which disappeared from the archaeological record by 700 CE. The bow's arrival in Oregon and Washington is linked to the appearance of smaller points (Hildebrandt and King, 2012).

Large permanent extended households formed on the Northwest Coast by around 1000 BCE, perhaps earlier. House sizes grew over subsequent centuries (Ames, 1995). Generally, the shared classic features of historic Northwest Coast culture are most strongly developed in the North and least in the southern part of its range. Large cedar plank houses, totem poles, large dugout canoes, wooden boxes, and elaborate masks were decorated in the distinctive art style of the region and concentrated in the northern part of the Northwest Coast. This area too is where marine resources are most seasonally abundant.

Unlike earlier houses that were sometimes round semi-subterranean structures, later houses were rectangular with heavy posts and beams and constructed from long, rigid cedar planks (Figure 11.2). Settlements with large structures were continuously occupied for many years. Canoes allowed well-organized work parties to move temporarily to seasonal-harvesting locations and to transport resources back for storage. The presence of heavy woodworking tools and harpoon technology indicates the use of large dugout canoes (Figure 11.4). Although direct evidence in the form of preserved canoes is not available, heavy celts, adzes, and mauls must have been intended for canoe and house construction.

FIGURE 11.2 Reconstructed Tlingit plank clan house, Totem Bight State Historical Park near Ketchikan, Alaska, 1966

CATHLAPOTLE

Cathlapotle is a major fur trade era Chinookan village site on the lower Columbia River. It is located on a U.S. Fish and Wildlife Service Refuge in the greater metropolitan areas of Portland, Oregon, and Vancouver, Washington. It was occupied between ca. 1350 CE and the 1830s. There were two rows of large Western red cedar plankhouses; the largest (House 1) is 53 x 10 m, the smallest (House 4) 11 x 8 m. Excavations focused on these two houses (Ames and Sobel, 2013; Sobel, 2011). The village's people played significant roles in the lower Columbia River fur-trade, as attested both by the village's frequent mention in contemporary Euroamerican accounts, including Lewis and Clark's extensive comments on their visit to the village on March 29, 1806, and by its rich fur trade artifact assemblage. The field work was conducted by Portland State University archaeological field schools under the direction of Kenneth Ames between 1991 and 1996.

The households and others in the region shared technology, economy, and social organization but pursued different strategies. House 1 at Cathlapotle emphasized some surplus food production while actively engaging in trade. In contrast, a contemporary large household at another site (Meier) produced massive surpluses of stored foods and specialized in the production of bone and wooden tools while House 4 at Cathlapotle pursued a generalist strategy. These different strategies were followed into the fur trade era. There was no standard Cathlapotle response to the Europeans. Each household, and in some cases, each household

FIGURE 11.3 The reconstructed Cathlapotle plank house near the site of Cathlapotle, Washington.
Ridgefield National Wildlife Refuge

segment, engaged in different ways. All suffered from the same series of epidemics, finally succumbing to malaria in the early-mid 1830s.

A modern plankhouse constructed in 2005–2006 was a major outgrowth of the project (Figure 11.3). Located in the same game refuge as Cathlapotle, the plankhouse is open to visitors during the summer months. It is used for interpretation and as a center for public education. The Chinook tribe uses it for private and public ceremonies.

Kenneth M. Ames

Boxes made of thin grooved and bent planks of cedar appeared as well (Figure 11.5). A single board was bent to form the sides, and another was sewn on to provide a bottom. These containers were made in many sizes, sometimes with tops, and used for storage and cooking. Their inside corners were sealed with pitch, and for those used in cooking, hot stones were emplaced to bring contents to a boil. This clever innovation filled the same functional need as pottery or basketry in other regions of North America. Late examples are sometimes quite large and often beautifully decorated.

Permanent communities emerged after 1800 BCE, evidenced by large cedar plank houses. Large houses imply large households, often lineages of dozens of related individuals. Large houses are also linked to large household production units, with all the competition, surplus production, and ranking that development would eventually entail. Typically, villages were organized by rows of

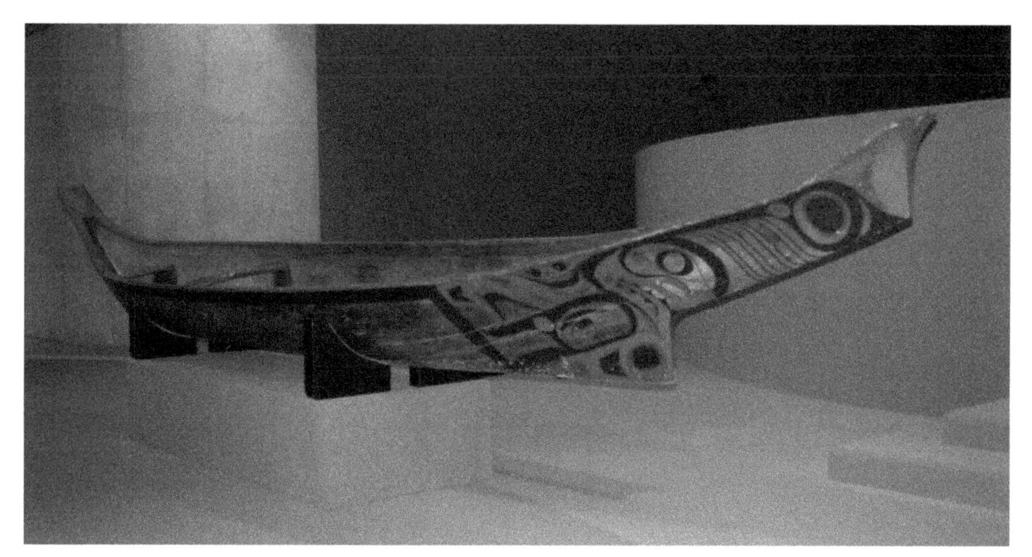

FIGURE 11.4 Northwest Coast canoe. Museum of Anthropology, University of British Columbia

FIGURE 11.5 Bent cedar boxes. Museum of Anthropology, University of British Columbia

FIGURE 11.6 A Northwest Coast copper, probably made from sheeting taken from the hull of a wrecked ship. Alaska State Museum, Juneau

plank houses, with the most highly ranked and imposing houses situated in the center(s) of the row(s). A single-row village was usually made up of households descended from a single ancestor. Two or more rows generally indicated that same number of extended kin groups in the community, as at the Paul Mason site of British Columbia (Fladmark et al., 1990: 238). We see in the heraldic art of coppers and façade decorations the ranking code that was understood all along the Northwest Coast in more recent centuries (Figure 11.6).

The most famous site along the southern Northwest Coast is Ozette at the northwestern tip of Washington's Olympic Peninsula. The site was a Makah whaling village just south of Cape Flattery. An earthquake in 1700 caused a landslide of mud that buried part of the village, preserving houses and thousands of artifacts under wet conditions. Preservation was so good that baskets, lines, bags, harpoons, boxes, toys, and many other items that would have normally disintegrated remained intact and well preserved (Ames, 2005b; Samuels, 1991; Samuels, 1994).

Natural erosion exposed part of the site by the 1970s and threatened to destroy the rest of it. For ten years, crews from Washington State University and the Makah community undertook rescue excavations. Over 55,000 artifacts were recovered from three buried houses, and many of these items are now on display in the Makah Museum at the Makah Cultural and Research Center on the nearby reservation. A majority of the artifacts are made of wood, which typically do not preserve well under ordinary archaeological conditions.

Ozette was occupied before Europeans visited the region with any frequency and before smallpox and other foreign diseases convulsed the population. Because the village was buried so rapidly, Ozette provides a rare archaeological moment in time, undisturbed by the normal cleanout that accompanies abandonment or the selective destruction from looting, in addition to remarkably preserved artifacts.

Culture, Language, and Identity

Northwest Coast

Historically, two social classes existed in most Northwest Coast societies: free people and slaves. War captives and their descendants comprised the slave class. Free people were often sorted further into three ranks: chiefs and chiefly families who formed an elite social stratum with many titles; a middle rank in which people held only a few titles; and commoners with no titles (Ames, 1995; Ames 2001).

Northwest Coast societies were organized more complexly than most hunter-gatherers, and they occupied permanent settlements, but they tended to be unstable chiefdoms. Most operated at the tribal level, with the most stable unit being the extended family household. Communities organized this way expanded up to about 2,000 inhabitants but usually not much higher (Ames and Maschner, 1999: 26). As in many other North American societies, this was the point at which tribal communities would split as the result of internal stresses.

Seasonal variability led to more elaborate controls on production and redistribution of resources, thereby selecting for the social and political adaptations documented by the nineteenth century. Many of these innovations were connected to deep-sea mammal hunting but did not spread to the Puget Sound and farther south. The more southerly environments did not support as much deep-sea mammal hunting and fishing (Nelson, 1990). After a long lag, some innovations, like the use of fish weirs, did spread south (Moss and Erlandson, 1998).

Household leaders controlled the production, storage, and redistribution of resources for the benefit of the whole kin group, for which they enjoyed high rank. Rank differentials between households were personified in the relative standings of their leaders. At the same time, there was a strong moral injunction against hoarding. Property and resources were expected to be used, not hoarded, and through strategic use and distribution, people gained prestige and power. These practices led to broader social ranking and elaborate ceremonies represented by the quintessential Northwest Coast cultural institution called the **potlatch.** Missionaries and government officials witnessed competitive potlatches and regarded these celebrations as wasteful. The complexity of the Northwest Coast societies also subverted the simplistic theories of nineteenth-century anthropologists, who could not explain the anomaly of wealthy hunter-gatherers.

Plentiful and reliable resources were necessary for ranking and chiefdoms to emerge. Reliable and *predictably* abundant resources were the essential economic base for the development of complex society and social inequality. Biological and archaeological evidence for the origins of ranking might have been the first appearance of cranial shaping and the use of labrets. Cranial shaping is a practice found in many cultures to mark one's status. It is achieved by binding the head of a young child so that the skull takes on a different shape, which is distinguishable from normal growth. In this case, rank was inherited at birth (ascribed) rather than earned (achieved) later on. Labrets were generally still worn by women in the nineteenth century (Ames, 2003; Moss, 1999). Unlike head shaping, these items could be acquired. But in practice, high-ranking youths had their lips pierced to receive small labrets at an early age, and increasingly large labrets replaced them as their wearers aged. In the eighteenth century, tattooing and knobbed hats also indicated high rank, but this evidence rarely shows up archaeologically.

The archaeological signatures of hierarchy are not present further south along the Northwest Coast in Oregon and northern California. In the southern part of the Northwest Coast, terrestrial resources were richer, resulting in a more diverse subsistence pattern. The peoples of the southern part of the Northwest Coast were not poor relations, just people whose circumstances and decisions were different from those prevailing farther north.

California

In 1492 there were no fewer than 64, and perhaps as many as 80, mutually unintelligible languages spoken in native California in a region of only 348,000 km^2 (134,000 mi^2). Sherburne Cook estimated the aboriginal population of California to have been 310,000±30,000, or about 10% of the total population of America, north of the Mexican desert at that time (Cook, 1978; Snow, 2001). In northwestern California, tribal territories of only 500–2,000 km^2 (190–770 mi^2) were common, about the size of a typical modern U.S. county. The highest densities were located in the central valley east of San Francisco, along the coast north of that city, and along the Santa Barbara coast (Heizer, 1966; Hornbeck, 1983).

Numerous small territories and local adaptations preclude generalizations about the archaeology of California. The many contrasting local sequences are identified by a vast array of diagnostic artifacts, often decorative items made from shell or stone.

California archaeology was once discussed in terms of broad early, middle, and late **horizon**s, long periods that do not actually conform to the standard definition of that term. They are now more commonly referred to as "periods." Early in the twentieth century, archaeologists divided California into at least 15 districts, grouped into five regions within the state (Gamble, 2015).

The California early period began after the passing of Paleoindians around 8050 BCE and extended until after 2500 BCE. Archaeological evidence is scarce for most of this long duration, much of it from scattered inconspicuous sites from the latter part of the period. The San Dieguito complex in the southernmost part of the state appears to mark the beginning of this period. California archaeologists often refer to a "Milling Stone Horizon" (7200–3000 BCE) when hand and milling stones (manos and metates) are the primary objects found in archaeological deposits (Fagan, 2003: 75, 94).

Although temporary leadership would have been necessary for the organization of seed harvesting, rabbit hunting, dolphin hunting, and other collective activities, California Archaic bands were largely egalitarian. The few documented burials contain grave offerings with no distinctions by gender, as both males and females were equally likely to be buried with milling stones. However, Fagan noted that the burial pattern eventually shifted such that women tended to be interred with milling stones while men were typically buried with weapons (Fagan, 2003: 98).

While theoretical models might predict that people living in the complex environmental mosaic of California should be expected to constantly broaden their subsistence base and to develop increasingly sophisticated ways to harvest and store seeds and other foods, this was not the case. It appears that men persisted in hunting big game, even when that activity was a less efficient expenditure of effort. Hunting remained a dominant theme in rock art and was well represented by faunal remains in habitation sites. But what might seem paradoxical to us may have been driven by the biological roles of men and women. Successful male hunters have always been valued more than unsuccessful ones in human societies, and it should be no surprise to find evidence of it (Hildebrandt and McGuire, 2002).

Botanical remains at the Skyrocket site in the western foothills of the Sierra Nevada reveal that the local environment became cooler and wetter after 3000 BCE, and this climate shift presented people with new opportunities. Grasslands interspersed with oak trees replaced sagebrush and juniper trees that had dominated during hotter drier times, and people living on this flank of the central valley responded by making greater use of acorns. Settlements became more substantial, and for the first time, groups began importing obsidian projectile points from the east and marine shells from the Pacific (Fagan, 2003: 99–101). It is unclear what larger-scale impacts environmental changes may have had on populations regionally. Some archaeologists speculate that the Hokan languages are the most ancient in the region and that Penutian languages expanded across central

California at about this time (Elsasser, 1978: 41). If the people speaking Penutian languages did expand at the expense of those speaking Hokan languages, they must have had some adaptive advantage that we have not yet recognized.

SKYROCKET

The Skyrocket site, in California's Central Sierra foothills lies in gold country. Between 1989 and 1994, the Royal Mountain King Mine company operated an open-pit mine using new technology to chemically float out gold. As part of their compliance to environmental laws, they paid for the partial excavation of a large archaeological site in the area of the largest pit. This project became a classic example of **CRM** excavation at its best. Excavators Roger La Jeunesse and John Pryor used earthmoving machinery to remove overburden, then revealed an astonishing 9,500 years of virtually continuous human occupation in places 12.5 ft (3.8 m) deep (La Jeunesse and Pryor, 1996; Fagan, 2003).

The earliest visitors, who used stemmed projectile points, settled around an ancient marsh fed by artesian springs that provided abundant water even in severe droughts. They consumed numerous acorns, pine nuts, and other plant foods. The excavators uncovered a 10 m (33 ft) square stone platform, built in about 7500 BCE, which extended into the neighboring marsh. The inhabitants carefully leveled the platform and built a large hearth on a baked clay layer. It remained in use until about 5000 BCE. Generations of visitors processed nuts and other plant remains with milling stones and hand stones. Most likely the remains were those of a base camp occupied by people who moved through the rich environments of the nearby Central Valley during the colder winter months.

A natural ridge in the bedrock protected the earliest settlement from massive flooding between about 5000 and 4000 BCE. By 3000 BCE, the inhabitants had built a new stone platform. The site was now a seasonal camp, with intensive exploitation of acorns after 2500 BCE. Human remains from this period reveal lower rates of infant mortality and longer life expectancies. Skyrocket remained in use until the mid-nineteenth century, just before direct European contact.

Brian Fagan

After 2500 BCE, California people produced larger numbers of shell artifacts, particularly beads and pendants of many types, which archaeologists have long used to sort out local and regional sequences. Huge shell middens along the southern California coast might signify much more than simple trash disposal. These extensive deposits, which sometimes include depressions resulting from house construction, are arguably evidence of episodic feasting (Gamble, 2017).

California Tribelets

Early communities of California were typically small, tribal in organization with low population densities. As populations increased and territories shrank, social entities referred to as "tribelets" formed, and in some instances, social ranking developed. Leaders who presided over some families enjoyed higher ranks than others in these miniature tribes. Ethnographic accounts revealed rigid social strata in some societies, including divisions of chiefs, lesser elites, commoners, and slaves. Archaeologically, high power and status were represented by shell and stone beads and amulets (King, 1978).

FIGURE 11.7 Reconstructed Hupa house from northwestern California

The mapping of subsistence, mortuary practices, projectile points, or house types produces map layers that are unlike each other, adding to the difficulty encountered when trying to generalize about California archaeology (Figure 11.7). Each class of traits produces its own distinctive spatial distribution when mapped against the underlying variation in California's microenvironments, again illustrating the consequences of cultural evolution. Many of California's small ancient populations evolved in place allowing archaeologists to track shifting adaptations more easily than if groups frequently relocated, in contrast to the Great Plains where groups moved around considerably (Chapter 9).

None of the plants exploited by people in California were subjected to genetic selection or selective nurturing so cultigens never evolved in the region and agriculture was not practiced. However, these people developed ever-finer basketry, eventually weaving containers so tightly that they were virtually waterproof. Fragile pottery was never a viable alternative to these fiber vessels. Pomo baskets were highly decorated with shell beads and bird feathers and are highly appreciated today, as are the many other art forms made by the native Californians.

Chumash Culture

The Chumash cultures of the Santa Barbara coast are an interesting case of the rise of chiefdoms in California with possible contacts from Polynesia. There were three branches and at least six

Chumash languages spoken by as many as 20,000 people when Europeans arrived (Goddard, 1996: 320; Shipley, 1978). The Chumash probably descended from the first Californians. At the time of first contact with Europeans the Chumash Indians had a sophisticated maritime technology, social stratification, and hereditary chiefs. Chiefs maintained their power through political and economic leadership. They were the owners of large plank canoes, which facilitated sea mammal hunting as well as long-distance trade and exchange along the California coast. The building, maintenance, and operation of canoes required large teams, so technology and sociopolitical organization reinforced one another. There has long been interest in knowing how long such large plank canoes and, by inference, hereditary chiefs, have been part of Chumash culture. Regrettably, canoes have been not preserved archaeologically. However, chipped-stone drills and natural asphalt calking have survived, so we now know that plank canoes were used by at least 700 CE (Gamble et al., 2002). Canoes of some sort must have a more ancient history because people were going back and forth to San Clemente Island 8,500 years ago.

The possibility of prehistoric trans-Pacific contacts has been a perennial topic of archaeological interest (Smith, 1953). Recent archaeological and linguistic evidence suggests the possibility that plank canoes, two-piece bone fishhooks, and words for these items might have been transmitted to the Chumash by seafaring Polynesians around 800 CE (Jones and Klar, 2005). Having reached such remote islands as Hawaii in the eastern Pacific around the same time (Hunt and Lipo, 2006), it would not be surprising if some Polynesian voyagers washed up on the California shore. However, many archaeologists remain skeptical. The contact, if it occurred in California, did not have a pervasive effect on the course of North American Indian history. Whatever the origins of the plank canoe were, the taking of sea mammals gradually declined over the last few millennia, possibly due to overhunting (Arnold and Bernard, 2005; Colten and Arnold, 1998).

The question arises as to what kinds of canoes were being used on open water prior to the development of plank canoes. A possible answer comes from Baja California, where composite canoes with driftwood log bottoms and bundled reed sides were still being used to navigate the 23 km (14 mi) between the mainland and Isla Cedros in historic times (Des Lauriers, 2005). This watercraft was sturdy and serviceable, even on open water, and it might be a form used elsewhere along the coast before the introduction of plank canoes.

The challenges entailed by the building, maintenance, and use of large plank canoes required organized labor. The chronology of canoe use and the formation of Chumash chiefdoms may have coincided, but the synchronization of these developments remain debatable (Arnold and Green, 2002; Gamble, 2002; Gamble et al., 2002). These demands were complicated by increasing conflict, indicated by larger numbers of individuals found with projectile points embedded in their skeletal remains. The bow and arrow appeared in California sometime after 500 CE, and the formation of chiefdoms might have been linked in part to organized efforts in conflict control (Arnold, 2001; Lambert and Walker, 1991).

Art and Symbolism

Northwest Coast

The Northwest Coast is justifiably famous for its distinctive native artistic traditions. Zoomorphic designs are equally at home on cylindrical totem poles, the flat surfaces of boxes, house façades, and Chilkat blankets (Figure 11.8). Three-dimensional forms can occur as decorations, for example,

FIGURE 11.8 Some Northwest Coast art motifs

bowls or spoon handles, or as portable statuettes. The shape of the eye is key, for its curves repeat in other contexts. Animals are often split and splayed, and their identifying elements are sometimes rearranged to create abstract images. Anthropomorphic and zoomorphic forms are sometimes skeletonized, and there is a strong tendency to fill all the available space rather than leave an empty background. Artistic impulses were also expressed in clothing and bodily decoration, including tattooing, cranial shaping, and labrets (discussed above).

California and Baja California

Human crania dissociated from their bodies have been found in central Californian sites, often called "trophy heads" in the older archaeological literature. Recently, these findings have been related to Native American worldviews and the practice of ancestor veneration (Eerkens et al., 2016).

The Chumash area of southern California is known for elaborate rock art. The Chumash who lived in the interior produced elaborate and colorful pictographs on the walls and ceilings of caves, which attract visitors today (Figure 11.9). The Chumash constituted a large and vibrant culture, but Spanish colonists concentrated the people in mission sites in the eighteenth century, where epidemics eroded their numbers over the years. Consequently, the specific meanings of their pictographs are now difficult to recover without first-hand knowledge of the symbolism.

CHUMASH PAINTED CAVE

Located northwest of Santa Barbara, California, is a remarkable example of Native American rock art. Nestled in an oak-shaded canyon near the headwaters of Maria Ygnacia Creek, Chumash Painted Cave is among the smallest of California's state parks. A security fence, installed in the early twentieth century, protects the Native art from vandalism, but a viewing portal permits visitors to obtain an unrestricted observation of the pictographs. The polychrome paintings of red, white, and black circular symbols and strange, otherworldly figures are quite striking. Multiple painting events are discernable, and the enhancements by aboriginal artists over time together present an unforgettable mosaic of color and pattern over the curving back walls of the rock shelter (De Soto, 2008; Grant, 1993).

The meanings behind the paintings remain mysterious. Many explanations have been offered in the century and a half since the earliest descriptions were published. Certainly there must have been a commonly understood significance of this art to Chumash people. Indeed, many of the painted symbols exemplify a style that is widespread throughout the region where Chumash languages were spoken. By the time that anthropologists began to inquire regarding the meaning behind commonly recurring motifs, descendants could only answer that at the time of the Winter Solstice, they remembered that there were elderly men who went into the mountains to conduct rituals and make paintings.

Painted Cave is one of the few Chumash rock art sites with a known place name – *'alaxulux'en* (Figure 11.9) . Despite the best efforts by linguists to etymologize this name, its suggested

FIGURE 11.9 Chumash Painted Cave pictographs. Courtesy of John R. Johnson

translation, "that which goes around," is as inscrutable as are the purpose of the paintings themselves. It is likely that the art was created by members of the *'antap*, the Chumash secret society who conducted sacred ceremonies at the time of the Winter Solstice and who were expressing some aspect of Chumash cosmology through their imagery (Hyder, 1989).

John R. Johnson

Pictographs in shallow caves and rock shelters from Baja California recently have attracted considerable attention. Images include geometric designs, hand prints, and representations of humans, deer, mountain sheep, antelopes, mountain lions, seals, and various smaller animals (Crosby, 1992; Grant, 1974).

Resilience and Collapse

European exploration and settlement of the Northwest Coast came late compared to the rest of the continent. For three centuries after Columbus, there were only sporadic and brief visits by explorers before they moved on to other locations. Vitus Bering came in 1741, followed by Spanish expeditions and James Cook in 1777. Fur traders began stopping along the coast in the latter part of the eighteenth century, which led to greater interest in the region by the Russians and British. Russians eventually established outposts at Kodiak Island, Sitka, and as far south as Fort Ross on the California coast. Following the American Revolution, British and American trading ships increasingly stopped along the Northwest Coast, collecting great quantities of furs from sea otters and other animals and leaving behind beads, guns, cloth, other trade goods, and eventually lethal diseases.

It was not until the early nineteenth century that European expansion brought widespread change to the Indian cultures of the Northwest Coast. The sea otter was driven nearly to extinction by the 1830s, and the fur trade shifted to interior game species. Euro-American settlers later following the Oregon Trail began moving into the region, displacing Indian communities already reduced by epidemics. Many Northwest Coast communities survive today as First Nations in both Canada and the United States.

Spanish colonization of California led to the reduction of many Indian communities, with the remaining few concentrated around Catholic missions. A number of these communities survive today, even after having been culturally merged and profoundly changed by the dominant colonial culture. The processes through which all this played out are a current topic of anthropological and archaeological research.

Glossary

CRM Cultural Resource Management, also called cultural heritage management. Studies conducted in compliance with legislation requiring consideration of archaeological and historical resources prior to development projects.

horizon A brief but widespread archaeological phenomenon that serves as a convenient stratigraphic marker.

potlatch Any of various practices of status-enhancing gift-giving or conspicuous consumption on the Northwest Coast.

References

Ames, K.M. (1985). Hierarchies, Stress and Logistical Strategies among Hunter-Gatherers in Northwestern North America. In: T.D. Price and J.A. Brown, eds. *Prehistoric Hunter-Gatherers: the Emergence of Cultural Complexity*. Orlando, FL: Academic Press.

Ames, K.M. (1995). Chiefly Power and Household Production on the Northwest Coast. In: T.D. Price and G.M. Feinman, eds. *Foundations of Social Inequality*. New York: Plenum Press.

Ames, K.M. (2001). Slaves, Chiefs and Labour on the Northern Northwest Coast. *World Archaeology*, 33, pp. 1–17.

Ames, K.M. (2002). Going by Boat: The Forager-Collector Continuum at Sea. In: B. Fitzhugh and J. Habu, eds. *Beyond Foraging and Collecting: Evolutionary Change in Hunter-Gatherer Settlement Systems.* New York: Kluwer Academic/Plenum Publishers.

Ames, K.M. (2003). The Northwest Coast. *Evolutionary Anthropology*, 12, pp. 19–33.

Ames, K.M. (2005a). Intensification of Food Production on the Northwest Coast and Elsewhere. In: D. Duer and N.J. Turner, eds. *Keeping It Living: Traditions of Plant Use and Cultivation on the Northwest Coast of North America.* Vancouver: University of British Columbia Press.

Ames, K.M. (2005b). The Place of Ozette in Northwest Coast Archaeology. In: D.L. Welchel, ed. *Ethnobotany and Wood Technology.* Ozette Archaeological Project Research Report III. Seattle, WA: National Park Service.

Ames, K.M., and Maschner, H.D.G. (1999). *Peoples of the Northwest Coast: Their Archaeology and Prehistory.* New York: Thames and Hudson.

Ames, K.M., and Sobel, E.A. (2013). Chinookan Households. In: R. Boyd, K.M. Ames, and T. Johnson, eds. *Chinookan Peoples of the Lower Columbia River.* Seattle: University of Washington Press.

Anderson, D.G. (2005). Why California? In: M. Hegmon and B.S. Eiselt, eds. *Engaged Anthropology: Research Essays on North American Archaeology, Ethnobotany, and Museology.* Ann Arbor: University of Michigan Museum of Anthropology.

Arnold, J.E. (2001). Social Evolution and the Political Economy in the Northern Channel Islands. In: J.E. Arnold, ed. *The Origins of a Pacific Coast Chiefdom: The Chumas of the Channel Islands.* Salt Lake City: University of Utah Press.

Arnold, J.E., and Bernard, J. (2005). Negotiating the Coasts: Status and the Evolution of Boat Technology in California. *World Archaeology*, 37, pp. 109–131.

Arnold, J.E., and Green, T.M. (2002). Mortuary Ambiguity: The Ventureño Chumash Case. *American Antiquity*, 67, pp. 760–771.

Baumhoff, M.A. (1978). Environmental Background. In: R.F. Heizer, ed. *California.* Washington, DC: Smithsonian Institution.

Bicho, N.F., Haws, J.A., and Davis, L.G., eds. (2011). *Trekking the Shore: Changing Coastlines and the Antiquity of Coastal Settlement.* New York: Springer.

Cannon, A., and Yang, D.Y. (2006). Early Storage and Sedentism on the Pacific Northwest Coast: Ancient DNA Analysis of Salmon Remains from Namu, British Columbia. *American Antiquity*, 71, pp. 123–140.

Colten, R.H., and Arnold, J.E. (1998). Prehistoric Marine Mammal Hunting on California's Northern Channel Islands. *American Antiquity*, 63, pp. 679–701.

Cook, S.F. (1978). Historical Demography. In: R.F. Heizer, ed. *California.* Washington, DC: Smithsonian Institution.

Coupland, G., Bilton, D., Clark, T., Cybulski, J.S., Frederick, G., Holland, A., Letham, B., and Williams, G. (2016). A Wealth of Beads: Evidence for Material Wealth-Based Inequality in the Salish Sea Region, 4000–3500 Cal B.P. *American Antiquity*, 81, pp. 294–315.

Crosby, H.W. (1992). *The Cave Paintings of Baja California: Discovering the Great Murals of an Unknown People.* San Diego, CA: Sunbelt Productions.

De Soto, E.Y. (2008). Chumash Painted Cave State Historic Park. In: F.H. Kennedy, ed. *American Indian Places: A Historical Guidebook.* New York: Houghton Mifflin.

Des Lauriers, M.R. (2005). The Watercraft of Isla Cedros, Baja California: Variability and Capabilities of Indigenous Seafaring Technology along the Pacific Coast of North America. *American Antiquity*, 70, pp. 342–360.

Eerkens, J.W., Bartelinnk, E.J., Brink, L., Fitzgerald, R.T., Garibay, R., Jorgenson, G.A., and Wiberg, R.S. (2016). Trophy Heads or Ancestor Veneration? A Stable Isotope Perspective on Disassociated and Modified Crania in Precontact Central California. *American Antiquity*, 81, pp. 114–131.

Elsasser, A.B. (1978). Development of Regional Prehistoric Cultures. In: R.F. Heizer, ed. *California.* Washington, DC: Smithsonian Institution.

Erlandson, J.M. (1994). *Early Hunter-Gatherers of the California Coast.* New York: Plenum Press.

Erlandson, J.M., and Glassow, M.A., eds. (1997). *Archaeology of the California Coast During the Middle Holocene.* Los Angeles, CA: Institute of Archaeology, UCLA.

Erlandson, J.M., and Moss, M.L. (2001). Shellfish Feeders, Carrion Eaters, and the Archaeology of Aquatic Adaptations. *American Antiquity*, 66, pp. 413–432.

Fagan, B.M. (2003). *Before California: An Archaeologist Looks at Our Earliest Inhabitants.* Lanham, MD: Rowman & Littlefield.
Fedje, D.W., Mackie, Q.X., Dixon, E.J., and Heaton, T.H. (2004). Late Wisconsin Environments and ArchaeolgoicalVisibility on the Northern Northwest Coast. In: D.B. Madsen, ed. *Entering America: Northeast Asia and Beringia Before the Last Glacial Maximum.* Salt Lake City: University of Utah Press.
Fladmark, K.R., Ames, K.M., and Sutherland, P.D. (1990). Prehistory of the Northern Coast of British Columbia. In: W. Suttles, ed. *Northwest Coast.* Washington, DC: Smithsonian Institution.
Gamble, L.H. (2002). Archaeological Evidence for the Origin of the Plank Canoe in North America. *American Antiquity*, 67, pp. 301–315.
Gamble, L.H. (2015). Subsistence Practices and Feasting Rites: Chumash Identity after European Colonization. *Historical Archaeology,* 49, pp. 115–135.
Gamble, L.H. (2017). Feasting, Ritual Practices, Social Memory, and Persistent Places: New Interpretations of Shell Mounds in Southern California. *American Antiquity*, 82, pp. 427–451.
Gamble, L.H., Walker, P.L., and Russell, G.S. (2002). Further Considerations on the Emergence of Chumash Chiefdoms. *American Antiquity*, 67, pp. 772–777.
Goddard, I., ed. (1996). *Languages.* Washington, DC: Smithsonian Institution.
Grant, C. (1974). *Rock Art of Baja California.* Los Angeles, CA: Dawson's Book Shop.
Grant, C. (1993). *The Rock Paintings of the Chumash: A Study of a California Indian Culture.* Santa Barbara, CA: Santa Barbara Museum of Natural History.
Heizer, R.F. (1966). *Languages, Territories and Names of California Indian Tribes.* Berkeley: University of California Press.
Hildebrandt, W.R., and King, J.H. (2012). Distinguishing Between Darts and Arrows in the Archaeological Record: Implications for Technological Change in the American West. *American Antiquity*, 77, pp. 789–799.
Hildebrandt, W.R., and McGuire, K.R. (2002). The Ascendance of Hunting During the California Middle Archaic: An Evolutionary Perspective. *American Antiquity*, 67, pp. 231–256.
Hobler, P.M. (1990). Prehistory of the Central Coast of British Columbia. In: W. Suttles, ed. *Northwest Coast.* Washington, DC: Smithsonian Institution.
Hornbeck, D. (1983). *California Patterns: A Geographical and Historical Atlas.* Mountain View, CA: Mayfield.
Hunt, T.L., and Lipo, C.P. (2006). Late Colonization of Easter Island. *Science*, 311, pp. 1603–1606.
Hyder, W.D. (1989). *Rock Art and Archaeology in Santa Barbara County.* San Luis Obispo, CA: San Luis Obispo County Archaeological Society.
Jones, T.L., Fitzgerald, R.T., Kennett, D.J., Miksicek, C.H., Fagan, J.L., Sharp, J., and Erlandson, J.M. (2002). The Cross Creek Site (CA-SLO-1797) and Its Implications for New World Colonization. *American Antiquity*, 67, pp. 213–230.
Jones, T.L., and Klar, K.A. (2005). Diffusionism Reconsidered: Linguistic and Archaeological Evidence for Prehistoric Polynesian Contact with Southern California. *American Antiquity*, 70, pp. 457–484.
Jones, T.L., and Klar, K.A., eds. (2007). *California Prehistory: Colonization, Culture, and Complexity.* New York: Rowman & Littlefield.
King, C. (1978). Protohistoric and Historic Archaeology. In: R.F. Heizer, ed. *California.* Washington, DC: Smithsonian Institution.
La Jeunesse, R.M., and Pryor, J.H. (1996). Archaeological Investigations at the Skyrocket Site, CA-Cal-629/630: The Royal Mountain King Mine Project. *Proceedings of the Society for California Archaeology*, 4, pp. 159–191.
Lambert, P.M., and Walker, P.L. (1991). Physical Anthropological Evidence for the Evolution of Social Complexity in Coastal Southern California. *Antiquity*, 65, pp. 963–973.
Laylander, D., and Moore, J., eds. (2006). *The Prehistory of Baja California: Advances in the Archaeology of the Forgotten Peninsula.* Gainesville: University Press of Florida.
Lepofsky, D., Smith, N.F., Cardinal, N., Harper, J., Morris, M., White, G.E., Bouchard, R., Kennedy, D.I.D., Salomon, A.K., Puckett, M., and Rowell, K. (2015). Ancient Shellfish Mariculture on the Northwest Coast of North America. *American Antiquity*, 80, pp. 236–259.
Maschner, H.D.G., and Reedy-Maschner, K.L. (1998). Raid, Retreat, Defend (Repeat): The Archaeology and Ethnohistory of Warfare on the North Pacific. *Journal of Anthropological Archaeology*, 17, pp. 19–51.
Morgan, C. (2012). Modeling Modes of Hunter-Gatherer Food Storage. *American Antiquity*, 77, pp. 714–736.

Moss, M.L. (1999). George Catlin among the Nayas: Understanding the Practice of Labret Wearing on the Northwest Coast. *Ethnohistory*, 46, pp. 31–65.

Moss, M.L., and Erlandson, J.M. (1992). Forts, Refuge Rocks, and Defensive Sites: The Antiquity of Warfare along the North Pacific Coast of North America. *Arctic Anthropology*, 29, pp. 73–90.

Moss, M.L., and Erlandson, J.M. (1998). A Comparative Chronology of Northwest Coast Fishing Features. In: K. Bernick, ed. *Hidden Dimensions: The Cultural Significance of Wetland Archaeology*. Vancouver: University of British Columbia Press.

Nelson, C.M. (1990). Prehistory of the Puget Sound Region. In: W. Suttles, ed. *Northwest Coast*. Washington, DC: Smithsonian Institution.

Porcasi, J.F., and Fujita, H. (2000). The Dolphin Hunters: A Specialized Prehistoric Maritime Adaptation in the Southern California Channel Islands and Baja California. *American Antiquity*, 65, pp. 543–566.

Prentiss, A.M., Foor, T.A., Cross, G., Harris, L.E., and Wanzenried, M. (2012). The Cultural Evolution of Material Wealth-Based Inequality at Bridge River, British Columbia. *American Antiquity*, 77, pp. 542–564.

Rosales-López, A., and Fujita, H. (2000). *La Antigua California Prehispánica: La Vida Costera en El Conchalito*. Mexico City: Instituto Nacional de Antropología e Historia.

Samuels, S.R., ed. (1991). *House Structure and Floor Midden*. Ozette Archaeological Project Research Report I. Pullman: Department of Anthropology, Washington State University.

Samuels, S.R., ed. (1994). *Fauna*. Ozette Archaeological Project Research Report II. Pullman: Department of Anthropology, Washington State University.

Schalk, R.F. (1981). Land Use and Organizational Complexity Among Foragers of Northwestern North America. In: S. Koyama and D.H. Thomas, eds. *Affluent Foragers: Pacific Coasts East and West*. Osaka: National Museum of Ethnology.

Shipley, W.F. (1978). Native Languages of California. In: R.F. Heizer, ed. *California*. Washington, DC: Smithsonian Institution.

Smith, M.W., ed. (1953). *Asia and North America: Transpacific Contacts*. Salt Lake City, UT: Society for American Archaeology.

Snow, D.R. (2001). Setting Demographic Limits, The North American Case. In: Z. Stancic, and T. Veljanovski, eds. *Computing Archaeology for Understanding the Past*. Oxford: British Archaeological Reports.

Sobel, E.A. (2011). The Exchange Expansion Model of Contact Era Change on the Northwest Coast: An Archaeological Test Using Obsidian Data from the Lower Columbia River. *Journal of Anthropological Archaeology*, 31, pp. 1–21.

12

THE GULF RIM AND THE CARIBBEAN ISLANDS

The Gulf of Mexico and the Caribbean Islands are maritime environments to which Native Americans adapted in a variety of ways, setting them apart from the interior Eastern Woodlands to the north, Mexico and Central America to the west, and mainland South America to the south. Domesticates from Mesoamerica and South America led to food production and were linked to the development of complex societies in some areas. Chiefdoms developed without agriculture in areas where natural resources were exceptionally rich. Wide water or desert gaps in the long circum-Gulf Rim restricted long-distance travel and trade between the Eastern Woodlands, Mesoamerica, and Cuba, yet there were similarities imposed by the Gulf environments (White and Weinstein, 2008). Cultures of the Gulf and Caribbean regions were among the first to be devastated by warfare, disease, and enslavement following settlement of the Greater Antilles by Spanish colonists (1492 and later), the Cortés expedition to Mexico (1519), and the de Soto expedition (1539–1543) into the Southeast.

Environment and Adaptation

The Gulf Coast

The Gulf Coast is a long, curving coastline with many indentations and considerable environmental variation, like the North American West Coast, except that it curves back on itself, forming the Gulf of Mexico. Like the West Coast, the Gulf Rim is set apart from the lands lying behind it by the maritime character of the Gulf Lowlands.

Sea levels were lower around the Gulf at the end of the Pleistocene. With warming conditions and receding glaciers, sea levels rose during the Holocene and stabilized around 4000 BCE, at which time barrier islands and associated resource-rich zones formed. This made the Gulf Coast environments more attractive to hunter-gatherers after 4000 BCE and set the stage for later developments (Widmer, 2005).

Maritime environments are different from interior ones and those that encircle large bodies of saltwater stand apart from the inland regions at their backs. The world's greatest such region is the Mediterranean Sea and the rim of resource-rich land that surrounds it. North America's only

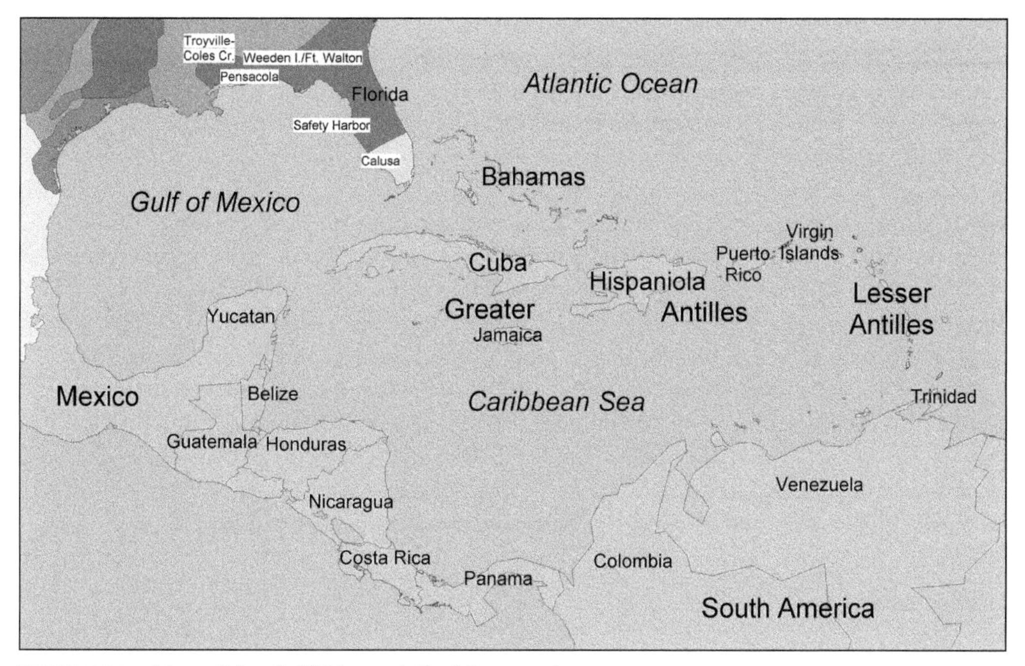

FIGURE 12.1 Map of the Gulf Rim and Caribbean region

comparably large marine body is the Gulf of Mexico, defining a maritime region separate from the rest of the continent. The Gulf is nearly encircled by land, and boat travel around its rim has been possible for millennia. This coastal province is not a uniform ecological zone but a residual ring made up of maritime margins of three other regions: Mesoamerica, the Eastern Woodlands, and the Greater Antilles. Distant offshore sea currents promote travel clockwise around the Gulf, while countercurrents closer to shore may have facilitated boat travel in the opposite direction (Wilkerson, 2005).

Cuba is located in the southeastern mouth of the Gulf (Figure 12.1). The first inhabitants of the Greater Antilles reached Cuba and shortly after reached Hispaniola, from the Yucatan Peninsula, Honduras, and/or Guatemala approximately 4000 BCE (Wilson et al., 1998). With lower sea levels, a series of small exposed islands existed between the coasts of Honduras and Nicaragua, and Cuba and Jamaica. These islands constituted the tips of the Nicaraguan Rise, an underwater carbonate ridge, which may have facilitated travel by Archaic canoeists between Central America and the Greater Antilles (Roksandic, 2016).

The Caribbean Islands

Most of the islands between Puerto Rico and Venezuela are included in the Lesser Antilles. Geologically, Puerto Rico and the Virgin Islands are grouped with the Greater Antilles (Lewis et al., 1990). Trinidad is the largest of the Caribbean Islands south of Puerto Rico and is considered part of the South American mainland; it separated from that mainland in the early post-Pleistocene with rising sea level (Bellizzia and Dengo, 1990). The Caribbean Islands present considerable ecological diversity, ranging from xerophytic scrub to lush tropical rain forest. It is into this context of ecological diversity that humans moved, settled, and dispersed over eight millennia, beginning around 6000 BCE.

Cultural trajectories documented in Mesoamerica and the Southeast occurred in the Antilles as well. Food production and settled life on Puerto Rico was initially organized along kinship lines. Shifts in mortuary practices were documented through the Ceramic Age. Prior to around 600 CE, the dead were buried in kin-managed communal cemeteries. After 600 CE, burials were increasingly placed in smaller, more private places close to or in the floors of domestic quarters (Curet and Oliver, 1998). Spanish descriptions of sixteenth-century practices reveal elites accorded elaborate funerals consistent with this later trend. Ancestor veneration and adherence to the cosmological system of the spirit world known as **cemíism** was a unifying thread through approximately 2,000 years of social and political changes in Puerto Rico and possibly parts of the Lesser Antilles (Oliver, 2009; Siegel, 2010). With the emergence of hierarchical society and institutionalized social inequality, nobility abandoned earlier communal burial practices and focused on ancestor veneration within a more-narrow elite context. The core belief system of cemíism remained intact, spanning a trajectory through many centuries of egalitarian society to the incipient formation and eventual elaboration of complex society (Figure 12.2).

Demography and Conflict

Because the West Indies are composed of a curvilinear arc of relatively closely spaced islands they were considered as stepping stones for migration waves (Rouse, 1986; Rouse, 1992). There were numerous independent episodes of human dispersals into the Antilles. Initial colonization came from two independent directions. The earliest solid archaeological evidence for human occupations comes from Oropuche Lagoon along the west coast of Trinidad (Boomert, 2000). A handful of sites reflect a broad-spectrum foraging, collecting, fishing, and hunting adaptation dating to approximately 6000 BCE. Assemblages consist of bone projectile points, peccary teeth fashioned into fishhooks, ground stone pestles and manos, faceted edge grinders, and stone anvils. This Early Banwari Trace complex has been linked to the Alaka and El Conchero complexes located in coastal swamp, marsh, or riverine settings of northwestern Guyana and the Paria Peninsula of eastern Venezuela, respectively (Boomert, 2000: 68–74). After a long pause of about 2,500 years, the Lesser Antilles were colonized for the first time by c. 3500 BCE. The earliest settlers of the West Indies might have been responsible for the local extinctions of sloths and manatees (Keegan, 1995).

Another route of entry into the islands came from Yucatan; people settled the Greater Antilles approximately 4500 BCE, although evidence for early occupations on Jamaica is lacking. By approximately 500 BCE and possibly earlier, agriculturally oriented pottery-producing communities originating in the Orinoco Valley settled the islands from Trinidad through Puerto Rico (Rouse, 1992; Siegel, 1991a). There was some mixing of these people with earlier populations but distinctive cultures persisted as well.

Within the islands, an expansion began around 600 CE. Having settled Puerto Rico, people began establishing settlements across Hispaniola and into Cuba and the Bahamas. Whether these dispersals represented population expansion and replacement of hunter-gatherers versus absorption and enculturation remains unknown.

Groups of the mainland Gulf Rim seemed to have been influenced by developments in the American midcontinent except in southern Florida. Those latter groups may have been more influenced by ideas or cultigens from South American peoples. Distinctively organized mound complexes in Gulf Rim settlements were associated with elevated population levels and eventually chiefdom formations.

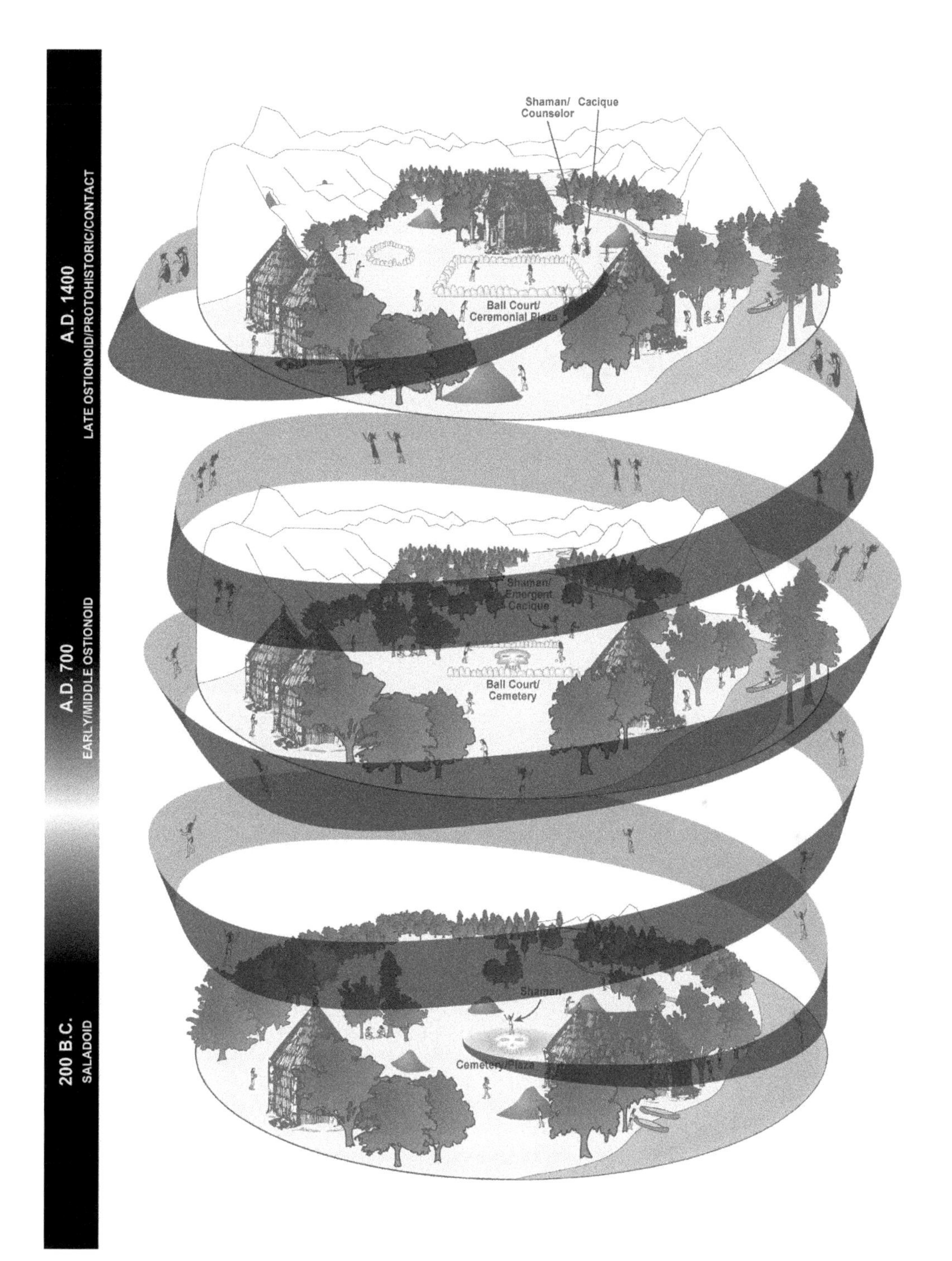

FIGURE 12.2 Evolution of leadership roles and plaza space in the context of cemíism in pre-Columbian Puerto Rico (from Siegel, 2010: Fig. 13)

Subsistence and Economy

It was traditionally believed that Archaic cultures of the Caribbean consisted of mobile bands of foragers, collectors, hunters, and fishers who tread lightly on landscapes, made no pottery, and did not engage in plant management or horticulture. As recovery methods and analytical techniques became more sophisticated, evidence is emerging for landscape modification if not management, small-scale horticulture, and in some areas the use of pottery during the Archaic (Newsom and Wing, 2004; Pagán-Jiménez et al., 2015; Rodríguez Ramos et al., 2008; Siegel et al., 2015).

By 500 BCE or earlier, new groups of settlers from the Orinoco Valley moved into the islands from Trinidad through Puerto Rico. This was the Saladoid series of cultures, named after the Saladero type site (Venezuela) excavated by Irving Rouse and José Cruxent (Rouse and Cruxent, 1963). Saladoid cultures have been traditionally assigned to the Early Ceramic Age (Siegel, 1989). Arriving to landscapes that had been previously modified by Archaic occupants, Saladoid colonists brought well-developed agricultural practices from South America, along with a sophisticated ceramic industry and a settled village-community lifestyle. Large settlements with thick midden deposits, mounds, and plazas were generally located in coastal or near-coastal settings. Saladoid adaptive strategies consisted of a mixed economy with reliance on the cultivation of root crops (manioc or yuca, yams, batata, age, yautia, arrowroot, llerén, canna), followed by seed plants (maize, beans, squash). These people took full advantage of the deep-sea and near-shore marine and mangrove resources through fishing, collecting, and foraging (Newsom and Wing, 2004).

By 600 CE, settlement patterns became more varied, with both interior and coastal settings occupied. Incipient settlement hierarchies have been documented. The earliest Caribbean ball courts date to this time (Alegría, 1983; Siegel, 1999; Siegel, 2010). Changes in ceramic styles, settlement patterns, and sociopolitical organization mark the beginning of the Late Ceramic Age (ca. 600–1500 CE). At this time, Ceramic Age settlers from Puerto Rico and perhaps other islands to the east began moving into Hispaniola, Jamaica, and Cuba and shortly thereafter the Bahamas. When the Spanish arrived in the New World, chiefdoms were present across the Greater Antilles and some islands of the Lesser Antilles (Siegel, 2004; Siegel, 2011). These sociopolitical formations were similar in complexity to Mississippian chiefdoms discussed in Chapter 7.

The Gulf of Mexico is environmentally and culturally heterogeneous and three gaps impeded movement around its rim. Sabal and other palms are found along most of the Gulf Coast, and no part of it is exempt from devastation in the warm months of hurricane season. Barrier islands and mangroves occur around much of the Gulf. The Tropic of Cancer separates the subtropical North from the tropical South, and crops like manioc could not prosper north of the line. The dry south Texas and Mexican coast north of the Tropic of Cancer supported a thin native population in 1492. The Texas barrier islands trap hypersaline lagoons up to eight times saltier than the sea and far less productive. The near-desert gap on land and the low marine productivity between Mesoamerica and the Eastern Woodlands created a barrier to easy human interactions, as did water gaps separating Yucatan, Cuba, and Florida (White, 2005b:11).

Some rare contacts across these gaps occurred over the millennia, including tropical cultigens brought into the Eastern Woodlands. Cultigens including maize, tobacco, and beans may have been carried to the Eastern Woodlands at various times, possibly by way of the Antilles (Riley et al., 1990; Siegel, 1991b). Tobacco was quickly adopted across North America. Papaya and chiles may have spread to Florida from the Antilles although they failed to be adopted permanently. Cotton was widely used for textile weaving in the U.S. Southwest; even though wild cotton grows in southern Florida, peoples of the Southeast made do with other fibers (Widmer, 1974). Domesticated cotton was available in Mesoamerica by 1500 BCE, but it was not cultivated in the Southeast until the colonial era (White, 2005a: 306–307).

The manufacture and use of pottery is earlier in northern and western South America than elsewhere in the Americas. Fiber-tempered ceramics appear by 2500 BCE in the Southeast, earlier than in Mesoamerica (White and Weinstein, 2008: 236). Many archaeologists infer that pottery was invented independently in the Southeast. If it spread there via the Antilles, it was by the spread of technology, not of a migrating population carrying it (Clark and Knoll, 2005: 284–288).

Manioc was cultivated throughout the Antilles, but there is no evidence for its use in the Southeast, perhaps owing to its requirements for a tropical or subtropical climate. Regional distributions of plant domesticates were linked to a balance between environmental constraints of specific plant taxa and socioeconomic needs of the human communities.

Architecture and Technology

Early Mound Building

Earthen mound building and pottery making came early to the Gulf region, but it took longer for maize to replace native crops. In northern Louisiana, the mounds at Watson Brake date as early as 3400 BCE, and Poverty Point was established by 1600 BCE (see Chapter 6). There is no clear connection between these moundbuilders and those in the Great Lakes area somewhat later. No evidence links the Gulf mound constructions directly to the Olmec moundbuilders of coastal Mexico, who started building earthen mounds around the same time. Yet all of these people were laying similar architectural foundations, both conceptually and in design.

The Gulf lowlands were productive resource zones for hunter-gatherers. The hot coast was most productive, with terrestrial and marine plants and animals. In some areas people were still living by hunting, fishing, and gathering wild foods when the first Spaniards arrived. Sociopolitically, the historic Calusa of the Florida southwest coast were organized into chiefdoms despite lacking domesticated crops.

In contrast, the Olmecs of coastal Mexico were heavily reliant on domesticated crops (see Chapter 13), double cropping maize and other plants, laying the foundation for the later Maya and Mexican states. Maize spread northward into the Eastern Woodlands and around the northern Gulf Coast in the first two centuries CE, more than two millennia after ceramics appeared in the Southeast. It would be centuries before maize became a staple in the region. Agriculture, ceramics, architecture, and chiefdom polities did not all necessarily develop or spread together. Details of shifting human adaptations in the region were contingent on local factors. The more we know about Amerindian societies around the Gulf Coast, it is clear that they evolved piecemeal.

Previously, archaeologists believed that a gap existed of several centuries between the decline of Hopewell and the rise of Mississippian in the Eastern Woodlands. It is clear now that many cultures bridged that gap, including along the northern Gulf Coast. Research today addresses continuity and change between the Hopewell tribes and later Mississippian chiefdoms, especially regarding the shift from reliance on local domesticates and wild resources by tribal societies to later chiefdoms dependent on Mesoamerican-derived domesticates. Links have been documented between the use of domesticates and associated architectural traditions.

Troyville-Coles Creek Culture

A prime example is found in the Troyville-Coles Creek Culture in the lower Mississippi Valley. Hopewell was waning in the northern Eastern Woodlands by 400 CE, and influences from its trading network in the Southeast gradually disappeared. Troyville-Coles Creek arose in the lower Mississippi Valley and along the Gulf Coast as Hopewell expired, persisting until 1100 CE. It later evolved into a regional variant of Mississippian culture (see Chapter 7).

Troyville-Coles Creek towns are notable for flat-topped mounds arranged around plazas. This pattern became a widespread feature of Mississippian towns. Major sites near rivers usually have five to nine mounds, one typically much larger than the others. Smaller communities usually had three or fewer mounds and many smaller hamlets had none (Gibbon, 1998: 171–173).

Weeden Island–Fort Walton Cultures

The trajectory of Weeden Island to Fort Walton and Safety Harbor in northern Florida also illustrates the emergence of agriculture, monumental architecture, and chiefdoms from simpler antecedents along the northeastern Gulf Coast. Simple farming cultures persisted across the Eastern Woodlands after the collapse of the Hopewell trading network. One of these, Swift Creek culture in Alabama and Georgia, gave rise to Weeden Island along Florida's Gulf Coast and the lowland portions of Alabama and Georgia.

Weeden Island (200–1000 CE) overlapped in time with Hopewell (Milanich, 1994: 155–241). Like Troyville-Coles Creek people and the builders of the Toltec Mounds in Arkansas, they constructed early platform mounds, an architectural form that became more elaborate during the later Mississippian period. Weeden Island included at least five regional, interacting variants. Some were reliant on maize by 500 CE, and others by approximately 750 CE. Weeden Island evolved into or was replaced in part of its range by Fort Walton by around 1000 CE.

Weeden Island people also built smaller burial mounds, reminiscent of earlier Adena and Hopewell mounds. Typically, a pit was excavated into which were deposited cremated remains and offerings. Rocks and clay were piled over the grave, resulting in mounds up to 15 m (50 ft) wide by 6 m (20 ft) high. Occasionally isolated skulls are found in mound fill, possibly from sacrificed individuals.

Fort Walton evolved from Weeden Island around 1000 CE, developing into chiefdom polities supported by intensive agriculture. While earlier Weeden Island farmers probably practiced swidden agriculture, planting crops in hills scattered across recently cleared fields, Fort Walton farmers planted row crops in more permanent fields. Mesoamerican beans were introduced at this time. Maize, squash, and beans became major staples across the Southeast, providing protein thereby reducing the need for meat and reliance on hunting. Sunflowers, nuts, and a range of other foods made for a diverse and nutritious diet. Fort Walton communities exhibited early forms of hierarchical political organization associated with chiefly societies. They even sported some of the symbolism borrowed from Mississippian centers in the interior of the Eastern Woodlands (Milanich, 1994: 364, 377). Interactions between tribal and chiefdom communities may have triggered processes of social and political complexity in cultures like Weeden Island, earlier than they might have otherwise (Anderson, 1999: 226). Lake Jackson is a typical Fort Walton mound site (Figure 12.3).

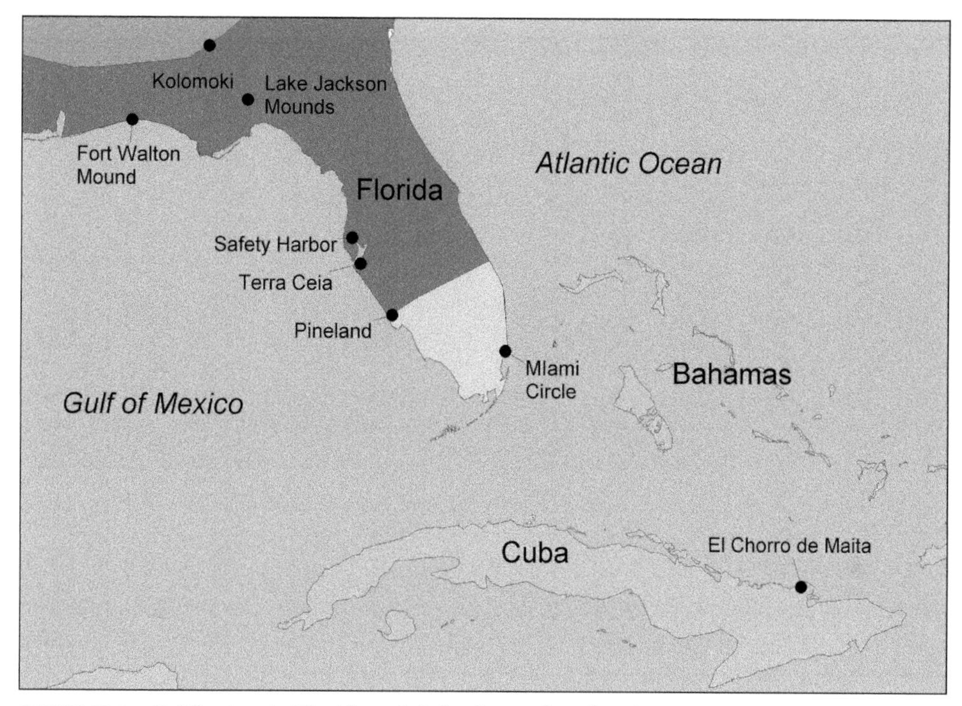

FIGURE 12.3 Public sites in Florida and Cuba featured in this chapter

LAKE JACKSON MOUNDS

Late prehistoric chiefdoms in northwest Florida, southwest Georgia, and southeast Alabama are represented by Fort Walton material culture, a variant of the Mississippian adaptation seen across the Southeast, representing the most complex indigenous societies north of Mexico. Fort Walton dates from 1000 CE to European contact and colonization. It features large towns, flat-topped "temple" mounds and plazas, smaller settlements, and ceramics with grit, sand, or grog temper, not crushed shell like most other Mississippian wares. Other distinctions are six-pointed open bowls and the lack of chipped-stone tools.

Lake Jackson Mounds (Site 8Li1) is the most spectacular Fort Walton ceremonial center, located on the north side of Tallahassee, Florida, and today a well-interpreted state park (Figure 12.4). It had at least seven mounds, one or more large plazas, and residential areas. Mound 2 is 11 m high and 83 m × 95 m at the base. High-status mound burials of women and men thought to have been chiefs included elaborately engraved copper plates, marine-shell beads, and other exotic objects of the Southeastern Ceremonial Complex, a shared set of artifacts and symbols depicting powerful, yet poorly understood, political and religious ideas. Fort Walton chiefdoms were socially ranked and probably matrilineal but may not have been economically stratified. They cultivated maize and other crops and continued fishing and shellfishing; gathering fruits and nuts; hunting deer, turkey, turtles, and other game; and building wattle-and-daub houses. On the coast, they did not farm but collected aquatic resources and probably brought whelk shells or dried yaupon holly tea leaves inland to trade

FIGURE 12.4 Lake Jackson, a Fort Walton mound site in northern Florida. Courtesy of Nancy Marie White

with farmers for maize. Fort Walton survived for about a century after the Spanish arrived in the early 1500s, then disappeared (Ashley and White, 2012; Marrinan and White, 2007; Willey, 1999).

Nancy Marie White

Safety Harbor

Safety Harbor evolved from another variant of Weeden Island around 900 CE in the area from Tampa Bay northward but, unlike Fort Walton, continued to emphasize wild resources. Each platform-mound settlement was probably the center of a polity, likely representing a weak chiefdom. These weak chiefdoms, which survived until Spanish times, were never as complex as the Fort Walton chiefdoms. Safety Harbor sites are generally small and dispersed, lacking evidence of intensive agriculture. The central west coast of Florida was rich in wild resources, so maize never became a major part of the Safety Harbor diet (Milanich, 1994: 398–399). Although Safety Harbor sites have yielded pottery and artifacts of copper, shell, and stone that bear symbols of the Southeastern Ceremonial Complex, they do not rival those of the more Mississippian-influenced cultures to the north and west. The Madira Bickel platform mound in the Terra Ceia site near Palmetto, Florida, is a good example.

SAFETY HARBOR

The Safety Harbor site is located on Phillippi Point that extends into Old Tampa Bay and at the north end of the town of Safety Harbor. It occupies more than a mile of shoreline in Philippe Park, which is maintained by Pinellas County Parks and Conservation Resources.

Since 1936, it has been considered the type site for the Safety Harbor Culture of west peninsular Florida. The Safety Harbor Culture is how archaeologists refer to the Mississippian

(900–1725 CE) peoples who occupied the region from the Withlacoochee River (Citrus County) on the north to Charlotte Harbor on the south (Mitchem, 2012). The phrase "type site" indicates that the features, layout, and artifacts are considered typical of all Safety Harbor Culture sites. This locality has a large platform mound at the easternmost edge (the foundation for the chief's house), with a burial mound at the northwest end. Between and around these earthworks was the village area.

Archaeological research began in 1929, when Matthew W. Stirling of the Smithsonian Institution's Bureau of American Ethnology carried out test excavations and returned the next year to excavate the burial mound. Although results were never reported thoroughly, some of the skeletal remains have been studied. The presence of metal artifacts indicated the mound was still used after Spanish contact. The best-reported excavations were undertaken in 1948 and 1949 (Griffin and Bullen, 1950). Excavations in the village area by local groups in the 1960s were never reported, and most of the artifacts and records have been lost.

The site is a National Historic Landmark. It is undoubtedly the village of Tocobaga, visited by Pedro Menéndez de Avilés in 1566 (Worth, 2014: 260–271). Menéndez established a small garrison, but by 1568 it was destroyed, the soldiers killed, and the entire village abandoned.

Jeffrey M. Mitchem

Belle Glade

Several sites in the Belle Glade area around Lake Okeechobee are known as "big circle" sites, the oldest dating to the first millennium BCE. They consist of large circular earthworks with attached linear ones radiating from them. Mounds were often placed at the ends of the radiating linear earthworks. Large circular ditches appear to have been excavated for drainage since groundwater was near the surface. These structures might suggest some sort of agriculture, but other explanations are possible, and there is little convincing evidence for cultivation in southern Florida (Milanich, 1998: 113–122).

Data from the Fort Center site and others like it suggest that its unusual architecture might have been introduced across the Gulf from Mexico as early as 450 BCE. Some controversial pollen evidence suggests the presence of maize in these sites (Milanich, 1994: 287–291). Farming did not become a major pursuit in the area, and Belle Glade did not evolve beyond the big circle stage.

There is great diversity among archaeological sites in the Glades region. Shell middens and earth middens mark sites where seasonal resources were gathered. Elsewhere, burial mounds were formed from sand or stone. Locally abundant plant, land animal, or fish resources were exploited (Milanich, 1994: 308–311).

Located on the Florida southwest coast, Key Marco was a wet site where artifacts made from normally perishable materials, including wood and fiber, were beautifully preserved (Figure 12.5). Surviving wooden artifacts include painted and inlaid masks, tablets, plaques, and statuettes (Milanich, 1994: 304–308). The site was excavated over a century ago, and since then the island has been almost entirely covered by modern development.

The Miami Circle

Archaeological testing in advance of major construction in 1998 led to the discovery of the enigmatic Miami Circle site (Figure 12.6) in downtown Miami, serving as an example of twenty-first-century

FIGURE 12.5 Kneeling human-feline effigy figure made of wood, 15 cm (6 in) tall, Key Marco, Florida. Courtesy of the National Museum of Natural History

archaeology. The site is an 11.5-m (38-ft) circle of 600 post molds containing 24 shallow, irregularly shaped basins. Radiocarbon dating places the occupation to 300 BCE. However, this part of Miami was heavily industrialized; the circle features could be remnants of more-recent activities now mixed with older wood samples during construction and demolition, only one of many controversies attached to the site.

While the Miami area was Tequesta Indian territory in the sixteenth century, there is little to link that or any tribe to the site. Various stakeholders came forward during the cultural resource management investigations. They included professional archaeologists, modern American Indian groups, state and local governments, federal agencies, developers, business interests, and citizen groups. The case illustrates both the ambiguity of many archaeological finds and the complications that arise when they become politicized. The site was purchased and preserved at great expense by Miami-Dade County, but in early 2007, it was once again threatened, this time by a collapsing sea wall.

Pensacola Culture

Pensacola developed in the western Florida panhandle and adjacent coastal parts of Alabama and Mississippi. It evolved from a generalized culture closely related to Weeden Island, but with greater influences from interior Mississippian cultures (Brown, 2003). Pensacola shows an unusual

FIGURE 12.6 Oblique view of Miami Circle feature, August 2000. Courtesy of the Florida Division of Historical Resources

combination of Gulf Coast and Mississippian traits. Some archaeologists also see connections with the Huastecan culture of coastal Mexico (Brose, 2003).

Bottle Creek is a large Pensacola site located on a low swampy island north of Mobile, Alabama, with at least 18 earthen mounds. Five mounds are arranged around a central plaza. The site was established after 1100 CE, with its main occupation from 1250 to 1550 CE. It is difficult to reach on foot, seemingly an unlikely place to locate a ceremonial center. However, the settlement would have been accessible by dugout canoe, a swift mode of transportation.

The Antilles

The trajectory from tribal to chiefly political organization is evident in changing community architecture in portions of the Antilles, especially Puerto Rico. During the Saladoid periods egalitarian communities established settlements with unlandscaped central plazas that also served as burial grounds. These plazas were typically surrounded by a series of mounds or mounded middens, into which the most elaborate artifacts fabricated by the settlement occupants were funneled constituting ritual deposits.

By 700 CE, the central plazas of some villages were landscaped and rudimentary ball courts were constructed; these early ball courts also served as cemeteries. The more-structured plazas provided emerging chieftains the architectural spaces they needed to assert their growing elite status (Curet, 1996). This appears to have made such centers both places of contest and places that were themselves contested (Siegel, 1999). The processes by which chieftains and their closest relatives gradually accrued power and prestige were generally the same as they were in other times and locations. Leading families strategically arranged marriages, orchestrated public rituals, and to the extent possible managed the distribution of wealth all in efforts to solidify and promote their power and prestige. Located near the modern city of Ponce, Puerto Rico, Tibes is a good example of one of these early civic-ceremonial centers.

TIBES CEREMONIAL CENTER

The Ceremonial Center of Tibes, under the administration of the City of Ponce, Puerto Rico, is one of the oldest sites of its kind in the Caribbean. Located just north of the city, approximately 8 km from the shore, Tibes was established on the alluvial terraces of the Portugués River (Curet and Stringer, 2010). The settlement is composed of several cultural deposits and nine stone structures (ball courts and plazas) (Figure 12.7). The quasi-quadrangular Plaza Principal in the center of the site covers an area of 1,500 m^2, and a ball court (Batey del Cemí) to its southeast measures 76 m by about 15 m (Alvarado Zayas and Curet, 2010). Based on radiocarbon dates, Tibes was occupied from 500 CE to around 1270 CE, spanning the late Saladoid and Elenan Ostionoid periods. The monumental structures all postdate the Saladoid period. Excavations conducted in the 1970s uncovered two clusters of burials: one under the Plaza Principal and the second under Ball Court 3. Both sets of burials date to the Saladoid period, thus predating the stone structures. Elenan Ostionoid burials were generally located throughout the site. This evidence suggested to many archaeologists that the initial occupations of Tibes reflected an egalitarian community, while the later (c. 900–1100 CE) more formally structured spaces represented some form of political centralization and social stratification.

Recent research, however, has failed to find clear evidence of social stratification or the accumulation of wealth and sumptuary items. Some valued objects such as exotic food (guinea pigs), shell, and stone ornaments are also scarce. Excavations of the building remains and cooking areas point to their ceremonial role in the settlement, perhaps during festivals, feasts, and gatherings. Researchers hypothesize that these centers represent the development of a communal, ritual space built under egalitarian and multiethnic conditions (Curet and Torres, 2010).

L. Antonio Curet

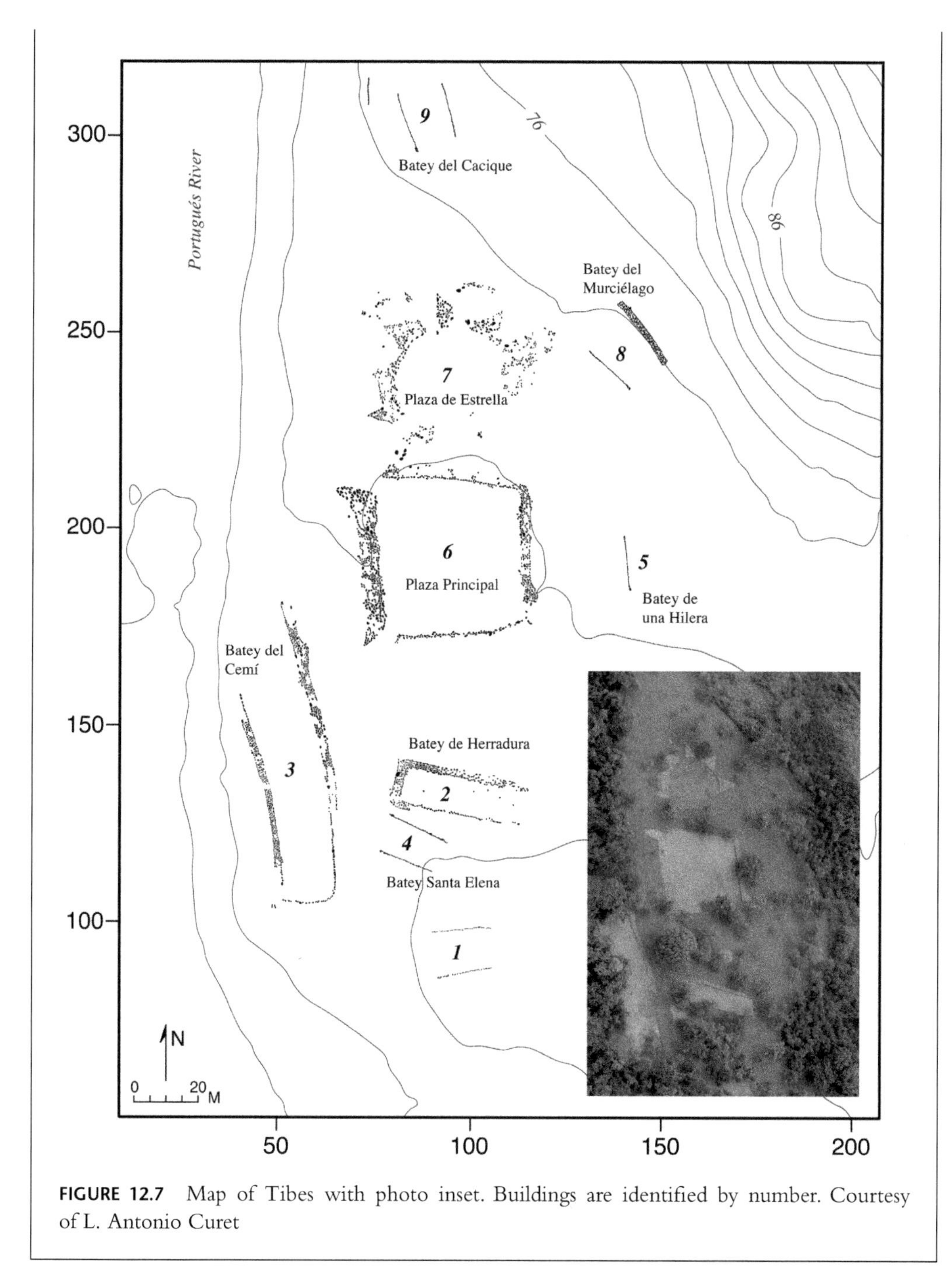

FIGURE 12.7 Map of Tibes with photo inset. Buildings are identified by number. Courtesy of L. Antonio Curet

The centuries after 1200 CE saw the production of stone collars and elbows, possibly copies of cloth pads used in the ball game, not unlike the stone yokes of the Mexican Gulf Coast. The objects appear to be associated with chiefly residences more than ball courts, so perhaps like stools, they were symbols of power (Curet, 1996). During this late pre-Columbian and protohistoric period, the ball courts on Puerto Rico and Hispaniola became more elaborate and diverse in construction

FIGURE 12.8 North wall of the Jácana site plaza. Courtesy of David Diener and New South Associates

and iconography than previously. Burials were located in areas other than the court plazas, although recent excavations in the Jácana site near the south coast of Puerto Rico produced many human burials in one of the largest ball courts documented for the island (Espenshade, 2014) (Figure 12.8). Jácana has a long occupational history, the burials have not been dated, and it is unknown whether they predate or are contemporaneous with the construction and use of the ball court.

Culture, Language, and Identity

Cultures were variable within and around the Gulf Rim and the Caribbean Islands. The Calusas provide an excellent example. Native ethnobotanically useful taxa were productive in southern Florida, and the indigenous peoples of the region never adopted agriculture. Settlements were situated close to reliable concentrations of native plants. Although groups in South Florida were removed from the greater Mississippian developments in the interior of the continent, they were well-positioned to potentially receive South American goods and ideas by way of the Antilles. Their nonagricultural adaptation persisted after hunting and gathering had been replaced by domestic food production across much of eastern North America.

THE PINELAND SITE COMPLEX

Located on the northwestern coast of Pine Island, the Pineland Site complex represents the second largest town of the native Calusa Indian people of southwestern Florida. First occupied about 50 CE, by the 1500s the town consisted of several domiciliary mounds, ponds, and canals. The largest of the Calusa burial mounds was located at Pineland, which was also the origin point of the engineered 4-km-long Pine Island Canal that traversed the entire width of Pine Island (Figure 12.9). Pineland was occupied by the Calusa until 1702.

When Spaniards arrived in the 1500s, the Calusa controlled the entire southern Florida peninsula and drew tribute from other polities such as the Ais, Jeaga, Mayami, Muspa, and

FIGURE 12.9 Calusa burial mound on Pine Island. Courtesy of William H. Marquardt

Tequesta. The Spaniards described a stratified society divided into nobles and commoners, with hereditary leadership, tributary patronage–clientage that extended throughout South Florida, ritual and military specialists, far-ranging trade, an accomplished artistic tradition, complex religious beliefs and ritual practices, and effective subsistence practices that supported thousands of people and allowed for a sedentary residence pattern. For nearly two centuries after contact, the Calusa maintained their identity and beliefs, repulsing European attempts to conquer and convert them to Christianity. The Calusa were the only Native American fisher-gatherer-hunters to achieve the social and political complexity of a true kingdom (MacMahon and Marquardt, 2004; Marquardt, 2014; Marquardt and Walker, 2013).

Today much of the site complex remains and is operated by the Florida Museum of Natural History as the Randell Research Center. It is located at 13810 Waterfront Drive, Pineland. The one-mile-long Calusa Heritage Trail offers access to several mounds and a canal as well as lush native vegetation and wildlife. The Trail is open seven days a week from sunup to sundown. Museum-quality interpretive signs help visitors connect with the Calusa and their ancestors who lived at the site for some 1,700 years. Guided tours are offered twice daily during peak season (January–April).

William H. Marquardt

The Calusas built linear and circular shell mounds on low-lying island and mainland locations in the vicinity of Fort Myers. Some are over 100 m (330 ft) long with steep sides and up to 6 m (20 ft) in height. The Calusas and their ancestors resided on or near these big middens, sometimes cutting canals from open water to gain access by canoe.

The ancestral Calusahatchee culture became established after sea levels stabilized around 700 BCE. Subsistence shifted increasingly toward marine resources in the ensuing centuries. The reliable supply of rich marine, terrestrial, and freshwater resources precluded the adoption of plant cultivation. Soil and climatic conditions make agriculture impractical, probably explaining why the Olmec phenomenon was not repeated here (Widmer, 1988).

By 300 CE, pressures to regulate, manage, and redistribute the complex array of resources led to the rise of hereditary chieftains. As was the case along the Northwest Coast (Chapter 11), seasonally abundant marine resources and population pressure selected for chiefly sociopolitical formations in the absence of agriculture.

Ancestors of the founding Ceramic Age cultures of the Caribbean Islands originated in the Orinoco Valley of Venezuela. Greater Amazonia had a long history of population movements, language distributions, and ethnogenesis prior to the first Ceramic Age migrations into the islands by ca. 500 BCE or perhaps earlier. Donald W. Lathrap wrote the visionary statement on Amazonian prehistory, the broad outlines of which are still relevant (Lathrap, 1970). Based on linguistic and archaeological analysis, Lathrap concluded that after thousands of years of population dispersals within Amazonia, bearers of one of the major language families, Arawakan, first moved into the islands around 500 BCE, although there has been some debate as to the reliability of employing historical linguistics in the context of the fluid social dynamics documented in the archaeological and ethnographic records of greater Amazonia (Rooevelt, 1997; Roosevelt, 2018; Wilson, 2007). Other scholars have discussed details of the Arawakan language in the Caribbean (Álvarez Nazario, 1996; Arrom, 2000; Taylor, 1977).

Art and Symbolism

The Taínos, the historic descendants of Saladoid culture, provide a fine example of the significance of symbolic art. Taíno craftspeople carved wooden "**zemi**s" (or "cemis") from trees they believed contained spirits. Stools and statues carved in the shapes of humans, birds, and other animals were common, but relatively few survive (Saunders and Gray, 1996). Small personal or domestic zemis were fewer after 600 CE, and large ones were more common. This was probably tied to the growing importance of the ancestors of chieftains and their families, who were evermore public and powerful. More paraphernalia appeared after 1200 CE, and later Spanish sources describe it as being controlled and used by chieftains, their assistants, and religious specialists (Curet, 1996). Only chieftains could take the cohoba **hallucinogen** and commune with the supernatural. Farming and natural resources produced a bounty that made it all possible, and the internal drivers of human nature, social and environmental circumscription, and elevated levels of warfare resulted in a spiral of increasing social inequality.

Island geography helps us understand the historic native cultures of the Antilles, much as it helps illuminate ecology. Most of the Caribbean Islands are small, perhaps too small for their native population densities to have tested the organizational limits of tribal organization. Puerto Rico is the smallest of the Greater Antilles. Given the deeply dissected terrain, the unstable nature of chiefly polities in general, and other studies of social dynamics on pre-Columbian Puerto Rico, Siegel argued that the entire island was almost certainly divided into a series of competing sociopolitical entities, or chiefdoms, shortly before the arrival of Europeans. Based on rank-size and spatial analysis of known ball courts, he suggested that Puerto Rico was divided into at least four to six polities (Siegel, 2011).

Reconstructions based on documentary evidence suggests the presence of five to six chiefdoms on Hispaniola at the time of Spanish contact (Wilson, 1990). One estimate suggests the total population of the island was 380,976 (Keegan, 1992: 112). An overall population of that size would result in chiefdoms ranging from approximately 63,000 to 76,000 people each, assuming five to six chiefdoms. Those demographics are six to eight times greater than the theoretical maximum of 10,000 people manageable for chiefdom polities (see Chapter 1). Given the absence of state organization in the

Antilles, it is likely that the total native population on Hispaniola was considerably smaller than 400,000 or more chiefdoms were present than reconstructed from ethnohistoric data. Alternatively, the island may have been occupied by a combination of chiefly and tribal-based societies simultaneously, an intriguing but to-date unverifiable scenario given current archaeological knowledge.

Islanders in the Lesser Antilles were part of the general theme and variations of the West Indies, but for centuries have often been called "Caribs," a term of disparagement initially intended to set them apart. Apparently, all of the island people spoke languages of the Arawakan family (Keegan, 1996: 276–279; Wilson, 1999). Those people who lived in the Lesser Antilles were ethnically similar to the Taínos of the Greater Antilles, but they lived on islands too small for larger populations and the formation of chiefdoms. Upon arrival of the Spanish and shortly after the English, French, and Dutch, the lives of the indigenous Antilleans were dramatically and permanently altered.

EL CHORRO DE MAÍTA

Located in northeastern Cuba, the El Chorro de Maíta site covers nearly 3.45 hectares. This large native settlement was occupied from the thirteenth century CE through the arrival of Spanish colonists. The community was subjected to the Spanish ***encomienda*** system in the first half of the sixteenth century. Forced labor was extracted from indigenous people, supposedly in exchange for religious instruction. The site is one of only a few in the Caribbean where the *encomienda* process has been examined archaeologically (Valcárcel Rojas, 2016).

The site features a central plaza that was converted into a colonial-period cemetery containing remains of more than 130 individuals (Figure 12.10). Archaeological data indicate that the cemetery was used in the wake of high epidemic mortality (Weston and Valcárcel Rojas, 2016). Interred individuals include indigenous Cubans and people with Mesoamerican,

FIGURE 12.10 El Chorro de Maíta, showing a partial reconstruction of the indigenous village. Courtesy of Roberto Valcárcel Rojas

mestizo, and African ancestries (Laffoon, 2012). Given their geographic origins, demographic profile, and burial treatments, some individuals may have been indigenous slaves imported by the Spanish who resided in or near El Chorro. The absence of cranial modifications, Christian ritual burial treatment, and individuals dressed in European clothing or interred with European objects suggest indoctrination focused on elite indigenous adults and children. There is also evidence that local indigenous people sought ways to preserve their traditional burial practices or to integrate them with European customs.

Artifacts of gold and of a gold and copper alloy (guanín/tumbaga) were found in association with the remains of an indigenous woman of local origin. These artifacts came from Colombia and may have been given to the woman by the Spaniards, who sometimes used them as trade items and to establish links with Antillean indigenous elites.

Roberto Valcárcel Rojas

Smallpox, measles, and other European diseases decimated significant proportions of the native populations in the islands sooner than elsewhere in the Americas simply because permanent colonization was earliest there and with it came children. Epidemics lethal to the natives were childhood diseases in Europe, and children who survived them were later immune as adults. European diseases were not dangerous to Indians so long as the explorers left children at home and crews were effectively quarantined by long ocean voyages. But Spanish colonists brought their families to the West Indies resulting in the transmission of diseases into Indian communities and subsequent high mortality rates (Snow and Lanphear, 1988). It has been commonly assumed that diseases, enslavement, and systematic murder resulted in the extinction of indigenous cultures in the Caribbean. However, recent genetics research among current residents of the Caribbean is showing the presence of Amerindian genomes similar to those found in pre-Columbian skeletal assemblages from the same region (Martínez-Cruzado, 2010; Schroeder et al., 2018).

Resilience and Collapse

The Spanish followed by other Europeans introduced horses, cattle, pigs, goats, sheep, and chickens intentionally, rats and mice unintentionally (Crosby, 1972). Grapes and cereal crops did not do well, but sugarcane flourished. Maize and other American domesticates combined with selected European crops produced a new agricultural complex in the New World. Other aspects of different cultures blended to form a uniquely new **creole** culture. Europeans reacted to the demographic collapse of Amerindians by importing African slaves. By 1520 Africans dominated the labor force, thereby contributing to the cultural mosaic of the islands that defines the modern West Indies (Watts, 1987).

Spanish missionization in northern Florida led to more intensive use of maize by natives than previously (Hutchinson et al., 1998). The historic Timucuas lived in independent polities spread over much of northern Florida. Spanish missions were established among Timucua villages and change came earlier to these people than to most others north of Mexico. As a two-directional process, the Spanish and Timucua adopted each other's practices. However, a formative creole society of mixed ancestry was aborted due to tremendous population losses among the indigenous population from smallpox and other diseases (Milanich, 1996).

The fates of the northern Gulf Rim cultures were similar. Some disappeared as organized societies, their remnants becoming refugees joining with slightly more fortunate regional communities. The Calusas and Timucuas of Florida disappeared, and the peninsula was repopulated by former Creeks and other refugees, who came to be known as Seminoles.

Glossary

cemíism An Antillian cosmological system involving the spirit world and ancestor veneration. See **zemi**.

creole A culture of mixed ancestry, usually in a colonial setting.

hallucinogen A drug that induces hallucinations.

zemi Also "cemí" Among Taíno cultures, zemies were considered to be spirits that delivered cosmological power. Icons of them were fabricated from wood, stone, shell, pottery, bone, and cotton.

References

Alegría, R.E. (1983). *Ball Courts and Ceremonial Plazas in the West Indies.* Yale University Publications in Anthropology 79. New Haven, CT: Yale University Department of Anthropology.

Alvarado Zayas, P., and Curet, L.A. (2010). Tibes: History and First Archaeological Work. In: L.A. Curet and L.M. Stringer, eds. *Tibes: People, Power, and Ritual at the Center of the Cosmos.* Tuscaloosa: University of Alabama Press.

Álvarez Nazario, M. (1996). *Arqueología lingüística: estudios modernos dirigidos al rescate y reconstrucción del Arahuaco Taíno* .San Juan: Editorial de la Universidad de Puerto Rico.

Anderson, D.G. (1999). Examining Chiefdoms in the Southeast: An Application of Multiscalar Analysis. In: J.E. Neitzel, ed. *Great Towns and Regional Polities in the Prehistoric American Southwest and Southeast.* Albuquerque: University of New Mexico Press.

Arrom, J.J. (2000). *Estudios de lexicología Antillana.* San Juan: Editorial de la Universidad de Puerto Rico.

Ashley, K., and White, N.M., eds. (2012). *Late Prehistoric Florida. Archaeology at the Edge of the Mississippian World.* Gainesville: University Press of Florida.

Bellizzia, A., and Dengo, G. (1990). The Caribbean Mountain System, Northern South America; A Summary. In: G. Dengo and J.E. Case, eds. *The Caribbean Region. The Geology of North America, Vol. H.* Boulder, CO: Geological Society of America.

Boomert, A. (2000). *Trinidad, Tobago and the Lower Orinoco Interaction Sphere: An Archaeological/Ethnohistorical Study.* Alkmaar, NL: Cari.

Brose, D.S. (2003). Foreword. In: I.W. Brown, ed. *Bottle Creek: A Pensacola Culture Site in South Alabama.* Tuscaloosa: University of Alabama Press.

Brown, I.W., ed. (2003). *Bottle Creek: A Pensacola Culture Site in South Alabama.* Tuscaloosa: University of Alabama Press.

Clark, J.E., and Knoll, M. (2005). The American Formative Revisited. In: N. M. White, ed. *Gulf Coast Archaeology: The Southeastern United States and Mexico.* Gainesville: University Press of Florida.

Crosby, A.W. (1972). *The Columbian Exchange: Biological and Cultural Consequences of 1492.* Westport, CT: Greenwood Press.

Curet, L.A. (1996). Ideology, Chiefly Power, and Material Culture: An Example from the Greater Antilles. *Latin American Antiquity*, 7, pp. 114–131.

Curet, L.A., and Oliver, J.R. (1998). Mortuary Practices, Social Development, and Ideology in Precolumbian Puerto Rico. *Latin American Antiquity*, 9, pp. 217–239.

Curet, L.A., and Stringer, L.M., eds. (2010). *Tibes: People, Power, and Ritual at the Center of the Cosmos.* Tuscaloosa: University of Alabama Press.

Curet, L.A., and Torres, J. (2010). Tibes and the Social Landscape: Integration, Interaction and the Community. In: L.A. Curet and L.M. Stringer, eds. *Tibes: People, Power, and Ritual at the Center of the Cosmos.* Tuscaloosa: University of Alabama Press.

Espenshade, C.T., ed. (2014). *The Cultural Landscape of Jácana: Archaeological Investigations of Site PO-29, Municipio de Ponce, Puerto Rico.* New South Associates Technical Report 2058. Jacksonville, FL: U.S. Army Corps of Engineers, Jacksonville District.

Gibbon, G., ed. (1998). *Archaeology of Prehistoric Native America: An Encyclopedia.* New York: Garland.

Griffin, J.W., and Bullen, R.P. (1950). *The Safety Harbor Site, Pinellas County, Florida.* Gainesville: Florida Anthropological Society.

Hutchinson, D.L., Larsen, C.S., Schoeninger, M.J., and Norr, L. (1998). Regional Variation in the Pattern of Maize Adoption and Use in Florida and Georgia. *American Antiquity*, 63, pp. 397–416.
Keegan, W.F. (1992). *The People Who Discovered Columbus: The Prehistory of the Bahamas*. Gainesville: University Press of Florida.
Keegan, W.F. (1995). Modeling Dispersal in the Prehistoric West Indies. *World Archaeology*, 26, pp. 400–420.
Keegan, W.F. (1996). West Indian Archaeology. 2. After Columbus. *Journal of Archaeological Research*, 4, pp. 265–294.
Laffoon, J. (2012). *Patterns of Paleomobility in the Ancient Antilles. An Isotopic Approach*. PhD dissertation, Leiden University.
Lathrap, D.W. (1970). *The Upper Amazon*. London: Thames and Hudson.
Lewis, J.F., Draper, G., Bourdon, C., Bowin, C., Mattson, P., Maurrasse, F., Tagle, F., and Pardo, G. (1990). Geology and Tectonic Evolution of the Northern Caribbean Margin. In: G. Dengo and D.T. Case, eds. *The Caribbean Region. The Geology of North America, Vol. H*. Boulder, CO: Geological Society of America.
MacMahon, D.A., and Marquardt, W.H. (2004). *The Calusa and Their Legacy: South Florida People and Their Environments*. Gainesville: University Press of Florida.
Marquardt, W.H. (2014). Tracking the Calusa: A Retrospective. *Southeastern Archaeology*, 33, pp. 1–24.
Marquardt, W.H., and Walker, K.J., eds. (2013). *The Archaeology of Pineland: A Coastal Southwest Florida Site Complex, ca. A.D. 50–1710*. Gainesville: University Press of Florida.
Marrinan, R.A., and White, N.M. (2007). Modeling Fort Walton Culture in Northwest Florida. *Southeastern Archaeology*, 26, pp. 292–318.
Martínez-Cruzado, J.C. (2010). The History of Amerindian Mitochrondrial DNA Lineages in Puerto Rico. In: S.M. Fitzpatrick and A.H. Ross, eds. *Island Shores, Distant Past: Archaeological and Biological Approaches to the Pre-Columbian Settlement of the Caribbean*. Gainesville: University Press of Florida.
Milanich, J.T. (1994). *Archaeology of Precolumbian Florida*. Gainesville: University Press of Florida.
Milanich, J.T. (1996). *The Timucua*. Cambridge: Blackwell.
Milanich, J.T. (1998). *Florida's Indians from Ancient Times to the Present*. Gainesville: University Press of Florida.
Mitchem, J.M. (2012). Safety Harbor: Mississippian Influence in the Circum-Tampa Bay Region. In: K. Ashley and N.M. White, eds. *Late Prehistoric Florida: Archaeology at the Edge of the Mississippian World*. Gainesville: University Press of Florida.
Newsom, L.A., and Wing, E.S. (2004). *On Land and Sea: Native American Uses of Biological Resources in the West Indies*. Tuscaloosa: University of Alabama Press.
Oliver, J.R. (2009). *Caciques and Cemí Idols: The Web Spun by Taíno Rulers between Hispaniola and Puerto Rico*. Tuscaloosa: University of Alabama Press.
Pagán-Jiménez, J.R., Rodríguez Ramos, R., Reid, B.A., Van Den Bel, M., and Hofman, C.L. (2015). Early Dispersals of Maize and Other Food Plants into the Southern Caribbean and Northeastern South America. *Quaternary Science Reviews*, 123, pp. 231–246.
Riley, T.J., Edging, R., and Rossen, J. (1990). Cultigens in Prehistoric Eastern North America: Changing Paradigms. *Current Anthropology*, 32, pp. 525–541.
Rodríguez Ramos, R., Babilonia, E., Curet, L.A., and Ulloa, J. (2008). The Pre-Arawak Pottery Horizon in the Antilles: A New Approximation. *Latin American Antiquity*, 19, pp. 47–63.
Roksandic, I. (2016). The Role of the Nicaraguan Rise in the Early Peopling of the Greater Antilles. In: I. Roksandic, ed. *Cuban Archaeology in the Caribbean*. Gainesville: University of Florida Press.
Roosevelt, A.C. (1997). *The Excavations at Corozal, Venezuela: Stratigraphy and Ceramic Seriation*. Yale University Publications in Anthropology 83. New Haven, CT: Yale University Department of Anthropology.
Roosevelt, A.C. (2018). Review of Handbook of Ceramic Symbols in the Ancient Lesser Antilles by L. Waldron. *Latin American Antiquity*, 29, pp. 413–414.
Rouse, I. (1986). *Migrations in Prehistory: Inferring Population Movement from Cultural Remains*. New Haven, CT: Yale University Press.
Rouse, I. (1992). *The Tainos: Rise and Decline of the People Who Greeted Columbus*. New Haven, CT: Yale University Press.
Rouse, I., and Cruxent, J.M. (1963). *Venezuelan Archaeology*. New Haven, CT: Yale University Press.
Saunders, N.J., and Gray, D. (1996). Zemís, Trees, and Symbolic Landscapes: Three Taíno Carvings from Jamaica. *Antiquity*, 70, pp. 801–812.
Schroeder, H., Sikora, et al. (2018). Origins and Genetic Legacies of the Caribbean Taino. *Proceedings of the National Academy of Sciences of the United States of America*, 115, pp. 2341–2346.

Siegel, P.E., ed. (1989). *Early Ceramic Population Lifeways and Adaptive Strategies in the Caribbean.* BAR International Series 506. Oxford: British Archaeological Reports.

Siegel, P.E. (1991a). Migration Research in Saladoid Archaeology: A Review. *The Florida Anthropologist*, 44, pp. 79–91.

Siegel, P.E. (1991b). On the Antillean Connection for the Introduction of Cultigens into Eastern North America. *Current Anthropology*, 32, pp. 332–334.

Siegel, P.E. (1999). Contested Places and Places of Contest: The Evolution of Social Power and Ceremonial Space in Prehistoric Puerto Rico. *Latin American Antiquity*, 10, pp. 209–238.

Siegel, P.E. (2004). What Happened After A.D. 600 on Puerto Rico? Corporate Groups, Population Restructuring, and Post-Saladoid Social Changes. In: A. Delpuech and C.L. Hofman, eds. *Late Ceramic Age Societies in the Eastern Caribbean.* Oxford: Archaeopress.

Siegel, P.E. (2010). Continuity and Change in the Evolution of Religion and Political Organization on Pre-Columbian Puerto Rico. *Journal of Anthropological Archaeology*, 29, pp. 302–326.

Siegel, P.E. (2011). Competitive Polities and Territorial Expansion in the Caribbean. In: L.A. Curet and M.W. Hauser, eds. *Islands at the Crossroads: Migration, Seafaring, and Interaction in the Caribbean.* Tuscaloosa: University of Alabama Press.

Siegel, P.E., Jones, J.G., Pearsall, D.M., Dunning, N.P., Farrell, P., Duncan, N.A., Curtis, J.H., and Singh, S.K. (2015). Paleoenvironmental Evidence for First Human Colonization of the Eastern Caribbean. *Quaternary Science Reviews*, 129, pp. 275–295.

Snow, D.R., and Lanphear, K.M. (1988). European Contact and Indian Depopulation in the Northeast: The Timing of the First Epidemics. *Ethnohistory*, 35, pp. 15–33.

Taylor, D. (1977). *Languages of the West Indies.* Baltimore, MD: Johns Hopkins University Press.

Valcárcel Rojas, R. (2016). *Archaeology of Early Colonial Interaction at El Chorro de Maíta, Cuba.* Gainesville: University Press of Florida.

Watts, D. (1987). The West Indies: Patterns of Development, Culture and Environmental Change Since 1492. Cambridge Studies in Historical Geography 8. Cambridge: Cambridge University Press.

Weston, D., and Valcárcel Rojas, R. (2016). Communities in Contact: Health and Paleodemography at El Chorro de Maíta, Cuba. In: I. Roksandic, ed. *Cuban Archaeology in the Caribbean.* Gainesville: University of Florida Press.

White, N.M. (2005a). Discontinuities, Common Foundations, Short-Distance Interactions, and Sporadic Long-Distance Connections around the Gulf of Mexico. In: N.M. White, ed. *Gulf Coast Archaeology: The Southeastern United States and Mexico.* Gainesville: University Press of Florida.

White, N.M. (2005b). Prehistoric Connections around the Gulf Coast. In: N.M. White, ed. *Gulf Coast Archaeology: The Southeastern United States and Mexico.* Gainesville: University Press of Florida.

White, N.M., and Weinstein, R.A. (2008). The Mexican Connection and the Far West of the U.S. Southeast. *American Antiquity*, 73, pp. 227–277.

Widmer, R.E. (1974). A Survey and Assessment of Archaeological Resources on Marco Island, Collier County, Florida. *Miscellaneous Project Report Series.* Tallahassee: Florida Division of Archives, History, and Records Management.

Widmer, R.E. (1988). *The Evolution of Calusa: A Nonagricultural Chiefdom on the Southwest Florida Coast.* Tuscaloosa: University of Alabama Press.

Widmer, R.E. (2005). A New Look at the Gulf Coast Formative. In: N.M. White, ed. *Gulf Coast Archaeology: The Southeastern United States and Mexico.* Gainesville: University Press of Florida.

Wilkerson, S.J.K. (2005). Rivers in the Sea: The Gulf of Mexico as a Cultural Corridor in Antiquity. In: N.M. White, ed. *Gulf Coast Archaeology: The Southeastern United States and Mexico.* Gainesville: University Press of Florida.

Willey, G.R. (1999). *Archeology of the Florida Gulf Coast.* Gainesville: University Press of Florida.

Wilson, S.M. (1990). *Hispaniola: Caribbean Chiefdoms in the Age of Columbus.* Tuscaloosa: University of Alabama Press.

Wilson, S.M., ed. (1999). *The Indigenous People of the Caribbean.* Gainesville: University Press of Florida.

Wilson, S.M. (2007). *The Archaeology of the Caribbean.* New York: Cambridge University Press.

Wilson, S.M., Iceland, H.B., and Hester, T.R. (1998). Preceramic Connections Between Yucatan and the Caribbean. *Latin American Antiquity,* 9, pp. 342–352.

Worth, J.E., ed. (2014). *Discovering Florida: First-Contact Narratives from Spanish Expeditions along the Lower Gulf Coast.* Gainesville: University Press of Florida.

13

MESOAMERICA

In the varied landscape of tropical rainforests, snow-capped mountains, coastal habitats, and scrub vegetation of the southernmost part of North America, numerous civilizations rose to power and constituted the most complex societies of ancient North America. In a region known as Mesoamerica, the well-known Olmecs, Zapotecs, Teotihuacanos, Maya, Mixtecs, Aztecs, and many other sophisticated societies built their cities and towns at various points in its history. This region includes the central and southern parts of Mexico, the Central American countries of Guatemala and Belize, and parts of Honduras and El Salvador (Figure 13.1). Archaeologists generally divide Mesoamerica into two areas: (1) peoples who lived west of the Isthmus of Tehuantepec were culturally Mexican, and (2) those who resided east of the Isthmus of Tehuantepec were culturally Maya.

Five broad periods define the cultural evolution of Mesoamerica (Table 13.1). Early migrants to the region during the Paleoindian period left subtle traces of their presence on the landscape (Chapter 3). Postglacial foraging cultures of the Archaic (8000–2000 BCE) (Chapter 4) utilized cave sites where experimentation with early domesticates occurred. This chapter will focus on the succeeding Formative, Classic, and Postclassic periods. The Formative (or Preclassic) period (2000 BCE–300 CE) witnessed the development of chiefdoms and **city-state**s out of the earlier less-complex societies. The best-known of these chiefdoms are the Olmecs who flourished in the Gulf Lowlands of Mexico, but complex societies also developed in the highland region of Oaxaca, Mexico, at the site of San José Mogote in western Mexico, and in the Maya Lowlands. During the Classic period (250–900 CE), Maya city-states thrived in the Peten lowlands, while the impressive city-state of Teotihuacan dominated the Basin of Mexico, and Monte Albán controlled the Oaxaca highlands. The Postclassic period (900–1519 CE) witnessed the growth of city-states of the Yucatan Peninsula (López Austin and López Luján, 2001; Stuart and Stuart, 1993) and the rise of empires, such as the Toltecs in highland Mexico, the Mixtecs in Oaxaca, the Aztecs in the Basin of Mexico, and the Tarascans in western Mexico (Pollard, 2016).

Environment and Adaptation

Mesoamerica includes the lands south of the northern Mexico deserts (from roughly the Tropic of Cancer) to western Honduras and El Salvador, encompassing about 900,000 km^2 (347,000 mi^2). The northern border of Mesoamerica has changed through time due to variation in rainfall (Evans,

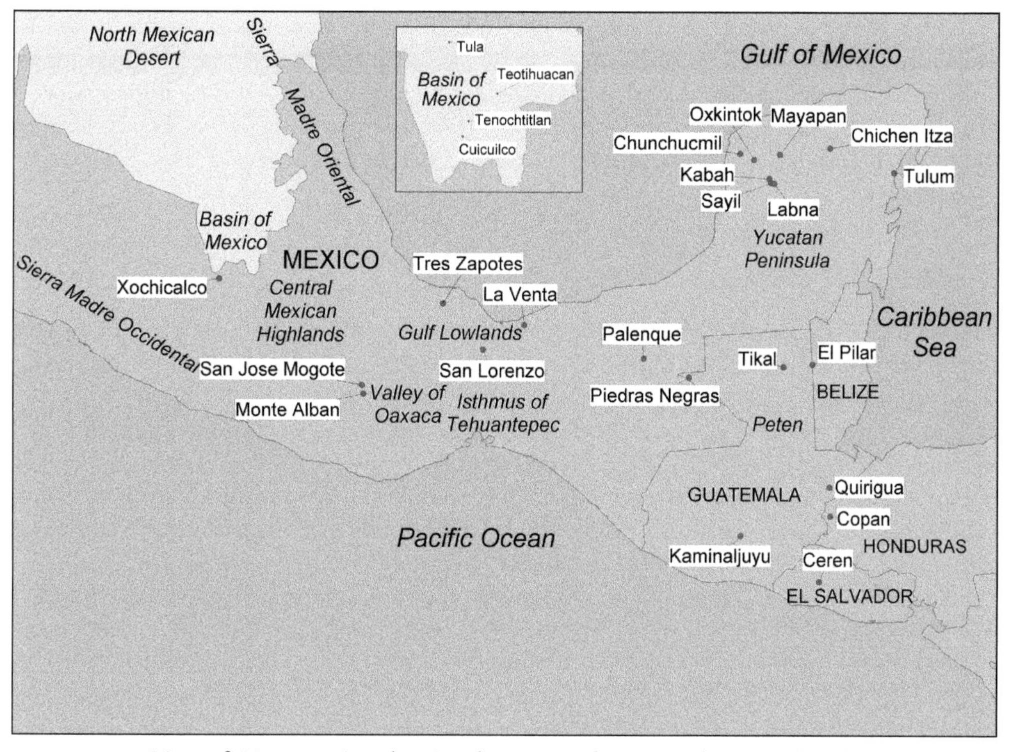

FIGURE 13.1 Map of Mesoamerica showing locations of major cultures and archaeological sites mentioned in the chapter

TABLE 13.1 Five main time periods in Mesoamerican chronology along with well-known ancient cultures and key sites

Period	*Dates*	*Sample of Ancient Cultures and Major Sites*
Paleoindian	?-8000 BCE	(Chapter 3)
Archaic	8000–2000 BCE	(Chapter 4)
Formative	2000 BCE–300 CE	Cuicuilco, Olmec, San José Mogote, Teuchitlán, Preclassic Maya
Classic	250–900 CE	Maya, Teotihuacan, Zapotec, Teuchitlán
Postclassic	900–1519 CE	Aztec, Cholula, Mixtec, Postclassic Maya, Tarascan, Toltec

2013: 49). This demarcation is significant for maize, which became the dominant agricultural crop sustaining large, dense populations.

Geologically, Mesoamerica is a dynamic tectonic zone. Earthquakes periodically shake the region and volcanoes, such as Popocatepetl and Volcán de Fuego, blow their tops. Both types of events have been responsible for creating and destroying the archaeological record and have had profound effects on migrations throughout Mesoamerica's history.

Altitude plays a critical role in the climate of Mesoamerica and defines three main climatic zones: *tierra caliente* (hot lands), *tierra templada* (temperate lands), and *tierra fría* (cold lands). In the cold highlands, summer temperatures are pleasant in the thin air and plants thrive under nearly daily thundershowers. Winters are cool and dry. Coastal lowlands are wetter, the air is heavy, and summers are very hot.

Central Mexico consists of a V-shaped arrangement of two mountain ranges connected by a high plateau and flanked by coastal lowlands. It is bounded on the east by the Sierra Madre Oriental and the Sierra Madre Occidental on the west. Deserts, known as the "Gran Chichimeca" after the **Chichimec** hunter-gatherers who lived there, lie open to the north. At the southern end of the great V lies the Basin of Mexico, a high-altitude plateau now mostly occupied by Mexico City.

Highland Basin of Mexico

The Basin of Mexico was a region of considerable potential to pre-Hispanic populations. The floor of this elevated plain is just under 2,240 m (7,350 ft) in elevation, surrounded by high mountains on three sides and open to the north toward the desert. Before the Spanish dug a canal to drain it, the centerpiece of the closed basin was a huge, brackish lake, sometimes subdivided into separately named lakes but just as often referred to in the aggregate as Lake Texcoco. The shallow lake was almost 70 km (43 mi) across from south to north. The southern part of the basin receives twice as much seasonal rainfall, and that portion of the lake was fed by many streams and springs, making it less brackish than its northern end. Aztec engineers built a 13-km (8-mi) dike across the basin's waist to raise the lake level and freshen the water in the south and west portions of the lake (Sanders, 2004).

While irrigation was necessary in the drier northern part of the basin, the southern part was suited to dry farming. Lower temperatures and moisture restricted farming to land near the lake, and even today, farming is unproductive on upper slopes, where it is too cold, or in low-lying areas where the settling frost shortens the growing season.

The Guatemalan highlands are similar to those of Mexico, except that they are more tropical and without snow in their higher elevations. Forested volcanic mountains provided fertile soils for Maya farmers on a landscape that still trembles periodically and where volcanic eruptions continue to occur.

Highlands in Oaxaca, Mexico

The Oaxaca Valley 400 km (250 mi) to the southwest of the Basin of Mexico, was the setting for the Zapotecs and the Mxtecs. The Zapotecs, who are still numerous, built the great mountaintop city of Monte Albán, as well as dozens of other smaller centers around the Y-shaped valley, at a lower elevation than the Basin of Mexico. The valley is warm and fertile, favoring conditions for farming communities. The valley encompasses 1,500 km^2 (580 mi^2) of arable land at an average elevation of 1,500 m (4,900 ft). Winter frost is rare at that elevation and the June to October wet season brings abundant rain. Climate and soil in the Valley of Oaxaca allowed for two crops a year. Irrigation prevented crop failure in the frequent years of low rainfall.

The Gulf Lowlands

Along the Gulf Coast of Mexico are the hot steamy lowlands of Veracruz and Tabasco. Numerous mountain rivers flow through coastal swamps and into the Gulf. With heavy annual rainfall of up to 3 m (10 ft), agriculture was productive in this region, and rubber and cacao were plentiful. This low-lying area was home to the well-known Olmec people (Blomster and Cheetham, 2017; Cyphers, 2012), as well as the later Huastecas.

The Maya Lowlands

The Peten lowlands of Guatemala were home to many of the largest Classic Maya centers, which flourished until around 900 CE. Much of the region is still covered by dense tropical rain forests that are hot and wet for most of the year. They were plentiful in jaguar pelts, quetzal feathers, cacao, rubber, and other commodities necessary and symbolically meaningful to the ancient way of life.

To the north, the Yucatan Peninsula of Mexico and Belize is a low shelf of limestone that provides ample building supplies and raw materials for tools. In areas of high rainfall, tropical rain forests dominate, but in the northern Yucatan, rainfall is low and scrub vegetation is the norm. Over much of the northern region, **karst** features (**cenote**s and caves), rather than rivers, drain the landscape. The Postclassic Maya are best known from this area. The Maya thrived throughout the lowlands and built their stone cities in both the north and the south, and they effectively utilized the ample coast line for trade between inland and coastal areas.

Demography and Conflict

Millions of people thrived in Mesoamerica before Spanish contact in 1519 CE. Their numerous cultures are spectacularly represented in the archaeological record. The tectonically dynamic landscape affected demography, settlement, and conflict throughout Mesoamerica's long history.

Complexity in the Formative

The Olmec heartland lies on the Gulf Coast side of the Isthmus of Tehuantepec, where inhabitants built large centers during the Formative period. The "People of the Rubber" are famous for the colossal stone sculpted heads (Figure 13.2). They are equally well-known for early complexity and sophistication in ceramics and stone. The Tuxtla Mountains, the source of the basalt that Olmec carvers used for their massive heads and other monuments, lie just east of one of the major Olmec centers, Tres Zapotes.

Olmec centers emerged from a population boom fueled by the productive cultivation of highland domesticates in a natural hothouse. Most of the Olmec people lived in individual farmsteads with thatched houses and associated structures. Their rulers recruited labor from the lower ranks to build centers, provided in exchange for elaborate placation and manipulation of supernatural forces. Lower-ranking farmers produced the agricultural surpluses needed to sustain the higher ranks and were assured a certain future and occasional festivals.

Prior to 500 BCE, San José Mogote was the major center in the Oaxaca highlands. Most other settlements were small-scale farming communities that raised maize, avocados, beans, and squash as their primary crops. Although the valley was agriculturally rich, most luxury goods were imported, and it was a node in the far-flung Olmec trade network. Imports included, obsidian, jade, feathers, shell, cacao, and gold. In exchange the Oaxaca people produced much-desired magnetite mirrors and pottery (Marcus and Flannery, 1996).

Located in the southwest of the Basin of Mexico, Cuicuilco flourished during the Late Formative, along with many other smaller competing centers, but the burgeoning city-state was nearly destroyed by an eruption from the nearby volcano, Xitle. The community and its infrastructure were falling into ruin when Xitle erupted a second time and lava flowed across the city, enveloping the lower portion of the great pyramid and covering everything else. The Xitle disaster finished Cuicuilco and forced a shift in the political center of gravity in the Basin of Mexico. Teotihuacan, located in the northeast of the Basin of Mexico, had been secondary to Cuicuilco up

FIGURE 13.2 Colossal Olmec Basalt Head 10 at San Lorenzo, Mexico. Courtesy of Ann Cyphers

to this point. It soon became the center of new growth in the years leading up to 300 CE and then the sixth largest city in the world in only three centuries (Evans, 2013: 213–215).

The metropolis of Teotihuacan was larger by far than all other Mesoamerican centers of its time. Plentiful springs for irrigation, fertile soils, and abundant raw materials attracted farming populations to the area, especially after the fall of Cuicuilco (Evans and Nichols, 2016). The city grew from a small Formative-period population to become the dominant force in the Basin of Mexico during the Classic Period.

Monte Albán: From Formative to Classic Center

Complex societies also developed in the Valley of Oaxaca. Monte Albán, the principal Zapotec city-state, was founded around 500 BCE and expanded by conquest beyond the valley as early as 300 BCE, before it consolidated its power in the main valley (Spencer and Redmond, 2001). These developments occurred during the heyday of Epi-Olmec trade and exchange, resulting in Olmec influences in the city. San José Mogote was nearly abandoned by this time and the inhabitants of the valley formed a confederation in response to growing levels of warfare; Monte Albán was built as a defensive stronghold on a summit in the valley center.

The population of the mountaintop center increased to 17,000. The number of small supporting communities grew from 51 to 86 and the residents of the surrounding landscape topped 24,000. Monte Albán was a primate center, bigger by far than any of the communities around it and clearly a major city-state by 200 BCE.

MONTE ALBÁN

Monte Albán, the ancient Zapotec capital, was founded around 500 BCE on a prominent hill located at the confluence of the three small valleys that together form the Valley of Oaxaca. It was first excavated in the 1930s, by preeminent Mexican archaeologist Alfonso Caso, who initiated a true scientific investigation in Oaxaca. The site's most relevant feature is the Principal Plaza, an impressive square in the city center, lined by monumental temples. Architectural features include massive stone platforms topped by temples. **Talud-tablero**, seen also at Teotihuacan, sports local ornamentation that gives the buildings a unique style in Mesoamerican architecture. More than 2,000 agricultural and domestic terraces surrounded the plaza, providing the infrastructure for living and food production.

Around 500 CE, urban expansion resulted in at least ten more monumental compounds and dispersed powerful families along the increasingly widespread city limits. Monte Albán, a truly urban capital of its time, lasted 13 centuries. It was a planned city, whose emergence was only possible by control from a ruling class at the top of a pyramidal social structure, or a true state. In many cases, governors were also priests, so the ruler was identified as a supreme being.

The economic and power base of the city was derived from tribute coming from many communities across Oaxaca. Monte Albán was positioned at the center of a complicated exchange system (obsidian, mica, ceramics). Religion was managed through the ritual calendar. A strong political network included close relationships with Teotihuacan, giving the rulers power to control locals, conquer surrounding territories, and expand regional authority of the Zapotecs.

The decline of Monte Albán started around 850 CE, after an abandonment period. By 1400 CE, the Mixtecs appeared in the valleys and took over some of the emblematic monuments of the ancient city.

Nelly M. Robles García

Maya City-States in the Lowlands

The Maya ascended in eastern Mesoamerica by at least 3000 BCE, with the introduction of maize and manioc. By 1000 BCE, numerous Mayan-speaking groups with their agriculture, technology, and cosmology began to transform the natural environment of the Peten lowlands into a complex mosaic of forest gardens (Ford and Nigh, 2015). Patterns of raised and canalized fields that are detectable in aerial imagery date to at least this time (Pohl et al., 1996). Complex Maya societies began to emerge by 600 BCE, their growing centers probably dependent upon raised fields in some areas and water storage in others (French and Duffy, 2016; Scarborough and Gallopin, 1991). These literate societies emerged from earlier chiefdoms over the course of two centuries, 230–430 CE. Eventually more than four dozen city-states resided in the steamy Maya lowlands, before their decline at the end of the Classic period. Maya population shifted north to the Yucatan Peninsula during the Postclassic, where several city-states absorbed migrating populations and new ones were founded.

The Postclassic Toltecs

The Toltec capital of Tula was a center on the fringe of the desert in central Mexico, and was initially founded around 700 CE as a lime-producing community. Agriculture along this northern edge of the Basin of Mexico required irrigation. With the addition of **Náhuatl**-speaking immigrants from farther north, forced southward by climate change, Tula developed into a full-blown city-state of 60,000 people during the early part of the Postclassic period, from 900 to 1175 CE.

Rise of the Aztecs

From where did the Aztecs come? Their mythical place of origin was Aztlan "Place of the Herons" far to the north of modern-day Mexico City. The people who called themselves the Mexica were the last to arrive in the Basin of Mexico around 1250 CE. By the time they arrived, the best real estate was occupied, so they settled on an undesirable hill known as Chapultepec "Grasshopper Hill."

Initially, the Mexica were subjects to various city-states and were regarded as bad neighbors. They frequently fled from the armies of outraged kings of nearby city-states and in 1325 CE retreated to a swampy island in Lake Texcoco. There they founded the twin cities of Tenochtitlan and Tlatelolco on land no one else wanted. According to their origin myth, an eagle led them to the island and then landed on a cactus with a snake in its beak, a symbol that adorns the modern Mexican flag.

A succession of six emperors, ***tlatoani***, from Itzcoatl to Motecuhzoma II, built the empire by systematically attacking and subjugating tributary city-states and smaller centers. By 1519 CE, the largest Mesoamerican empire straddled both coasts. When the Spanish arrived in 1519, Tenochtitlan had been filled, raised, and expanded to an island city of 12–15 km^2 (4.6–5.8 mi^2). There were many city-states that the Mexica did not conquer, despite persistent efforts. Tlaxcala and various Tarascan polities are particularly famous for having resisted Mexica conquest.

Subsistence and Economy

Plant domestication in Mesoamerica provided the economic foundation for the development of the first complex societies in North America. People domesticated squash, pumpkins, maize (from wild teosinte), beans, avocados, chili peppers, cacao, cotton, amaranth, gourds, and sapotes. In several cases, two or more species of these domesticates were cultivated. In the Basin of Mexico farmers made use of ***chinampas***, fertile raised fields built on lake margins. In forested areas people cleared temporary fields called ***milpas***, allowing them to regain fertility during multi-year periods of rest, a form of swidden agriculture.

Several bean species were essential for satisfying most of their protein requirements. Dogs that were bred for their meat and wild deer represented minor contributions of protein. Some Mesoamerican domesticates spread northward to become important staple crops, discussed in previous chapters.

Architecture and Technology

From wattle-and-daub houses to the stone skyscrapers of the tropical rain forest, Mesoamerican architecture is readily identifiable. House remains are most numerous on the landscape, though the spectacular temples and palaces are most well-known from a variety of different cultures and time periods. Absent from Mesoamerican technology were the wheel (except in miniature animal effigies or toys), metal tools, and draft animals. Nevertheless, indigenous populations were inventive and resourceful in their use of available materials.

Olmec Centers

San Lorenzo is the oldest of three great Olmec centers, spanning the Early Olmec period from roughly 1500 to 900 BCE.

SAN LORENZO

The heart of Olmec civilization is found at the archaeological site of San Lorenzo, Veracruz, set in the tropical wetlands of the southern Gulf Coast of Mexico. During its extraordinary, complex development from 1800 to 1000 BCE, San Lorenzo fueled profound transformations in the social fabric of the coastal region and beyond. As the first political and economic city in Mesoamerica, its population of nearly 12,000 inhabitants was organized as a stratified social hierarchy of ruling elite, noble, and common people. The marked division of labor included food producers and specialists such as sculptors, drillers, crafters, builders, religious and military leaders, traders, ballplayers, and administrators.

The thematic imagery in Olmec monumental stone art illustrates the existence of powerful, hierarchical lineages backed by divine legitimation. The well-known hallmark of this art style is the colossal head, and, of the 17 known heads, the city of San Lorenzo boasts ten of these ruler portraits (Figure 13.2). The monolithic monumental stone throne, the seat of power, is another icon of sovereigns (Figure 13.3). Smaller sculptures include the human figure, the most common representation, followed by zoomorphic and supernatural images, **stelae**, boxes, and stone columns.

FIGURE 13.3 Olmec throne at La Venta, Mexico

Of all Early Formative communities in Mesoamerica, San Lorenzo was the only one with strong hereditary rulers with a proclivity for organizing large labor mobilizations. Stone monument transport from the neighboring mountains required a huge labor force that was surpassed only by the unparalleled construction of the great terraced plateau in the heart of the city, considered one the largest buildings in the ancient world.

San Lorenzo waned due to several inter-connected causes, including competition with other communities, environmental changes, forced labor practices, power struggles, problems in food production, and ideological crises. The result was a population exodus that began around 1000 BCE at the same time that La Venta, in the Mexican state of Tabasco, began its rise to power as the second Olmec capital.

Ann Cyphers

La Venta rose to prominence as San Lorenzo declined. This center was built during the Late Olmec period from around 900 to 400 BCE. The site was constructed atop a salt dome, a relatively dry sandy rise in what is otherwise low, swampy terrain (Bernal, 1969). The central complexes lie on an axis that deviates 8° west of true north. Complex A to the north has both massive offerings and three large serpentine mosaics laid out as gigantic geometric masks (Figure 13.4). The axis of the site points south toward the nearest high mountain, while the offerings on the north might represent the sea, which lies a few kilometers in that direction (Tate, 1999).

The Mexican Highlands

Cuicuilco, on the southwest side of Lake Texcoco in the Basin of Mexico, appeared to have a bright future. The local polity built a large pyramid with an unusual circular footprint, whereas most

FIGURE 13.4 Olmec jaguar mosaic of serpentine at La Venta, Mexico

Mesoamerican pyramids were square or rectangular in plan, even at this early date. The earliest stages of construction consisted of adobe. Later stages were made of rubble faced with rounded river cobbles and boulders. Residents of Cuicuilco enlarged the pyramid to a diameter of 118 m (387 ft) and a height of 23 m (75 ft), after two expansion episodes that left earlier stages buried deeply within. With each building episode, a large altar was added to the newly created surface, resulting in a stratigraphic sequence of surfaces and altars. Each altar was probably protected by a temple constructed of wood or wattle-and-daub. By 150 BCE, approximately 10,000 people occupied the surrounding community, one-ninth of the entire population of the Formative-period Basin of Mexico.

Teotihuacan

The Teotihuacanos organized their large city on a grid system. One major feature is a wide grand avenue oriented 15°30' east of true north. It is along this major throughway that the largest pyramids were built and palaces were constructed.

The Pyramids of the Moon and the Sun are two of the largest structures in the New World, however evidence is lacking that either was dedicated to a particular deity, as was the case for the later Aztecs. The Pyramid of the Moon was built in seven stages, each covering the previous one. Initial construction of it began around 100 CE, whereas the Pyramid of the Sun was begun around 150 CE (Figure 13.5). The tops of the pyramids were flat plastered surfaces, perhaps indicating that they were used for open rituals and performances rather than as places for enclosed temples. Humans were sacrificed to commemorate each new construction episode. Some of the victims were finely dressed and bore headdresses and opulent jewelry, while others were naked and bound, and in some cases, decapitated.

The Temple of Quetzalcoatl was constructed inside a huge walled compound. Earlier buildings were demolished to make way for it around 200 CE. Two hundred people, including 20 men

FIGURE 13.5 The Pyramid of the Sun and the Avenue of the Dead, as seen from the Pyramid of the Moon, Teotihuacan. Courtesy of Linda R. Manzanilla

wearing lavish decorations, were sacrificed and buried under the fill of the new building (Cabrera Castro et al., 1991). The flat-topped pyramid was apparently designed as a ritual platform. The compound around it known as the Ciudadela was twice the size of a modern sports stadium, big enough to hold the entire population of the city on special occasions.

The front of the temple's main structure was later covered by a smaller addition, thereby preserving its elaborate façade. Archaeologists later removed the back of the addition to expose the façade, and the classic talud-tablero architecture is now one of the most popular sights in the city. Great stone masks project out from the tablero portion of each terrace.

The large Teotihuacan archaeological mapping project produced a highly detailed description of this great city (Millon, 1973). The urban area covers about 20 km^2 (8 mi^2), an area comparable to downtown Washington, DC. About 2,000 apartment complexes, housing 60–100 residents each, were arrayed around the central urban core (Manzanilla and Barba, 1990). At its peak, Teotihuacan's population was probably between 100,000 and 150,000.

Monte Albán

A major landscaping project was undertaken to flatten the main plaza of this mountaintop city. Outcrops were taken down and low spots were filled over an area the size of six modern football fields. Buildings were then constructed on and around the plaza and a ball court was built in its northeastern corner. The final configuration of the city took form by around 300 CE (Figure 13.6).

FIGURE 13.6 Monte Albán, Mexico, from the South Platform, Building J in the foreground. The ball court is near the tree in the distant right

Arrow-shaped Building J, just north of the South Platform, is adorned with inscriptions celebrating military conquests (Peeler and Winter, 1995).

Classic Maya

Elite Maya architecture was founded on dressed and carved stone blocks that were stacked and mortared into lavish palaces and steep-sided terraced pyramids. Temple structures typically surmounted the towering pyramids, and these were made to look even taller through the addition of latticed roof combs. The Maya made use of the corbelled vault for ceilings and roofs rather than a true arch. This kind of vault has an A-shaped cross section and depends upon the stacking of heavy stone counterweights atop thick walls. Temples, pyramids, platforms, palaces, ball courts, plazas, and residences make up the core of Maya city-states. Dotting the plazas are stelae, stone monoliths designed to commemorate major events. Over time, Maya buildings lost their paint, but they were once plastered and painted in dramatic colors, especially red and the famous Maya blue (Arnold et al., 2008; José-Yacamán et al., 1996).

Tula

The architects of Tula drew upon ideas shared across a long strip of Mesoamerica, extending from the Basin of Mexico to the northern Yucatan Peninsula (Ringle et al., 1998). Their tastes ran to modest stone pyramids, ball courts, and spacious colonnaded halls. Low reliefs of jaguars, eagles, and warriors decorated the walls of their principal sites. A few undecipherable glyphs have been documented and inscriptions have not been recovered.

West Mexico

West Mexico, a vast region sprawling across Nayarit, Jalisco, Colima, Michoacán, and western Guerrero, is known for its shaft tombs and distinctive funerary pottery (Beekman and Pickering, 2016; Foster and Gorenstein, 2000). Metallurgy was initiated in this region around 650 CE (West, 1994). From there the smelting and casting of copper, gold, and silver spread to other Mexican and Maya centers, but was not used in great quantities and did not revolutionize tool-making.

Public architecture was built in the distinctive Teuchitlán tradition, which was also depicted in the form of charming ceramic scale models (Beekman, 2000). During the Late Formative and Early Classic, people of the Teuchitlán polity constructed ball courts, residences of elites and commoners, unique circular temples, and shaft tombs to bury their ancestors (Beekman, 2016).

Tenochtitlan

When the Spanish arrived, about 80 buildings comprised the walled ceremonial core of the Aztec capital city, including temples, palaces, dormitories, ball courts, skull trophy racks, clubhouses, and platforms for dancing and ritual combat. Gardens and even a zoo were present. Causeways with draw bridges linked the island capital to the mainland and aqueducts brought in fresh water. Palaces were splendid residences for the elites: Motecuhzoma's residence was 2.4 hectares (6 acres) in area, dwarfing even the largest residential compound at earlier Teotihuacan (Evans, 2013). Most people lived in residential wards called "**calpultin**" (plural of "**calpulli**"), social units into which the city's inhabitants organized themselves.

The "Templo Mayor" dominated the city. Seven major construction episodes were documented, each covering and preserving earlier structures. Two temples were located at the top of the pyramid's double staircase, the one to the north dedicated to Tlaloc and the one on the south to Huitzilopochtli. Lavish offerings were found in several places, some placed on the steps of earlier structures that were covered by additions and renovations (López Luján, 2005).

Culture, Language, and Identity

When the Spanish arrived in 1519, Highland Mexico was dominated by Aztecs (Mexica) and other groups who spoke Náhuatl. West of the Aztecs lived the Tarascans and to the southeast, in Oaxaca, were the Zapotecs and the Mixtecs. Huastecs, Totonacs, Otomis, and many other groups were living in large provinces along the coasts and in pockets of the highlands. The highlands of Guatemala and the lowlands of the Peten and the Yucatan Peninsula were the domain of Mayan-speaking peoples, but referencing this array of related cultures with a single term should not be taken to mean that they were a homogeneous group (Macri, 2017). A diverse range of Maya and other groups built major centers in the Peten, Yucatan, Guatemalan highlands, and eastward to western Honduras and El Salvador. Only a few of the extraordinary cultures are highlighted below.

Classic Maya City-States

Several major independent city-states of Mayan-speaking peoples existed during the Classic period with warfare and power politics existing between competing dynasties. Epigraphers have compiled dynastic lists from Classic Mayan glyphs (Houston et al., 2001; Martin and Nikolai, 2008; Schele, 1992). Ambitious local leaders drove this competition, which was expressed in architecture and monuments designed to extol and memorialize the accomplishments of the royalty in whose honor they were erected. Three major centers, discussed below, exemplify the variability that is often masked by using the term "Maya." These polities were initiated during the Preclassic period, rose to power during the Classic, and drastically waned in influence and ultimately abandoned by the Postclassic period.

Tikal

Maya rulers of Tikal lived in opulence and presided over a center of great beauty with palaces, temples, plazas, ball courts, and other monumental architecture. Two opposing, tall, and steeply sided temples dominated the main plaza, which contained numerous stelae (Figure 13.7). Its population numbered around 120,000 within its domain, and its rulers may have commanded the labor and tribute of thousands more. A long and wide earthwork surrounded a large area of Tikal and its outlying regions. It may have been used for defense or water management, among other possible functions (Webster et al., 2013).

Palenque

Palenque is famous for its beautiful architecture with elegant mansard roofs. The center is dominated by two imposing structures: the Palace with a spectacular reconstructed tower and the Temple of the Inscriptions (Figure 13.8), which houses the Tomb of K'inich Janaab

FIGURE 13.7 Temple of the Giant Jaguar (Temple I) at Tikal, Guatemala

Pakal I (603–683 CE), Palenque's most famous king. The lid of his sarcophagus bears glyphs and representation of a maize plant growing out of the abdomen of a recumbent man. The remains of King Pakal himself were bedecked in jade; a mosaic mask covered his face and jade bracelets adorned his arms and legs.

FIGURE 13.8 Temple of the Inscriptions, burial tomb of King K'inich Janaab Pakal I. Palenque, Mexico. Courtesy of Marlon Shota Gonlin

PALENQUE

Originally named *Lakam-ha'*, "the place of abundant water," the ancient city of Palenque was the political capital of a large territory that included sections of the modern southern Mexican states of Chiapas and Tabasco. Built on a series of natural terraces of the first escarpments of the northern mountains of Chiapas, the Palencanos developed a sophisticated system of channels, aqueducts, and stone bridges that controlled five streams across the terraces, which eventually flow into verdant tracts irrigated by the Michol River.

Ongoing research on Palenque's urban growth identified two early villages (Late Formative period, circa 450 BCE) that later merged into one larger settlement during the Early Classic period (150–600 CE). During the following 250 years, the power of the local ruling dynasty grew tremendously. Rulers commissioned sumptuous temples, an exceptional palace profusely decorated with stucco friezes, royal tombs, stone tablets with lengthy hieroglyphic inscriptions, a ball court, and mansions, some of which can be viewed during a visit to this site. Archaeologists disagree over the causes of Palenque's collapse. The city was rapidly abandoned after 800 CE and covered by the tropical forest until its re-discovery during the eighteenth century (González Cruz, 2011; López Bravo and Venegas Durán, 2012).

Archaeological research and monument maintenance may cause some sections of the city to be closed when visiting. Tourists are encouraged to walk through the plazas and enjoy the ancient buildings such as the Group of the Crosses (Temples of the Cross, the Sun, and

FIGURE 13.9 The Palace at Palenque, Mexico. Courtesy of Roberto López Bravo

the Foliated Cross) and the North Group, the Palace (Figure 13.9), and the Ball Court. More experienced visitors can hike through the jungle to see waterfalls and buildings still covered in tropical rainforest.

Roberto López Bravo

Copan

Copan is located in westernmost Honduras and is the southernmost city of the Classic Maya. Its rulers presided over 20,000 to 25,000 subjects who occupied several fertile river valleys (Webster et al., 2005). The largest valley is where the Maya chose to build the Principal Group that contained the grand palaces, temples, ball courts, and tombs. Sixteen kings ruled over Copan in its nearly 400 years of dynastic history. Copan is well known for its extraordinary hieroglyphic staircase on a temple (Figure 13.10) that contains the longest-known Mayan inscription (Fash, 1992; Fash, 1991; Schele, 1992).

Much research on Classic Maya producer households has been conducted, so we know a great deal about how the majority of people lived during this time period. They were agriculturalists, part-time craftspeople, and laborers for the building of pyramids and palaces. They conducted their own rituals in addition to participating in those of the entire kingdom. The commoners at Copan had access to sharp obsidian tools, grinding stones for milling maize, and some fancy ceramics in addition to their everyday wares. They built their perishable residences, kitchens, and storehouses, on small stone platforms and arranged these structures around patios to accommodate their extended families (Gonlin, 2004; Gonlin, 2007; Gonlin, 2012).

Others in the Maya area constructed buildings of adobe, such as the inhabitants of La Joya de Cerén, El Salvador. This small community was covered by volcanic ash around 660 CE, resulting in extraordinary preservation that reveals details of everyday life (Sheets, 2006). Residents cultivated a wide range of plants, including manioc and maize, and had access to cacao and other exotic items considered to be the purview of only the elite (Dixon, 2013).

The Aztecs

Aztec society was highly stratified, with a king who held the title of *tlatoani* and other members of the nobility forming a hereditary top rank of society. Commoners were comprised of farmers,

FIGURE 13.10 The Hieroglyphic Staircase at Copan, Honduras

craft specialists, and artisans who lived in the residential calpultin of Tenochtitlan and performed the day-to-day work of the city. They paid taxes and provided services to the noble class and in exchange received protection and basic services. Skilled artisans could rise to high positions even if they were not of noble birth, and those who chose to become warriors could rise to quasi-noble rank through extraordinary military achievement.

Traders called "***pochteca***" were the wealthiest group of commoners. They traveled long distances to acquire luxury goods for the nobility, frequently enriching themselves in the process. They were allowed to own slaves, thus affording them much of the same lifestyle as nobles. Near the base of the social hierarchy were the "mayeque," destitute commoners bound to noble lords like serfs. The lowest of the low were the "tlacotin," who through debt had fallen into servitude. The Spanish thought they were slaves, but mayeques could own property and buy their way out of servitude if their fortunes improved. Tlacotin children were born free of debt, so the idea of hereditary slavery was foreign to the Aztecs.

Aztec armies typically fought as highly decorated, massed infantry units (Anawalt, 1992). Warriors wore elaborate armored costumes and fought at close quarters using wooden slashing swords edged with razor-sharp obsidian blades. While the purpose of Aztec leaders might have been to expand the empire and acquire more tribute, goals of individual soldiers were to fight well and capture enemy warriors for sacrifice. Although they had the bow and arrow, they retained the spear thrower (atlatl) using it as a military weapon owing to the effectiveness of Aztec armor. Special atlatl army units directed clouds of spears toward opposing forces, over the heads of their own advancing infantry. The spears could penetrate armor that otherwise stopped arrows.

Art and Symbolism

Mesoamericans invented two forms of symbolic communication, including the use of iconography and inscriptions, both of which are integral to artistic expression. The art styles can readily be identified through **epigraphy** due to certain elements that characterize numerous groups of this culture area. One of the most pervasive symbols of power was the jaguar (*Panthera onca*), a large feline that roams the lowland forests at night. The jaguar was associated with the Olmecs in the Formative through to the Aztecs in the Postclassic. Jade (jadeite) and other green stones were difficult to work, but highly desired. Such materials were fashioned into numerous *objets d'art*, and jade beads were placed in the mouths of the dead (Evans, 2013: 135). Art, religion, and politics were intricately tied together for ancient Mesoamericans, so it is no surprise that jaguars and jade are associated with divine rulership.

The Mesoamerican Ball Game

The ball game was a vital feature of Classic Mesoamerican civilization. It symbolized the battle between life and death, good and evil. Abundant archaeological evidence in the form of ball courts (Figure 13.11), preserved balls, figurines of ball players, paintings of players on ceramics, and carvings in stone are found throughout Mesoamerica (Whittington, 2001). An early Formative-period ball court in the Paso de la Amada site in coastal Chiapas, Mexico, dates to at least 1400 BCE (Hill et al., 1998). Many later Mesoamerican sites have ball courts, the grandest of which is in the Postclassic Maya site of Chichén Itzá. Playing fields vary considerably in size and shape, but the typical plan is in the form of the letter "I", with the primary playing area within the long axis.

Most balls were made from the latex sap of the lowland rubber tree (*Castilla elastica*). By mixing latex with sap from the vine of a species of morning glory, the slippery polymers in raw latex could be turned into a resilient rubber. This substance in turn was molded into grapefruit-sized bouncy rubber balls (Hosler et al., 1999).

Some ball courts, such as at Chichén Itzá and Copan, featured stone loops for scoring on either side of the main playing area. Others, such as those at Monte Albán and Tula, lacked them

FIGURE 13.11 The ball court at Copan, Honduras. Note the rings on the slanted sides

and scores might have been achieved by putting the ball in the end zone. In the Aztec version, points could also be awarded to the opposite team if a player failed to return the ball after only one bounce or allowed it to go out of bounds (Day, 2001). Like soccer, the rules prohibited use of the hands. Players had to advance the ball with their feet, legs, and hips, and there is some evidence of special padding for protection.

Teotihuacan did not have the typical ball court (García Cook and Merino Carrión, 1998), but it did have at least one carved monument that might have served as a goal, raising the possibility that the great Avenue of the Dead was used to play ball games. Perhaps the game played at this great city was conducted in open areas with players sporting bats, as pictured in a mural from the Tepantitla compound (Cowgill, 2015: 151).

Olmec Art and Symbolism

Olmec art and culture contained the roots of many themes identified in later Mesoamerican cultures. Images of later Mesoamerican deities were already present in the Formative, as evidenced by Las Limas Monument I (Figure 13.12). The seated human figure with a **were-jaguar** baby in its lap is decorated with the symbols for four gods, each a representation of a god known from later Mesoamerican cultures.

Tres Zapotes, the third great Olmec center, represents the last phase of the Olmec sequence, 400 BCE–400 CE, which archaeologists often refer to as the Epi-Olmec (Diehl, 2004: 8). The later Olmecs were using the calendrical system upon which the Classic Maya would elaborate, the **Long Count**. A Long Count date is carved into Stela C at Tres Zapotes (Figure 13.13), consisting of a count of days beginning at a mythological starting point in the distant past, August 13, 3114

FIGURE 13.12 Las Limas figure, a seated Olmec adult holding a were-jaguar baby and inscribed with glyphs of ancient Mesoamerican deities. Courtesy of Michael D. Coe

BCE, using the **vigesimal** system (base 20). This notation represents multiples of 20 (1–20–400), rather than 10 (1–10–100) in the decimal system. The Mesoamerican vigesimal system uses dots (ones) and bars (fives) to represent numbers.

The Olmecs and later Maya made one adjustment to the basic count. To bring the third place of the Long Count into rough correspondence with the solar calendar, they stipulated that it had 360 days rather than the 400 normally expected in vigesimal arithmetic. A Tun is equal to 18 Uinal rather than 20 Uinal. Each unit has a name, increasing in quantity from the Kin (quantity of 1) to the Baktun (Table 13.2). The date on the stela is read from the bottom up – 18, 16, 6, 16 – indicating that the count was for a date 18 Kin, 16 Uinal, 6 Tun, 16 Katun. A piece broken from the top was recovered and found to have 7 Baktun carved on it, for a date equivalent to September 2, 32 BCE or 18. 16. 6. 16. 7.

Zapotec Art and Symbolism

The earliest monuments at Monte Albán show clear evidence of Olmec influences. A gallery of prisoners (Danzantes) in the southwest corner of the main plaza depicts dozens of sacrificial victims, not dancers, but corpses with limbs akimbo. Closed eyes, conspicuously missing genitals,

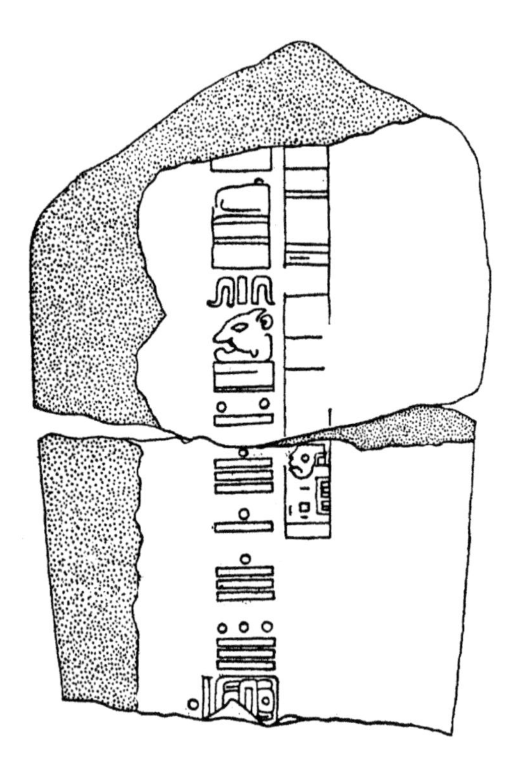

FIGURE 13.13 Stela C, Tres Zapotes, Mexico. The upper portion was missing when originally uncovered, but it was later discovered

TABLE 13.2 Simplified Long Count and the Stela C date, Tres Zapotes. This date [18.16.6.16.7] is equivalent to September 2, 32 BCE

Long Count Structure					*Tres Zapotes Stela C Inscription*		
20 Katun	=	1 Baktun	=	144,000 days	[7 Baktun]	=	[1,008,000 days]
20 Tun	=	1 Katun	=	7,200 days	16 Katun	=	115,200 days
18 Uinal	=	1 Tun	=	360 days	6 Tun	=	2,160 days
20 Kin	=	1 Uinal	=	20 days	16 Uinal	=	320 days
		1 Kin	=	1 day	18 Kin	=	18 days

and curlicues of flowing blood reveal the true nature of the low relief carvings. There would eventually be 320 of them, and more like them at other smaller centers around the Valley of Oaxaca.

Early inscriptions show that the Zapotecs at Monte Albán employed calendrical notation and writing. Later inscriptions show Zapotec leaders meeting with visitors wearing distinctive Teotihuacan costumes, complete with tassel headdresses probably representative of ambassadors (Marcus, 1980; Marcus, 1992).

Teotihuacan Art and Symbolism

James Langley has found about 120 signs on murals and pottery at Teotihuacan that appear to comprise a notational system, although the elaborate calendrics of some contemporaneous cultures are missing. Karl Taube has conducted considerable research into the symbols at Teotihuacan, concluding that some may reference different compounds. To George Cowgill these symbols identify districts, neighborhoods, or provinces of Teotihuacan. It is likely that many features of the Mesoamerican calendars were used at this city as well, although perhaps administrators chose to write on perishable materials rather than in stone (Cowgill, 2015; Langley, 1991; Taube, 2000; Taube, 2011).

Classic Maya Art and Symbolism

Classic Maya ceramics tell us much about culture and politics. Cylindrical vessels bear courtly scenes and glyphs that commemorate significant events in the lives of the elites. Special spouted vessels were used for preparing chocolate drinks from cacao (Powis et al., 2002). Chocolate was an important ritual drink in the earliest Maya monumental centers and might have been used by the Olmecs as well.

Maya religion pervaded their art, politics, economy, and daily lives. Elites depicted themselves laden with icons on stone panels, painted murals, and cylindrical pottery vessels. In typical Mesoamerican fashion they identified themselves with deities, often more than one, and conflated deities with each other (Gillespie and Joyce, 1998). Metaphor, transformation, and shifting identities were commonplace.

Maya writing appears on various media: stone, ceramic, and paper. Hundreds of glyphic inscriptions are preserved on buildings and monuments. Glyphs were also painted on pottery, particularly cylindrical vessels that displayed elaborate scenes of historic significance. Maya glyphs also appear on other small portable stone, shell, bone, and ceramic objects. Maya scribes compiled a large but unknown number of fan-folded books, which are referred to as **codices**. Most of the books that survived until the sixteenth century were burned by Spanish religious zealots. Only three of the thirteen indisputably pre-Hispanic books that have survived in Mesoamerica are Maya; the others come from highland Mexico. The Dresden, Madrid, and Paris Codices are known by the names of the cities where they are now housed. A fourth book, the Grolier **Codex**, surfaced in 1971, and has been authenticated by leading Mayanists (Baudez 2002; Coe et al. 2015).

Maya writing is both syllabic and phonetic; symbols can represent either individual syllables or sounds. Epigraphers have now deciphered the majority of Mayan glyphs. Historical information that rulers always wanted to preserve and advertise were typically recorded: dynastic lists, births, accessions, deaths, and their military accomplishments (Houston, 1989; Houston et al., 2001).

Maya Calendars

The Classic Maya kept track of time in three ways: the **Tzolkin** is the 260-day ritual calendar, the **Haab** is the 365-day solar calendar, and the vigesimal-based Long Count described for the Tres Zapotes Stela C inscription. The Maya also understood the cycles of the moon and Venus, and they were able to predict eclipses (Aveni, 2018; Baudez, 2002; Spinden, 1928).

The 260-day Tzolkin calendar approximated the period of human gestation (Earle and Snow, 1985). The calendar worked through the permutation of 20 day names and 13 god names (Table 13.3). Counting the two lists together the god names (represented here as numbers) begin to repeat after 13. The day after the first completion of 20 day names on 7 Ahaw would be 8 Imix. The two lists run like this for 260 days, at the end of which 1 Imix begins again and the cycle starts over (Satterthwaite, 1965).

The Maya simultaneously tracked the 260-day Tzolkin cycles and the solar year using the 365-day Haab calendar. The Haab calendar was computed by using 18 month names, 20 day names

TABLE 13.3 Tzolkin cycle of 20 day names shown as a permutation with the first and part of the second cycle of 13 gods

God	*Day Name*	*God*	*Day Name*
1	Imix (Waterlily)	11	Chuen (Frog)
2	**Ik (Wind)**	12	**Eb (Skull)**
3	Akbal (Night)	13	Ben (Corn stalk)
4	Kan (Corn)	1	Ix (Jaguar)
5	Chicchan (Snake)	2	Men (Eagle)
6	Cimi (Death head)	3	Cib (Shell)
7	**Manik (Hand)**	4	**Caban (Earth)**
8	Lamat (Venus)	5	Etznab (Flint)
9	Muluc (Water)	6	Kawak (Storm cloud)
10	Oc (Dog)	7	Ahaw (Lord)

(numbered 0–19 as in modern computing), and 5 (occasionally 6) extra days to fill out the solar year. All of these elements had their own glyphs, and the calendar was organized as 18 units of 20 days each. The first day on the Haab calendar was 0 Pohp.

When the two calendars cycled together, every day had a compound designation with four elements, such as 1 Ik 0 Pohp. The same dates coincided every 52 years, or every 18,980 days. This cycle was the 52-year Calendar Round that was vital to the Maya and many other Mesoamerican cultures. Only 52 of the 260 days of the Tzolkin can ever occur with 0 Pohp, the first day of the solar year. These are days in which the names Ik, Manik, Eb, or Caban appear (bolded in Table 13.3). Some later derivative calendars used these designations as shorthand names for the 52 solar years in the Calendar Round, avoiding the complicated details of the Classic Maya calendar. The Long Count provided a linear day count to accompany the cycles of the 52-year Calendar Round. The ruler of a Classic Maya city-state would often record a great accomplishment in the Tzolkin, the Haab, and the Long Count calendars simultaneously.

Aztec Art and Symbolism

Aztec religion was a powerful tradition in the service of political objectives. Aztec views of the world were imbued with religious overtones. Ideology was steeped in metaphor and ordered by pervasive dualism: life-death, male-female, light-dark, day-night, fire-water, and so forth. The basic concept of teotl, "deity" or "sacred power," was a status that they initially attributed even to the strange-looking Spanish invaders. The crowded pantheon of gods was presided over by Ometeotl, who was both male "Ometecuhtli" and female "Omecihuatl." Other gods were often paired for a variety of reasons. Each was assigned a domain of jurisdiction and each had a place in the 260-day ritual calendar. Thirteen gods were lords of daylight while nine were lords of darkness. Deities could transform themselves from one deity to another, take alternative names, become more than one at the same time, and some were thought of as versions of others.

To maintain the world order, Aztecs made sacrifices to the gods, some of which involved cutting beating hearts from living people. There were also sacrifices of a less dramatic kind. **Auto-sacrifice** might involve the voluntary letting of one's own blood or some other act. The essence was in the symbolic unity of the sacrificed, the sacrificer, and the deity for whom the sacrifice was performed.

Aztec calendrics and mathematics followed the standard elements of the earlier Mesoamerican systems, although the Mexica modified them for their specific purposes. The key to understanding the Mexica calendrical system is the **Tonalpahualli**, the 260-day ritual calendar that was equivalent to the Maya Tzolkin calendar. The two were used in the same way, by simultaneously counting off 20 day names and thirteen numbers. One's birthday in this calendar was part of one's name, carrying with it divinatory predictions in much the same way as astrological predictions did in Europe.

Resilience and Collapse

Mesoamerican archaeology provides many examples of long-term cultural resilience, as well as many cases of political and economic collapse. A few of the best-known cases provide examples.

TEOTIHUACAN

During the first six centuries CE, Teotihuacan emerged as the first multiethnic metropolis of central Mexico. It was an exception in Mesoamerica, as most corporate societies are: it was a huge urban development (ca. 20 km^2) with a population of ca. 125,000 people. The urban center is surrounded by rural sites in the Basin of Mexico, without a well-developed settlement hierarchy. It was the capital of a particular type of state, what I call "the octopus type," with the city as the head and corridors of ally sites linked to sumptuary-goods provisioning regions, as the tentacles; a site that controlled the green obsidian of the Pachuca Range; and a center of pilgrimage (Manzanilla, 2017).

The city had a ritual and administrative core around the Street of the Dead, where the three main pyramids were set. The next ring displayed the ca. 22 neighborhood centers with the different apartment compounds of the corporate groups surrounding each of them (Manzanilla, 2009). The outer ring displayed the foreign ethnic enclaves of people from Oaxaca, Michoacán, and Veracruz. The city may have been divided into four districts.

Two main phases of Teotihuacan's history are represented by superimposed construction levels in many different sectors of the city: the Tlamimilolpa phase (200–350 CE) with polychrome paintings in public areas, and the Xolalpan phase (350–550 CE), this last referred to as the "urban renewal" by René Millon, buildings mostly painted in red (Millon, 1973).

The city had a corporate organization at the base (the corporate groups), as well as at the summit of this society (perhaps a ruling council). The neighborhood centers managed by the intermediate elite constituted a competitive and exclusionary aspect of this society, which may have torn down its corporate nature (Manzanilla, 2015). Teotihuacan´s core was burned by ca. 550 CE perhaps as the result of an internal revolt, as no evidence of invasions are found. One problem still unsolved is how Teotihuacan was ruled.

Linda R. Manzanilla

The fall of Teotihuacan occurred when the central public buildings were burned and the religious shrines within them systematically destroyed. Palaces were burned and idols smashed, but while the resident population dropped significantly as a result of the conflict, the city was not deserted. Many residential compounds survived the burning, but the city declined as the preeminent Mesoamerican center it had been. If outsiders were responsible they did not choose to occupy the city afterward, for there is no evidence of invasion. Nearby in the highlands but later in time, Xochicalco was sacked and burned around 900 CE, and Tula met a similar fate around 1150 CE.

The Classic Maya Collapse

Dominant Classic Maya centers, including Palenque, Piedras Negras, Quirigua, and Copan, stopped erecting dated monuments after 822 CE. Tikal and others in the northern Peten held out longer. By 910 CE all lowland Maya cities had collapsed politically, marking the end of the Classic period in the region. The collapse of Maya civilization occurred for numerous interrelated reasons (Webster, 2002).

In some cases, political hierarchies collapsed but populations were left intact, as at Copan (Paine and Freter, 1996). Elsewhere, entire city-states were wiped out or dispersed by warfare. At some centers, environmental factors played a role, whereas in others, catastrophe came in the form of conquest from the outside or revolution from within. The Maya collapse was not a single event nor an orchestrated series of events, but an extended process that unfolded over at least 150 years (Webster, 2002).

The Maya Lowlands experienced a severe and prolonged drought around 850 CE (Haug et al., 2003; Hodell et al., 2001; Iannone, 2014; Shaw, 2003; Webster, 2014) that accounted for the decline of some centers. Other centers had ever-increasing populations to feed on agricultural lands that were becoming more scarce and depleted. Evidence for chronic and disruptive warfare comes from Cancuén, Guatemala, where remains of nearly three dozen members of the royal family were murdered and dumped into a shallow pool at the foot of a temple around 800 CE. Similar events occurred at many cities over the course of a century. Within seven decades only one center remained, and the area was largely depopulated (Demarest et al., 1997).

The collapse was not as pervasive on the Yucatan Peninsula. In northwestern Yucatan, the population of the Chunchucmil city-state grew to as high as 60,000, and for a time, it was a thriving center of trade. But its success brought attacks from competitors. Chunchucmil's last major construction was a hastily built 2-km (1.25 mi) stone barricade surrounding the city's core. Bruce Dahlin concluded that like other centers with such barricades, Chunchucmil was overrun and then deserted, its inhabitants annihilated or dispersed, never to return (Dahlin, 2000).

Several large autonomous city-states had existed in the Puuc region, including Oxkintok, Uxmal, Chac, Sayil, Kabah, and Labna. Teotihuacan indirectly influenced their development from 300–600 CE (Smyth and Rogart, 2004). Uxmal was politically dominant during the late ninth century, however by 950 CE, it fell out of power and as at all of the other Puuc cities, grand elite activities ceased (Dunning and Kowalski, 1994).

The city-states of Chichén Itzá and Tulum fared better than the Peten centers. Dahlin argued that people at Chichén Itzá had access to a wider range of nearby resources. Agricultural production did not suffer as much in northern Yucatan and marine resources were available along the coast. Trade and tribute allowed for the circulation of resources. Political organization and military power overcame the effects of environmental disaster (Dahlin, 2002).

The Maya persisted in northern Yucatan and the Guatemalan highlands after the collapse of Classic Maya city-states in the Peten (Restall, 1997). The Maya not only thrived on the Yucatan Peninsula following the Peten collapse, there is little evidence for cultural discontinuity in the region. The populations of the Peten region declined, and there must have been at least some out-migration, but there was no such decline on the northern peninsula.

Chichén Itzá was a multiethnic, cosmopolitan city-state capital for over three centuries, 700–1020 CE.(Andrews, 1990; Andrews et al., 2003; Cobos, 2016). Hieroglyphic inscriptions dating to 800–1000 CE at Chichén Itzá include patronyms identifying principal families. These family names persisted beyond the arrival of Spaniards five centuries later.

CHICHÉN ITZÁ

Chichén Itzá was first described by the Spanish conquerors in the sixteenth century and charmed the attention of American as well as European explorers during the nineteenth century. In the twentieth century, archaeologists initiated serious scientific studies of Chichén Itzá, and the results of systematic research suggest that this pre-Hispanic community was a pre-industrial city with dispersed urbanism.

The permanent occupation of the settlement began around 600 CE. During the next three centuries, Chichén Itzá witnessed a rapid process of urbanization, which included significant population growth, social and economic differentiation, hieroglyphic texts, paramount rulers, and a planned and spatially organized settlement with a center located at the Monjas architectural complex. Between 900 and 1100 CE, Chichén Itzá reached its apogee and a new site-center located north of the Monjas architectural complex arose. This new center consisted of an artificial platform known as the Great Terrace. Several sumptuous structures were built on top of this artificial feature, which include El Castillo (Figure 13.14), the Great Ball Court, the skull-rack or *Tzompantli*, the Temple of the Warriors, a gallery-patio structure known as *El Mercado*, and the Venus platform. The Great Terrace and its associated buildings are connected via a causeway to a natural sinkhole, known as the Sacred Cenote. It was utilized by the inhabitants of Chichén Itzá as one of their main water sources. However, due to severe droughts that reached their peak in the eleventh century, the Sacred Cenote became a place to perform human sacrifices. The goal of these sacrifices was to propitiate the rain god, Chac, so that he could guarantee a rainy season sufficient to ensure the growth of maize. After 1100 CE, and during the next four centuries, Chichén Itzá along with its Sacred Cenote, witnessed numerous pilgrims performing ritual ceremonies. However, this cultural practice was stopped after the arrival of the Spaniards.

Rafael Cobos

FIGURE 13.14 El Castillo at Chichén Itzá, Mexico. Courtesy of Rafael Cobos

The nearby city-state of Mayapan was probably already founded and poised to predominate when Chichén Itzá collapsed politically in the eleventh century (Andrews et al., 2003; Milbrath and Peraza Lope, 2003). Mayapan's central feature is a copy of El Castillo on a smaller scale. The inhabitants of this late city-state built a defensive wall that enclosed about 4.2 km^2 (1.6 mi^2). Over 4,000 structures, mostly residences, were packed into this fortified compound, enough for a population of perhaps 12,000 people. Mayapan was one of the last of the short-lived warring cities on the northern Yucatan Peninsula. It collapsed in 1441 CE.

Glossary

auto-sacrifice The voluntary letting of one's own blood by cutting one's earlobe, tongue, or penis; bloodletting.

calpulli (pl. calpultin) A social unit used to organize the inhabitants of Aztec cities; Nahuatl for "great house."

cenote Yucatecan Mayan word for "sinkhole."

Chichimec Any of the hunter-gatherer people of northern Mexico.

chinampa Large, raised agricultural beds in swampy land.

city-state A state polity built around a city and its immediate environs.

codex (pl. codices) An ancient manuscript book. In Mesoamerica, a codex was commonly made from bark paper, painted, and folded like an accordion.

epigraphy The study of inscriptions.

Haab The 365-day Classic Maya solar calendar.

karst A limestone landscape characterized by many caves and sinkholes.

Long Count The calendar system based on an origination date of August 13, 3114 BCE.

milpa A Maya agricultural clearing.

Náhuatl A language of the Uto-Aztecan family that was spoken by the Aztecs and other groups in central Mexico.

pochteca A professional class of Aztec merchants.

stela (pl. stelae) A free-standing stone monument bearing inscriptions.

talud-tablero A central Mexican architectural style featuring a flat panel (tablero) above a sloping lower wall (talud).

tlatoani Náhuatl word meaning "ruler."

Tonalpahualli The Aztec 260-day ritual calendar.

Tzolkin The Classic Maya 260-day ritual calendar.

vigesimal A counting system based on units of 20.

were-jaguar A being who is a combination of a human and a jaguar.

References

Anawalt, P.R. (1992). Ancient Cultural Contacts between Ecuador, West Mexico, and the American Southwest: Clothing Similarities. *Latin American Antiquity,* 3, pp. 114–129.

Andrews, A.P. (1990). The Fall of Chichén Itzá: A Preliminary Hypothesis. *Latin American Antiquity*, 1, pp. 258–267.

Andrews, A.P., Andrews, E.W., and Robles Castellanos, F. (2003). The Northern Maya Collapse and its Aftermath. *Ancient Mesoamerica*, 14, pp. 151–156.

Arnold, D.E., Branden, J.R., Williams, P.R., Feinman, G.M., and Brown, J.P. (2008). The First Direct Evidence for the Production of Maya Blue: Rediscovery of a Technology. *Antiquity*, 82, pp. 151–164.

Aveni, A.F. (2018). Night in Day: Contrasting Ancient and Contemporary Maya and Hindu Responses to Total Solar Eclipses. In: N. Gonlin and A. Nowell, eds. *Archaeology of the Night: Life After Dark in the Ancient World.* Boulder: University Press of Colorado.

Baudez, C.F. (2002). Venus y el Códice Grolier. *Arqueología Mexicana*, 10, pp. 70–79.
Beekman, C.S. (2000). The Correspondence of Regional Patterns and Local Strategies in Formative to Classic Period West Mexico. *Journal of Anthropological Archaeology*, 19, pp. 385–412.
Beekman, C.S. (2016). Conflicting Politcal Strategies in Late Formative to Early Classic Central Jalisco. In: S. Kurnick and J. Baron, eds. *Political Strategies in Pre-Columbian Mesoamerica.* Boulder: University Press of Colorado.
Beekman, C.S., and Pickering, R., eds. (2016). *Shaft Tombs and Figures in West Mexican Society: A Reassessment.* Tulsa, OK: Thomas Gilcrease Institute of American History and Art.
Bernal, I. (1969). *The Olmec World.* Berkeley: University of California Press.
Blomster, J.P., and Cheetham, D. (2017). *The Early Olmec and Mesoamerica: The Material Record.* Cambridge: Cambridge University Press.
Cabrera Castro, R., Sugiyama, S., and Cowgill, G.L. (1991). The Templo de Quetzalcoatl Project at Teotihuacan. *Ancient Mesoamerica*, 2, pp. 77–92.
Cobos, R., ed. (2016). *Arqueología en Chichén Itzá: Nuevas Explicaciones.* Mérida: Ediciones de la Universidad Autónoma de Yucatán.
Coe, M., Miller M., Houston S., and Taube, K. (2015). The Fourth Maya Codex. In: C. Golden, S. Houston, and J. Skidmore, eds. *Maya Archaeology 3.* San Francisco, CA: Precolumbia Mesoweb Press.
Cowgill, G.L. (2015). *Ancient Teotihuacan: Early Urbanism in Central Mexico.* Cambridge: Cambridge University Press.
Cyphers, A. (2012). *Las bellas teorías y los terribles hechos: controversias sobre los Olmecas del Preclásico Inferior.* Mexico City: Instituto de Investigaciones Antropológicas, Universidad Nacional Autónoma de Mexico.
Dahlin, B.H. (2000). The Barricade and Abandonment of Chunchucmil: Implications for Northern Maya Warfare. *Latin American Antiquity*, 11, pp. 283–298.
Dahlin, B.H. (2002). Climate Change and the End of the Classic Period in Yucatan. *Ancient Mesoamerica*, 13, pp. 327–340.
Day, J.S. (2001). Performing on the Court. In: E.M. Whittington, ed. *The Sport of Life and Death: The Mesoamerican Ballgame.* New York: Thames and Hudson.
Demarest, A.A., O'Mansky, M., Wolley, C., Van Tuerenhout, D., Inomata, T., Palka, J., and Escobedo, H. (1997). Classic Maya Defensive Systems and Warfare in the Petexbatun Region. *Ancient Mesoamerica*, 8, pp. 229–253.
Diehl, R.A. (2004). *The Olmecs: America's First Civilization.* New York: Thames and Hudson.
Dixon, C.C. (2013). *Farming and Power: Classic Period Maya Manioc and Maize Cultivation at Cerén, El Salvador.* PhD dissertation, University of Colorado.
Dunning, N.P., and Kowalski, J.K. (1994). Lords of the Hills: Classic Maya Settlement Patterns and Political Iconography in the Puuc Region, Mexico. *Ancient Mesoamerica*, 5, pp. 63–95.
Earle, D., and Snow, D.R. (1985). The Origin of the 260-Day Calendar: The Gestation Hypothesis Reconsidered in Light of Its Use among the Quiche-Maya. In: M. Robertson and V. Fields, eds. *Fifth Palenque Round Table, 1983.* San Francisco, CA: Pre-Columbian Art Research Institute.
Evans, S.T. (2013). *Ancient Mexico & Central America: Archaeology and Culture History.* London: Thames & Hudson.
Evans, S.T., and Nichols, D.L. (2016). Water Temples and Civil Engineering at Teotihuacan, Mexico. In: N. Gonlin and K.D. French, eds. *Human Adaptation in Ancient Mesoamerica: Empirical Approaches to Mesoamerican Archaeology.* Boulder: University Press of Colorado.
Fash, B.W. (1992). Late Classic Architectural Sculpture Themes in Copan. *Ancient Mesoamerica*, 3, pp. 89–104.
Fash, W.L. (1991). *Scribes, Warriors and Kings.* New York: Thames & Hudson.
Ford, A., and Nigh, R. (2015). *The Maya Forest Garden: Eight Millennia of Sustainable Cultivation of the Tropical Woodlands.* New York: Routledge.
Foster, M.K., and Gorenstein, S. (2000). *Greater Mesoamerica: The Archaeology of West and Northwest Mexico.* Salt Lake City: University of Utah Press.
French, K.D., and Duffy, C.J. (2016). Measuring the Impact of Land Cover Change at Palenque, Mexico. In: N. Gonlin and K.D. French, eds. *Human Adaptation in Ancient Mesoamerica: Empirical Approaches to Mesoamerican Archaeology.* Boulder: University Press of Colorado.
García Cook, A., and Merino Carrión, B.L. (1998). Cantona: urbe prehispanica el altiplano central de Mexico. *Latin American Antiquity*, 9, pp. 191–216.

Gillespie, S.D., and Joyce, R.A. (1998). Deity Relationships in Mesoamerican Cosmologies: The Case of the Maya God L. *Ancient Mesoamerica*, 9, pp. 279–296.
Gonlin, N. (2004). Methods for Understanding Classic Maya Commoners: Structure Function, Energetics, and More. In: J.C. Lohse, and F.J. Valdez, eds. *Ancient Maya Commoners*. Austin: University of Texas Press.
Gonlin, N. (2007). Ritual and Ideology Among Classic Maya Rural Commoners at Copan, Honduras. In: N. Gonlin and J.C. Lohse, eds. *Commoner Ritual and Ideology in Ancient Mesoamerica*. Boulder: University Press of Colorado.
Gonlin, N. (2012). Production and Consumption in the Countryside: A Case Study from the Late Classic Maya Rural Commoner Households at Copan, Honduras. In: J.G. Douglass and N. Gonlin, eds. *Ancient Households of the Americas: Conceptualizing What Households Do*. Boulder: University Press of Colorado.
González Cruz, A. (2011). *La Reina Roja: Una tumba real. México D.F.* Mexico City: Consejo Nacional para la Cultura y las Artes, INAH, Turner.
Haug, G.H., Günther, D., Peterson, L.C., Sigman, D.M., Hughen, K.A., and Aeschlimann, B. (2003). Climate and the Collapse of Maya Civilization. *Science*, 299, pp. 1731–1735.
Hill, W.D., Blake, M., and Clark, J.E. (1998). Ball Court Design Dates Back 3,400 Years. *Nature*, 392, pp. 878–879.
Hodell, D.A., Brenner, M., Curtis, J.H., and Guilderson, T. (2001). Solar Forcing of Drought Frequency in the Maya Lowlands. *Science*, 292, pp. 1367–1373.
Hosler, D., Burkett, S. L., and Tarkanian, M. J. 1999. Prehistoric Polymers: Rubber Processing in Ancient Mesoamerica. *Science*, 284, 1988–1991.
Houston, S.D. (1989). *Maya Glyphs*. Berkeley: University of California Press.
Houston, S.D., Mazariegos, C., and Stuart, D., eds. (2001). *The Decipherment of Ancient Maya Writing*. Norman: University of Oklahoma Press.
Iannone, G., ed. (2014). *The Great Maya Droughts in Cultural Context: Case Studies in Resilience and Vulnerability*. Boulder: University Press of Colorado.
José-Yacamán, Rendón, L., Arenas, J., and Serra Puche, M.C. (1996). Maya Blue Paint: An Ancient Nanostructured Material. *Science*, 273, pp. 223–225.
Langley, J.C. (1991). The Forms and Usage of Notation at Teotihucan. *Ancient Mesoamerica*, 2, pp. 285–298.
López Austin, A., and López Luján, L. (2001). *El pasado indígena*. Mexico City: El Colegio de México.
López Bravo, R., and Venegas Durán, B.J. (2012). Continuidad y cambios en la vida urbana de la Antigua Lakamha' (Palenque). *Arqueología Mexicana*, 19, pp. 38–43.
López Luján, L. (2005). *The Offerings of the Templo Mayor of Tenochtitlan*. Albuquerque: University of New Mexico Press.
Macri, M.J. (2017). Differentiation among Mayan Speakers: Evidence from Comparative Linguistics and Hieroglyphic Texts. In: B.J. Beyyette and L.J. Lecount, eds. *"The Only True People": Linking Maya Identities Past and Present*. Boulder: University Press of Colorado.
Manzanilla, L.R. (2009). Corporate Life In Apartment and Barrio Compounds at Teotihuacan, Central Mexico: Craft Specialization, Hierarchy and Ethnicity. In: L. Manzanilla and C. Chapdelaine, eds. *Domestic Life in Prehispanic Capitals. A Study of Specialization, Hierarchy and Ethnicity*. Museum of Anthropology Memoir 46. Ann Arbor: University of Michigan.
Manzanilla, L.R. (2015). Cooperation and Tensions in Multiethnic Corporate Societies Using Teotihuacan, Central Mexico, as a Case Study. *Proceedings of the National Academy of Sciences*, 112, pp. 9210–9215.
Manzanilla, L.R. (2017). *Teotihuacan, Ciudad Excepcional de Mesoamérica*. Mexico City: El Colegio Nacional.
Manzanilla, L.R., and Barba, L. (1990). The Study of Activities in Classic Households: Two Case Studies from Coba and Teotihuacan. *Ancient Mesoamerica*, 1, pp. 41–49.
Marcus, J. (1980). Zapotec Writing. *Scientific American*, 242, pp. 50–64.
Marcus, J. (1992). *Mesoamerican Writing Systems, Propaganda, Myth, and History in Four Ancient Civilizations*. Princeton, NJ: Princeton University Press.
Marcus, J., and Flannery, K. (1996). *Zapotec Civilization*. New York: Thames & Hudson.
Martin, S., and Nikolai, G. (2008). *Chronicle of the Maya Kings and Queens*. New York: Thames & Hudson.
Milbrath, S., and Peraza Lope, C. (2003). Revisiting Mayapan: Mexico's las Maya Capital. *Ancient Mesoamerica*, 14, pp. 1–46.
Millon, R., ed. (1973). *Urbanization at Teotihuacán, Mexico*. Austin: University of Texas Press.

Paine, R.R., and Freter, A. (1996). Environmental Degradation and the Classic Maya Collapse at Copan, Honduras (A.D. 600–1250). *Ancient Mesoamerica*, 7, pp. 37–47.

Peeler, D.E., and Winter, M. (1995). Building J at Monte Albán. *Latin American Antiquity*, 6, pp. 362–369.

Pohl, M.E.D., Pope, K.O., Jones, J.G., Jacob, J.S., Piperno, D.R., deFrance, S.D., Lentz, D.L.G., John A., Danforth, M.E., and Josserand, J.K. (1996). Early Agriculture in the Maya Lowlands. *Latin American Antiquity*, 7, pp. 355–372.

Pollard, H.P. (2016). Ruling "Purépecha Chichimeca" in a Tarascan World. In: J. Baron, and S. Kurnick, eds. *Political Strategies in Pre-Columbian Mesoamerica*. Boulder: University Press of Colorado.

Powis, T.G., Valdez, F.J., Hester, T.R., Hurst, W.J., and Tarka, S.M.J. (2002). Spouted Vessels and Cacao Use among the Preclassic Maya. *Latin American Antiquity*, 13, pp. 85–106.

RestalL, M. (1997). *The Maya World*. Palo Alto, CA: Stanford University Press.

Ringle, W.M., Gallareta Negrón, T., and Bey, G.J.I. (1998). The Return of Quetzalcoatl: Evidence for the Spread of a World Religion during the Epiclassic Period. *Ancient Mesoamerica*, 9, pp. 183–232.

Sanders, W.T. (2004). The Basin of Mexico as a Habitat for Pre-Hispanic Farmers. In: F. Solis, ed. *The Aztec Empire*. New York: Guggenheim Museum.

Satterthwaite, L. (1965). Calendrics of the Maya Lowlands. In: G.R. Willey, ed. *Handbook of Middle American Indians: Archaeology of Southern Mesoamerica*. Austin: University of Texas Press.

Scarborough, V.L., and Gallopin, G.G. (1991). A Water Storage Adaptation in the Maya Lowlands. *Science*, 251, pp. 658–662.

Schele, L. (1992). The Founders of Lineages at Copan and Other Maya Sites. *Ancient Mesoamerica*, 3, pp. 135–144.

Shaw, J.M. (2003). Climate Change and Deforestation: Implications for the Maya Collapse. *Ancient Mesoamerica*, 14, pp. 157–167.

Sheets, P. (2006). *The Cerén Site: An Ancient Village Buried by Volcanic Ash in Central America*. Belmont: Thomson Wadsworth.

Smyth, M.P., and Rogart, D. (2004). A Teotihuacan Presence at Chac II, Yucatan, Mexico: Implications for Early Political Economy of the Puuc Region. *Ancient Mesoamerica*, 15, pp. 17–47.

Spencer, C.S., and Redmond, E.M. (2001). The Chronology of Conquest: Implications of New Radiocarbon Analyses from the Cañada de Cuicatlán, Oaxaca. *Latin American Antiquity*, 12, pp. 182–202.

Spinden, H.J. (1928). *Maya Inscriptions Dealing with Venus and the Moon*. Buffalo: Buffalo Society of Natural Sciences.

Stuart, G.S., and Stuart, G.E. (1993). *Lost Kingdoms of the Maya*. Washington, D.C.: National Geographic Society.

Tate, C.E. (1999). Patrons of Shamanic Power: La Venta's Supernatural Entities in Light of Mixe Beliefs. *Ancient Mesoamerica*, 10, pp. 169–188.

Taube, K.A. (2000). *The Writing System of Ancient Teotihuacan*. Washington, D.C.: Center for Ancient American Studies.

Taube, K.A. (2011). Teotihuacan and the Development of Writing in Early Classic Central Mexico. In: E.H. Boone and G. Urton, eds. *Scripts, Signs, and Notational Systems in Pre-Columbian America*. Washington, D.C.: Dumbarton Oaks.

Webster, D. (2002). *Fall of the Ancient Maya*. New York: Thames & Hudson.

Webster, D. (2014). Maya Drought and Niche Inheritance. In: G. Iannone, ed. *The Great Maya Droughts in Cultural Context: Case Studies in Resilience and Cultural Context*. Boulder: University Press of Colorado.

Webster, D., Freter, A., and Gonlin, N. (2005). *Copan: The Rise and Fall of an Ancient Maya Kingdom*. Fort Worth, TX: Harcourt Brace & Company.

Webster, D., Murtha, D.T., Straight, K.D., Jay, S., Martinez, H., Terry, R.E., and Burnett, R. (2013). The Great Tikal Earthwork Revisited. *Journal of Field Archaeology*, 32, pp. 41–64.

West, R.C. (1994). Aboriginal Metallurgy and Metalworking in Spanish America: A Brief Overview. In: A.K. Craig and R.C. West, eds. In *Quest of Mineral Wealth: Aboriginal and Colonial Mining and Metallurgy in Spanish America*. Baton Rouge: Department of Geography and Anthropology, Louisiana State University.

Whittington, E.M., ed. (2001). *The Sport of Life and Death: The Mesoamerican Ballgame*. New York: Thames & Hudson.

14

ARCHAEOLOGY IN THE MODERN WORLD

North American archaeology today is different from what it was a century ago. It is now a profession with several career trajectories. At the beginning of the twentieth century, archaeology was largely the domain of wealthy white men, but legislation, economics, and shifts in national cultures resulted in fundamental changes over the ensuing decades. In the United States, President Theodore Roosevelt signed the Antiquities Act on June 8, 1906, which provided for the protection of archaeological sites on federal land and authorized the president to designate important federally owned sites or regions as National Monuments (Harmon et al., 2006). Protection has become an increasingly controversial process as commercial interests have come into conflict with archaeological preservation, as the recent case of Bears Ears National Monument illustrates.

Archaeology was conducted mainly by personnel in universities and museums until the Great Depression, which led to a boom in field archaeology. Federal work programs like the Works Progress Administration (WPA) and the Civilian Conservation Corps (CCC) sometimes focused on archaeological excavations, which were often conducted by people with little prior training but with surprising skill and accuracy. Huge collections and records from these projects are still being analyzed by archaeologists today.

Another significant change in American archaeology was stimulated by federal legislation requiring the mitigation of adverse effects of any federally funded project on archaeological resources. There are several such laws, and the lead agency for archaeology, the National Park Service, has compiled them in a government publication for handy reference. The Archaeological Resources Protection of Act (ARPA) was enacted in 1979. In addition to requiring government agencies to protect archaeological resources, ARPA criminalized looting on public or Indian land (Anonymous, 2002: 144). As a result of increasingly stronger regulatory antiquities and heritage oversight, professional archaeologists were employed by government agencies and private consulting firms that provided Cultural Resource Management (**CRM**) services in the U.S. and Heritage Resource Management (**HRM**) firms in Canada.

BEARS EARS

The Antiquities Act is an important tool for protecting the natural and cultural landscapes embodied in the public lands of the United States. President Theodore Roosevelt signed that Act in 1906. Since September of that year, 16 presidents have used the Antiquities Act to establish more than 150 national monuments. On December 4, 2017, President Donald Trump used the Antiquities Act – unlawfully, say legal scholars – to remove nearly two million acres from Bears Ears and Grand Staircase-Escalante National Monuments in Utah (Figure 14.1).

Archaeology Southwest's response is as a plaintiff in one of the lawsuits against the reversal of Bears Ears. They seek to protect the entire 1.35-million-acre national monument that President Barack Obama established on December 28, 2016, legally and with broad prior consultation. In doing so they argue that they are also acting to protect the Antiquities Act itself.

Since the Antiquities Act became law, only Bears Ears National Monument came into being through the efforts of a tribally led coalition of five Native American nations. This is the Bears Ears Inter-Tribal Coalition: Navajo Nation, Pueblo of Zuni, Hopi Tribe, Ute Mountain Ute, and Ute Indian Tribe.

The Bears Ears proclamation honored the values and priorities of native peoples, peoples whose past suffuses the monument's lands. Further, the Bears Ears National Monument proclamation gave those tribes a powerful voice in managing and protecting those lands. This honors tribal history, sovereignty, and connections to this landscape.

Archaeology Southwest's goal is to support tribal communities and their connections to these natural and cultural landscapes since time immemorial. Its goal is to ensure that their stories in and of the land are not only protected but also shared and celebrated with all Americans, because we all share ownership of the public lands that hold these stories (Doelle, 2018).

William H. Doelle

FIGURE 14.1 Procession Panel at Bears Ears National Monument. Courtesy of Rebecca Simon

The archaeological profession has subsequently grown rapidly. There are probably 10,000 professional archaeologists working in the United States today. Most new opportunities are not in traditional teaching posts or museum positions but rather in CRM and HRM. The successes of modern archaeology have created many new careers, but they have also generated huge quantities of curated artifacts, databases, and documents. Coping with this massive amount of information and distilling it for the benefit of the public that has paid for it through tax dollars have become major challenges for archaeology. Another new challenge is the proper training and preparation of the next generation of archaeologists. Every U.S. state and territory has a State Historic Preservation Office charged with managing CRM reports. For example, the Massachusetts Historical Commission, which oversees such work for one of the smaller states, accumulated a bibliography of 3,632 such reports by September 2015 (Simon, 2016). Federally recognized Indian tribes have their own equivalent offices. Canada has parallel offices at the provincial and national levels. Mexico has the Instituto Nacional de Antropología e Historia, with branch offices around the country. The island nations of the Caribbean have their own archaeological programs. Public interest in archaeological heritage is growing everywhere.

The Society for American Archaeology was founded in 1934, and it has grown to become the largest organization of professional and avocational archaeologists in North America. Sister organizations include the Archaeological Institute of America, the Society for Historical Archaeology, and the Archaeology Division of the American Anthropological Association. Together, these four organizations sponsor the Register of Professional Archaeologists. Most U.S. states and Canadian provinces have societies for both avocational archaeologists and councils of professional archaeologists. These groups generally work together on a range of projects in archaeological preservation, research, and public and advocacy outreach.

The Archaeological Conservancy was founded in 1980 as a national nonprofit organization dedicated to the preservation of archaeological sites in the United States. The Conservancy has saved hundreds of archaeological sites in the face of development projects. At the same time, it is not always clear how to ensure preservation of that heritage. For example, while preservation of archaeological sites from looting and accidental damage is an important goal, it is not clear what should be done when the damage is being created by similarly protected animal populations. Some coastal sites are threatened not only by climate change but by seals and sea lions that are also at risk (Braje et al., 2011). Finding the solutions for these and other complex problems define the future of American archaeology.

Environment and Adaptation

Modern American archaeology has taken up many scientific challenges, some of which are related to the effects of global climate change. Archaeology can reveal much about the effects of long-term changes on past human populations and provide some prediction of future effects on the populations of today (Kintigh et al., 2014)

It is ironic that climate change is creating new opportunities for archaeology. With its long-term perspective, archaeology may contribute to understanding the effects of climate change on humans and cultures. Further, global warming is producing new data. Ice patches are shrinking, resulting in the release of long-frozen archaeological evidence (Lee and Puseman, 2017).

Demography and Conflict

The European invasion of America began in earnest after the voyages of Christopher Columbus, but Columbus was not the first visitor to contact Native Americans whose ancestors peopled these continents thousands of years previously. Spanish explorers might have been preceded by Polynesians (Chapter 11), but if so, there had been little impact. More significant was the temporary Norse colonization of Newfoundland five centuries before Columbus. The Norse ventured across the North Atlantic from Norway and settled in Iceland, Greenland, and eventually Newfoundland during the warm spell known as the Medieval Maximum. The Norse colonized the Faroe Islands and reached Iceland by 874 CE, probably as family groups traveling in cargo ships with all of their livestock and belongings. Many came from the Hebrides and Scotland, and most families appear to have brought Irish slaves.

The technological advantage of the Vikings is to be found mainly in their ships, which had clinker-built hulls characterized by narrow overlapping planks joined by iron rivets, such that the whole vessel had long, graceful lines. The strakes were split from curved logs, not sawn, so that none of the natural strength of the wood was lost. The hulls were light, strong, and flexible. Ships designed for war and travel were low, narrow, and fast, whereas cargo ships were higher, wider, and slower (Roesdahl, 1991). Cargo ships ranged 16–25 m (53–82 ft) in length and could carry 18–38 tons.

Norse occupation in Greenland was concentrated around two settlements, Osterbygd and Vesterbygd, the eastern and western colonies, both of which provide evidence of Norse lifeways. Bands of West Greenland Inuits were scattered near the Norse settlements, and initially relations between the two cultures were cordial but cautious. The Norse brought their own cultural traditions that included agriculture and animal husbandry, both of which were viable, if just barely, along the Greenland coast during the Medieval Maximum. They built houses, barns, and Christian churches of stone, and eked out a living without shifting to an adaptation more similar to that of their Inuit neighbors.

Norse people in Greenland supplied furs and walrus ivory to Iceland and Norway but there were no towns or trading centers established in either Greenland or Iceland. Neither did they have kings or earls. Instead they were quasi-republics run by assemblies of chieftains. Although local populations were low, in the range of band or tribal societies, they maintained their traditional chiefdom form of government.

The Norse subsisted on fish, sea mammals, birds, and other game in addition to domesticates. From burial remains of the Greenland Norse, the teeth show heavy tooth wear but few dental caries of the sort that typically afflict people with high-carbohydrate diets, indicating little to no reliance on grains.

Trade and exchange between the Norse and the Inuits ceased around 1480 CE after the onset of the Little Ice Age. Norse colonies in Greenland dwindled as the growing season shortened and wheat crops failed. The Norse withdrew from their colonies in America, but their departure was probably only indirectly related to the Little Ice Age. Their primary trade resource was walrus ivory, allowing them to acquire goods from northern Europe. When cheaper African elephant ivory became available in Scandinavia, Greenlander Norse traders were unable to compete, and their inability to acquire cash to buy imports led to economic decline. The survivors eventually moved to Iceland (McGovern, 1994).

What Columbus called "the other world" in 1492 presented the Spanish and other Europeans with many things that dashed the constrained certainties of their most cherished religious beliefs. Here was a world in which outlandish and completely unanticipated things abounded, like hummingbirds, turkeys, poison ivy, monkeys that could hang by their tails, coyotes, chocolate, rattlesnakes, maize, and birch bark canoes (to name just a few). For their part, Native Americans were just as astonished by the things the hairy pale men from Europe brought with them: iron, horses, gunpowder, sails, smallpox, and pigs (again to name just a few). These and other things were the currencies of an interchange that would play out over the course of the centuries that followed (Crosby, 1972). Some were beneficial, while others were detrimental, arguably the most horrendous being the introductions of catastrophic epidemics and the rise of race-based slavery. Archaeology contributes to the understanding of all of these processes.

The Colonial Experience

The collision of the world's cultures in North America began in 1492 CE, and it continues today. Prior to 1492, the peoples of Eurasia and Africa were not aware of the continents that Columbus would call "the other world." Similarly, the peoples of the Americas had no idea that the continents and cultures of the Eastern Hemisphere existed prior to European ships arriving to their shores. Despite separate histories, both evolved from small bands of hunter-gatherers to states and empires, the peoples of the two worlds being remarkably similar in many fundamental ways by 1492. To understand how those similarities arose independently promotes comparisons of and inquiry into processes of cultural evolution. The desire for those insights and understandings drives many of the questions asked by modern archaeologists working in North America.

LA ISABELA

La Isabela was the first European city in the Americas, established by Christopher Columbus in 1493. The site is today a Dominican National Park and Museum near the town of Luperón on the Dominican Republic's north coast. The location was chosen somewhat hastily after Columbus returned in 1493 to La Navidad (in Haiti), where in 1492, he had left the crew of the shipwrecked *Santa María* in a large Taíno village. Finding the crew dead and the town burned, the Spaniards fled 160 km to the east to settle La Isabela. Columbus arrived with 1,500 male settlers, including nobles who had recently fought in the Spanish *Reconquista*, craftsmen, and laborers. They built an essentially medieval town covering about 5 hectares (12.4 acres), surrounded by an earthen defensive wall. Inside were a large storehouse (the *alhóndiga*), a church, a large fortified house for Columbus himself, and about 200 small, palm-thatched huts for the settlers. Builders used the medieval Andalucian technique of *tápia* (rammed earth or *pisé*) to construct the major building walls over stone foundations. Remnants of these buildings have survived.

La Isabela was well-provisioned with resources needed to sustain life in an utterly alien environment (Figure 14.2). Crafts documented archaeologically include blacksmithing, pottery production, carpentry, masonry, metal smelting, and lime burning (Deagan and Cruxent, 2002). Colonists, however, complained constantly that there was nothing to eat, despite their location in a rich fisheries and manioc-production zone.

Columbus's original dream of creating a trade entrepot faded when it became evident that the resources they sought were simply not available. Hostilities between Spaniards and Taínos began almost immediately, and combined with hunger and disappointing gold yield, provoked mutinies and desertions. The town was gradually abandoned, and by 1498, La Isabela had been moved to the south coast, where Santo Domingo is located today.

Kathleen Deagan

FIGURE 14.2 Columbus house at La Isabela

In its earliest stages, the clash of cultures in North America played out as an unequal contest of arms. Europeans brought horses, guns, and steel armor, and native armies initially used their traditional tactics that had been successful in the past rather than different ones to deal with the new invader, a conservative strategy that favored the Europeans. By the time the armies of Aztec Emperor Motecuhzoma learned how to thwart the Spanish invaders, Cortés had recruited nearby competing city-states to his banner. More devastating for the Mexicans, immigrant Spanish children had brought smallpox with them to Cuba, and a single infected soldier was among Cortés's reinforcements in 1520. The disease spread almost unchecked through the native Highland Mexican population, with horrendous consequences.

The introduction of lethal diseases by early explorers from the Old World was catastrophic for Native American populations. Unfortunately, recognition of this terrible consequence of sixteenth-century contacts entailed inaccurate assessments of the scope and consequences of early epidemics. These resulted in unrealistic estimates for the sizes of American Indian populations prior to 1492 CE, discussed later.

The history of North America is often presented as the history of exploration by Euroamericans, the settlement of a land largely converted to wilderness after its abandonment by decimated and dislocated Native Americans (Fisher, 2004; Goetzmann and Williams, 1992). Regions like central Pennsylvania had never before looked like they did when the first Euroamerican settlers settled there. The American Indians who had long modified it with fire and hoe had been gone for decades, long enough for it to become the wilderness it had not been since the end of the Pleistocene. Little wonder that history books celebrate Daniel Boone's discovery and travels through the Cumberland Gap. The traces of ancient Indian paths he was following were by then almost too faint for him to see, but the trail he blazed was hardly a new one.

In some regions, American Indians were spared the worst of the initial diseases, and European expeditions therefore did not have to negotiate new wilderness. Francisco Vasquéz de Coronado in

1540–1542, Hernando de Soto in 1539–1542, and even the much later expedition by Meriwether Lewis and William Clark from 1804–1806 found American Indian cultures not yet ravaged by epidemics. DeSoto followed well-worn trails through belts of productive farmland of the Southeast, moving from town to town in what was clearly not wilderness. But epidemics soon followed.

ETOWAH

Etowah is a large Mississippian-period town located in the northwestern corner of Georgia. It covers 22 ha (54 ac), has six earthen platform mounds, and today is a state park maintained by the Georgia Department of Natural Resources (Figure 14.3).

Etowah began as a modest place. It was established in the eleventh century CE as different groups from the surrounding region joined to form a new kind of community. The town included distinct neighborhoods and a public area where mound building, feasting, and public events were held. For reasons currently unknown, people left the site sometime after 1200 CE.

People returned around 1250 CE, and in the next century, Etowah reached its peak in size, complexity, and influence in the wider region. Considerable labor was devoted to formalizing the settlement and enlarging its monuments, creating three large mounds, clay-lined plazas, an encircling palisade wall, and ditch. At this time, some people were interred with elaborately decorated ritual objects and regalia in Mound C. These objects bear symbolic imagery and often are made of materials not found in the local area. The palisade wall and portions of the town were burned by unknown attackers near the end of the fourteenth century CE, ending the Etowah polity.

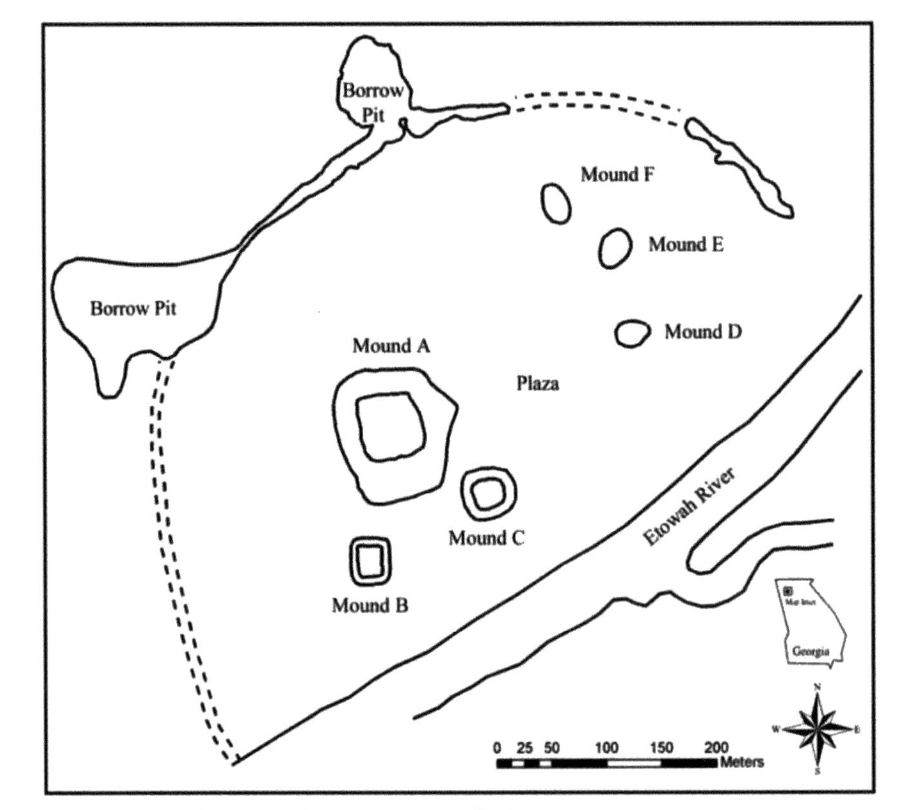

FIGURE 14.3 Plan of the Etowah site. Courtesy of Adam King

People returned a century later and established yet another community. Only one of the old monuments, Mound B, was reused, but three new, smaller mounds (D, E, and F) were constructed. Etowah was visited by Hernando de Soto in 1540. Within a few decades of that visit Etowah was abandoned for the last time, as European diseases led to the demise of local polities and the movement of survivors to eastern Alabama (King, 2003; Milanich and Hudson, 1993: 221–224).

Adam King

Russians colonized Alaska in the eighteenth century, and they explored the West Coast as far south as California. Epidemics spread behind these contacts as well. The Russians gave up their colonizing efforts in 1867, when they sold their American interests to the United States.

The earliest records of European colonial efforts in North America often tell us much about colliding cultures before they began to substantially modify each other and before epidemics converted the interactions into an unequal contest. The mounted tribes of the Great Plains did not exist until after the Spanish introduced horses in the seventeenth century. The mountain men of the Rockies did not exist until after Lewis and Clark explored the area in the nineteenth century. The best-known nations of the Southeast did not exist until after the dislocations and cultural consolidations of the seventeenth century. Spanish missions in the Southeast, Southwest, and California conditioned the gradual subjugation of native communities in those regions (Lightfoot et al., 2013; Mathers et al., 2013; Robinson, 2013). Franciscan and Jesuit missionaries brought similar changes to the Northeast. Through it all, American Indians experienced dislocations and shrinking numbers. The later history of the colonial period is characterized by a decline in American Indian population sizes that did not reverse toward recovery until around 1900 CE.

MISSION SANTA CATALINA DE GUALE

Santa Catalina de Guale (pronounced "Walley") was built in the 1560s as an outpost of St. Augustine, capital of Spanish Florida. For a century, this was the northernmost Spanish settlement on the eastern seaboard. Mission Santa Catalina was effectively vanished after being overrun by British-sponsored slave raiders in 1680.

For three centuries, adventurers and scientists searched unsuccessfully for this long-lost Spanish mission. Using random sampling and remote sensing techniques on St. Catherines Island, Georgia, it took us five years to find this extraordinarily well-preserved Franciscan mission – hiding in plain sight beneath 14 inches of hurricane debris. We had driven over it dozens of times.

Decades of scientific excavations at Mission Santa Catalina revealed a central sacred compound, laid out along a rigid grid plan. The mission church flanked the western side of the main plaza, and at least 431 people were buried inside (Figure 14.4). Across the plaza stood the communal kitchen and the friary, where friars and lay brothers lived cloistered lives according to the rules of their Franciscan order.

More than simply a Spanish settlement, Mission Santa Catalina was also a fully functioning Guale town, governed by an interlocking set of hereditary and elected native leaders. Archaeology demonstrates the fluid blends of Franciscan theology that played out in the context of continuing Mississippian beliefs and materiality. This Spanish colonial-Mississippian hybrid provided the external support necessary to maintain the authority of hereditary chiefs, who negotiated the details and nuances of daily mission life.

FIGURE 14.4 Excavation of the Santa Catalina church. Courtesy of David Hurst Thomas

A near total demographic collapse and English-sponsored slave raids in the late seventeenth century ultimately doomed Mission Santa Catalina, but the colonial strategy facilitated the survival of ancient chiefly lineages and Mississippian style social systems long after the total demise of indigenous polities in the interior Southeast.

David Hurst Thomas

The inexorable expansion of French, English, Dutch, and Spanish colonies in the East and the Caribbean; the Spanish in Mesoamerica, the Southwest, and California; and the Russians in Alaska and along the Northwest Coast invariably displaced American Indian communities. Some congregated around missions, either forcibly or from desperation due to cultural breakdown. Others moved away from colonists, seeking to preserve traditional lifeways beyond the reach of the invaders. Some Iroquoians and Algonquians relocated westward through the Great Lakes basin or into the Midwest. Some Pueblo communities relocated away from Spanish colonial outposts to places as remote as western Kansas (Beck and Trabert, 2014).

Other American Indian communities remained in their traditional homelands. These tended to evolve as European tools, architectural forms, crops, and domesticated animals were selectively integrated with traditional ones. Change also followed the development of economic and marriage linkages between natives and newcomers (Hunter et al., 2014). The demographic complexity of modern America both informs and complicates shared heritages. Integration of archaeology and ancient DNA studies is producing many new insights and a more detailed understanding of past demographic and cultural variables (Johannsen et al., 2017).

Subsistence and Economy

The two-way flow of domesticates and technology across the Atlantic after 1492 is often referred to as the "Columbian exchange." All parts of the world contributed to the interchange, a complex history of exotic contributions that probably can be seen most easily in national cuisines. Medieval diets in Europe were particularly bland, and it is not hard to understand why spices from India and Indonesia captured the interest of European cooks. It seems impossible to imagine a world today without chocolate, maize (corn), beans, pumpkins, tomatoes, or avocados, yet all of these were American crops that were unknown elsewhere until after 1492.

Tobacco, the first tropical plant to become widespread in North America, was an immediate hit with Europeans in the second half of the sixteenth century. Smoking was taken back to Europe and promoted there as a health benefit. Soon Europeans were making smoking pipes from white ball clay and selling them wherever their ships traveled, including North America. The potent tobacco used by North American Indians, *Nicotiana rustica*, was replaced by the milder West Indian *Nicotiana tabacum* in Virginia's fields, and that remains the main ingredient in modern tobacco products.

Clay smoking pipes were not common in highland Mexico until the time of the Toltecs, 900–1175 CE. Inscriptions and paintings indicate that cigars or tubular pipes were smoked earlier by Classic Maya (Robicsec, 1978), but smoking pipes were common in eastern North America well before that (Porter, 1948; Weaver, 1972:213). Tobacco is a South American plant, so if it became well established in California and the Eastern Woodlands before it did so in Mesoamerica, it was probably carried into North America either along the West Coast, by way of the Caribbean islands, or both. Claims have been made for smoking pipes in Olmec sites and other early contexts in Mesoamerica, but these finds typically reference artifacts in private collections, where dating and documentation are suspect. In fact, so much of the archaeological evidence of smoking involves artifacts that are attractive to looters and collectors that archaeology may never be able to provide a clear history of what is arguably one of the worst widespread habits ever practiced by human beings. Nevertheless, tobacco was on the leading edge of the Columbian exchange.

Other species involved in the Columbian exchange were more benign. Domesticated plants, animals, technology, and habits flowed both ways between the Eastern and Western Hemispheres from the sixteenth century on. European farmers waited impatiently for new American crops to try out in their fields. Some took root, but many others did not. Potatoes became an Irish staple, and tomatoes became indispensable to Italian cuisine. In exchange, American Indian communities planted orchards of peach and apple trees. Colonial settlers created new American foodways based on crops and animal domesticates from all of these sources. The Pilgrims of Massachusetts quickly developed a hybrid agriculture that featured both maize and wheat, both turkeys and chickens, both squash and apples, drawing upon domesticates that were to them both new and old. It is no exaggeration to say that the cultures of North America today are hybrids that would not exist but for fervent interactions and exchanges over the last five centuries. Recent genetic research indicates that dog breeds brought by colonists have almost completely replaced native American dogs (Leathlobhair, 2018).

Architecture and Technology

An electronic map of North America that accompanies this book on the Companion Website locates about 500 archaeological sites that are well-protected and open to the public. These places are important archaeological resources for everyone, especially descendants of those who once built and occupied them (Kennedy, 2008).

Stone projectile points have long been picked up and displayed by collectors. However, under federal and state laws, finders are not necessarily keepers. Anything found on public land is public property, and taking it for private purposes is theft. So too is the collection and possession of artifacts from private property without explicit permission of the property owner. Artifacts, the finite and irreplaceable evidence of changes in technology over millennia, deserve careful study and preservation in museums or other research repositories.

The Columbian exchange led to whole new classes of artifacts. For example, the magical power attributed to marine shells and beads made them popular trade items from both coasts into the interior regions of North America for centuries (Bradley, 2011; Bradley, 1992; Whalen, 2013). When Dutch and English colonists introduced iron saws and drills that could be adapted to work shell, small standardized tubular shell beads called wampum quickly became widespread, especially in the Northeast. Simple strings of wampum were soon supplemented by elaborate belts of white and blue wampum, which became ritual currency for political and religious interactions between Indian nations as well as between them and Europeans. When faced with shortages of coinage, wampum even took on currency functions in the colonial Northeast.

Indians who moved westward away from colonies on the Atlantic Coast encountered other Indian communities with whom they had to forge new relationships. They soon found that they also had to contend with advancing European scouts and entrepreneurs following them. Innovative strategies evolved to facilitate communications and social interactions, including the development of sign language, trading jargons, and **calumet** ceremonialism. Commonly called a "peace pipe," the calumet served as the centerpiece of ritual designed to promote trade and formal relationships between individuals of differing language and cultural origins (Rodning, 2014).

Missionary efforts by Europeans led to new architectural forms, new artifact traditions, and new kinds of descendant communities. Historical documentation often falls short of sufficiently describing and explaining these phenomena, so they too are now central themes in archaeological research.

Culture, Language, and Identity

Even in the face of devastating population decline prior to 1900 CE, the Indians north of Mexico were able to more-or-less maintain their unique cultural identities by playing the colonial powers off each other. This balancing act changed in the East when the British expelled France from virtually the entire continent with the Treaty of Paris, which concluded their war over North America in 1763. Surviving North American Indians were subjects of either England or Spain after that date, with decreasing political leverage. This changed very little as various colonies became independent of European powers beginning in the 1770s. Fortunately for native peoples of what is now the United States, the 1787 Constitution gave special status to American Indian nations. This provision has played a significant role in their long-term survival, as well as in the conduct of modern archaeology. Similar histories have played out in Canada, Mexico, and the Caribbean nations, each in its own way.

American Indian groups typically retreated in the face of European colonization during the first three centuries of contact. Epidemics reduced their populations until around 1900, and the allure of gunpowder, steel, and state political organizations made Europeans impossible to resist over the long term. Spanish colonial administration moved quickly to subjugate the native peoples of Mexico, Guatemala, and the southwestern United States. Spanish colonists did not settle North America in great numbers, although a considerable amount of intermarriage occurred with American Indians. Many native communities survived in culturally modified form, and a large fraction of the Spanish-speaking population of North America came to be made up of mestizos, people of mixed European and American Indian ancestry. This era of Native American history has recently become the subject of research by historical archaeologists (Eiselt and Darling, 2012).

History also played out differently in the United States and Canada. French-speaking colonists from Quebec frequently intermarried with the First Nations, but intermarriage was rarer in the United States and western Canada. Instead, a frontier formed between Indian country and the mostly Dutch- and English-speaking colonies of the East Coast of North America.

The independent nations that arose from European colonies expanded or contracted to their current boundaries in the nineteenth century. American Indian communities either retreated in the face of this expansion or were confined to small remnants of their former territories. Western Indian tribes often ceded large amounts of land to the United States in the treaties of the nineteenth century. But they also retained large parcels as reservations, which are typically maintained today for the joint use of enrolled tribal members. A similar process unfolded in Canada, where Indian-owned lands are referred to as "reserves." Canadian reserves tend to be smaller residential communities, with their Indian residents retaining access to nearby unreserved lands. In Mexico and elsewhere in Mesoamerica native communities persisted, often in areas far from centers of population and political power. Their survival was partly because their settlements and subsistence practices were similar to those of the dominant Hispanic culture.

Generally, Indian reservations in the United States were located within what already were or would become states under the terms of the U.S. Constitution, but states had no jurisdiction over them unless it was specifically conveyed to them by the federal government. Tribes located inside the boundaries of the original 13 colonies were in ambiguous circumstances throughout the nineteenth and most of the twentieth century because it was advantageous to the founding states to consider surviving Indian communities as exempt from the provisions of the federal Constitution. Some of these states made their only treaties with tribes within their boundaries, believing that they were not subject to the same constitutional restrictions as the western states. Legal cases in the late twentieth century led the courts to decide that such tribes were in fact not exempt from the constitutional provision and laws that built upon it, a decision that has led to several outcomes advantageous to the Indians. Illegal treaties between some states and Indian tribes have been overturned, and other old treaties remain in question.

Indian relations with U.S. federal and state governments during the nineteenth century generally resulted in Indians losing land and independence (Banner, 2005) (see Chapter 1, Figure. 1.5). State and imperial organizations out-compete chiefdoms, tribes, and bands. When they conflict or simply do business with each other, the more complex of them almost always prevails to the detriment of the less complex. Indian nations withdrew to smaller territories in the nineteenth century or those territories shrank as other interests whittled away at them. Their often-poor conditions are well known, and some authors have compared reservations to concentration camps. However, many Native American nations would have disappeared completely and individual American Indians would have had to merge into the general U.S. population over time had reservations not preserved their home bases.

NAGPRA

It was common for human skeletons, including but not limited to American Indian ones, to be displayed in museums through most the of the twentieth century. The Smithsonian Institution's National Museum of Natural History once displayed an entire wall of human skulls. As American Indians became more vocal regarding their civil rights, such exhibits were increasingly targeted by Indian activists. Exhibits of human skeletons, Indian or otherwise, gradually disappeared from museums and archaeological sites in the U.S. and Canada.

At the same time Native American organizations petitioned Congress for new legislation protecting unmarked graves and mandating the return of human remains and sacred objects known to be affiliated with living federally recognized tribes. Archaeology was shifting away from excavation and toward preservation around the same time, so the two stakeholder groups found common cause. American Indians, archaeologists and politicians crafted the language of the Native American Graves Protection and Repatriation Act (**NAGPRA**), which was enacted in 1990. The new law required federal funding for the analysis, description, and inventorying of thousands of boxed skeletons to determine which tribes should be notified. In many cases, it was an opportunity to complete important analyses.

NAGPRA required that human remains linked to extant federally recognized tribes be offered for repatriation, along with associated funerary offerings. Coverage was also extended to sacred objects, whether or not they came from graves. The law provided for creation of a committee to decide disputed claims, but it left open the question of how to treat skeletal remains that were clearly American Indian but could not be identified with a specific living community. Archaeologists increasingly reach out to descendant communities when oral tradition can clarify or supplement understanding, discussed in earlier chapters (Colwell-Chanthaphonh, 2009; Hermann et al., 2017; Simon, 2017).

Art and Symbolism

Today the art of American Indians past and present is widely appreciated and avidly collected. One can see deep symbolic traditions and modifications applied by recent artisans. The National Museum of the American Indian, which celebrates these traditions, opened in the late twentieth century. It joined other Smithsonian museums that cover various aspects of archaeology and its allied disciplines. Similar efforts led to Canada's National Museum of History and Mexico's Museo Nacional de Antropología. Supporting these national centers are a vast number of state, provincial, and local institutions dedicated to the archaeology of native North America (Kennedy, 2008).

Resilience and Collapse

The size of the North American native population around 1500 CE has been the subject of considerable scholarly debate. Attempts to estimate population sizes based on historical records have typically underestimated them because so few records predate the virulent epidemics that often swept ahead of European explorers and journalists. Crowd infections resulted when trans-Atlantic crossing times shortened to a month and colonists began bringing their families (Snow and Lanphear, 1988). Shorter crossings and larger crews ended the effective quarantine of early voyages, and the presence of European children ensured that childhood diseases were present as well. Nearly everywhere the first Europeans traveled, they inadvertently introduced diseases, after which native communities they contacted were devastated. Local mortality rates were often catastrophic, 60% or greater for smallpox alone (Jones, 2014).

Altogether North America probably had a population approaching 8.5 million in 1492 (Snow, 2001), similar to Russell Thornton's estimates and consistent with what we know about the continent's human capacity at that time (Thornton, 1987; Thornton and Marsh-Thornton, 1981). The long decline that followed did not bottom out until around 1890, when the American Indian population in the United States stood at only 228,000 (Thornton and Marsh-Thornton, 1981: 48). This decline was dreadful no matter what the precise population figure might have been before 1492 CE. Artificially inflating the initial figure does not make the accomplishments of Native North Americans any more impressive or their devastating population decline any more tragic.

Modern American Indians

Against the odds, and contrary to most expectations, American Indian cultures rebounded strongly in the twentieth century. Over 5 million self-identified Native Americans were registered in the 2000 United States national census, more than the number living in just the United States in 1492. The number of people of Indian descent is undoubtedly higher than the total number of formally enrolled tribal members; in any case, it is clear that more American Indians live in the United States today than when Columbus arrived in the New World. This has been a remarkable reversal of the downward demographic trend prior to around 1900.

In 1999, Canada set off a large portion of the previously unincorporated Northwest Territories as a new province, one dominated by its scattered population of around 30,000 Inuit residents. Nunavut is the newest province of the Canadian confederation.

In twentieth-century Mexico, the lands around many traditional Indian communities were converted into collective "*ejidos*," but this system was abandoned by the end of the century. Special status is conferred on indigenous communities in Mexico and Guatemala, although they have not been allocated territorial set-asides as have Native Americans in the United States or Canada.

The legal cases of the late twentieth century made it clear that most federally recognized tribes on reservation lands in the United States were not governed by state laws. Exceptions were made in cases where the federal government explicitly delegated law enforcement on reservations to state authorities. Under U.S. law, the regulation of gambling and other activities falls within the domain of the states. Many Indian reservations are not covered by state prohibitions on gambling or prohibited from selling untaxed tobacco and gasoline. Consequently, many Indian tribes opened casinos and other income-generating enterprises on their lands. Such reservations located near urban centers have often become quite successful, although the flow of money sometimes has been linked to corruption. The Abramoff scandal of 2005 involved millions of dollars of Indian casino money and the bribery of some Washington politicians. Wealthy Washington, DC lobbyist Jack Abramoff and his cronies defrauded Native American tribes of approximately 85 million dollars, purportedly representing Indian groups in their efforts to establish casinos on tribal reservation lands.

Many traditional American Indians have objected to the money-making schemes that reservation status has made possible, fearing the corrupting influences of money earned from selling tax-free gasoline and cigarettes as well as the larger profits derived from casinos. In cases like the Abramoff scandal, their concerns appear to have been accurate. On the positive side, the National Museum of the American Indian in Washington, DC was partly financed by the financial successes of several contributor tribes. The opening of the museum occasioned the convergence of American Indians from the entire Western Hemisphere, but especially from the United States. Building on the lifeways, traditions, and belief systems of numerous Native American groups, the museum takes a forward-looking perspective, emphasizing that American Indian societies are thriving in the twenty-first century.

Hundreds of American Indian communities reside on and off reservations or reserves in North America. Information can be found by searching online for "Native American Nations." In some cases, native languages are still spoken by community members. Elsewhere, programs have been established to record and preserve endangered languages. In many cases, languages have become extinct. In communities that no longer speak native languages, traditional customs are often still preserved. These are proudly expressed at periodic convocations called "**powwows**," where native crafts, foods, costumes, and dancing are featured (Figure 14.5).

Some American Indians enjoy productive careers as artists. They typically blend traditional motifs and materials with more contemporary ones, and some have achieved high standing in the international art world. Native artists of the Southwest are especially well known, in addition to individuals from the Northwest Coast, the Northeast, and other regions of the continent.

A century ago no one was certain that American Indians would survive to the twenty-first century. Well-intended officials of the day were preaching assimilation, bureaucrats were advocating the dissolution of reservations, and some elderly Indian leaders were predicting the demise

FIGURE 14.5 Tepee camp at Lame Deer, Montana, powwow, showing both traditional and modern technology. Courtesy of Dolores and Tom Elliott

of native cultures. Aging Indian leaders sometimes turned heirlooms into museum objects in the belief that this was the only way native lifeways and traditions could be preserved for the future. Anthropologists scrambled to record details of American Indian cultures before they disappeared. These dismal prognostications assumed that American Indian cultures were static systems, incapable of adapting to shifting social, economic, and political conditions. Like all human cultures, native communities are dynamic and ever-changing systems that respond to changes in internal and external circumstances. How tribal groups will evolve going forward is unknown, but we can be sure that they will be part of the cultural fabric defining America a century from now.

Archaeology and American Indians

Relations between early archaeologists and American Indians were often contentious, and the search for common ground has taken many years. Denigration of American Indians, looting of their ancestral graves, dismissal of their oral traditions, and other offenses plagued relations until late in the twentieth century. The Society for American Archaeology elected Arthur C. Parker, an American Indian, as its first president in 1934. Unfortunately, that step did not immediately lead to better relations between American Indians and archaeologists, who were mostly men of European descent. In recent decades, American archaeologists as a group have become more diverse, including an increasing number of American Indians. Combined with new ethical standards, the growth of nonacademic archaeology, and the vigorous growth of archaeology as a scientific discipline are all leading to a new, more inclusive, and rigorous profession.

There is now a sense of cooperation between archaeologists and American Indians. Vitriolic dismissals of archaeological science, like native activist Vine Deloria's assertion that "Indians came first via the Bering Strait [is] a myth with little to recommend it" are fading (Thomas, 2000:xv). So too are outdated positions like early twentieth-century anthropologist Robert Lowie's contention that American Indian oral tradition is worthless as a source of information for scientific research (Lowie, 1915). Oral traditions have become sources for testable hypotheses in archaeological science, increasingly recognized by mainstream archaeologists (Crowell and Howell, 2013). As more American Indians become archaeologists, the perceived clash between science and oral tradition will continue to fade (Gidwitz, 2007; Grier and Shaver, 2008; Watkins, 2003).

The Americas were first peopled over 140 centuries ago by hunter-gatherers expanding eastward out of Siberia, equipped with keen intelligence, lethal weapons, warm clothing, companion dogs, and a healthy curiosity. When the long age of Pleistocene winter finally waned, the following Holocene epoch brought relatively greater stability and predictability to the world's environments. This change in turn relaxed constraints on human ingenuity and mobility patterns, and the long slowly accelerating shift to plant and animal domesticates, and larger human populations unfolded wherever natural resources enabled.

In the Americas, civilizations pre-dating 1492 CE have been documented archaeologically that arose independently from other areas of the world. The remarkable similarities between the New and Old Worlds after fourteen millennia of separate evolution tells us much about ourselves as a species.

Globalization is not a process unique to our modern world. It began more than five centuries ago. If it is fair to say that Columbus discovered America for Europe in 1492 CE, then it is also fair to say that the unnamed American Indians in the party Columbus introduced to the king of Portugal the following spring were the American discoverers of Europe. One day in the fall of 1492, two groups of people stood staring at each other on an island in the Bahamas, saying in each of their own languages something like, "Who *are* those people?" The rest is history, of course. The ever-quickening exchange of vocabulary, plants, animals, ideas, technology, and germs that followed was a form of frenzied globalization that has continued ever since.

The sharp edges of culture contact in North America have finally dulled. Professional archaeology now involves much broader participation, and there is a growing appreciation that conclusions based on evidence are preferable to those rooted in ideology. The archaeology of North America is not just for or about American Indians; these chapters have shown that it is much more than that.

Archaeologists are sometimes told by earnest and well-intentioned people that the study of the past is a waste of time and money. As historians will attest, asserting that looking to the future is better than to the past is wrong. Most of the colossal mistakes made in human history have been by people who failed to learn key lessons from their past. Trajectories of the past partially determine our future; likewise, gaining insight into our future is not possible without an understanding of where we came from – our past. Archaeology is vital for understanding not only the origins and development of complex societies in general but also the persistence of the numerous culturally diverse threads found in the skein defining modern human culture. North American archaeology is worth exploring because America before 1492 CE is most accessible through archaeological science. "Without the instruments and accumulated knowledge of the natural sciences … the world is too remote from ordinary experience to be merely imagined" (Wilson, 1999: 76–77). The North American landscape also contains a record of all those people who came to the New World post-1492 CE. In total, North American archaeology provides a multi-textured view of the ambitions, agendas, strategies, hopes and desires, failures and successes, and outcomes resulting from approximately 14 millennia of human behavior.

Glossary

calumet Commonly called a "peace pipe," used in social, economic, and political ritual.

CRM Cultural Resource Management, a branch of professional archaeology conducted by private companies and government agencies in the United States.

HRM Heritage Resource Management, a branch of professional archaeology conducted by private companies and government agencies in Canada.

NAGPRA The Native American Graves Protection and Repatriation Act.

powwow A traditional American Indian convocation or performance.

References

Anonymous. (2002). *Federal Historic Preservation Laws.* Washington, DC: National Center for Cultural Resources, National Park Service.

Banner, S. (2005). *How the Indians Lost Their Land.* Cambridge: Belknap Press.

Beck, M.E., and Trabert, S. (2014). Kansas and the Postrevolt Puebloan Diaspora: Ceramic Evidence from the Scott County Pueblo. *American Antiquity*, 79, pp. 314–336.

Bradley, J.W. (2011). Re-visiting Wampum and Other Seventeenth-Century Shell Games. *Archaeology of Eastern North America*, 39, pp. 25–51.

Bradley, R.J. (1992). Marine Shell Exchange in Northwest Mexico and the Southwest. In: J.E. Ericson and T.G. Baugh, eds. *The American Southwest and Mesoamerica: Systems of Prehistoric Exchange.* New York: Plenum Press.

Braje, T.J., Rick, T.C., Erlandson, J.M., Megan, A., and Delong, R.L. 2011. Conflicts in Natural and Cultural Resource Management: Archaeological Site Disturbances by Seals and Sea Lions on California's Northern Channel Islands. *Journal of Field Archaeology*, 36, pp. 312–321.

Colwell-Chanthaphonh, C. (2009). Reconciling American Archaeology & Native America. *Daedalus*, 138(2), pp. 94–104.

Crosby, A.W. (1972). *The Columbian Exchange: Biological and Cultural Consequences of 1492.* Westport, CT: Greenwood Press.

Crowell, A.L., and Howell, W.K. (2013). Time, Oral Tradition, and Archaeology at Xakwonoowú. *American Antiquity,* 78, pp. 3–23.

Deagan, K., and Cruxent, J.M. (2002). *Columbus's Outpost Among the Taíno,* New Haven: Yale University Press.

Doelle, W.H. (2018). Back Sight. *Archaeology Southwest,* 32, p. 64.

Eiselt, B.S., and Darling, J.A. (2012). Vecino Economics: Gendered Economy and Micaceous Pottery Consumption in Nineteenth Century Northern New Mexico. *American Antiquity,* 77, pp. 424–448.

Fisher, R., ed. (2004). *National Geographic Historical Atlas of the United States.* Washington, DC: National Geographic Society.

Gidwitz, T. (2007). A Different History. *Archaeology,* 60, pp. 28–32.

Goetzmann, W.H., and Williams, G. (1992). *The Atlas of North American Exploration: From the Norse Voyages to the Race to the Pole.* New York: Swanston Publishing.

Grier, C., and Shaver, L. (2008). The Role of Archaeologists and First Nations in Sorting Out Some Very Old Problems in British Columbia, Canada. *The SAA Archaeological Record,* 8, pp. 33–35.

Harmon, D., McManamon, F.P., and Pitcaithley, D.T., eds. (2006). *The Antiquities Act: A Century of American Archaeology, Historic Preservation, and Nature Conservation.* Tucson: University of Arizona Press.

Hermann, E., Nathan, R., Rowe, M., and McLeary, T. (2017). Bacheeishdíio (Place Where Men Pack Meat). *American Antiquity,* 82, pp. 151–167.

Hunter, R., Silliman, S.W., and Landon, D.B. (2014). Shellfish Collection and Community Connections In Eighteenth-Century Native New England. *American Antiquity,* 79, pp. 712–729.

Johannsen, N.N., Larson, G., Meltzer, D.J., and Vander Linden, M. (2017). A Composite Window into Human History. *Science,* 356, pp. 1118–1120.

Jones, E.E. (2014). Spatiotemporal Analysis of Old World Diseases in North America, A.D. 1519–1807. *American Antiquity,* 79, pp. 487–506.

Kennedy, F.H. (2008). *American Indian Places: A Historical Guidebook.* New York: Houghton Mifflin.

King, A. (2003). *Etowah: The Political History of a Chiefdom Capital.* Tuscaloosa: University of Alabama Press.

Kintigh, K.W. et al. (2014). Grand Challenges for Archaeology. *American Antiquity,* 79, pp. 5–24.

Leathlobhair, M.N. et al. (2018). The Evolutionary History of Dogs in the Americas. *Science,* 361, pp. 81–85.

Lee, C.M., and Puseman, K. (2017). Ice Patch Hunting in the Greater Yellowstone Area, Rocky Mountains, USA: Wood Shafts, Chipped Stone Projectile Points, and Bighorn Sheep (*Ovis canadensis*). *American Antiquity,* 82, pp. 223–243.

Lightfoot, K.G., Panich, L.M., Schneider, T.D., Gonzalez, S.L., Russell, M.A., Modzelewski, D., Molino, T., and Blair, E.H. 2013. The Study of Indigenous Political Economies and Colonialism in Native California: Implications for Contemporary Tribal Groups and Federal Recognition. *American Antiquity,* 78, pp. 89–104.

Lowie, R. (1915). Oral Tradition and History. *American Anthropologist,* 17, pp. 597–599.

Mathers, C., Mitchem, J.M., and Haecker, C.M., eds. (2013). *Native and Spanish New Worlds: Sixteenth-Century Entradas in the American Southwest and Southeast.* Tucson: University of Arizona Press.

McGovern, T. (1994). Management for Extinction in Norse Greenland. In: C. Crumley, ed. *Historical Ecology: Cultural Knowledge and Changing Landscapes.* Santa Fe, NM: School for Advanced Research.

Milanich, J.T., and Hudson, C. (1993). *Hernando de Soto and the Indians of Florida.* Gainesville: University Press of Florida.

Porter, M.N. (1948). *Pipas precortesianas: introducción de Chita de la Calle.* Mexico City: Acta Antropológica.

Robicsec, F. (1978). *The Smoking Gods: Tobacco in Maya Art, History, and Religion.* Norman: University of Oklahoma Press.

Robinson, D. (2013). Polyvalent Metaphors in South-Central California Missionary Processes. *American Antiquity,* 78, pp. 302–321.

Rodning, C.B. (2014). Cherokee Towns and Calumet Ceremonialism in Eastern North America. *American Antiquity,* 79, pp. 425–443.

Roesdahl, E. (1991). *The Vikings.* New York: Penguin Books.

Simon, B. (2016). *Bibliography of Archaeological Survey & Mitigation Reports.* Boston: Massachusetts Historical Commission.

Simon, M.L. (2017). Reevaluating the Evidence for Middle Woodland Maize from the Holding Site. *American Antiquity*, 82, pp. 140–150.

Snow, D.R. (2001). Setting Demographic Limits, The North American Case. In: Z. Stancic and T. Veljanovski, eds. *Computing Archaeology for Understanding the Past.* Oxford: British Archaeological Reports.

Snow, D.R., and Lanphear, K.M. (1988). European Contact and Indian Depopulation in the Northeast: The Timing of the First Epidemics. *Ethnohistory*, 35, pp. 15–33.

Thomas, D.H. (2000). *Skull Wars.* New York: Basic Books.

Thornton, R.G. (1987). *American Indian Holocaust and Survival: A Population History Since 1492.* Norman: University of Oklahoma Press.

Thornton, R.G., and Marsh-Thornton, J. (1981). Estimating Prehistoric American Indian Population Size for the United States Area: Implications of the Nineteenth Century Population Decline and Nadir. *American Journal of Physical Anthropology*, 55, pp. 47–53.

Watkins, J.E. (2003). Beyond the Margin: American Indians, First Nations, and Archaeology in North America. *American Antiquity*, 68, pp. 273–285.

Weaver, M.P. (1972). *The Aztecs, Maya, and Their Predecessors: Archaeology of Mesoamerica.* New York: Seminar Press.

Whalen, M.E. (2013). Wealth, Status, Ritual, and Marine Shell at Casas Grandes, Chihuahua, Mexico. *American Antiquity*, 78, pp. 624–639.

Wilson, E.O. (1999). *Consilience.* New York: Vintage Books.

INDEX

Note: Page numbers in **bold** or *italics* indicate tables or figures